Placing Prints: New Developments in the Study of Print, 1400–1800

Brill's Studies on Art, Art History, and Intellectual History

General Editor

Walter S. Melion (*Emory University*)

VOLUME 74

The titles published in this series are listed at *brill.com/bsai*

Placing Prints: New Developments in the Study of Print, 1400–1800

Edited by

Bryony Bartlett-Rawlings
Naomi Lebens

BRILL

LEIDEN | BOSTON

On the cover: *Exlibris of Jan Ponętowski*, Woodcut (Figure 9.3), Paul Sandby after Pietro Fabris, View of Arco Felice, 1777, Aquatint (detail of Figure 4.6), School of Mantegna, *The Elephants, from 'The Triumph of Caesar'*, c.1484–92, Engraving (detail of Figure 10.8), Map of Paris, Jan Ziarnko's etching reworked, edited by Nicolas Berey, 1693, Etching and Engraving (detail of Figure 7.10) and Lymphatic System of the Liver of a Dog, 1627, Woodcut (Figure 5.5).

The Library of Congress Cataloging-in-Publication Data is available online at https://catalog.loc.gov
LC record available at https://lccn.loc.gov/

Typeface for the Latin, Greek, and Cyrillic scripts: "Brill". See and download: brill.com/brill-typeface.

ISSN 1878-9048
ISBN 978-90-04-26511-0 (hardback)
ISBN 978-90-04-70383-4 (e-book)
DOI 10.1163/9789004703834

Copyright 2024 by Koninklijke Brill BV, Leiden, The Netherlands.
Koninklijke Brill BV incorporates the imprints Brill, Brill Nijhoff, Brill Schöningh, Brill Fink, Brill mentis, Brill Wageningen Academic, Vandenhoeck & Ruprecht, Böhlau and V&R unipress.
All rights reserved. No part of this publication may be reproduced, translated, stored in a retrieval system, or transmitted in any form or by any means, electronic, mechanical, photocopying, recording or otherwise, without prior written permission from the publisher. Requests for re-use and/or translations must be addressed to Koninklijke Brill BV via brill.com or copyright.com.

This book is printed on acid-free paper and produced in a sustainable manner.

Contents

List of Illustrations   VII
Abbreviations   X
Notes on Contributors   XI

Introduction   1
Bryony Bartlett-Rawlings and Naomi Lebens

PART 1
The Art of Print: Approaches and Attitudes

1   Mark(et)ing Expertise: the Goldsmith-engraver in the Low Countries
and the Use of House Marks   27
Oliver Kik

2   Theory of Printmaking in the Early Modern Age   56
Barbara Stoltz

3   Poussin and the Theory of Hatching   75
Ben Thomas

4   Paul Sandby and Reproductive Printmaking   93
Ann V. Gunn

5   Not for the Feeble of Mind! Color-printed Illustrations in European
Medical Literature, 1500–1850   117
Ad Stijnman

PART 2
The Reception of Print: Circulation and Use

6   Multiplied Madonnas—Strategies of Commercializing Raphael
in Print   143
Anne Bloemacher

CONTENTS

7 Copying Motifs and Reworking Printing Plates as Part of the French Royal Propaganda in the First Half of the 17th Century   162
   Małgorzata Biłozór-Salwa

8 Displaying Gift-Giving: Thesis Prints in the Spanish Netherlands   188
   Gwendoline de Mûelenaere

9 Jan Ponętowski's Print Albums in the Jagiellonian Library in Cracow: an Early Print Collection in Moravia and the Kingdom of Poland   213
   Magdalena Herman

10 A "Great and Valuable Collection": Sir Joshua Reynolds (1723–1792) and His Prints   241
    Donato Esposito

Bibliography   273
Index   299

Illustrations

0.1 Abraham Bosse, *La Galerie du Palais*, *c.*1638, etching   2

1.1 Hans Schmuttermayer, *Fiallenbuchlein*, fol. 1, 1489   28

1.2 Alart Du Hameel, *Monstrance*, *c.*1484–85, engraving   31

1.3 Alart Du Hameel, *Gothic Baldachin*, *c.*1478–1507, engraving   33

1.4 Master WA, *Flying Buttress*, *c.*1470–80, engraving   35

1.5 Ludger Tom Ring the Elder, *Portrait of an Architect*, *c.*1520, oil on panel   36

1.6 Petrus Christus, *A Goldsmith in his Shop*, 1449, oil on panel   40

1.7 Adam Kraft, *Sacrament House* (detail), 1493–96, Nuremberg, St Lorenz   42

1.8 Anton Pilgram, *Organ Loft*, 1510–15, Vienna, St Stephan   42

1.9 Albert Dürer the Elder, *Self-Portrait*, 1486, silverpoint on prepared paper   43

1.10 Israel van Meckenem, *Self-portrait with his wife*, *c.*1490, engraving   44

1.11 Quinten Metsys, *St Anne tryptich* (detail), 1508–09, oil on panel   47

4.1 Paul Sandby, *East View of Edinburgh Castle*, 1753, etching   98

4.2 Paul Sandby, *South View of Bothwell Castle*, 1751 and 1753, etching   98

4.3 Paul Sandby after Thomas Pownall, *A View of the Falls on the Passaick, or second River, in the Province of New Jersey*, 1761, hand coloured etching and engraving   100

4.4 Paul Sandby after Thomas Sandby, *The Great Bridge over the Virginia River*, 1754–58, etching and engraving   102

4.5 Paul Sandby and Edward Rooker after John Collins, *A Morning Scene of the Forest with Rinaldo on the Bank of the Enchanted River c.*1757–60, etching and engraving   104

4.6 Paul Sandby after Pietro Fabris, *View of Arco Felice*, 1777, aquatint   107

4.7 Archibald Robertson after Pietro Fabris, *A View of the Ruins of the Temple of Bacchus*, 1777, aquatint   107

4.8 Paul Sandby after David Allan, *The Opening of the Carnival at Rome*, 1780–81, aquatint   109

4.9 William Watts after Paul Sandby, *Duchess of Athol's Seat near Charlton in Kent*, 1777, engraving   113

4.10 Paul Sandby, *Pont-y-Pair over the River Conway above Llanrwst in the County of Denbigh*, 1776, aquatint   113

5.1 Jan L'Admiral, *Preparations of the Skin and Nail of a Black Woman*, 1737, Mezzotint   124

5.2 Jacques-Fabien Gautier-Dagoty, *Muscles of the Back: Partial Dissection of a Seated Woman, Showing the Bones and Muscles of the Back and Shoulder*, 1746, Mezzotint   124

ILLUSTRATIONS

5.3 Angelique Briçeau, *Les Fosses du Cerveau et du Cervelet Recourvertes de la Dure-Mere*, 1786, etching with crayon engraving 125

5.4 *Amputation of the Right Lower Leg of a Man*, 1559, woodcut 126

5.5 *Lymphatic System of the Liver of a Dog*, 1627, woodcut 127

5.6 Stassel after Charles Billard, *Muguet de l'Estomac et de l'OEsophage*, 1828, etching 128

5.7 Themoteo Antonio and I. L. Sailliar, *Symptoms of Skin Disease Caused by Mites*, 1807, etching 134

5.8 James S. Stewart, *Symptoms of Syphilis*, 1814, dotting 135

6.1 Marcantonio Raimondi, *Madonna on Clouds (B.52)*, engraving 144

6.2 Marcantonio Raimondi, *Madonna on Clouds (B.53)*, engraving 145

6.3 Raphael, *Madonna di Foligno*, 1511/12, oil on canvas 147

6.4 Marcantonio Raimondi, *Madonna on Clouds (B.47)*, engraving 151

6.5 Giovanni Antonio da Brescia, *Madonna on Clouds*, engraving 155

6.6 Marcantonio Raimondi, *Parnassus*, engraving 157

7.1 Jan Ziarnko, *The Assembly of the Estates-General in 1614*, state II, 1615, etching and engraving 166

7.2.a Jan Ziarnko, *The Assembly of the Estates-General in 1614* (detail), state I, 1614, etching 168

7.2.b Jan Ziarnko, *The Assembly of the Estates-General in 1614* (detail), state II, 1615, etching and engraving 168

7.3 Jan Ziarnko, *Assembly of Notables in Rouen*, state I, 1617, etching 171

7.4 Jan Ziarnko, *Assembly of Notables in Rouen*, state III, 1617, etching and engraving 173

7.5 Jan Ziarnko, *Almanac for the year 1617*, 1616, etching and engraving 176

7.6 *The victory over the English troops by the royal army*, broadsheet with Jan Ziarnko's etching reworked, edited by Michel de Mathonière, 1627, etching and engraving 178

7.7 Jan Ziarnko, *Map of Paris*, 1616, etching 180

7.8 *Portrait of Henry IV*—detail from Jan Ziarnko, *Map of Paris*, 1616, etching 181

7.9 *Portrait of Maria de Medici*—detail from Jan Ziarnko, *Map of Paris*, 1616, etching 182

7.10 *Map of Paris*, Jan Ziarnko's etching reworked, edited by Nicolas Berey, 1693, etching and engraving 184

8.1 Richard Collin after Abraham van Diepenbeeck, *Young Man Offering his Thesis*, c.1675, engraving 191

8.2 Schelte a Bolswert after Abraham van Diepenbeeck (and Peter Paul Rubens?), *Thesis Dedicated to Sigismund III Vasa, King of Poland*, 1628, engraving 193

8.3 *Advertisement for Droste Cocoa Powder*, after 1904 197

8.4 Attributed to Rogier Van der Weyden, Frontispiece to the *Chroniques de Hainaut* dedicated to Philip the Good, 1447–1448, presentation miniature 199

ILLUSTRATIONS IX

8.5 Giotto di Bondone and workshop, *The Stefaneschi Altarpiece* (verso), *c.*1320, tempera on panel   200

8.6 Giotto di Bondone and workshop, *The Stefaneschi Altarpiece* (detail)   201

8.7 Michel Natalis after Bertholet Flémalle, *Thesis of Henri Hatzfeldt, Count of Gleichen*, 1663, engraving   201

8.8 Michel Natalis after Cornelis Schut, *Thesis Defended by George Nicolaus and Wolffgang Andreas, Barons of Rosenberg*, 1643, engraving   204

8.9 Michel Natalis after Cornelis Schut, *Thesis Defended by George Nicolaus and Wolffgang Andreas, Barons of Rosenberg* (detail)   205

8.10 Paul Pontius after Abraham van Diepenbeeck, *Thesis of Claudius, Count of Collalto*, 1645, engraving   207

8.11 Jean Frosne, *Nous Allons à l'An Pire*, 1653, engraving   209

9.1 Signets on the front and back covers of the album *Typus Ecclesiae Catholicae*   220

9.2 Supralibros on the front and back covers of the album *Solitudo Sive Vitae Patrum Heremitarum Monasticae Sacrae Professionis ...*   221

9.3 *Exlibris of Jan Ponętowski*, woodcut   227

9.4 Sheet with Hans Collaert and Adriaen Huybrechts, *Corporal and Spiritual Works of Mercy*, before 1582, engraving   227

9.5 *Sheet stamped with sixteen plates depicting various subjects*, before 1582, engraving   229

9.6 Anonymous, *Homini Christiani Ecstasis*, before 1582, engraving on silk   235

9.7 Maarten de Vos, Adriaen Collaert and Gerard de Jode, *The Allegory of Fire*, *c.*1582, hand-coloured engraving   238

10.1 Giovanni Benedetto Castiglione, *Noah and the Animals entering the Ark*, *c.*1650–55, monotype   244

10.2 Theodorus van Kessel after Titian, *Charles v*, engraving   246

10.3 Pierre Drevet after Hyacinthe Rigaud, *Louis Dauphin de Bourgogne*, 1707, engraving   247

10.4 Josias English after William Dobson, *William Dobson*, *c.*1649, etching   249

10.5 Giuseppe Marchi, *James Harrington Esqr. Author of the Oceana*, mezzotint   250

10.6 Marcantonio Raimondi, *Venus, Mars, and Cupid*, 1508, engraving   253

10.7 Rembrandt, *Christ Presented to the People ('Ecce Homo')*, 1655, Drypoint on Japan paper   261

10.8 School of Mantegna, *The Elephants, from 'The Triumph of Caesar'*, *c.*1484–92, engraving   263

10.9 Giulio Campagnola, *Saint John the Baptist*, *c.*1505, engraving   264

10.10 Francesco Rosselli after Sandro Botticelli, *The Assumption of the Virgin*, *c.*1490, engraving   265

Abbreviations

BJ	Biblioteka Jagiellońska Cracow
BJC	Biblioteka Jasnogórska Częstochowa
KAA	Kathedraalarchief Antwerp
NA	Národní archiv Prague
MZA	Moravský zemský archiv Brno
ZAO-OL, AO	Olomouc, Zemský archiv v Opavě, pobočka Olomouc, fond Arcibiskupství olomoucké

Notes on Contributors

Oliver Kik
is an art historical researcher at the Royal Institute for Cultural Heritage in Brussels (KIK-IRPA), where he specializes in sixteenth-century visual culture in the Habsburg Low Countries. He studied art history at the universities of Ghent and Utrecht. In his dissertation, defended at the universities of Leuven and Utrecht, he focused on the role of Netherlandish visual artists in the architectural design practice during the first half of the sixteenth century. Some of his research interests are Netherlandish humanist culture, early modern print production, architectural and ornamental language, and cross-media collaborations. He is a member of the Royal Academy of Archaeology of Belgium and has contributed to several exhibition catalogues and edited volumes on early modern Netherlandish art and architecture.

Barbara Stoltz
studied History of Art and Italian Literature at the Philipps Universität Marburg and at the Università Ca' Foscari di Venezia. She was a PhD-student at the Kunsthistorisches Institut in Florence, working on the theory of art and literature critics within Federico Zuccaro's drawings to the Divine Comedy (*Gesetz der Kunst—Ordo der Welt. Federico Zuccaros Dante-Zeichnungen*, 2011). From 2009 to 2015 she worked on a DFG-project about the theory of printmaking in the Renaissance and habilitated in 2020. Recently her book on theory of printmaking was published, entitled: *Die Kunst des Schneidens und die gedruckte Zeichnung. Theorie der Druckgraphik in der Kunstliteratur des 16. und 17. Jahrhunderts, Merzhausen* (Ad picturam 2023). Currently she is lecturer at the Universtät Marburg and is working on art theory, especially on the interrelations between renaissance and postmodern theory of arts.

Ben Thomas
is Reader in Art History at the University of Kent. He is currently working on a book about prints entitled Multiple Histories. Recent publications include Edgar Wind and Modern Art: In Defence of Marginal Anarchy (2020), Humphrey Ocean (2019) and Drawing Together (2017).

Ann V. Gunn
taught Museum and Gallery Studies at the University of St Andrews. She has published on 18th–20th century British art, and on research and scholarship in museums. She is author of *The Prints of Wilhelmina Barns-Graham. A Complete*

Catalogue (2007), and *The Prints of Paul Sandby* (*1731–1809*): *A Catalogue Raisonné* (2015). She is currently researching the life and collections of Rt. Hon. Charles Greville (1749–1809), connoisseur, town planner, mineralogist, and horticulturist.

Ad Stijnman

(PhD University of Amsterdam, Fellow of the Royal Historical Society in London) is an independent scholar of historical printmaking processes, specialising in manual intaglio printmaking techniques. He has lectured and published widely on the subject, including his seminal *Engraving and Etching 1400–2000: A History of the Development of Manual Intaglio Printmaking Processes* (2012). Together with Elizabeth Savage he co-authored and co-edited *Printing Colour 1400–1700: History, Techniques, Functions and Receptions* (2015). He has curated museum exhibitions on medieval prints, early modern color prints, and Rembrandt etchings printed on Japanese paper. He recently prepared parallel exhibitions on European color prints and book illustrations from the hand-press period in the Herzog August Library (Wolfenbüttel) and the Herzog Anton Ulrich-Museum (Braunschweig) in 2019–20.

Anne Bloemacher

is Assistant Professor of Art History at the University of Münster, where she completed her PhD in 2012 with a thesis on Raphael and Marcantonio Raimondi (funded by the German National Academic Foundation), published as a monograph in 2016 (Deutscher Kunstverlag). Together with Mandy Richter and Marzia Faietti she has edited and contributed to a volume on "Sculpture in Print" (Brill: 2021). Her main research areas are early modern prints and Italian and Northern Renaissance Painting and Sculpture. She is currently pursuing research for her new book on the artist's hands.

Małgorzata Biłozór-Salwa

PhD, is an art historian and Curator of Old Master Drawings at the Print Room of the University of Warsaw Library. She interned in the graphic collection departments of the British Museum, Musée du Louvre and Biblioteca Apostolica Vaticana. Her principal areas of interest are early modern drawings and print culture in Europe. She is the author of numerous publications including catalogues of the Print Room collections (Italian and Polish drawings) and the recent monograph of Jan Ziarnko/Jean le Grain (2021).

Gwendoline de Mûelenaere

NOTES ON CONTRIBUTORS XIII

is a postdoctoral researcher in history of art at Université catholique de Louvain in Belgium. Her current project focuses on the handling of early modern prints produced in the Southern Low Countries. Prior to that, she studied the illustrated lecture notebooks from the Old University of Louvain. She obtained a PhD at the UCLouvain, for which she carried out an iconographical study of seventeenth-century thesis prints. Her book Early Modern Thesis Prints in the Southern Netherlands was published by Brill in 2022.

Magdalena Herman

(PhD) is a research assistant at the Institute of Art History, University of Warsaw. She was a principal investigator in the research project "The Print Collection of Jan Ponętowski in the Jagiellonian Library in Cracow" supported by the National Science Centre (Poland). Her thesis on Jan Ponętowski's prints collection was awarded the Polish Prime Minister's Prize for outstanding doctoral dissertations and the Polish Art Historians Association Prize for works of young scholars. She has also authored several book chapters and journal articles. Her work has focused on the materiality of printed images, book bindings and print collecting in the second half of the sixteenth century.

Donato Esposito

is an academic and curator who specialises in 18th and 19th-century art, collecting and taste. From 1999 to 2004 he worked as curator in the Department of Prints and Drawings at the British Museum and was in 20012–13 an Andrew W. Mellon Fellow at the Metropolitan Museum of Art, New York. He has published widely on the art collection formed by Reynolds including catalogue essays for exhibitions in Plymouth in 2009–10 (which he also co-curated) and Edinburgh in 2018. Recently, he has reconstructed Reynolds' former home at 47 Leicester Square, London with special regard to the disposition and storage of his varied artworks, from sculpture to works on paper.

Introduction

Bryony Bartlett-Rawlings and Naomi Lebens

The etching of *La Galerie du Palais* (*c.*1637–1640) by the prolific Parisian print-maker Abraham Bosse (*c.*1604–1676) offers an imagined scene, based on Pierre Corneille's (1606–1684) comic play of the same name, of well-to-do shoppers browsing among the market stalls in the fashionable arcades of Paris's Le Palais de Justice (Fig. 0.1). From left to right, a man is being shown a copy of Tristan L'Hermite's (*c.*1601–1655) courtly romance, *La Mariane* (1637), at a bookseller's stall; a gentleman displays a printed fan to three ladies before a mercer's stall; and a young couple stroll arm in arm before a lingerie stall selling collars, cuffs and other items of personal linen. Below, in a ruled border inside of the print's illusionistic frame, a poem describes the scene in rhyming couplets, concluding: "*Tout ce que l'Art humain a jamais inventé, / Pour mieux charmer les sens par la galanterie, / Et tout ce qu'ont d'appas la Grace et la beauté, / Se descouvre à nos yeux dans cette Gallerie.*" [Everything that human art has ever invented, / To best charm the senses with gallantry, / And all the attractions of grace and beauty, / Can be seen before our eyes in this Gallery].

The entire gallery is, of course, Bosse's invention and it is filled with further fruits of his creation. Bosse illustrated the frontispiece to L'Hermite's *La Marianne* and the mercer in the image is occupied taking down a box from a shelf bearing the inscription: "*evantails de Bosse*" [Bosse's Fans]. Bosse also published three fan-prints in 1637/1638, which were intended to be cut out and pasted onto a handle or folded and mounted upon overlapping sticks—demonstrating the important, and often overlooked, role of prints produced to make objects of practical use.[1] Encountered in the material context of *La Galerie*, however, Bosse sets his prints in relationship to the objects in the marketplace around them. At the bookseller's stall, the fashionable customer overlooks serious philosophical texts by authors such as Cicero and Seneca to converse over *La Marianne*, the light contemporary tragedy illustrated by Bosse. The promenading couple to the right gesture towards the group admiring one of Bosse's fans before the mercer's stall. Hanging prominently from

---

1   André Blum, *L'Oeuvre Gravé d'Abraham Bosse* (Paris: 1924), nos. 158, 169, 170 (see also no. 1333 for a circular fan design of unknown date). An unfinished fan design by Bosse is discussed in Craig Hartley, "An Unfinished Fan by Abraham Bosse", *Print Quarterly*, Vol. 10, No. 4 (1993): 402. On the phenomenon of early modern printed objects, see *Altered and Adorned: Using Renaissance Prints in Daily Life*, exhibition catalogue, ed. Kimberly Nichols and Suzanne Karr Schmidt (Chicago: 2011).

FIGURE 0.1   Abraham Bosse, *La Galerie du Palais*, c.1638, etching

the woman's skirt are a mirror and a timepiece, symbols of vanity and ephemerality. The implied rebuke refers equally to the shoppers' flirtations and the products they peruse. Unlike the durable tomes stacked away on the booksellers' shelves, Bosse presents his prints as fripperies: the subjects of fleeting attention that act as grounds for social exchanges of dubious moral integrity. Nevertheless, Bosse's print of *La Galerie* reveals all such "human art" to our eyes.

La Galerie du Palais is a rare example of what might be termed a self-reflective print. It shows Bosse "placing" his printed wares in a precise context where he imagines them operating in a wider material and social world. He produced similarly enlightening prints illustrating the contemporary platemaking and printing processes for etchings and engravings.[2] The information with which we are provided by Bosse is carefully staged, but our insight is rarely so comprehensive. The inherent complexities in the manufacture, sale and use of

---

2   Abraham Bosse, *Cette figure vous montre Comme on Imprime les planches de taille douce* (The Intaglio Printers) (1642) and *Graveurs en taille douce au burin et a leaue forte* (The Etcher and the Engraver) (1643). Blum, *Abraham Bosse*, nos. 205 and 356.

INTRODUCTION

print, often involving multi-faceted networks of specialist craftsmen, artists, publishers, sellers and consumers, are frequently obscure and have led to confusion about the "place" of print in modern scholarship.

Traditionally, the history of printmaking has fallen in the space between art history and the history of the book. Multiple and often "reproductive" in nature, prints have long been marginalized in art historical scholarship in favor of the traditional "high" arts. Yet prints of all kinds, and often printed sheets bearing both text and image like Bosse's *La Galerie*, provide an essential source of information for scholars across a range of academic disciplines. In this context, a greater understanding of the medium of print, as well as the multifaceted ways in which prints operated as agents of communication, remains essential.

The essays in this volume have been developed from selected papers delivered at the conference *Placing Prints: New Developments in the Study of Print 1400–1800*, organized at The Courtauld Institute of Art, London in 2016. The international conference brought together cross-disciplinary print scholars to share approaches and research with the aim of shaping our understanding of how this broad and complex field is developing. Building on seminal scholarship that has progressed the study of print significantly over the recent decades, the essays presented here continue to explore and deepen efforts to "place" prints into diverse social, historical and cultural contexts. A brief, and by no means exhaustive, overview of the current state of the field is offered to provide context for the organization of the present volume and the key issues raised in the essays, which are introduced in more detail below.

1 Developments in the Study of Print

That the advent of print revolutionized early modern European culture is the now seminal argument first put forward by Elizabeth Eisenstein.[3] Addressing herself predominantly to text, Eisenstein posited that works produced in an "age of print" were subject to new conditions of production which made them quantitatively and qualitatively different to anything that had existed before. Of primary importance to this was the quality of "fixity" that allowed multiple people access to the same information for the first time. Despite strong rebuttals by scholars who rejected the notion of a clean paradigm shift from a world dominated by manuscript, or stressed the fallible human elements that undermined standardization in early print, it is hard to overstate the importance of

---

3 Elizabeth Eisenstein, *The Printing Press as an Agent of Change: Communications and Cultural Transformations in Early-Modern Europe* (New York: 1980).

Eisenstein's concept of a new "print culture".[4] Attention was focused towards a hitherto neglected question: what were the main consequences of print technology on European society?

Detailed investigations have been made into the technical and practical aspects of print publishing, and the development of the printed book, by scholars including Michael Gieseke, and Lucien Febvre and Henri-Jean Martin.[5] Others continued to explore the broader relationship between print and processes of cultural, social and epistemological change.[6] Among these, the great French cultural historian, Roger Chartier, defined "print culture" in a narrower sense.[7] Uniting the traditional bibliographical concerns of book history with a broader exploration of print's cultural significance, and addressing a wider range of printed materials, he focused attention on the transformations caused by the social uses and users of print: on the "set of new acts that arose out of the production of writing and pictures in a new form". He argued that prints made in specific circumstances were subject to repeated acts of "appropriation" by individuals. The culture they created was neither stable nor universal. Due to the need for specificity when addressing such objects and encounters, Chartier saw the case-study method as a prerequisite for understanding the diverse roles assumed by prints in society. In a model echoed by the present volume (and many collections of conference proceedings), his edited book included studies on subjects as apparently diverse as the publishing careers of Franciscan hagiographic pamphlets; marriage charters in 17th-century Lyon; and a selection of printed materials connected to the taking of La Rochelle in 1628.

A specific focus on the use of prints was mirrored by early scholarship in the sphere of printed images. Hans Körner used the term "*Ortlosigkeit*" [placelessness] to describe the flexibility of single-sheet woodcuts that were not fixed

---

4   Harold Love, *Scribal Publication in Seventeenth-Century England* (Oxford: 1993); Walter J. Ong, *Orality and Literacy: The Technologizing of the Word* (London: 1982); Adrian Johns, *The Nature of the Book: Print and Knowledge in the Making* (Chicago and London: 1998). A debate between Eisenstein and Johns followed in two articles published in *The American Historical Review*, Vol. 107, No. 1 (1999). See Elizabeth Eisenstein, "An Unacknowledged Revolution Revisited", 87–105; Adrian Johns, "How to Acknowledge a Revolution", 106–126. The discussion, in defense of Eisenstein, was continued in the introduction by Sabrina Alcorn Baron, Eric N. Lindquist and Eleanor F. Shelvin to their edited volume: *Agent of Change: Print Culture Studies after Elizabeth L. Eisenstein* (Amherst and Boston: 2007).

5   Michael Gieseke, *Der Buchdruck in der frühen Neuzeit: Eine historische Fallstudie über die Durchsetzung neuer Informations- und Kommunikationstechnologie* (Frankfurt: 1991); Lucien Febvre and Henri-Jean Martin, *L'apparition du livre* (Paris: 1958).

6   Lodovica Braida, *Stampa e cultura in Europa tra xv e xvi secolo* (Rome: 2000); David McKitterick, *Print, Manuscript, and the Search for Order, 1450–1830* (Cambridge: 2005).

7   Chartier, *The Culture of Print*, 1.

INTRODUCTION
5

to any specific position but rather adapted and personalized by their users in numerous ways.[8] Prints of all types were glued to things, displayed on walls, stored in albums or boxes, pasted into books, colored, cut, and combined in complex ways.[9] Research by Suzanne Karr Schmidt, Susan Dackerman, Lorraine Daston and others has continued to reveal more about how prints were absorbed into different traditions and interactions, especially within the realm of scientific inquiry.[10]

Scholarship focusing more specifically on the art of the print has also moved on to give a deeper understanding of the medium and its culture than was originally provided in the traditional catalogues of "*peintre-graveur*" by Adam von Bartsch, Johann David Passavant, Max Lehrs, Friedrich Wilhelm Hollstein, Arthur Mayger Hind or Ivins's survey of the wide range of techniques used in printmaking prior to photography.[11] Ivins was one of the earliest scholars to explore print in a broader context, in his *Prints and Visual Communication* (1969), which focused on the wide range of techniques used in the history of printmaking whilst also considering the fundamental role of the medium as an agent of visual dissemination.[12] In their foundational text, *The Renaissance Print 1470–1520* (1994), David Landau and Peter Parshall evaluated documentary sources alongside carefully analysing individual prints to investigate early

---

8   Hans Körner, *Der Früheste Deutsche Einblattholzschnitt* (Mittenwald: 1979), 40.

9   Jan van der Waal's exhibition at the Museum Boijmans Van Beuningen in Rotterdam, *Prints in the Golden Age: From Art to Shelf Paper* (2006), was a novel attempt to recreate this variety of use by integrating acclaimed masterworks with every day prints in shared roles as wall coverings. Other exhibitions that have addressed the subject of use include Peter Parshall's and Rainer Schoch's, *The Origins of European Printmaking: Fifteenth-Century Woodcuts and their Public*, at the National Gallery of Art, Washington and the Germanisches Nationalmuseum, Nuremberg (2005–2006), and Suzanne Karr Schmidt's and Kimberly Nichols's *Altered and Adorned* at the Art Institute of Chicago (2011). On hand-coloured prints, see Susan Dackerman, *Painted Prints: The Revelation of Color in Northern Renaissance & Baroque Engravings, Etchings & Woodcuts* (Baltimore: 2002).

10   Schmidt, *Altered and Adorned; Prints and the Pursuit of Knowledge in Early Modern Europe*, exhibition catalogue, ed. Susan Dackerman and Lorraine Daston (Cambridge MA: 2011).

11   Adam von Bartsch, *Le Peintre Graveur*, 21 vols (Leipzig: 1803–1821); Johann David Passavant, *Le Peintre-Graveur*, 6 vols (Leipzig: 1860–1864); Max Lehrs, *Geschichte und Kritischer Katalog des Deutschen, Niederländischen und Französischen Kupferstichs im XV. Jahrhundert*, 16 vols (Vienna: 1908–1934); Arthur Mayger Hind, *Early Italian Engraving*, 7 vols (London: 1938–1948); Friedrich Wilhelm Hollstein, *Dutch and Flemish Etchings, Engravings and Woodcuts, ca. 1450–1700* (Amsterdam: 1949–); Friedrich Wilhelm Hollstein, *German Etchings, Engravings and Woodcuts, ca. 1450–1700* (Amsterdam: 1954–); William M. Ivins Jr, *Prints and Visual Communication* (Cambridge MA: 1969).

12   Ivins Jr, *Prints and Visual Communication*.

print culture.[13] Taking the frame of the Renaissance period in which print both matured as a medium and gained status as an object, they provide an in depth overview of all stages of print production and reception: from materials, making, artist's networks and distribution, through to the wide range of prints produced (including ephemeral prints as well as those regarded as works of art) and their publics. Michael Bury has also combined close analysis of objects and supporting primary sources to consider three main aspects of print production: techniques and materials, people and networks, and center.[14] He traced the developments of print production in the Italian peninsula from the years after Landau and Parshall's book into the Early Modern period, a time which saw the rise of larger publishing houses and the commercial print alongside smaller-scale print production.

Many subsequent authors have chosen to investigate one theme or question from the many raised in the surveys by Landau, Parshall and Bury. An important line of inquiry has been the center in which a work was made. A leading center in early print production was Venice, where the Gutenberg press was introduced in 1468 by the German Johann von Speyer (d. 1470) and the Frenchman Nicolas Jenson (c.1420–1480).[15] Rosa Salzberg, for instance, has assessed how cheap prints in the form of broadsides, pamphlets and fliers were issued in Venice from the late 15th century to provide entertainment and information to a wide audience.[16] In the northern sphere, such work is paralleled by scholars who have focused on the expansion of printmaking in the important 16th century center of Antwerp. The publishing house *Aux Quatre Vents*, opened by Hieronymus Cock (1518–1570) and his wife Volcxken Diericx (d. 1600) in 1548 has provided a particularly fruitful case for scholarly investigation, notably that of Timothy Riggs.[17] Jan van der Stock's more recent *Printing Images in Antwerp*.

---

13   David Landau and Peter Parshall, *The Renaissance Print 1470–1550* (New Haven and London: 1994).

14   Michael Bury, *The Print in Italy: 1550–1620* (London: 2001).

15   Bernd Roeck, "Venice and Germany: Commercial Contacts and Intellectual Inspirations", in *Renaissance Venice and the North: Crosscurrents in the Time of Bellini, Dürer, and Titian*, ed. Bernard Aikema and Beverly Louise Brown (London: 1999), 46; Henry Simonsfeld, *Der Fondaco dei Tedeschi in Venedig und die Deutsch-Venetianischen Handelsbeziehungen* (Stuttgart: 1887), 286–385.

16   Rosa Salzberg, *Ephemeral City: Cheap Print and Urban Culture in Renaissance Venice* (Manchester: 2014).

17   The standard work on *Aux Quatre Vents* remains Timothy Riggs's 1971 disseration at Yale University "Hieronymus Cock 1510–1570: Printmaker and Publisher in Antwerp at the Sign of the Four Winds", photocopy (Ann Arbour, Mich.: Xerox University Microfilms, 1974, 71–31.002). More recently Cock's publishing house was explored in the exhibition at the M-Museum, Leuven, and accompanying catalogue Joris van Grieken, Ger Luijten, Jan

INTRODUCTION

The Introduction of Printmaking in a City: Fifteenth Century—1585 (1998) has used the case study of one center to provide an in-depth investigation of early print culture. Presenting a meticulous analysis of the rich archival resources found in Antwerp's Archives, van der Stock not only gives an overview of the variety of printed objects, ranging from artistic to ephemeral prints, many of which are documented in Antwerps archives but have been lost over time, but also uses the sources he presents to chart the origins of print as a medium, considering the ways in which it became part of society while also looking at the development of the print publisher during this early period of print history.[18] Further comparisons can be drawn to seminal work on the printing trade in Rome, including on the publishing house of Antonio Lafreri (*c*.1512–1577) and, in the 17th and 18th centuries, of the De' Rossi family.[19]

By the 17th century, print publishing was operating on a much larger scale in many different centres across Europe. Case studies of publishing houses established in Dutch cities include that of Hendrick Goltzius (1558–1617) in Haarlem, Hendrick Hondius (1573–*c*.1650) in the Hague, Crispijn de Passe (1564–1637) in Utrecht, and Claes Jansz. Visscher (1587–1652) in Amsterdam.[20] Alexander Globe's study of the London printseller Peter Stent (*c*.1613–1665) examined surviving print catalogues from 1654 and added greatly to the store of knowledge on the mid-century trade in England, a subject which

---

van der Stock, *The Renaissance in Print* (Brussels: 2013). For an overview of Antwerp print-making, see Timothy Riggs and Larry Silver (ed.), *Graven Images: The Rise of Professional Printmakers in Antwerp and Haarlem, 1540–1640* (Evaston IL: 1993).

18   Jan van der Stock, *Printing Images in Antwerp. The Introduction of Printmaking in a City: Fifteenth Century—1585* (Rotterdam: 1998).

19   Valeria Pagani, "The Dispersal of Lafreri's Inheritance 1581–89—The De' Nobili-Arbotti-Clodio Partnership", *Print Quarterly*, 28, no. 2 (2011): 119–136; Rebecca Zorach, *The Virtual Tourist in Renaissance Rome: Printing and Collecting the Speculum Romanae Magnificentiae*, exhibition catalogue (Chicago: 2008); Peter Parshall, "Antonio Lafreri's *Speculum Romanae Magnificentiae*", *Print Quarterly*, Vol. 23, No. 1 (2006): 3–27; Landau and Parshall, *The Renaissance Print*, 166, 302–308; Christopher L. Witcombe, *Print Publishing in Sixteenth-Century Rome: Growth and Expansion, Rivalry and Murder* (Turnhout: 2008); Francesco Ehrle, *Roma Prima di Sisto v: La pianta di Roma du Perac-Lafrery del 1577, Contributo alla Storia del Commercio delle Stampe a Roma nel Secolo Sedicesimo et Diciasettesimo* (Rome: 1908). Francesca Consagra, "The De' Rossi Family Print Publishing Shop: A Study in the History of the Print Industry in Seventeenth-Century Rome" (PhD Thesis, The Johns Hopkins University, Baltimore: 1993).

20   Nadine Orenstein, Huigen Leeflang, Ger Luijten and Christiaan Schuckman "Print Publishers in the Netherlands", in *Dawn of the Golden Age: Northern Netherlandish Art 1580–1620*, exhibition catalogue, edited by Ger Luijten, Ariane van Suchtelen, Reinier J. Baarsen, and Walter Kloek (Amsterdam: 1993), 170–177; Nadine Orenstein, *Hendrick Hondius and the Business of Prints in Seventeenth-Century Holland* (Rotterdam: 1996).

has received attention in later surveys that extend into the 18th century and beyond.[21] The authority of Marianne Grivel's rigorous overview of the print trade in 17th-century Paris remains unchallenged, though it has been complemented by further work on individual print publishing dynasties, such as the unparalleled Mariette family.[22]

Dedicated research addressing individual printmakers has proven another welcome development in the field. Perhaps above all, the early printmakers Andrea Mantegna (c.1431–1506), Marcantonio Raimondi (1480–1534) and Albrecht Dürer (1471–1528) have attracted much research. The engravings of Mantegna have provided a case for understanding how printmaking provided the artist with a means to disseminate his work beyond the confines of the Gonzaga court in Mantua where he was employed, as well as how his prints were made.[23] Central to scholarship on Mantegna's prints has been the

---

21 Alexander Globe, *Peter Stent, London Printseller, a Catalogue Raisonné of his Engraved Plates and Books* (Vancouver: 1985). See also Timothy Clayton, *The English Print 1688–1802* (New Haven and London: 1997); Antony Griffiths, *The Print in Stuart Britain 1603–1689* (London: 1998); Sheila O'Connell, *The Popular Print in England 1550–1850* (London: 1999); Joseph Monteyne, *The Printed Image in Early Modern London: Urban Space, Visual Representation, and Social Exchange* (Aldershot: 2007); Michael Jones, *The Print in Early Modern England: An Historical Oversight* (New Haven and London: 2010); James Raven, *Publishing Business in Eighteenth-Century England* (Woodbridge and Rochester, NY: 2014).

22 Marianne Grivel, *Le Commerce de L'Estampe à Paris au XVIIᵉ Siècle* (Geneva: 1986). On the Mariette publishing dynasty, see Maxime Préaud, "La Dynastie Mariette", in Marie-Thérèse Mandroux-França and Maxime Préaud (eds.), *Catalogues de la Collection d'Estampes de Jean V, Roi du Portugal*, 3 vols (Lisbon and Paris: 1996–2003), i, 329–371; Maxime Préaud et al., *Dictionnaire des Éditeurs d'Estampes à Paris sous l'Ancien Régime* (Paris: 1987), 228–234. On Pierre Jean Mariette (1694–1774), who became a famous writer, art collector and engraver in his own right, see Kristel Smentek, *Mariette and the Science of the Connoisseur in Eighteenth-Century Europe* (Farnham: 2014).

23 On Mantegna's use of prints to disseminate his work see: Caroline Campbell, Dagmar Korbacher, Neville Rowley and Sarah Vowles, *Mantegna and Bellini: A Renaissance Family*, exhibition catalogue (London: 2018), 20; Konrad Oberhuber, "Mantegna and the Role of Prints: A Prototype for Artistic Innovation in the North and the South", in *Renaissance Venice and the North*, 145–49; Keith Christiansen, "The Case for Mantegna as Printmaker", *The Burlington Magazine*, Vol. 135, No. 1086 (1993): 604–612; Saverio Lomartire, *Andrea Mantegna e L'Incisione Italiana del Rinascimento nelle Collezioni dei Musei Civici di Pavia* (Milan: 2003); Paul Kristeller, *Andrea Mantegna* (London, New York and Bombay: 1901); Jacquelyn L. Sheehan, "Andrea Mantegna" in Jay A. Levenson, Konrad Oberhuber and Jacquelyn L. Sheehan, *Early Italian Engravings from the National Gallery of Art* (Washington: 1973). On the production of Mantegna's prints see: Suzanne Boorsch, "Mantegna and Engraving: What We Know, What We Don't Know, and a Few Hypothesis", in *Andrea Mantegna: Impronta del Genio* (*Atti del Convegno Internazional ed Studi: Padova, Verona, Mantova, 8, 9, 10 Novembre 2006*), i, ed. Rodolfo Signorini, Viviana Rebonato,

INTRODUCTION 9

question of whether their varied technique is the result of the artist engraving the plates himself or employing printmakers to do so.[24] Andrea Canova's discovery of a contract between Mantegna and Gian Marco Cavalli (1454–c.1508), dated 5 April 1475 records that the artist did employ an engraver to produce printing plates after some of his drawings and provides an invaluable insight into this early period of print production.[25] However, scholarship remains divided on the question of whether seven core prints were indeed made by Mantegna.[26] In his recent article "Revisiting Mantegna", Landau has looked at scholarship on Mantegna and related documents that were discovered

---

and Sara Tammaccaro (Florence: 2010), 415–437; David Landau, "Andrea Mantegna as Printmaker", in *Andrea Mantegna*, edited by Jane Martineau (London: 1992), 44–55; Suzanne Boorsch, "Mantegna and His Printmakers", in *Andrea Mantegna*, ed. Martineau, 56–66; Evelyn Lincoln, *The Invention of the Italian Renaissance Printmaker* (New Haven and London: 2000), 17–43; Landau and Parshall, *The Renaissance Print*, 65–71, 112–116.

24 Giovanni Agosti, *Su Mantegna. 1, La Storia dell'Arte Libera la Testa* (Milan: 2005), 69; Patricia A. Emison, "The Raucousness of Mantegna's Mythological Engravings", *Gazette des Beaux-Arts*, 6, No. 124 (1994): 159–176. The seven prints attributed to Mantegna's hand by Paul Kristeller have been accepted in some scholarship on Mantegna as by the artist with prints that betray a different hand being grouped together as by his school. See also: Ronald W. Lightbown, *Mantegna: With a Complete Catalogue of Paintings, Drawings and Prints* (Oxford: 1986), 489–493; Zucker, *Early Italian Masters*, XXV, 73–134, no. 2506.1–2506.31; Levenson, Oberhuber, and Sheehan, *Early Italian Engravings*, 165–233; Hind, *Early Italian Engraving*, V, 3–31, nos. 1–27.

25 ASMn, Notarile, Galeazzo Giudici, 76, 5 April, 1475. The contract is published in full in: Andrea Canova, 'Gian Marco Cavalli incisore per Andrea Mantegna e altre notizie sull'oreficeria e la tipografia a Mantova nel XV secolo', *Italia medioevale e umanistica*, XLII, 2001, 149–151. See also: Andrea Canova, 'Andrea Mantegna e Gian Marco Cavalli: nuovi documenti mantovani', *Italia medioevale e umanistica*, XLIII, 2002, 201–229.

26 The two polemics were addressed by separate essays in the 1992 catalogue of the Royal Academy exhibition on Andrea Mantegna, with David Landau arguing the case of the artist as a printmaker and Suzanne Boorsch proposing that other printmakers were in fact responsible for engraving his plates. See: Landau "Andrea Mantegna as Printmaker" and Boorsch, "Mantegna and His Printmakers". That Mantegna was a printmaker has more recently been defended in: Christiansen, "The Case of Mantegna as Printmaker", 604–612. Oberhuber maintains Kristeller's attribution of seven prints, whilst also acknowledging the likelihood that Mantegna employed engravers. See also: Marzia Faietti, "Il segno di Andrea Mantegna" (2006), 14–44, Evelina Borea, *Lo Specchio dell'Arte Italiana: Stampe in Cinque Secoli*, i (Pisa: 2009), 23–25. Oberhuber, "Mantegna and the Role of Prints", 144–149; The likelihood that Mantegna employed engravers has recently been addressed in: Sarah Vowles and Dagmar Korbacher, "Drawing Conclusions: the Graphic work of Mantegna and Bellini", in *Mantegna and Bellini*, 78–79; Lincoln, *The Invention*, 38–39; Boorsch, "Mantegna and Engraving", 415–437; Andrea Canova, "Mantegna Invenit" in *Mantegna 1431–1506*, ed. Giovanni Agosti, and Dominique Thiébaut (Milan: 2008), 243–295; Sharon Gregory, *Vasari and the Renaissance Print* (Farnham: 2012), 12–16.

following the 1992 RA exhibition, alongside the prints themselves to investigate the authorship of these works as well as their production and reception.[27]

Little documentation survives on Marcantonio Raimondi and it is instead his prolific output of over 300 prints which offers a means to investigate printmaking in Bologna, Venice and Rome, the cities in which he was active. Marzia Faietti and Konrad Oberhuber have built a rich picture of the erudite circles of the university city of Bologna at the turn of the 16th century, where Marcantonio and his contemporaries Francesco (1444–1517) and Jacopo Francia (1484–1557) produced engravings informed by the study of classical antiquity.[28] Lisa Pon, meanwhile, has investigated Marcantonio's activity in two further centers where he is known to have worked, Venice and Rome. Focusing on Marcantonio's activity in Rome, Pon reassesses previous scholarship on how the printmaker's collaboration with Raphael, which produced around fifty engravings, was a vehicle to disseminate the latter's artistic ideas.[29] Debates about reproduction versus artistic invention, and the difference between "original" and "reproductive" engraving and etching, have also been central to print scholarship and criticism since Raimondi began to circulate Raphael's compositions in engravings.[30] The proceedings *Marcantonio Raimondi: il Primo Incisore di Raffaello* (2022) of the conference of the same name held to mark the 500th anniversary of Raphael's death, brings together leading scholarship to present a comprehensive study of printmaking at the time of Raphael, covering not only his partnership with Marcantonio but printmaking in the North as well as the reception and legacy of these prints in Europe in the eighteenth and nineteenth centuries.[31]

The wealth of surviving documents transcribed and published in three volumes on Dürer by Hans Rupprich (1956–1969), includes accounts by the artist and his contemporaries that offers an invaluable insight into printmaking

---

27   David Landau, "Revisiting Mantegna", *Print Quarterly*, 38, no. 3 (2021): 251–288.

28   Marzia Faietti, and Konrad Oberhuber, *Bologna e l'Umanesimo 1490–1510* (Bologna: 1988); Giancarlo Fiorenza, "Marcantonio Raimondi's Early Engravings: Myth and Imitation in Renaissance Bologna", in *Bologna. Cultural Crossroads from the Medieval to the Baroque: Recent Anglo-American Scholarship (Atti del Convegno Internazionale, Bologna 2011)*, ed. Gian Mario Anselmi, Angela De Benedictis and Nicholas Terpstra (Bologna: 2013), 13–25; Landau and Parshall, *The Renaissance Print*, 99–100.

29   Gregory, *Vasari*, 1–4, 23–30; Borea, *Lo Specchio*, i, 41–62; Witcombe, *Print Publishing*, 19–34; Lisa Pon, *Raphael, Dürer, and Marcantonio Raimondi: Copying and the Italian Renaissance Print* (New Haven and London: 2004) 67–68; Landau and Parshall, *The Renaissance Print*, 119–146.

30   See Rebecca Zorach and Elisabeth Rodini (ed.), *Paper Museums. The Reproductive Print in Europe, 1500–1800* (Chicago: 2005).

31   Anna Cerboni Baiardi and Marzia Faietti, *Marcantonio Raimondi: Il Primo Incisore di Raffaello* (Urbino: 2022).

INTRODUCTION   11

and distribution during the artist's lifetime.[32] The three-volume catalogue *Albrecht Durer: Das druckgraphische Werk* (2001–2004) edited by Rainer Schoch, Matthias Mende and Anna Scherbaum provides a definitive overview of Dürer's rolific output in the medium of print.[33] Scholarship has also noted Dürer's entrepreneurial skills in relation to how he developed the medium of print through engravings and woodcuts, and how the transmission of Dürer's art through print had a lasting impact on subsequent artists.[34]

Since the 1990s, Sound and Vision have launched a huge drive to catalogue the vast production of Dutch and Flemish and also German engravings and woodcuts as part of the New Hollstein catalogue series. This ongoing project has revisited and greatly expanded on Friedrich Hollstein's original initiative begun in 1949 to provide fully illustrated catalogues and new research on many of the key Dutch, Flemish and German print designers and printmakers active between 1450 and 1700, including Lucas van Leyden (1494–1533), Virgil Solis (1514–1562), Hendrick Goltzius, Rembrandt van Rijn (1606–1669), and Wenceslaus Hollar (1607–1677). Among the increasing attention paid to individual printmakers, Rembrandt is a special case. As Arthur M. Hind noted in his seminal *A History of Engraving & Etching*, the artist did more to explore the possibilities of the printmaking techniques he used than any before him.[35] Very likely a self-taught etcher, he intentionally varied the states of his etchings, printed them on exotic papers, and retouched prints by hand to create rarities for a clientele that valued unique impressions. His oeuvre and practice have received attention both in exhibition and as the subject of scholarly catalogues, crowned by Erik Hinterding's authoritative three-volume contribution to the New Hollstein series.[36]

---

32   Hans Rupprich, *Dürer Schriftlicher Nachlass*, 3 vols (Berlin: 1956–1969).

33   Rainer Schoch, Matthias Mende and Anna Scherbaum, editors, *Albrecht Durer: das drucksgraphische Werk*, 3 volumes (Munich: 2001).

34   Karoline Feulner, "The *Life of the Virgin*: Marketed, Plagiarized, and Copyrighted", in *Albrecht Dürer: His Art in* Context, exhibition catalogue, ed. Jochen Sander (Munich, London and New York: 2013), 234–259; Joseph Leo Koerner, 'Albrecht Dürer: a Sixteenth-Century *Influenza*', in *Albrecht Dürer and His Legacy: The Graphic Works of a Renaissance Artist*, ed. G. Bartrum (London: 2002), 22; Charles Talbot, "Dürer and the High Art of Printmaking," in *The Essential Dürer*, ed. Larry Silver and Jeffrey Chipps Smith (Philadelphia: 2010), 35–61; Giulia Bartrum, "Dürer Viewed by His Contemporaries", in *Albrecht Dürer and his Legacy*, ed. Giulia Bartrum (London: 2002), 9–17; Bartrum, *Albrecht Dürer and his Legacy*, 293–314; Aikema and Brown, *Renaissance Venice and the North*.

35   Arthur Mayger Hind, *A History of Engraving and Etching from the 15th Century to the Year 1914* (London: 1923), 170.

36   Erik Hinterding, *Rembrandt as an Etcher, Studies in Prints and Printmaking*, vi, trans. Michael Hoyle, 3 vols (Ouderkerk aan den Ijssel: 2006). The classic study of Rembrandt's printmaking methods is Christopher White, *Rembrandt as an Etcher: A Study of the Artist*

Print collections, both surviving and those documented in inventories, provide invaluable sources for researching the taste for prints as well as their distribution.[37] The collections of Philip II of Spain and his cousin Ferdinand II of Tyrol, Archduke of Austria shed light on the taste for prints in European courts during the 16th century.[38] Peter Parshall's investigation of surviving volumes of prints, documents the growing practice of collecting these works both amongst artists, humanist scholars and princely collectors such as Ferdinand, Archduke of Tyrol.[39] Michael Bury's essay "The Taste for Prints in Italy before 1600" (1985) carefully analyzes surviving inventories from the late 15th and 16th centuries to build an image of the rich collecting practices already evolving following the advent of print.[40] Similarly Mark McDonald's careful reading of the inventory of Ferdinand Columbus's collection, along with identifying works listed in the document builds a rich picture, not only of the diplomat's wide ranging taste reflecting the huge variety of printed objects available in the early 16th century, but also of an evident pattern between his diplomatic travels and collecting practices.[41]

More recently, McDonald has provided a ground-breaking full account, along with catalogue raisonné, of around 3000 prints in the collection of the Roman scholar and patron Cassiano dal Pozzo (1588–1657).[42] Cassiano selected and organized his prints on the basis of their subject, visual and textual elements, and the various meanings that could be generated by particular sequential arrangements. A remarkable proportion of his prints, compiled

---

at Work (London: 1969). For exhibition catalogues, see Erik Hinterding, Ger Luijten, and Martin Royalton-Kisch (eds.), *Rembrandt the Printmaker*, exhibition catalogue (Chicago: 2000); Clifford Ackley, *Rembrandt's Journey: Painter, Draftsman, Etcher*, exhibition catalogue (Boston: 2003); Robert Fucci, *Rembrandt's Changing Impressions*, exhibition catalogue (New York: 2015).

37 For a useful collection of recent essays on the subject, see Andrea M. Gáldy and Sylvia Heudecker (ed.), *Collecting Prints and Drawings* (Newcastle: 2018).

38 Peter Parshall, "The Print Collection of Ferdinand, Archduke of Tyrol", *Jahrbuch der Kunsthistorischen Sammlungen in Wien*, 78 (1982): 129–190; Jesus Maria González de Zárate, *Real Colecciòn de Estampas de San Lorenzo de El Escorial*, 10 vols (Madrid: 1992[–1]996); Mark P. McDonald, "The Print Collection of Philip II at the Escorial", *Print Quarterly*, 15, no. 1 (1998): 15–35.

39 Peter Parshall, "Art and the Theatre of Knowledge: The Origins of Print Collecting in Northern Europe", *Harvard University Art Museums Bulletin*, 2, no. 3 (1994): 7–36.

40 Michael Bury, "The Taste for Print in Italy to c.1600", *Print Quarterly*, 2, no. 1 (1985): 12–26.

41 Mark P. McDonald, *The Print Collection of Ferdinand Columbus 1488–1539: A Renaissance Collector in Seville*, 2 vols (London: 2004).

42 Mark P. McDonald, *The Print Collection of Cassiano dal Pozzo. Part I: Ceremonies, Costumes, Portraits and Genre*, 3 vols (London: 2016), and *Part II: Architecture, Topography and Military Maps*, 3 vols (London: 2019).

INTRODUCTION

across nine albums and many loose impressions, are not found in the existing literature and constitute important additions to the known works of major printmakers. Among the great 18th-century print collectors, the collection of King John v of Portugal (1689–1750), thought to have been totally destroyed by the Lisbon earthquake and fire of 1755, has been both partially rediscovered and reconstructed by Marie-Thérèse Mandroux-França and Maxime Préaud.[43] In contrast to earlier subject-based collecting, it reflects the growing emphasis on artists and designers in 18th-century collections, and on amassing and arranging prints to record the *oeuvres* of individual printmakers.[44] The proliferation of collecting practices during this century, extending to categories such as ephemera and across social strata, has also been subject to increasing attention.[45]

Scholarship has also seen a growing interest in the techniques and processes of print. While previous studies considered the processes involved in printmaking, these have often been for the supplementary purpose of aiding our understanding of the history of print.[46] Ad Stijnman has provided the first focused analysis in print scholarship of the different stages involved in printmaking between 1546 and 1979, from cutting and inking of plates through to the organization of workshops and trade of prints.[47] More recently, studies have focused on exploring the process of color print. The colored technique of chiaroscuro woodcuts, invented in Germany and developed both north and south of the Alps during the 16th century, was the subject of the exhibition "Chiaroscuro: Renaissance Woodcuts from the Collections of Georg Baselitz and The Albertina, Vienna" (Royal Academy, London: 2014).[48] In 2018, The National Gallery of Art, Washington offered a focused study of the technique

---

43   Mandroux-França and Préaud, *Catalogues de la collection d'estampes de Jean v*. See also Antony Griffiths, "The Prints of John v of Portugal", *Print Quarterly*, 22, no. 3 (2005): 334–338.

44   Antony Griffiths, "Print Collecting in Rome, Paris, and London in the Early Eighteenth Century", *Harvard University Art Museums Bulletin*, 2, no. 3 (1994): 37–58.

45   Gillian Russell, *The Ephemeral Eighteenth Century, Print, Sociability, and the Cultures of Collecting* (Cambridge: 2020); Adriano Aymonino, "The Musaeum of the First Duchess of Northumberland (1716–1776) at Northumberland House in London", in Susan Bracken, Andrea M. Gáldy and Adriana Turpin (ed.), *Women Patrons and Collectors* (Newcastle: 2012), 101–120.

46   See for example, Hind, *A History of Engraving and Etching*.

47   Ad Stijnman, *Engraving and Etching 1400–2000: A History of the Development of Manual Intaglio Printmaking Processes* (London: 2012).

48   Achim Gnann, David Ekserdjian and Michael Foster, *Chiaroscuro: Renaissance Woodcuts from the Collections of Georg Baselitz and The Albertina, Vienna*, exhibition catalogue (London: 2014).

in the Italian peninsula through the exhibition "The Chiaroscuro Woodcut in Renaissance Italy".[49] Elizabeth Savage and Ad Stijnman have further showcased growing scholarship within this previously overlooked area of print studies in their edited volume that highlights the various processes and uses for colour in print before Le Blon's invention of the trichromatic printing process *c.*1710.[50]

The very nature of print, employing different techniques to produce works of varying quality and function from adverts, pamphlets and broadsides through to reproductive and fine art has resulted in scholars taking a particular focus in the field. Such studies have included Zahira Véliz Bomford's essay on the role of print in Spanish art during the Golden Age, where artist's drew from exceptionally strong collections of print.[51] The recent volume of essays *Sculpture in Print, 1480–1600*, edited by Anne Bloemacher, Mandy Richter and Marzia Faietti, looks at the process and technique of translating sculpture into print.[52]

Relevant to all of the above developments in the field is the latest contribution by Antony Griffiths, *The Print before Photography* (2016).[53] The result of decades of research and reflection over his long tenure as Keeper of Prints and Drawings in the British Museum (1991–2011), this ground-breaking thematic survey provides a reference work rich with examples, archival detail and documentary sources for researchers from any field who engage with print. Griffiths takes 1550 as his starting date, this being both the point at which the development of trade in intaglio prints accelerated and one which follows directly on from the aforementioned *The Renaissance Print* by Landau and Parshall, its effective predecessor as the fundamental text on European print.

Reflecting the increasing "unity" of the international trade in prints during this later period, Griffiths abandons the chronological narrative of Landau and Parshall and divides his book into three main sections. The first, and longest, is on print production. It covers not just printing technologies, the printing capacity of copper plates and related costs, but also lettering, censorship, copying, reprinting, coloring, book illustration, and the survival and loss of prints. The second section deals with the various actors involved in the print trade,

---

49 Naoko Takahatake, *The Chiaroscuro Woodcut in Renaissance Italy*, exhibition catalogue (Los Angeles: 2018).

50 Elizabeth Savage and Ad Stijnman, *Printing in Colour 1400–1700* (Leiden: 2015).

51 Véliz Bomford, "The Authority of Prints in Early Modern Spain" (2008), 416–436.

52 Anne Bloemacher, Mandy Richter and Marzia Faietti (ed.), *Sculpture in Print, 1480–1600* (Leiden: 2021).

53 Antony Griffiths, *The Print before Photography: An Introduction to European Printmaking, 1550–1820* (London: 2016).

INTRODUCTION   15

from the printmakers, designers, and publishers (together with their networks
of financing, patronage, marketing and state and private publication) to buyers, and the figures involved in the iterant trade in cheap print. The third section examines the variety of ways in which prints were used and understood:
for display and storage, in collections, in early literature on prints, in the wider
art world, and in the internal hierarchy of print techniques. Finally, a brief
coda considers the print since 1820, a period just before photography "and the
processes that depend on it have made [print technologies] obsolete, and the
twentieth century steadily removed the pre-photographic print from everyday
view". Despite its encyclopedic content, Griffiths takes pains to emphasize that
he views print history as a discipline "still at a very early stage" and welcomes
future scholars to continue to develop the field.

2   Volume

Based in the early period of production explored in, and prior to, Griffiths'
The Print Before Photography, the individual essays in this volume respond
to this call. They are presented in a bi-part structure encompassing two over-
riding themes. Part One "The Art of Print" considers aspects of print production and their perceived "place" within a printmaker's practice; and Part Two
"The Reception of Print" addresses issues of circulation, reception and use
of prints in the hands of publishers and audiences. Of course, no such division can be absolute. In many cases, a natural link existed between the way in
which a print was conceived of and made, and how it was marketed and used.
Several essays in this volume will touch upon this. Some of the connections
between the subjects presented in this volume will be discussed briefly below,
however many more can be made and the two-part structure is intended to
allow the reader to draw further connections between the over-riding themes
covered in essays that span different centuries, countries and even continents.

    "The Art of Print: Approaches and Attitudes" includes essays which address
physical and intellectual aspects of printmaking. In the first essay by Oliver Kik,
we see how goldsmiths in the Low Countries and Germany from *c*.1470–1520
keenly embraced printmaking to disseminate their designs and technical
knowledge. Kik examines how the production of a new genre of ornament
prints intersected with developments in self-representation and professional
position of printmakers such as Alart DuHameel (*c*.1460–*c*.1506) and the anonymous Master W with the Key (active *c*.1465–1485).

    Understanding how prints have been "placed" in the hierarchy of artistic
media by artists themselves is an area that has received limited attention in

existing scholarship.[54] Barbara Stoltz's contribution builds on the interdisciplinary crossovers introduced by Kik with a detailed exploration of how printmaking was defined in comparison to other arts in the Renaissance period. Mining the writings of Benvenuto Cellini (1500–1571), Matthias Quad von Kinckelbach (1557–1613), Giorgio Vasari (1511–1574) and John Evelyn (1620–1706), she shows how the relative definitions of sculpture, painting and drawing expressed by these authors shaped their individual definitions of printmaking. The need for tackling the problems of print's "dual" nature that Stoltz identifies in these writings, it being both a sculpted process and yet a work on paper, is echoed in the contribution by Ben Thomas. Thomas investigates Nicolas Poussin's (1620–1706) somewhat negative attitude towards printmaking and the particular tensions he perceived between the printmaking techniques adopted by his contemporaries and the demands of translating painted compositions into print. Thomas offers new analysis of attempts to regularize engraving techniques in the prints and writings of French printmakers in Poussin's circle including Abraham Bosse, Claude Mellan (1598–1688), Robert Nanteuil (1623–1678) and Giles Rousselet (1610–1686).

Picking up on the theme of reproduction, Anne Gunn's exploration of Paul Sandby's (1731–1809) work as a printmaker in 18th-century England shows an artist keenly using printmaking and reproductive prints as a medium through which to distribute his works to a wider audience. Sandby's reproductive etchings are carefully examined in comparison to his later original aquatint projects in terms of technique, aesthetics and intention, and this is set into a wider discussion of contemporary attitudes towards reproductive printmaking.

In the final essay of this section, Ad Stijnman introduces the little studied area of color printed medical illustrations. Taking the 125 early modern medical books with colour printed illustrations conserved in the Herzog August Library, Wolfenbüttel as his source material, he considers the "place" these prints occupied between book illustrations and fine art prints and demonstrates how the continued development of color printing techniques played an important role in allowing specialized scientific prints to be more clearly read by their audience.

The essays in Part Two "The Reception of Print: Circulation and Use" further examine the functions of prints on the commercial marketplace and

---

54   See Griffiths, *The Print before Photography*, 446–465. Sharon Gregory makes a significant contribution in *Vasari and the Renaissance Print*, where she explores Vasari's writings on print published in his *Lives of the Artists* to show how prints were perceived during the 16th century.

INTRODUCTION   17

within the hands of the early modern consumer. In Anne Bloemacher's opening contribution, issues of audience and the commercial republishing of prints are investigated in the case of a series of engravings made after Raphael's *Madonna of Foligno* by Raimondi and Giovanni Antonio da Brescia (1540–1623). Through careful formal and contextual analysis, Bloemacher demonstrates how each "reproduction" used aesthetic and commercial strategies to increase the prints' appeal to specific markets and audiences. In the following essay, Małgorzata Biłozór-Salwa interrogates the practice of updating maps and broadsides by the Polish printmaker Jan Ziarnko (1575–1630) in 17th-century Paris. She demonstrates how both Ziarnko and his royal patrons were acutely aware of the power of print in distributing sensitive political messages to a wide audience, and of how carefully such changes to the plates were negotiated.

In contrast, the 17th-century broadsheets produced as thesis prints in the Southern Low Countries, the subject of Gwendoline de Mûelenaere's essay, were intended for a much smaller circulation within an intellectual elite. They were made in commemoration of the *disputatio*, or final exam of their degree, and intended to be presented as a gift from students to their professors. De Mûelenaere explores these acts of gift-giving, which were also expressed in the written dedications and the common device of the *mise-en-abyme* featured on the broadsides (in which the prints' own presentation to the student's sponsor is illustrated).

The volume closes with two studies of collecting practices at the beginning and end of the period covered by this book. Magdalena Herman offers insight into the rich culture of print collecting in Poland during the 16th century through her study of the collection of the erudite noble scholar Jan Ponętowski (*c.*1540–1598), gifted to the Jagiellonian library in Kraków in 1592. Comprising of eleven albums and over one thousand prints, Herman interrogates the logic and sequencing of the albums and considers how this reflected the activity and interests of a Polish nobleman entrusted with vital Church functions in post-Tridentine Moravia. The final essay by Donato Esposito investigates the use of prints by the English painter Sir Joshua Reynolds (1723–1792). Reynolds assembled a collection of over 10,000 prints of an extraordinary depth and range, with many prints related to other parts of his art collection, decorative schemes or artists connected with specific locations. Esposito explores how Reynolds' print collection supported the intellectual claims he made about art and revealed much about the privileged position he assumed. Closing by tracing the dissemination of the collection following Reynolds' death, it allows us to build an understanding of collecting practices of both individual collectors and museums into the 20th century.

Select Bibliography

Ackley, Clifford, *Rembrandt's Journey: Painter, Draftsman, Etcher*, exhibition catalogue (Boston: 2003).

Agosti, Giovanni, *Su Mantegna. 1, La Storia dell'Arte Libera la Testa* (Milan: 2005).

Aymonino, Adriano, "The Musaeum of the First Duchess of Northumberland (1716–1776) at Northumberland House in London", in Susan Bracken, Andrea M. Gáldy and Adriana Turpin (ed.), *Women Patrons and Collectors* (Newcastle: 2012), 101–120.

Baron, Sabrina, Eric N. Lindquist and Shelvin, Eleanor F. (ed.), *Agent of Change: Print Culture Studies after Elizabeth L. Eisenstein* (Amherst and Boston: 2007).

Bartrum, Giulia (ed.), *Albrecht Dürer and his Legacy: The Graphic Work of a Renaissance Artist*, exhibition catalogue (London: 2002).

Bartsch, Adam von, *Le Peintre Graveur*, 21 vols (Vienna: 1802–1821).

Blum, André, *L'Oeuvre Gravé d'Abraham Bosse* (Paris: 1924).

Boorsch, Suzanne, "Mantegna and His Printmakers", in *Andrea Mantegna*, edited by Jane Martineau (London: 1992), 56–66.

Boorsch, Suzanne, "Mantegna and Engraving: What We Know, What We Don't Know, and a Few Hypotheses", in *Andrea Mantegna: Impronta del Genio (Atti del Convegno Internazional ed Studi: Padova, Verona, Mantova, 8, 9, 10 Novembre 2006)*, i, ed. Rodolfo Signorini, Viviana Rebonato, and Sara Tammaccaro (Florence: 2010), 415–437.

Borea, Evelina, *Lo Specchio dell'Arte Italiana: Stampe in Cinque Secoli*, i (Pisa: 2009).

Bury, Michael, "The Taste for Prints in Italy to c.1600", *Print Quarterly*, 2, No. 1 (1985): 12–26.

Bury, Michael, *The Print in Italy: 1550–1620* (London: 2001).

Campbell, Caroline, Dagmar Korbacher, Neville Rowley, and Sarah Vowles, *Mantegna and Bellini: A Renaissance Family*, exhibition catalogue (London: 2018).

Canova, Andrea, "Mantegna Invenit" in *Mantegna 1431–1506*, ed. Giovanni Agosti, and Dominique Thiébaut (Milan: 2008), 243–295.

Canova, Andrea, 'Gian Marco Cavalli incisore per Andrea Mantegna e altre notizie sull'oreficeria e la tipografia a Mantova nel XV secolo', *Italia medioevale e umanistica*, XLII, 2001 149–181.

Canova, Andrea, 'Andrea Mantegna e Gian Marco Cavalli: nuovi documenti mantovani', *Italia medioevale e umanistica*, XLIII, 2002, 201–229.

Cerboni Baiardi, Anna, and Marzia Faietti, *Marcantonio Raimondi: Il Primo Incisore di Raffaello* (Urbino: 2022).

Chartier, Roger (ed.), *Les Usages de L'imprimé (XVe–XIXe siècle)* (Paris: 1987).

Chartier, Roger (ed.), *The Culture of Print: Power and the Uses of Print in Early Modern Europe*, translated by Lydia G. Cochrane (Cambridge: 1989).

Christiansen, Keith, "The Case for Mantegna as Printmaker", *The Burlington Magazine*, 135, no. 1086 (1993): 604–612.

INTRODUCTION

Clayton, Timothy, *The English Print 1688–1802* (New Haven and London: 1997).

Consagra, Francesca, "The De' Rossi Family Print Publishing Shop: A Study in the History of the Print Industry in Seventeenth-Century Rome" (PhD Thesis, The Johns Hopkins University, Baltimore: 1993).

Dackerman, Susan, *Painted Prints: The Revelation of Color in Northern Renaissance & Baroque Engravings, Etchings & Woodcuts* (Baltimore: 2002).

Dackerman, Susan & Daston, Lorraine (ed.), *Prints and the Pursuit of Knowledge in Early Modern Europe*, exhibition catalogue (Cambridge MA: 2011).

Eisenstein, Elisabeth, *The Printing Press as an Agent of Change: Communications and Cultural Transformations in Early-Modern Europe* (New York: 1980).

Eisenstein, Elizabeth, "An Unacknowledged Revolution Revisited", *The American Historical Review*, Vol. 107, No. 1 (1999): 87–105.

Ehrle, Francesco, *Roma Prima di Sisto V: Lapianta di Roma du Perac-Lafrery del 1577, Contributo alia Storia del Commercio delle Stampe a Roma nel Secolo Sedicesimo et Diciasettesimo* (Rome: 1908).

Emison, Patricia A., "The Raucousness of Mantegna's Mythological Engravings", *Gazette des Beaux-Arts*, 6, No. 124 (1994): 159–176.

Faietti, Marzia, and Oberhuber, Konrad, *Bologna e l'Umanesimo 1490–1510* (Bologna: 1988).

Feulner, Karoline, "The *Life of the Virgin*: Marketed, Plagiarized, and Copyrighted", in *Albrecht Dürer: His Art in Context*, exhibition catalogue, ed. Jochen Sander (Munich, London and New York: 2013), 234–259.

Fiorenza, Giancarlo, "Marcantonio Raimondi's Early Engravings: Myth and Imitation in Renaissance Bologna", in *Bologna. Cultural Crossroads from the Medieval to the Baroque: Recent Anglo-American Scholarship* (*Atti del Convegno Internazionale, Bologna 2011*), ed. Gian Mario Anselmi, Angela De Benedictis and Nicholas Terpstra (Bologna: 2013), 13–25.

Fucci, Robert, *Rembrandt's Changing Impressions*, exhibition catalogue (New York: 2015).

Gáldy, Andrea M., and Heudecker, Sylvia (ed.), *Collecting Prints and Drawings* (Newcastle: 2018).

Globe, Alexander, *Peter Stent, London Printseller, a Catalogue Raisonné of his Engraved Plates and Books* (Vancouver: 1985).

Gnann, Achim, Ekserdjian, David and Foster, Michael, *Chiaroscuro: Renaissance Woodcuts from the Collections of Georg Baselitz and The Albertina, Vienna*, exhibition catalogue (London: 2014).

González de Zárate, Jesus Maria, *Real Colecciòn de Estampas de San Lorenzo de El Escorial*, 10 vols (Madrid: 1992[–1]996).

Gregory, Sharon, *Vasari and the Renaissance Print* (Farnham: 2012).

Griffiths, Anthony, "Print Collecting in Rome, Paris, and London in the Early Eighteenth Century", *Harvard University Art Museums Bulletin*, 2, no. 3 (1994), 37–58.

Griffiths, Antony, *The Print in Stuart Britain 1603–1689* (London: 1998).

Griffiths, Antony, "The Prints of John V of Portugal", *Print Quarterly*, 22, no. 3 (2005), 334–338.

Griffiths, Anthony, *The Print before Photography: An Introduction to European Print-making, 1550–1820* (London: 2016).

Grivel, Marianne, *Le Commerce de L'Estampe à Paris au XVIIe Siècle* (Geneva: 1986).

Hartley, Craig, "An Unfinished Fan by Abraham Bosse", *Print Quarterly*, 10, no. 4 (1993), 402.

Hind, Arthur Mayger, *A History of Engraving and Etching from the 15th Century to the Year 1914* (London: 1923).

Hind, Arthur Mayger, *Early Italian Engraving*, 7 vols (London: 1938–1948).

Hinterding, Erik, Ger Luijten, and Royalton-Kisch, Martin (eds.), *Rembrandt the Print-maker*, exhibition catalogue (Chicago: 2000).

Hinterding, Erik, *Rembrandt as an Etcher, Studies in Prints and Printmaking*, VI, translated from the Dutch by Michael Hoyle, 3 vols (Ouderkerk aan den Ijssel: 2006).

Hollstein, Friedrich Wilhelm, *Dutch and Flemish Etchings, Engravings and Woodcutrs, ca. 1450–1700* (Amsterdam: 1949–).

Hollstein, Friedrich Wilhelm, *German Etchings, Engravings and Woodcuts, ca. 1450–1700* (Amsterdam: 1954–).

Ivins, William M. Jr, *Prints and Visual Communication* (Cambridge MA and London: 1969).

Johns, Adrian, "How to Acknowledge a Revolution", *The American Historical Review*, Vol. 107, No. 1 (1999): 106–126.

Johns, Adrian, *The Nature of the Book: Print and Knowledge in the Making* (Chicago and London: 1998).

Jones, Michael, *The Print in Early Modern England: An Historical Oversight* (New Haven and London: 2010).

Karr Schmidt, Suzanne and Nichols, Kimberly (ed.), *Altered and Adorned: Using Renaissance Prints in Daily Life*, exhibition catalogue (Chicago: 2011).

Koerner, Joseph Leo, 'Albrecht Dürer: a Sixteenth-Century *Influenza*', in *Albrecht Dürer and His Legacy: The Graphic Works of a Renaissance Artist*, ed. Giulia Bartrum (London: 2002), 18–38.

Körner, Hans, *Der Früheste Deutsche Einblattholzschnitt* (Mittenwald: 1979).

Kristeller, Paul, *Andrea Mantegna* (London, New York and Bombay: 1901).

Landau, David, "Revisiting Mantegna", *Print Quarterly*, 38, no. 3 (2021): 251–288.

Landau, David, "Andrea Mantegna as Printmaker", in *Andrea Mantegna*, ed. Jane Martineau (London: 1992), 44–55.

Landau, David and Parshall, Peter, *The Renaissance Print 1470–1550* (New Haven and London: 1994).

INTRODUCTION

Lehrs, Max, *Geschichte und Kritischer Katalog des Deutschen, Niederländischen und Französischen Kupferstichs im XV. Jahrhundert*, 16 vols (Vienna: 1908–1934).

Lightbown, Ronald W., *Mantegna: With a Complete Catalogue of Paintings, Drawings and Prints* (Oxford: 1986).

Lincoln, Evelyn, *The Invention of the Italian Renaissance Printmaker* (New Haven and London: 2000).

Lomartire, Saverio, *Andrea Mantegna e L'Incisione Italiana del Rinascimento nelle Collezioni dei Musei Civici di Pavia* (Milan: 2003).

Love, Harold, *Scribal Publication in Seventeenth-Century England* (Oxford: 1993).

Mandroux-França, Marie-Thérèse and Maxime Préaud (ed.), *Catalogues de la Collection d'Estampes de Jean V, Roi du Portugal*, 3 vols (Lisbon and Paris: 1996–2003).

McDonald, Mark P., "The Print Collection of Philip II at the Escorial", *Print Quarterly*, Vol. 15, No. 1 (1998): 15–35.

McDonald, Mark P., *The Print Collection of Cassiano dal Pozzo. Part I: Ceremonies, Costumes, Portraits and Genre*, 3 vols (London: 2016).

McDonald, Mark P., *The Print Collection of Cassiano dal Pozzo. Part II: Architecture, Topography and Military Maps*, 3 vols (London: 2019).

McDonald, Mark P., *The Print Collection of Ferdinand Columbus 1488–1539: A Renaissance Collector in Seville*, 2 vols (London: 2004).

Monteyne, Joseph, *The Printed Image in Early Modern London: Urban Space, Visual Representation, and Social Exchange* (Aldershot: 2007).

Oberhuber, Konrad, "Marcantonio Raimondi." *Bologna e l'umanesimo 1490–1510*, exhibition catalogue, edited by Marzia Faietti and Konrad Oberhuber (Bologna: 1988), 51–210.

Oberhuber, Konrad, "Mantegna and the Role of Prints: A Prototype for Artistic Innovation in the North and the South", in *Renaissance Venice and the North: Crosscurrents in the Time of Bellini, Dürer, and Titian* ed. Bernard Aikema and Beverly Louise Brown (London: 1999), 145–49.

O'Connell, Sheila, *The Popular Print in England 1550–1850* (London: 1999).

Orenstein, Nadine, Leeflang, Huigen, Ger Luijten and Christiaan Schuckman "Print Publishers in the Netherlands", in *Dawn of the Golden Age: Northern Netherlandish Art 1580–1620*, exhibition catalogue, ed. Ger Luijten, Ariane van Suchtelen, Reinier J. Baarsen, and Walter Kloek (Amsterdam: 1993).

Orenstein, Nadine, *Hendrick Hondius and the Business of Prints in Seventeenth-Century Holland* (Rotterdam: 1996).

Pagani, Valeria, "The Dispersal of Lafreri's Inheritance 1581–89—The De' Nobili-Arbotti-Clodio Partnership", *Print Quarterly*, 28, no. 2 (2011): 119–136.

Parshall, Peter, "The Print Collection of Ferdinand, Archduke of Tyrol", *Jahrbuch der Kunsthistorischen Sammlungen in Wien*, 78 (1982): 129–190.

Parshall, Peter, "Art and the Theatre of Knowledge: The Origins of Print Collecting in Northern Europe", *Harvard University Art Museums Bulletin*, 2, No. 3 (1994): 7–36.

Parshall, Peter, "Antonio Lafreri's *Speculum Romanae Magnificentiae*", *Print Quarterly*, 23, no. 1 (2006): 3–27.

Parshall, Peter and Rainer Schoch (ed.), *Fifteenth-Century Woodcuts and Their Public*, exhibition catalogue (New Haven and London: 2005).

Passavant, Johann David, *Le Peintre-Graveur*, 6 vols (Leipzig: 1860–1864).

Pon, Lisa, *Raphael, Dürer, and Marcantonio Raimondi: Copying and the Italian Renaissance Print* (New Haven and London: 2004).

Préaud, Maxime, et al., *Dictionnaire des Éditeurs d'Estampes à Paris sous l'Ancien Régime* (Paris: 1987).

Raven, James, *Publishing Business in Eighteenth-Century England* (Woodbridge and Rochester, NY: 2014).

Riggs, Timothy and Silver, Larry (ed.), *Graven Images: The Rise of Professional Printmakers in Antwerp and Haarlem, 1540–1640* (Evaston IL: 1993).

Roeck, Bernd, "Venice and Germany: Commercial Contacts and Intellectual Inspirations", in *Renaissance Venice and the North: Crosscurrents in the Time of Bellini, Dürer, and Titian* ed. Bernard Aikema and Beverly Louise Brown (London: 1999), 45–55.

Rupprich, Hans, *Dürer Schriftlicher Nachlass*, 3 vols (Berlin: 1956–1969).

Russell, Gillian, *The Ephemeral Eighteenth Century, Print, Sociability, and the Cultures of Collecting* (Cambridge: 2020).

Salzberg, Rosa, *Ephemeral City: Cheap Print and Urban Culture in Renaissance Venice* (Manchester: 2014).

Savage, Elizabeth and Stijnman, Ad, *Printing in Colour 1400–1700* (Leiden: 2015).

Simonsfeld, Henry, *Der Fondaco dei Tedeschi in Venedig und die Deutsch-Venetianischen Handelsbeziehungen* (Stuttgart: 1887).

Sheehan, Jacquelyn L., "Andrea Mantegna" in Jay A. Levenson, Konrad Oberhuber and Jacquelyn L. Sheehan, *Early Italian Engravings from the National Gallery of Art* (Washington: 1973).

Smentek, Kristel, *Mariette and the Science of the Connoisseur in Eighteenth-Century Europe* (Farnham: 2014).

Stijnman, Ad, *Engraving and Etching 1400–2000: A History of the Development of Manual Intaglio Printmaking Processes* (London: 2012).

Stock, Jan van der, *Printing Images in Antwerp. The Introduction of Printmaking in a City: Fifteenth Century—1585* (Rotterdam: 1998).

Takahatake, Naoko, *The Chiaroscuro Woodcut in Renaissance Italy*, exhibition catalogue (Los Angeles: 2018).

Talbot, Charles, "Dürer and the High Art of Printmaking," in *The Essential Dürer*, ed. Larry Silver and Jeffrey Chipps Smith (Philadelphia: 2010), 35–61.

Véliz Bomford, Zahira, "The Authority of Prints in Early Modern Spain", Hispanic Research Journal, Iberian and Latin American Studies, 9 (2008), 416–436.

Waal, Jan van der, *Prints in the Golden Age: From Art to Shelf Paper*, exhibition catalogue (Rotterdam: 2006).

White, Christopher, *Rembrandt as an Etcher: A Study of the Artist at Work* (London: 1969).

Witcombe, Christopher. L., *Print Publishing in Sixteenth-Century Rome: Growth and Expansion, Rivalry and Murder* (Turnhout: 2008).

Zorach, Rebecca and Elisabeth Rodini (ed.), *Paper Museums. The Reproductive Print in Europe, 1500–1800* (Chicago: 2005).

Zorach, Rebecca, *The Virtual Tourist in Renaissance Rome: Printing and Collecting the Speculum Romanae Magnificentiae*, exhibition catalogue (Chicago: 2008).

Zucker, Mark J., *Early Italian Masters*, vol. 25 (Commentary). Formerly Volume 13 (part 2). The Illustrated Bartsch, ed. Walter L. Strauss (New York: 1984).

PART 1

The Art of Print: Approaches and Attitudes

∵

CHAPTER 1

Mark(et)ing Expertise: the Goldsmith-engraver in the Low Countries and the Use of House Marks

Oliver Kik

In 1489, the Nuremberg-based goldsmith Hans Schmuttermayer (act. 1484–1520) published his *Fialenbüchlein*.[1] It was a small instruction manual, intended for his fellow craftsmen, on how to draw and design a gothic pinnacle starting from a geometrical ground plan and based on Euclidean rules of thumb. By using a simple geometrical figure (such as a square or a triangle), it was possible to deduce from the ground plan the widths and lengths of the entire structure. This followed a long tradition of similar model- and instruction books, of which the earliest known example is the 13th-century portfolio of Villard de Honnecourt (*c*.1230).[2] What differentiated Schmuttermayer's manual from its predecessors was the fact that it included two engravings, one showing a gothic pinnacle and the other an arch (Fig. 1.1). Schmuttermayer published the booklet himself and most likely provided the copperplates required for the engravings. Although he is not generally considered an engraver, Schmuttermayer is a modest representative of a late 15th-century phenomenon of goldsmiths disseminating their technical skills and knowledge via the new medium of engraved images.

The close connection between goldsmiths' workshops and the origins of the engraved image is a well-studied phenomenon.[3] By the middle of the

---

1   Lon Shelby, *Gothic Design Techniques: The Fifteenth-Century Design Booklets of Mathes Roriczer and Hanns Schmuttermayer* (Carbondale: 1977), 28–31.

2   Carl F. Barnes Jr., *The Portfolio of Villard de Honnecourt (Paris, Bibliothèque Nationale de France, MS Fr 19093): A New Critical Edition and Color Facsimile* (Farnham: 2009).

3   Max Lehrs, *Geschichte und kritscher Katalog des deutchen, niederlandischen un franzözischen Kupferstichs in XV. Jahrhundert*, vol. 1 (Vienna: 1908), 1–3; David Landau ans Peter Parshall, *The Renaissance Print, 1470–1550* (New Haven and London: 1994), 7–8; Joyce G. H. Zelen, "Zum Verhältnis des frühen Kupferstichs zur Goldschmiedekunst: der Salzburger Hausaltar des Meisters Perchtold" in: *Mit den Gezeiten. Frühe Druckgraphik der Niederlande*, ed. Tobias Pfeifer-Helke (Petersberg: 2013), 25–31; Ad Stijnman, *Engraving and Etching 1400–2000. A History of the Development of Manuel Printmaking Processes* (Houten: 2012), 30–33, situates the beginning of printmaking with the Master of the Playing Cards, *c*.1435. He does notice, however, that the hatchings made by early engravers are of a different nature than those seen in goldsmiths' engravings.

© KONINKLIJKE BRILL BV, LEIDEN, 2024 | DOI:10.1163/9789004703834_003

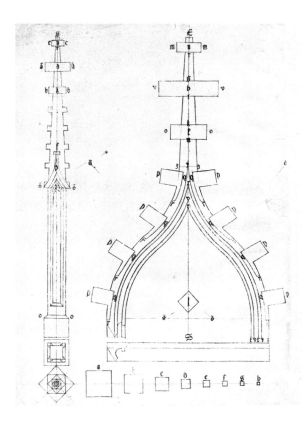

FIGURE 1.1
Hans Schmuttermayer, *Fiallenbuchlein*, fol. 1, 1489

15th century, stimulated by the introduction of the roller press and cheaper paper, gold- and silversmith tools traditionally used for figurative and decorative patterns on metalwork (burin and stylus) were increasingly adopted by craftsmen to produce printed media. Most early engravers shared a family background in the goldsmith's trade. A fellow-goldsmith of Hans Schmuttermayer in Nuremberg, Albrecht Dürer the Elder (c.1427–1502) watched as his son swapped this tradition for the printed image, thereby taking the medium to a hitherto unseen level of quality.[4] It should come as no surprise that, aside to playing cards and devotional prints, one of the most popular genres practiced

---

4   These goldsmiths were acquainted with one another; they are both named in a 1487 document, stating that a certain Hermann Laisner was in debt to both Hans Schmuttermayer and Albrecht Dürer (the Elder). Shelby, *Gothic Design Techniques*, 29. Schmuttermayer may also have influenced Dürer in writing a geometrical treatise in 1525, see: Thomas Eser, "A Different Early Dürer. Three Proposals", in *The Early Dürer*, exhibition catalogue, ed. Daniel Hess and Thomas Eser (New Haven and London: 2012), 25.

by these early goldsmith-engravers were ornament- and design prints.[5] Such prints were essential in disseminating both goldsmith and architectural designs. While models for ornaments and architectural plans had previously circulated among workshops in the form of sketchbooks, workshop designs and luxury presentation drawings, their role was swiftly overtaken by prints.[6] Prints served as patterns not only for goldsmiths but for a wide range of craftsmen and artists, including woodcarvers, architects, book illuminators, painters, and sculptors and they were also prized by early collectors as objects in their own right. Despite the well-established link discussed between goldsmiths' workshops and early print production in print scholarship, the genre of prints depicting goldsmiths' designs has received little attention. This essay will examine the phenomenon of the goldsmith-engraver in the Low Countries and, to a lesser extent, in Germany, between 1470 and 1520, focusing on the use of prints depicting goldsmiths' designs and their role as a medium through which to disseminate technical know-how. The use of monograms and house marks will also be discussed as a manifestation of professional pride and an indicator of the craftsman's awareness of their changing social position within the larger cultural framework of the early Renaissance artist.

1 Goldsmith-Engravers in the Low Countries

Little is known about the early developments of printmaking in the Low Countries during the late 15th century, prior to Lucas van Leyden's (1489/ 94–1533) entrance onto the Netherlandish printmaking stage in around 1510.[7] Many early engravers, such as Master IAM of Zwolle or Master FVB

---

5   The term *ornament print* covers a vast variety of works ranging from strictly decorative designs (e.g. candelabra decorations, foliage motifs of arabesques) to architectural fantasies and designs for metalwork. In this article, a distinction is made between ornament prints (i.e. prints representing predominantly decorative function patterns) and design prints (i.e. prints representing a design for metalwork, architecture, sculpture, etc.). On the terminology and applications of this specific type of prints, also see: Allison Stielau, "Intent and Independence: Late Fifteenth-Century Object Engravings", in: *Visual Acuity and the Arts of Communication in Early Modern Germany*, ed. Jeffrey Chipps Smith (Farnham: 2014), 21–42.

6   Janet S. Byrne, *Renaissance Ornament Prints and Drawings. The Metropolitan Museum of Art* (New York: 1981), 17–19; For the use of model books in medieval workshops, see: Robert W. Scheller, *Exemplum. Model-Book Drawings and the Practice of Artistic Transmission in the Middle Ages* (Amsterdam: 1995).

7   Jan van der Stock, *Printing Images in Antwerp. The Introduction of Printmaking in a City: Fifteenth Century to 1585* (Rotterdam: 1998); Tobias Pfeifer-Helke, editor, *Mit den Gezeiten. Frühe Druckgraphik der Niederlande* (Petersberg: 2013).

(*act.* 1480–1500), are known only by the initials or monograms with which they signed their prints. The earliest Netherlandish engraver who left a biographical trace is Alart Du Hameel (*c.*1449–1507). Du Hameel, who trained originally as a master mason, was active on several of the most prestigious building sites in the region of Brabant.[8] When the Brabantine gothic style was reaching its peak, Du Hameel was working as master mason at St John's Cathedral in Den Bosch. Between 1470 and 1490, he designed the south portal and the chapel of the celebrated Confraternity of Our Lady. He was subsequently appointed as building master (*magister operis*) at the church of St Peter in Leuven (1494–95). Like many of his colleagues, Du Hameel's practice exceeded pure architectural design and also involved designing micro-architecture, such as reliquaries, monstrances and other goldsmith's works.[9] As a designer of micro-architecture, Du Hameel may have also designed a sacrament house for the church of Our-Lady in Antwerp, which was to be executed by the sculptor Thomas Best between 1484 and 1487.[10] In 1484, the Cologne goldsmith Hendrik de Borchgrave (1456–1508) was contracted to create a costly new monstrance for the cathedral, following a design of Alart Du Hameel.[11]

Drawings like those mentioned in the contract of 1484 constituted an exclusive dialogue between designer, executor and commissioner. However, Du Hameel was keen on finding a much wider audience for his inventions by translating them into print. Considering his artistic network, it would not be unreasonable to assume that Du Hameel's plates were cut by local goldsmiths for whom the artist had made designs before. Du Hameel's engraving for a *Monstrance* (Fig. 1.2) may be based on the monstrance design he made in 1484 to be followed by Hendrik de Borchgrave. A second ornament print in

---

8   Since the term architect is not fully introduced in the Low Countries before Pieter Coecke van Aelst's translation of Sebastiano Serlio's Fourth Book on Architecture in 1539, the term master mason (*bouwmeester*) is less anachronistic. On the professional development of the architectural profession in the Low Countries, see: Merlijn Hurx, *Architect en Aannemer. De Opkomst van de Bouwmarkt in de Nederlanden 1350–1530* (Nijmegen: 2012), 36–43.

9   Oliver Kik, "From Lodge to Studio: Transmissions of Architectural knowledge in the Low Countries 1480–1530", in *The Notion of Painter-Architect in Italy and the Southern Low Countries*, edited by Piet Lombaerde (Architectura Moderna) 11 (Turnhout: 2014), 73–88.

10   KAA, Kerkrekeningen X (1493–1494), fol. 36r–37r. Fernand Donnet, *Notice Historique sur la Chapelle du T. S. Sacrement en l'Église Cathédrale d'Anvers* (Antwerp: 1924). Donnet does not mention a specific archival reference for this finding and the payment is not recorded in the church accounts. Du Hameel is only mentioned in an advisory role for the construction of the north tower by master mason Domien de Waghemakere.

11   Christian Verreyt, "Allart du Hamel of du Hameel", *Oud Holland*, 12 (1894) 1–8; Liesbeth Helmus, "Drie contracten met Zilversmeden", in: *In Buscoducis. Kunst uit de Bourgondische tijd te 's-Hertogenbosch*, ed. A. M. Koldeweij (Maarssen: 1990), 473–81.

FIGURE 1.2
Alart Du Hameel, *Monstrance*, c.1484–85, engraving

which the master mason demonstrated his abilities to incorporate the latest novelties in gothic style represents a *Gothic Baldachin* (Fig. 1.3). The concept for this print was vaguely based on the sacrament house in the choir of St Peter's at Leuven, designed and sculpted by the Leuven master mason Matheus de Layens (*c*.1430–83) in 1457. With its hexagonal shape, seemingly endless stacking of flying buttresses, pinnacles, and gilded leaf work, the sacrament house marked a new stage in the aesthetics of Brabantine gothic design. The intended audience for the print was most likely Du Hameel's fellow craftsmen with a shared interest in constructive geometry, which was so essential for the design of objects of an architectural nature: goldsmiths, engravers, painters, master masons, woodcarvers, ornamental sculptors, etc. The clearest indication of this intended audience for the print is the partially represented geometrical ground plan, present in both of Du Hameel's engravings, which allowed craftsmen to "read" the elevation as a representation of a three-dimensional object. This "*ad-quadratum*" representation method had a long tradition among architectural designers dating back to at least the 13th century.[12] Most gothic architectural drawings began with the construction of a geometrical ground plan, from which the elevation was later deduced. Sometimes, like in Du Hameel's *Gothic Baldachin*, the ground plan is only partially shown, indicated by the fraction one-eighth.[13]

It was not only master masons like Du Hameel who applied this constructive geometry; it was also essential to goldsmiths' design. This is demonstrated in the work of Master W with the Key (or Master WA) (*act*. 1470–90), named after his signature of a W with an A-shaped house mark, which in the 19th century was interpreted as a key.[14] Given that one of his prints depicts the heraldry of Charles the Bold (1433–77), we can assume he was a goldsmith active within the entourage of the Burgundian court. Two other series also point toward Burgundian patronage: one represents an almost encyclopedic typology of the Burgundian naval fleet, while a second series displays a Burgundian encampment with cavalry and infantry troops. Although Master WA has previously been identified as the Bruges goldsmith Willem van der Cruse, there is

---

12   Johann Josef Böker, *Architektur der Gotik/Gothic Architecture: Bestandskatalog der weltgrößten Sammlung an gotischen Baurissen im Kupferstichkabinett der Akademie der bildenden Künste Wien* (Munich: 2005); Shelby, *Gothic Design Techniques*, 32; Robert Bork, *Geometry of Creation* (Farnham: 2011).

13   For a reconstruction of the ground plan, see: Krista De Jonge, "'Scientie' and 'Experientie' dans le Gothique Moderne des Anciens Pays-Bas", in: *Le Gotique de la Renaissance*, edited by Monique Chatenet (Paris: 2010), 215.

14   Lehrs, 1895, *Der Meister WA: ein Kupferstecher der Zeit Carls des Kühnen* (Dresden: 1895); Wolfgang Boerner, *Der Meister W A* (Leipzig: 1929).

FIGURE 1.3
Alart Du Hameel, *Gothic Baldachin*, c.1478–1507, engraving

little more than the cross shape in his house mark to confirm this tentative suggestion.[15] The majority of his output consists of designs for goldsmiths, architects, woodcarvers, cabinetmakers and painters.[16] His prints reveal various applications of geometrical design, ranging from monstrances, and chalices, to architectural elements.

A comparative analysis of different impressions of the same print reveals that many of Master WA's printed designs were combined with geometrical ground plans. Often this element was subsequently cut off by later owners or collectors who were either unappreciative or ignorant of the relationship between the geometrical plan and the elevation. Further technical information is provided in Master WA's engraving depicting a *Flying Buttress* (Fig. 1.4). The piers, pinnacles and buttresses of the structure are all shown in an orthogonal elevation, with one exception: at the left side of the engraving, where the buttress seems to have been cut off, and instead the engraver chooses to show a cross-section. This allows the ground plan to be deduced by the geometrically schooled viewer. Template drawings of this kind were often used in gothic architectural design practice and were referred to as *berderen* in building contracts.[17] They were mostly made from wood or paper and were used by stonecutters during the building process. Templates like these can be seen in the background of an architect's portrait by Ludger Tom Ring the Elder (1496–1547) (Fig. 1.5).

Very early on, the design prints of Master W with the Key were copied extensively by Israel Van Meckenem (c.1455–1503), which indicates the growing demand for such models within the nascent print market. In the introduction of his *Fialenbüchlein*, Schmuttermayer explains he is writing his manual "for the instruction of our fellow men and all the masters and journeymen who use this high and noble art of geometry".[18] A similar audience to that discussed in relation to Du Hameel, of fellow craftsmen and practitioners of geometry, was intended for many of Master WA's printed designs. design prints; here discussed. The large size of some of the prints, however, might also suggest

---

15 André Wegener Sleeswyk, "De Graveur WA: een speurtocht", *Gens Nostra*, 49 (1994), 1–14.

16 Recently one of Master W with the Key's ornament prints was identified as the source for a painted mantle clasp on a panel by Gerard David, underlining the versatility of these design prints, see: Constanza Beltrami, "A print Source for a Painting by Gerard David", *The Burlington Magazine* 162, no. 1410 (2020), 748–755.

17 Hurx, *Architect en Aannemer* (see n. 9), 274–78.

18 "zutrost vñ vntterweysung vnnserm nachsten vñ allē maisteren vñ gesellen die sich diser hohen vñ freyen kunst der Geometria geprauchen ir gemute speculirung vnd ymaginacion", Lon Shelby, *Gothic Design Techniques*, 84.

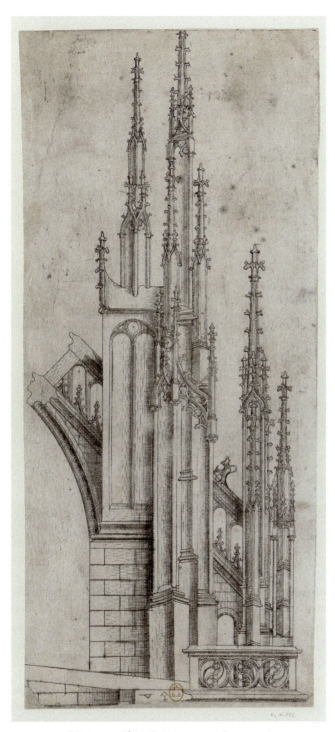

FIGURE 1.4 Master WA, *Flying Buttress*, c.1470–80, engraving

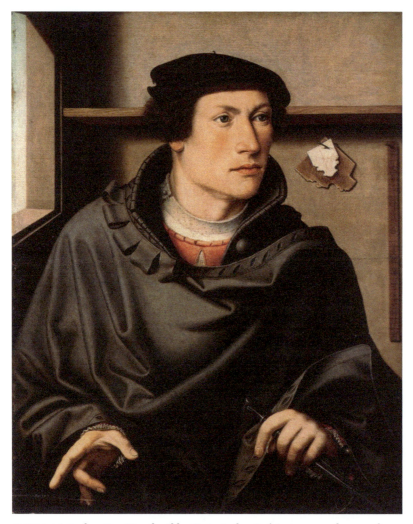

FIGURE 1.5   Ludger Tom Ring the Elder, *Portrait of an Architect*, c.1520, oil on panel

that they were collected as luxury objects.[19] Although there are no traces of early Netherlandish print collections or even workshop inventories that list prints among their possessions, an idea of their use for such a purpose can be obtained by looking at the later inventory of the *Basler Goldschmiederisse*. This collection, part of the Amerbach-Kabinett in Basel since 1578, consists

---

19   Du Hameel's *Monstrance* engraving, for example, consists of three separate plates, with a total height of 111 cm. This makes it one of the largest prints produced in its time. Designing, printing and mounting the image required some time and skill, which would have raised its market value and price considerably.

of the entire workshop stock of 709 prints and drawings and 773 goldsmith models once belonging to the Basel goldsmith Jörg Schweiger the Elder (*c.*1470–1533) and his son Jörg Schweiger the Younger (*d.* 1574).[20] It provides a unique insight into the portfolio of a goldsmith's workshop and includes many design prints of German goldsmith-engravers, such as Urs Graf (1485–1528), Martin Schongauer (1445–1491), Jörg Syrlin the Younger (1455–1521), and Israel van Meckenem. Furthermore, the collection includes a print by Master W with the Key, which represents the wooden case of a carved altarpiece.[21]

2 The Social Position of the Early Modern Goldsmith and Architect

Many goldsmiths in the Upper-Rhine area and the Low Countries made the engraving of copper plates for prints their main occupation or embraced this professional activity completely. This phenomenon had severe implications to the social standing of the artist, and also coincided with a flowering of humanist writings pertaining to the artistic identity of early modern craftsmen. To understand the full implications of this professional shift, from goldsmith to printmaker and in some cases painter, on the social ladder, it is first important to consider the social position of goldsmiths during the 15th-century. Both in the Upper-Rhine area and in the Burgundian Netherlands, the goldsmiths' profession was much appreciated for several reasons, and these artists were often among the wealthiest and most privileged of their time.[22]

One reason for this was the high status of patrons for goldsmiths' works which reflected onto the goldsmiths themselves. Ownership of gems, and precious metals was far beyond the means of the majority of the population and could only be afforded by the Court and the Church. Hugo van der Velde has compared the incomes and revenues of Gerard Loyet (*fl.* 1466–1502), goldsmith at the court of Charles the Bold with those of contemporary painters

---

20   Paul Tanner, *Das Amerbach-Kabinett. Die Basler Goldschmiederisse* (Basel: 1991).

21   Lehrs, *Geschichte und kritscher Katalog*, vol. 7, no. 88.59.II; Tanner, *Amerbach*, 89, no. 64. Although prints by Master W with the Key can also be found in other early modern collections, such as that of Hartmann Schedel and Ferdinand Columbus, they included no ornament prints. On these collections, see: Peter Fuhring, "'Colligete fragmenta, ne pereant': The Ornament Prints in the Columbus Collection" in: *The Print Collection of Ferdinand Colmumbus 1488–1539: A Renaissance Collector in Seville*, ed. Mark P. McDonald (London: 2004), 206–220; Béatrice Hernad (ed.), *Die Graphiksammlung des Humanisten Hartmann Schedel* (Munich: 1990), 35.

22   On the social position of the goldsmith in the Upper-Rhine area, see: Thomas Eser, "Der Gold- und Silberschmied. Edelmetall- und edelsteinverarbeitende Gewerbe", in *Handwerk im Mittelalter*, ed. Christine Sauer (Darmstadt: 2012), 43–55.

working in Flanders.[23] In 1467, Loyet received a payment of 1200 pounds for a golden statuette, which was presented as a votive gift from Charles the Bold to Liège Cathedral. By comparison, Hugo van der Goes received just 360 pounds for the completion of two Justice panels and a *Last Judgement*, commissioned by the city of Leuven in 1473.[24] Obviously, a large proportion of this cost difference is due to the intrinsic value of the materials. However, goldsmiths' work was also highly valued because it fulfilled an important role in state ceremony. In the Burgundian 'theatre state', goldwork, with its sheer splendor and magnificence, was an essential means to manifest the power and eloquence of the court.[25] Gold and silver dominate the inventories of the Burgundian treasury and goldwork was the favored gift *par excellence* in diplomatic meetings, where golden goblets or statuettes were frequently exchanged.[26] In the context of ecclesiastical commissions, goldwork and jewelry offered ultimate praise of the Lord, their intricate design and divine glitter could simply not be achieved in painting. The high value of the materials they worked with added to the goldsmith's social standing. Additionally, they were often Masters of the Mint, and thus had the right or privilege to cast new coins.[27] Both the income and prestige they gained from this activity was often considerable. Goldsmiths also took on the additional role of money changer, a profession that by the early 16th century had become infamous for its wealth.[28]

Goldsmiths, along with architectural designers, had a profound knowledge of (Euclidian) geometry. Whether it was a chalice, monstrance or church spire, its design required basic geometrical principles to calculate proportions, dimensions and stability. Since geometry was one of the seven Liberal Arts, it was regarded with higher esteem than other artistic activities, such as painting and sculpture, which were only considered minor mechanical arts.[29]

---

23 Hugo Van der Velden, *The Donor's Image. Gerard Loyet and the Votive Portraits of Charles the Bold* (Turnhout: 2000), 65–67.

24 Van der Velden, *The Donor's Image.*

25 For the term "Burgundian theatre state", see Wim Blockmans and Walter Prevenier, *The Promised Lands: The Low Countries under Burgundian Rule 1369–1530* (Pennsylvania: 1999).

26 Marina Belozerskaya, *Rethinking the Renaissance. Burgundian Arts Across Europe* (New York: 2002), 84–104; Marina Belozeskaya, *Luxury Arts of the Renaissance* (Los Angeles: 2005), 64–70.

27 Godelieve Van Hemeldonck (ed.), *Zilver uit de Gouden Eeuw van Antwerpen* (Antwerp: 1988), 30.

28 Raymond de Roover, *Money, Banking and Credit in Medieval Bruges* (Cambridge MA 1948), 171–344.

29 On the origins of the divisions between technical and mechanical arts, see: Pamela O. Long, *Openness, Secrecy, Authorship. Technical Arts and the Culture of Knowledge from Antiquity to the Renaissance* (Baltimore and London: 2001).

Although *Metallaria* (blacksmithing and metallurgy) was traditionally considered a mechanical art, the closer association of goldsmiths with the liberal art of *Geometria* lifted it to the level of a Liberal Art. It is precisely this geometrical knowledge that had such a tremendous impact on the social standing and self-image of other professions such as engravers or painters which is so-often associated with the emergence of the 'Renaissance' artist.

This privileged social position enjoyed by goldsmiths in 15th-century urban society is strongly reflected in the portraiture of the time. The earliest example in early Netherlandish painting is Jan van Eyck's 1436 *Portrait of Jan de Leeuw*.[30] The prominent Bruges goldsmith proudly displays his craftsmanship by presenting a golden ring to the viewer. Additionally, the picture's frame alludes to his craft, as Van Eyck expertly replicates in paint the goldsmith's incisions on a brass frame, which states the sitter's name, age and profession. The fact that Jan de Leeuw could commission his portrait from the official court painter of Duke Phillip the Good (1419–1467), delivers a clear message about the sitter's status. Much in the same tradition is Petrus Christus's (*c.*1410–1473) *Portrait of a Goldsmith in his Shop*—convincingly identified by Hugo van der Velden as the successful Bruges goldsmith Willem van Vlueten (*act.* 1432–62). He is portrayed in his workshop as he receives a visiting group of noblemen (Fig. 1.6).[31] With its elaborate display of jewelry, gems and precious metals, the portrait offers a clear impression of the wealth and social standing of the goldsmith. In these portraits, Van Eyck and Petrus Christus established a long tradition of professional goldsmith portraits that continued well into the 16th century.[32] At a time when only the uppermost elements of urban society and the Burgundian nobility were financially capable and socially permitted to be portrayed by the most celebrated painters of their time, goldsmiths were among the few craftsmen able to count themselves among this select group.

The self-representation of architects presents a comparable image of high professional esteem and self-confidence. Especially in Germany and Bohemia it was not uncommon for master masons to finish a commission by including a self-portrait within the architectural framework that they had designed (churches, pulpits, choir stalls, rood screens, etc.). One of the earliest and best-known examples of this is the sculpted self-portrait that the influential master mason Peter Parler (1330–99) included in the choir triforium of Prague's

---

30   Vienna, Kunsthistorisches Museum, inv. 946.

31   Metropolitan Museum of Arts, Robert Lehman Collection, inv. 1975.1.110. Hugo van der Velden, "Defrocking St Eloy: Petrus Christus's Vocational portrait of a goldsmith", *Simiolus*, 26 (1998), 243–61.

32   On goldsmiths' portraits in the Low Countries see: Van der Velden, *Defrocking St Eloy*, 261–269; Silver, "Massys and Money: The Tax Collectors Rediscovered", *Journal of Historians of Netherlandish Art*, 7, no. 2 (2015), 6–7.

FIGURE 1.6   Petrus Christus, *A Goldsmith in his Shop*, 1449, oil on panel

St Vitus Cathedral, thus putting himself on par with the similar portraits of his ecclesiastical and royal commissioners. Much in the same tradition is the self-portrait of the Nuremberg sculptor Adam Kraft (*d.* 1508), in the Sacrament House (1493–96) of the St Lorenz church.[33] In a place traditionally reserved for saints or apostles, the micro-architectural structure is carried on the shoulders

---

33   Michael Baxandall, *The Limewood sculptors of Renaissance Germany* (New Haven and London: 1980), 288.

of two masons on both sides, with Kraft's self-portrait impertinently placed in the middle, at a scale close to life-size (Fig. 1.7).[34] Proudly dressed in the clothes of his trade, he portrays himself holding his tools of creation: the mallet and chisel. A final example is that of Anton Pilgram (*c.*1460–1514/16), the sculptor and master mason of the building lodge of Vienna's St Stephan's Cathedral, who incorporated two self-portraits into the micro-architecture. Once, he peers out of an illusionistic window, at the bottom of the pulpit with a compass in his hands.[35] He appears a second time in an even bolder manner at the base of the organ loft (*c.*1510–15), built into the cathedral's north wall (Fig. 1.8). Even more than Parler or Kraft, Pilgram makes an unequivocal statement about both his reputation and his geometrical knowledge. Instead of holding tools of manual labour as Kraft does, Pilgram holds a compass and a T-square: instruments of the intellectual designing process at the drawing table. It is also no coincidence that both times his head is placed below complex geometrical structures; appearing at the base of a convoluted series of intersecting squares and topped by the vaults.[36] The entire structure is a showcase of the most intricate gothic geometry of its time, which literally seems to sprout and blossom from the architect's mind. Directly below the sculptor's polychrome self-portrait, he has placed his mason's mark, so that there can be no doubt whatsoever about his identity.

Ever since Jacob Burckhardt "re-invented" the Renaissance, the phenomenon of self-portraiture by painters has been considered as one of the key elements in the growing self-awareness and rising social status of the Renaissance artist.[37] In light of the present analysis of the goldsmith-engraver, it should come as little surprise that one of the most referenced instances of self-portraiture in northern European painting stems from the son of a goldsmith.[38] At the age of thirteen, in 1486, the young Dürer started a life-long practice

---

34   Susie Nash, *Northern Renaissance Art* (Oxford: 2008), 149; Achim Timmermann, *Real Presence: Sacrament Houses and the Body of Christ, c.1270–1600* (Architectura Medii Aevi 4) (Turnhout: 2009), 144–52; Ethan Matt Kavaler, *Renaissance Gothic* (New Haven and London: 2012), 173.

35   Pilgrim was most likely inspired by a similar sculptor's self-portrait at the base of the pulpit in Strasbourg Cathedral, designed by Hans Hammer (*c.*1440/5–1519) in 1484.

36   Kavaler, *Renaissance Gothic*, 175.

37   Frances Ames-Lewis, *The Intellectual Life of the Early Renaissance Artist* (New Haven and London: 2000), 209–242.

38   It should be noted that one of the earliest known instance of self-portraiture in Italian art is that of the sculptor and goldsmith Lorenzo Ghiberti (1378–1455)in the inclusion of his own likeness in the faming border the of the 'Gates of Paradise' that he made for the Baptistry in Florence between 1447–48.

FIGURE 1.7 Adam Kraft, *Sacrament House* (detail), 1493–96, Nuremberg, St Lorenz

FIGURE 1.8 Anton Pilgram, *Organ Loft*, 1510–15, Vienna, St Stephan

of self-portraiture. It was already in line with family tradition, however, as Dürer's father had also drawn his self-portrait in a meticulous silverpoint proudly portraying himself, holding a delicate golden statuette in his hand as a sign of his craft and skill (Fig. 1.9).[39] Joseph Leo Koerner writes: "If this

---

39   Vienna, Graphische Sammlung Albertina, inv. 4846.

FIGURE 1.9 Albert Dürer the Elder, *Self-Portrait*, 1486, silverpoint on prepared paper

FIGURE 1.10
Israel van Meckenem,
Self-portrait with his wife,
c.1490, engraving

is the self-portrait of Dürer the Elder (...), self-portraiture does not emerge in Germany single-handily in the art of Dürer the Younger, but rather is a practice shared by a Nuremberg goldsmith and his son".[40]

Rather than simply being a trope in the Dürer family, though, we have seen that the practice of self-portraiture stems from a longer tradition in the goldsmith's trade. Dürer the Elder's drawing recalls earlier portraits of goldsmiths by Van Eyck, Petrus Christus and Gerard David. In fact, in his 1524 family chronicle, Dürer writes about his father that he "spent a long time in the Netherlands learning from the great masters of his craft, and finally came to Nuremberg in the year 1455".[41] If Dürer the Elder went to the Netherlands in the middle of the 15th century, the best place to meet the great masters of his craft would have been Ghent or Bruges. It was perhaps here that he picked up the tradition of the goldsmith portrait. Goldsmith portraits seemed to have been customary in Germany as well, as is suggested from an engraving, dated between 1480 and 1490, by Israel van Meckenem, in which he is portrayed with his wife Ida (Fig. 1.10).[42] The unusual print shows a close-up of both sitter's heads against a floral backdrop and the lettering below "*figuratio facterum Israelis et Ida suis uxoris IVM*" (depicted are the faces of Israhel and his wife Ida). The Latin inscription on the fictive frame, calls to mind the Dutch inscription included on the frame of Jan van Eyck's portrait of Jan de Leeuw. Van Meckenem's portrait

---

40 Joseph Leo Koerner, *The Moment of Self-Portraiture in German Renaissance Art* (Chicago: 1993), 43.

41 Jeffrey Ashcroft, *Albrecht Dürer. Documentary Biography* (New Haven and London: 2017), vol. 1, 31.

42 Lehrs, *Geschichte und kritscher Katalog*, vol. 9, 1; Landau and Parshall, *The Renaissance Print*, 57.

should likewise be considered a statement of a goldsmith's self-fashioning, declared through the medium of print. A second print by Van Meckenem confirms this professional self-importance. Depicting a bearded man wearing an oriental turban, the print proudly states *"Israel van Meckenem Goldschmied"* ("Israhel van Meckenem, Goldsmith"), serving as a professional calling card of his skill.[43] The enormity of Van Meckenem's print output, including many design prints, might lead one to suspect that engraving had become his main professional activity, yet the goldsmith-engraver was still inclined to stress his abilities as a goldsmith.[44]

3   Leaving Their Mark

Further analysis of goldsmith-engravers' signatures reveals how long-standing craft traditions were transferred into the new medium of printed images. Notwithstanding some notable exceptions like Jan van Eyck and Colyn de Coter (*act.* 1480–1525), signing or monogramming works of art was a practice mostly employed by master masons, sculptors, silver- and goldsmiths and cabinet-makers.[45] Before Albrecht Dürer trademarked his print production with his famous AD-monogram, a whole generation of goldsmiths, sculptors and architectural designers had used their monograms and family house marks both as self-promotional tools of expertise and as quality control. Martin Schongauer signed all his 115 prints known to us today with his initials "M S", separated by a cross.[46] Although the initials are a reference to the engraver's name, the cross in the centre seems to be a family house mark, since his brother, the goldsmith-engraver Ludwig Schongauer (*c.*1450–1494), used the very same cross between his initials on his prints. Similarly, Alart Du Hameel's prints are signed with his surname, followed by his house mark. On some occasions, the word *Bosche* is added to Du Hameel's prints, as a reference to the city where he worked in between 1478 and 1494.[47] This recalls the standard signing practice used by silver- and goldsmiths in many Netherlandish cities. The product was

---

43   Lehrs, *Geschichte und kritscher Katalog*, vol. 9, 5.

44   Zelen, *Zum Verhältnis*, 30; Landau and Parshall, The Renaissance Print 56–63.

45   Tobias Burg, *Die Signatur. Formen und Funktionen vom Mittelalter bis zum 17. Jahrhundert* (Münster: 2007). On the use of signatures in the Low Countries, see: Ruben Suykerbuyck, *Sign of Times. A Concise History of the Signature in Netherlandish painting 1432–1575* (Unpublished MA Thesis; Utrecht: 2013).

46   Tobias Burg, "Signaturen in der frühen Drückgraphik" in *Künstlersignaturen von der Antike bis zur Gegenwart*, ed. Nicole Hegener (Petersberg: 2013), 284–85.

47   This is analogous to Hieronymus Bosch's signing practice, whose surname was Van Aken.

signed with the mark of the individual master (an initial or a house-mark) and the city mark.[48] Sometimes a third mark was added by the guild as an extra quality check of the alloy. On Du Hameel's *Monstrance*, his largest and most luxurious print, he exceptionally signed it with his first name in gothic lettering, followed by his house mark. At the base of the monstrance, the city's name s' HERTOGEN BOSCH is mentioned in full, rather than just the more commonly abbreviated form "Bosche". As Marisa Bass has recently noted, Du Hameel's self-representation in this print goes even further.[49] Curling around the base of the engraved object is a banderol proclaiming Du Hameel's personal motto: "*non desino*" (I do not cease). Although the writing style for the city and his own name sometimes differs from print to print, the one thing that appears on all of Du Hameel's known prints is the idiosyncratic house mark. On prints from a highly-reputed master builder, the use of a house mark was a transferrable sign of professional pride and geometrical skill as a designer, much in the same way as the anonymous Master W with the Key used his monogram. Most likely Master WA was a Netherlandish goldsmith, sculptor or mason whose name started with a W, which was then followed by his personal house mark.

The practice of using house marks as a sign of social standing and technical expertise was not only transferred to engraving, but also to painting. Very similar to the career path taken by Albrecht Dürer, is that of the renowned Antwerp painter, Quinten Metsys (1466–1530) who was the son of the Leuven blacksmith, Joos Metsys the Elder (*d.* 1482). Quinten's eldest brother, also called Joos (*act.* 1481–1529), was master mason of the prestigious new church of St Peter in Leuven, and as such, he was responsible for the delivery of the new design plans for the church's west facade.[50] In 1491, Quinten Metsys is first mentioned as a painter in the records of the Antwerp Guild of St Luke, without any record of his having served an apprenticeship with an Antwerp painter.[51] Little is known about the period between his being mentioned in the guild records and his

---

48   In Antwerp, for example, this was customary since 1382. Van Hemeldonck, ed., *Zilver*, 26–27. Silver- and goldsmiths in Den Bosch did not have an individual guild until 1503. Here as well, it was stipulated that every object should bare a master's mark, a year mark and a city mark, see: A. M. Koldeweij, "Goud- en zilversmeden te 's-Hertogenbosch" in: *In Buscoducis. Kunst uit de Bourgondische tijd te 's-Hertogenbosch* ed. A. M. Koldeweij (Maarssen: 1990), 464–481, 608–9.

49   Marisa Bass, "Hieronymus Bosch and his Legacy as 'Inventor'", in *Beyond Bosch. The Afterlife of a Renaissance Master in Print, eds.* Marisa Bass and Elizabeth Wyckoff (Saint Louis: 2015), 20–24.

50   Kik, *From Lodge to Studio*, 82–84.

51   Philippe Félix Rombouts and Théodore Van Lerius, *De Liggeren en andere historische archieven van het Antwerpse Sint-Lukasgilde*, vol. 1 (Antwerp: 1864–76), 43.

MARK(ET)ING EXPERTISE							47

FIGURE 1.11
Quinten Metsys, *St Anne tryptich* (detail), 1508–09, oil on panel

first dated altarpiece in 1509, *The St Anne Altarpiece*, already a mature work.[52] The painting was commissioned by the Fraternity of St Anne for the same church in Leuven for which his brother was designing the architectural plans. In the outer left wing, an inscription reads: *QUINTE METSYS SCREEF DIT 1509* (*Quinten Metsys wrote this*) (Fig. 1.11). Often omitted in the literature is the hour glass-shaped masons' mark placed before the year.[53] Perhaps intentionally, the signature is also placed upon an architectural element, which is right above a window looking out on what seems to be a hypothetical version of the north tower of Antwerp's church of Our-Lady.[54] The fact that the son of a goldsmith and the brother of a master mason signs his work with a house mark should leave no doubt about the message the artist thought to communicate: besides being a good painter, he wanted to state his ample experience in geometry and its applications. In fact, Metsys never fully left the goldsmith trade, since he

52   Brussels, Koninklijk Museum voor Schone Kunsten van België, inv. 2784. Andrée De Bosque, *Quinten Metsys* (Brussels: 1975), 92–100; Larry Silver, *The Paintings of Quinten Massys with Catalogue Raisonné* (Oxford: 1984), 35–45, 199–204; Raoul Slachmuylders, "De Triptiek van de Maagdschap van de Heilige Anna", *Quinten Metsys en Leuven* (Arca Lovaniesis artes atque historiae restans documenta) 33 (Leuven: 2007), 85–120.
53   De Bosque interprets the sign as "Anno". See: De Bosque, *Quinten Metsys*, 99. However, in an anonymous copy of Metsys's *Money Changers*, in Brussels, the same mason's mark appears on a slip of paper sticking out of a book. Brussels, Koninklijk Museum voor Schone Kunsten van België, inv. 7356. It may be possible that this copy was made after another version from Metsys' workshop which also included the house mark. The oeuvre of Marinus van Reymerswaele shows adequately that there was a market for this new secular genre piece. Several versions would not have been uncommon for Metsys' workshop practice which did not shy away from making several versions for the developing Antwerp art market.
54   Although the Antwerp tower was only completed in 1521, Joos Metys was in close contact with both Rombout II Keldermans and Domien de Waghemakere, the architects responsible for the tower's design; see: Kik, *From Lodge to Studio*, 84.

remained active as a designer of portrait medallions.[55] In 1491, the same year as his registration in the Antwerp painters' guild, Metsys cast a bronze medallion with the portrait of his sister-in-law Cristina Metsys (*d.* 1518).[56] In 1519, when he had already established himself and enjoyed a long and successful career as a painter, Metsys cast a bronze medallion with the likeness of Erasmus (*c.*1466–1536).[57] Erasmus shared copies of the medallion with his humanist circle and carried on an extensive correspondence about it with Dürer's patron Willibald Pirckheimer (1470–1530).[58] Given his experience as a draftsman and a goldsmith, one can only wonder why no prints of Quinten Metys are known today, or at least none bearing his house mark.[59] Similar to Metsys's career path is that of the Bruges painter Lanceloot Blondeel (1498–1561).[60] In 1519, he started a successful career as a painter when he was inscribed as a master painter in the Bruges guild of St Luke. Before 1519, however, he was already active as a mason, as one learns from the eulogizing poem written in the year of his death by the Bruges poet Eduard de Dene (1505–76):

> Here lays buried the body of Lanceloot Blondeel / First he was at work as a mason and a great artist with the mason's trowel / after which he became a painter / following Apelles's brush in painting / thus completing himself in Architecture.[61]

Describing Blondeel as an artist (*Constenare*) with his trowel, seems most likely in this context to refer to his experience in the Liberal Art of geometry.[62] Blondeel himself took great pride in his background as a mason, as he consistently signed his work with a monogram of his initials LAB in combination with a

---

55 Victor Tourneur, "Quintin Metys, Médailleur", *Revue Belge de Numismatique*, 72 (1920), 139–160; Luc Smolderen, "Quintin Metsys Médailleur d'Erasme", *Scrinium Erasmianum*, ed. Joseph Coppens (Brussels: 1969), vol. 1, 513–525; De Bosque, *Quinten Metsys*, 59–70.

56 Antwerp, Museum Mayer Van den Bergh, inv. 2353.

57 Brussels, Koninklijke Bibliotheek Albert I, inv. 21.

58 De Bosque, *Quinten Metsys*, 59–61.

59 His son, Cornelis Metsys (1510–1556), would enjoy a career as an engraver, see: Jan van der Stock, *Cornelis Metsys. Grafisch Werk* (Brussels: 1985).

60 Eva Tahon, *Lanceloot Blondeel* (Bruges: 1988).

61 'Hier light. tvleesch begrauen van Landslood blondeel voormaels werckman ghevveist / met maetsers truweel groot constenare / schilder gheworden der naer Reyn naervolgher in pictura Apelles pincheel vvetenlick inde Architecture gheheel'. Walter Waterschoot and Dirk Coigneau, "Eduard de Dene, Testament Rhetoricael", *Jaarboek Koninklijke soevereine hoofdkamer van rhetorica De Fonteine te Gent* 2 (1976–77), 22.

62 On the shifting meaning of the word artist, see: Krista De Jonge, "The Court Architect as Artist in the Southern Low Countries", *Nederlands Kunsthistorisch Jaarboek* 59 (Zwolle: 2010), 111–35.

MARK(ET)ING EXPERTISE 49

picture of a trowel. The list of late fifteenth-century and early sixteenth-century engravers or painters who share a family or personal background as architects or goldsmiths is extensive.[63] Arguably it is even possible to speak of a professional pattern. These craftsmen's backgrounds were not regarded as shameful. Instead, artists signing with their monograms, house marks and even working tools advertised their ability to design complex geometrical structures, which made them professional artists in the literal sense of the word, as practitioners of the *Liberal Arts*.

4 Epilogue

Over the course of the 16th century, this appreciation for technical and geometrical backgrounds would change and a reversal of values governing the hierarchy of the arts would gradually take place. Under the growing influence of Italian art theory, the role of painting would become more prominent and the 'art' of the goldsmith would come to be dismissively regarded as manual labour. In fact, Albrecht Dürer would be one of the first to regard painting as a Liberal Art, elevated by the appropriation of geometrical science, as he states in one of the prefaces to his treatise on human proportions.[64] In his family chronicle of 1523, Dürer tells the often-quoted story of how his father took him out of school to teach him the goldsmith's craft: "And by the time I could do competent work, I felt myself more drawn towards painting than to goldsmith's work. I put this to my father, but he was not pleased, because he rued the time I had wasted learning to be a goldsmith".[65] By the time he rewrote his own history, Dürer had already stayed in Venice and met Jacopo de'Barbari (1460–1516) and probably Luca Pacioli (*c*.1447–1517), which radically altered his art theoretical views.[66] It is from this period forward he was hailed as the Northern or German Apelles. By distancing himself from his goldsmith background, Dürer forged a dichotomy of intellectual liberal art versus manual labour in favour of painting. The same debate took place in the Low Countries around the middle of

---

63   For the Low Countries alone, this list would include Jan Gossart, Lanceloot Blondeel, Quinten Metsys, Jan Rombouts, Frans and Cornelis Floris, Cornelis Cort and Gillis II Coignet.

64   Ashcroft, *Albrecht Dürer*, vol. 2, 710.

65   Ashcroft, *Albrecht Dürer*, vol. 1, 35.

66   Ulrich Pfisterer, "Dürer in Discourse: Art Theories around 1500 and the Paths They Took North and South of the Alps", *Albrecht Dürer. His Art in Context* ed. Jochen Sander (Munich, London and New York: 2013), 376–82.

the 16th century.[67] Decisive in the changing attitude towards painting was the Liège humanist milieu around the painter Lambert Lombard (c.1505–1566).[68] Lombard's art theoretical thinking was strongly influenced by his Italian travels (1537–38) and more importantly by Giorgio Vasari (1511–1574), with whom he corresponded in 1565 about art.[69] Vasari's triad of *Disegno* (painting, sculpture and architecture) had no place for goldsmith's work and would change our view of how art is perceived. Lombard's Vasarian perspective strongly influenced the following generation of artists, among whom were his pupils Frans Floris (1517–70), Willem Key (c.1515–68) and Hendrik Golzius (1558–1617). He also taught the Bruges humanist and amateur painter Domenicus Lampsonius (1532–99).

Among the first contributions to Northern art history is Lampsonius' *Pictorum Aliquot Celebrium Germaniae Inferioris Effigies* of 1572, a collection of twenty-three laudatory poems on Netherlandish painters, each accompanied by portrait engravings published by Hieronymus Cock.[70] Particularly relevant to our present discussion of the goldsmith-engraver is the poem and engraving dedicated to Quinten Metsys. Lampsonius tells us how Metsys was "a rough Cyclop Blacksmith before, but through love he was able to leave the blows of the anvil for the pleasing strokes of the paint brush".[71] Lampsonius clearly regarded his background as son of a blacksmith as a major obstacle in his path to becoming a painter. Influenced by Vasari's endeavors to add painting

---

67 Zirka Zaremba Filipczak, *Picturing Art in Antwerp 1550–1700* (Princeton: 1987); Walter S. Melion, *Shaping the Netherlandish Canon* (Chicago: 1991); Hessel Miedema, "De ontwikkeling van de kunsttheorie in de Hollandse Gouden Eeuw I: Het Begin; de Zuidelijke Nederlanden", *Oud Holland*, vol. 125 (2012), 102–15.

68 Godelieve Denhaene, *Lambert Lombard. De Renaissance en humanisme te Luik* (Antwerp: 1990); Edward H. Wouk, "Reclaiming the Antiquities of Gaul: Lambert Lombard and the History of Northern Art", *Simiolus*, 36 (2012), 35–65.

69 Gianni Carlo Scolia and Caterina Volpi, *Da van Eyck a Brueghel. Scritti sulle arti di Domenico Lamsonio* (Turin: 2001), 34–40.

70 Melion, *Netherlandish Canon*, 143–59.

71 The full text reads: "Before I used to be a Cyclopean smith, but when a wooing painter began to love on an equal footing with me, and the cautious girl objected to me that she liked the heavy thundering of hammers less than the silent paintbrush, love made me a painter. A tiny hammer, which is the sure note of my paintings, alludes to this. Thus, when Venus had asked Vulcan for arms for her son, you, greatest of poets, made a painter out of a smith." ("*Ante faber fueram Cyclopeus; ast ubi mecum / Ex aequo pictor coepit amarsi procus / Seque graves tuditum tonitrus postferre silent / Peniculo obiecit cauta puella mihi / Pictorem me fecit amor. tudes innuit illud / Exiguus, tabulis quae nota certa meis / Sic ubi Vulcanum nato Venus arma rogarat / Pictorem e fabro summe Poeta facis*"). Dominicus Lampsonius, *Pictorum Aliquot Celebrium Germaniae inferioris effigies* (Antwerp: 1572), fol. 9.

to the canon of liberal arts, Lampsonius presents Metsys' career change as the evolution of a mere craftsman into that of a learned artist, ignoring the high status bestowed upon the goldsmith profession and geometrical designers at the time.

The fact that geometrical professions increasingly became involved in print design had serious repercussions. Not only did their designs find a larger market, inspiring fellow craftsmen, it initiated an evolution in the role geometry could play in the visual arts. Architect-engravers like Alart du Hameel or goldsmith-engravers such as Master WA represent a social pattern that was instrumental in the dissemination of technical knowledge among different professional groups that were often separated by guild regulations. This scientific knowledge was demonstrated and promoted by the use of house marks and professional tools in early signatures. For this new generation of engravers and painters, their geometrical know-how added an intellectual and economic value to their mark and burin, with a wide range of applications, for example architectural design, linear perspective and even cartography. The professional shift would also influence the dissemination of attitudes towards art and the self-image of the craftsman as an artist.[72]

Select Bibliography

Primary Sources

Lampsonius, Dominicus, *Pictorum Aliquot Celebrium Germaniae inferioris effigies* (Antwerp: 1572).

Secondary Sources

Ames-Lewis, Francis, *The Intellectual Life of the Early Renaissance Artist* (New Haven and London: 2000).

Ashcroft, Jeffrey, *Albrecht Dürer. Documentary Biography* (New Haven and London: 2017).

Barnes, Carl F. Jr., *The Portfolio of Villard de Honnecourt (Paris, Bibliothèque Nationale de France, MS Fr 19093): a new critical edition and color facsimile* (Farnham: 2009).

---

72   Setting these developments in a wider European context, it does not happen to have been a coincidence that the development of geometrical linear perspective in Italy was conceived by artists whose family backgrounds were rooted in geometrically oriented professions. For example, Brunelleschi was the son of a goldsmith and Andrea Mantegna the son of a carpenter. See: Howard Burns, "The Painter-Architect in Italy during the Quattrocento and Cinquecento", in *The Notion of Painter-Architect*, 1–8.

Bass, Marisa, "Hieronymus Bosch and his Legacy as 'Inventor'", in *Beyond Bosch. The Afterlife of a Renaissance Master in Print*, exhibition catalogue, ed. Marisa Bass and Elizabeth Wyckoff, Saint Louis Art Museum (Saint Louis: 2015), 11–32.

Baxandall, Michael, *The Limewood Sculptors of Renaissance Germany* (New Haven and London: 1980).

Belozerskaya, Marina, *Rethinking the Renaissance. Burgundian Arts Across Europe* (New York: 2002).

Belozerskaya, Marina, *Luxury Arts of the Renaissance* (Los Angeles: 2005).

Beltrami, Constanza, "A Print source for a painting by Gerard David", *The Burlington Magazine*, 162, no. 1410 (2020), 748–755.

Böker, Johann Josef, *Architektur der Gotik/Gothic Architecture: Bestandskatalog der weltgrößten Sammlung an gotsichen Baurissen im Kupferstichkabinett der Akademie der bildenden Künste Wien* (Munich: 2005).

Bork, Robert, *Geometry of Creation* (Farnham: 2011).

Bosque, Andrée De, *Quinten Metsys* (Brussels: 1975).

Blockmans, Wim, and Walter Prevenier, *The Promised Lands: The Low Countries under Burgundian Rule 1369–1530* (Pennsylvania: 1999).

Burg, Tobias, *Die Signatur. Formen und Funktionen vom Mittelalter bis zum 17. Jahrhundert* (Münster: 2007).

Burg, Tobias, "Signaturen in der frühen Drückgraphik" in *Künstlersignaturen von der Antike bis zur Gegenwart*, ed. by Nicole Hegener (Petersberg: 2013), 284–85.

Burns, Howard, "The Painter-Architect in Italy during the Quattrocento and Cinquecento", in: *The Notion of Painter-Architect in Italy and the Southern Low Countries* (Architectura Moderna) 11 (Turnhout: 2014), 1–8.

Byrne, Janet S., *Renaissance Ornament Prints and Drawings. The Metropolitan Museum of Art* (New York: 1981).

Coppens, Joseph (ed.), *Scrinium Erasmianum* 2 vols (Brussels: 1969).

Denhaene, Godelieve, *Lambert Lombard. De Renaissance en humanisme te Luik* (Antwerp: 1990).

Donnet, Fernand, *Notice Historique sur la Chapelle du T. S. Sacrement en l'Église Cathédrale d'Anvers* (Antwerp: 1924).

Eser, Thomas, "Der Gold- und Silberschmied. Edelmetall- und edelsteinverarbeitende Gewerbe", *Handwerk im Mittelalter*, ed. Christine Sauer (Darmstadt: 2012), 43–55.

Eser, Thomas, "A Different Early Dürer. Three Proposals", in: *The Early Dürer*, exhibition catalogue, ed. Daniel Hess and Thomas Eser (New Haven and London: 2012), 18–29.

Filipczak, Zirka Zaremba, *Picturing Art in Antwerp 1550–1700* (Princeton: 1987).

Fuhring, Peter, "'Colligete fragmenta, ne pereant': The Ornament Prints in the Columbus Collection" in: *The Print Collection of Ferdinand Colmumbus 1488–1539: A Renaissance Collector in Seville*, ed. Mark P. McDonald (London: 2004), 206–220.

Helmus, Liesbeth, "Drie contracten met Zilversmeden", in: *In Buscoducis. Kunst uit de Bourgondische tijd te 's-Hertogenbosch*, ed. A. M. Koldeweij (Maarssen: 1990), 473–81.

Hemeldonck, Godelieve Van editor, *Zilver uit de Gouden Eeuw van Antwerpen* (Antwerp: 1988).

Hernad, Béatrice (ed.), *Die Graphiksammlung des Humanisten Hartmann Schedel* (Munich: 1990).

Hurx, Merlijn, *Architect en Aannemer. De Opkomst van de Bouwmarkt in de Nederlanden 1350–1530* (Nijmegen: 2012).

De Jonge, Krista, "'Scientie' and 'Experientie' dans le Gothique Moderne des Anciens Pays-Bas", in *Le Gotique de la Renaissance*, edited by Monique Chatenet (Paris: 2010), 199–216.

De Jonge, Krista, "The Court Architect as Artist in the Southern Low Countries", *Nederlands Kunsthistorisch Jaarboek* 59 (Zwolle: 2010): 111–135.

Kavaler, Ethan Matt, *Renaissance Gothic* (New Haven and London: 2012).

Kik, Oliver, "From Lodge to Studio: Transmissions of Architectural knowledge in the Low Countries 1480–1530", in *The Notion of Painter-Architect in Italy and the Southern Low Countries* (Architectura Moderna) 11 (Turnhout: 2014), 73–88.

Koerner, Joseph Leo, *The Moment of Self-Portraiture in German Renaissance Art* (Chicago: 1993).

Koldeweij, A. M. (ed.), *In Buscoducis. Kunst uit de Bourgondische tijd te 's-Hertogenbosch* (Maarssen: 1990).

Koldeweij, A. M., "Goud- en zilversmeden te 's-Hertogenbosch" in: *In Buscoducis. Kunst uit de Bourgondische tijd te 's-Hertogenbosch* ed. A. M. Koldeweij (Maarssen: 1990), 464–481.

Landau, David and Peter Parshall, *The Renaissance Print, 1470–1550* (London: 1994).

Lehrs, Max, *Der Meister W A: ein Kupferstecher der Zeit Carls des Kühnen* (Dresden: 1895).

Lehrs, Max, *Geschichte und kritscher Katalog des deutchen, niederlandischen un franzözischen Kupferstichs in XV. Jahrhundert* 9 vols (Vienna: 1908–34).

Long, Pamela O., *Openness, Secrecy, Authorship. Technical Arts and the Culture of Knowledge from Antiquity to the Renaissance* (Baltimore and London: 2001).

McDonald, Mark, P. (ed.), *The Print Collection of Ferdinand Colmumbus 1488–1539: A Renaissance Collector in Seville* 2 vols (London: 2004), 206–220.

Melion, Walter S., *Shaping the Netherlandish Canon. Karel Van Mander's Schilder-Boeck* (Chicago: 1991).

Miedema, Hessel, "De ontwikkeling van de kunsttheorie in de Hollandse Gouden Eeuw I: Het Begin; de Zuidelijke Nederlanden", *Oud Holland* 126, no. 1 (2012): 102–115.

Nash, Susie, *Northern Renaissance Art* (Oxford: 2008).

Pfisterer, Ulrich, "Dürer in Discourse: Art Theories around 1500 and the Paths they Took North and South of the Alps", in *Albrecht Dürer. His Art in Context*, ed. Jochen Sander (Munich, London and New York: 2013), 376–382.

Rombouts, P. and T Van Lerius, *De Liggeren en andere historische archieven van het Antwerpse Sint-Lukasgilde*, 2 vols (Antwerp: 1864–76).

Roover, Raymond de, *Money, Banking and Credit in Medieval Bruges* (Cambridge MA: 1948).

Sauer, Christine, editor, *Handwerk im Mittelalter* (Darmstadt: 2012), 43–55.

Scheller, Robert W., *Exemplum. Model-Book Drawings and the Practice of artistic Transmission in the Middle Ages* (Amsterdam: 1995).

Scolia, Gianni Carlo & Caterina Volpi, *Da van Eyck a Brueghel. Scritti sulle arti di Domenico Lamsonio* (Turin: 2001).

Shelby, Lon, *Gothic Design Techniques: The Fifteenth-Century Design Booklets of Mathes Roriczer and Hanns Schmuttermayer* (Carbondale: 1977).

Silver, Larry, *The Paintings of Quinten Massys with Catalogue Raisonné* (Oxford: 1984).

Silver, "Massys and Money: The Tax Collectors Rediscovered", *Journal of Historians of Netherlandish Art*, vol. 7, no. 2 (2015).

Slachmuylders, Raoul, "De Triptiek van de Maagdschap van de Heilige Anna", *Quinten Metsys en Leuven* (Arca Lovaniesis artes atque historiae restans documenta) 33 (Leuven: 2007), 85–120.

Smolderen, Luc, "Quintin Metsys Médailleur d'Erasme", *Scrinium Erasmianum*, ed. Joseph Coppens (Brussels: 1969), vol. 1, 513–525.

Stielau, Allison, "Intent and Independence: Late Fifteenth-Century Object Engravings" in *Visual Acuity and the Arts of Communication in Early Modern Germany*, ed. Jeffrey Chipps Smith (Farnham: 2014), 21–42.

Stijnman, Ad, *Engraving and Etching 1400–2000. A History of the Development of Manuel Printmaking processes* (Houten: 2012).

Stock, Jan Van der, *Cornelis Metsys. Grafisch Werk* (Brussels: 1985).

Stock, Jan van der, *Printing Images in Antwerp. The Introduction of Printmaking in a City: Fifteenth Century to 1585* (Rotterdam: 1998).

Suykerbuyck, Ruben, *Sign of Times. A concise history of the signature in Netherlandish painting 1432–1575* (Unpublished MA Thesis; Utrecht: 2013).

Tahon, Eva, *Lanceloot Blondeel* (Bruges: 1988).

Tanner, Paul, *Das Amerbach-Kabinett. Die Basler Goldschmiederisse* (Basel: 1991).

Tourneur, Victor, "Quintin Metys, Médailleur", *Revue Belge de Numismatique*, 72 (1920), 139–160.

Timmermann, Achim, *Real Presence: Sacrament Houses and the Body of Christ, c.1270–1600* (Architectura Medii Aevi) 4 (Turnhout: 2009).

Velden, Hugo Van der, "Defrocking St Eloy: Petrus Christus's Vocational portrait of a goldsmith", *Simiolus*, 26 (1998): 243–269.

Velden, Hugo Van der, *The Donor's Image. Gerard Loyet and the Votive Portraits of Charles the Bold* (Turnhout: 2000).

Verreyt, Christian, "Allart du Hamel of du Hameel", *Oud Holland*, 12 (1894), 1–8.

Wegener Sleeswyk, André, "De Graveur WA: een speurtocht", *Gens Nostra*, 49 (1994), 1–14.

Wouk, Edward H., "Reclaiming the antiquities of Gaul: Lambert Lombard and the history of northern art", *Simiolus*, 36 (2012): 35–65.

Zelen, Joyce G. H., "Zum Verhältnis des frühen Kupferstichs zur Goldschmiedekunst: der Salzburger Hausaltar des Meisters Perchtold", in *Mit den Gezeiten. Frühe Druckgraphik der Niederlande*, ed. Tobias Pfeifer-Helke (Petersberg: 2013), 25–31.

CHAPTER 2

Theory of Printmaking in the Early Modern Age

Barbara Stoltz

1   Introduction

A discussion about the theory of printmaking in the early modern age presumes the existence of ample and profound reflection in historical sources.[1] Some single texts, comments and poems on this art from the end of the 15th and beginning of the 16th century, the first significant period of printmaking, have been preserved. One of the most prominent is that by Erasmus of Rotterdam (*c.*1466–1536) regarding Albrecht Dürer (1471–1528), in which he describes printmaking as the "art of black lines", comparing Dürer's prints to the art of Apelles.[2] The first known treatise on printmaking is Abraham Bosse's (1604–1676) *Traicté des maniers de graver* from 1645, which can certainly be defined more as a technical text about printmaking than a discourse reflecting on the art.[3] It is only John Evelyn's (1620–1706) *Sculptura: Or the History and Art of Chalcography and Engraving in Copper* from 1662 that provides the

---

1   This article presents some results of an extensive project about printmaking theory in the Renaissance, on which the author worked within a DFG-project (Deutsche Forschungsgemeinschaft, STO 907/1) and which is now published in the book: Barbara Stoltz, *Die Kunst des Schneidens und die gedruckte Zeichnung: Theorie der Druckgraphik in der Kunstliteratur des 16. und 17. Jahrhunderts* (Merzhausen 2023). The following articles also presented results from the project: Idem, "Das Bild-Druckverfahren in der frühen Neuzeit", *Marburger Jahrbuch für Kunstwissenschaft*, vol. 39 (2012), 93–117; idem, "*Disegno* versus *Disegno stampato*: Printmaking Theory in Vasari's *Vite* (1550–1568)", *Journal of Art Historiography*, vol. 7, December (2012), 1–20; idem, "Ars Nova? Die Neue Kunst? Die Bedeutung der Druckgraphik in der Kunstliteratur des 15. und des frühen 16. Jahrhunderts" in *Ars Nova. Frühe Kupferstiche aus Italien*, ed. Gudula Metze (Petersberg: 2013) S. 19–29.

2   "*Durerus quanquam & alias admirandus, in monochromatis, hoc est nigris lineis, quid non exprimit? Umbras, lumen, splendorem, eminentias, depressiones (…). Haec felicissimis lineis iisque nigris sic ponit ob oculos, ut si colorem illinas, iniuriam facias operi. Annon hoc mirabilius, absque colorum lenocinio prestare, quod Apelles praestitit colorum praesidio.*" Desiderius Erasmus of Rotterdam, *De recta Latini Graecique sermonis pronuntiatione Des. Erasmi dialogus* (Paris: 1528), 28r. For a discussion of early texts on printmaking including those of Erasmus and Pomponio Gaurico (1481/1482–1530), see: Stoltz, *Ars Nova*, 19–28; Norberto Gramaccini and Hans Jakob Meier, *Die Kunst der Interpretation. Italienische Reproduktionsgraphik 1485–1600* (Berlin and Munich: 2009), 443–358.

3   Abraham Bosse, *Traicté des manières de graver en taille douce sur l'airin* (Paris: 1645).

© KONINKLIJKE BRILL BV, LEIDEN, 2024 | DOI:10.1163/9789004703834_004

first full account of the definition, criticism and history of printmaking.[4] This was followed by a more prominent treatise, Filippo Baldinucci's (1625–1696) *Cominciamento e progresso dell'arte dell'intagliare in Rame* from 1686.[5]

Reading Evelyn and Baldinucci, it emerges that both texts reflect, elaborate and build on a long tradition of writing about printmaking. It is true that between the beginning of the 16th century, when a few observations were made, and the middle of the 17th century, when full treatises started to appear, no specific books were written about printmaking. But the topic was already a regular feature of art literature, beginning with Giorgio Vasari's (1511–1574) *Vite* in its two editions, from 1550 and 1568, and followed by treatises such as those by Benvenuto Cellini (1500–1571), Karel van Mander (1548–1606), Giovanni Baglione (*c*.1573–1643) and Giovanni Pietro Bellori (1613–1696).[6] In these texts, we find specific chapters about printmakers and printmaking. There are also treatises where printmaking is directly or indirectly integrated within theoretical discourses about art. This is especially the case in the work of Giovanni Paolo Lomazzo (1538–1592).[7] All of these texts demonstrate that printmaking already had an important role within the theory of art in the early modern age.

2 The Definition of Printmaking

To understand what the theory of printmaking consisted of in the Renaissance it is important to look very briefly at art theory of the time. The literature, for example of Giovan Battista Alberti (1404–1472) and Benedetto Varchi (1503–1565) in the 15th and 16th century, established art theory and set out its main issues: they are concerned with the question of the development of the

---

4   John Evelyn, *Sculptura: Or the History and art of Chalcography and Engraving in Copper* (London: 1662).

5   Filippo Baldinucci, *Cominciamento e progresso dell'arte dell'intagliare in Rame* (Firenze: 1686).

6   Giorgio Vasari, *Le vite de più eccellenti architetti, pittori, et scultori italiani, da Cimabue insino a' tempi nostri* (Florence: 1550); idem, *Le vite de' più eccellenti pittori, scultori, e architettori: con i ritratti loro et con l'aggiunta delle Vite de' vivi, & de' morti dall'anno 1550 insino al 1567... Di nuovo dal medesimo riviste et ampliate* (Florence: 1568); Benvenuto Cellini, *Due Trattati. Uno intorno alle otto principali arti dell'oreficeria. L'altro in materia dell'Arte della Scultura; dove si veggono infiniti segreti nel lavorar le Figure di Marmo, & nel gettare di Bronzo* (Florence: 1568); Karel van Mander, *Het Schilder-Boeck waer in Voor eerst de leerlustighe Iueght den grondt der Edel Vry Schilderconst in Verscheyden deelen Wort Voorghedraghen* (Haarlem: 1604); Giovanni Baglione, *Le Vite de' Pittori, Scultori et Architetti. Dal Pontificato di Gregorio XIII del 1572. In fino a' tempi di Papa Urbano Ottavo nel 1642* (Rome: 1642); Giovanni Pietro Bellori, *Le Vite de' Pittori, Scultori, ed Architetti moderni* (Rome: 1672).

7   Giovanni Paolo Lomazzo, *Trattato dell'Arte de la Pittura, di Gio. Paolo Lomazzo, Milanese Pittore. Diviso in sette libri. Ne' quali si contiene tutta la Theorica, & la prattica d'essa pittura*, Milan 1584; idem, *Idea del tempio della pittura di Gio. Paolo Lomazzo pittore* (Milan: 1590).

arts and their improvement, the definitions of single art forms and their functions; but they also discuss the virtues of the artists, above all their intellectual and manual efforts, and finally the rules and norms of art production.[8] These rules and norms go from a broad view of the general aims of art, such as the concept of imitation, to single questions concerning artistic images, such as the norm of decorum (*decoro*). As soon as printmaking became an important part of art production in the Renaissance, it also became a topic in relation to which all these issues could be debated.[9] However, the main question that appears in treatises from the 16th to the 17th century is that of what printmaking actually is. This arises within an analysis of the principles and essential rules of single art forms, such as painting, sculpture and architecture, and it is intensified in discussions that compare painting and sculpture, such as the well-known *paragone* discourses in Benedetto Varchi's lessons and later treatise *Due Lezzioni* from 1549. These discussions divide art generally into the two main fields of *pictura* and *sculptura*, into which the different kinds of arts, such as glass-painting or *intarsia*, are classified.[10]

The key problem with the definition of printmaking is its dual nature: the fact that the actual work of art is done on the plate but it is visible only in its impression on paper.[11] Authors of Renaissance art treatises who wrote about printmaking were aware of a duty to define it, but its two-fold nature and the firm categories of *pictura* and *sculptura* often led them to focus either solely on the plate or solely on the printed paper. Therefore, they attributed printmaking

---

8 Giovanni Battista Alberti, *De pictura/Della pittura* (1435/6); first print Basel: 1540, Benedetto Varchi, *Due Lezzioni* (Firenze: 1549).

9 Vasari makes clear that printmaking had become an important part of the arts. He declares at the end of the chapter of the "Life of Marcantonio", published in the second edition of the *Vite* in 1568, that he wrote this "long but necessary discourse in order to 'satisfy' scholars of the arts and admirers of printmaking": ("... *ho voluto fare questo lungo si, ma necessario discorso, per sod(d)isfare non solo agli studiosi delle nostre arti, ma tutti coloro ancora che di cosi fatte opere si dilettano*.") Giorgio Vasari, *Le vite de' più eccellenti pittori, scultori, e architettori* (Florence: 1568), vol. 2, chapter "Marcantonio Bolognese", 312. Vasari already discussed printmaking in the first edition of *Vite* of 1550, for example he wrote chapters about engraving and *chiaroscuro*-woodcuts in the "Introduction to the Arts". These chapters are repeated unchanged in the second edition of 1568. The two chapters will be discussed below. For a discussion on printmaking in the first and second edition of Vasari's *Vite* see: Stoltz, *Disegno versus Disegno stampato*, 3–11.

10 See Beat Wyss, "Der Paragone. Spielregeln des Kunstsystems" in *Streit. Domäne der Kultur*, ed. Irmgard Bohunovsky-Bärnthaler (Klagenfurt: 2006), 31–55. On the *paragone*-discussion regarding Varchi and artists such as Michelangelo and Cellini see Paola Barocchi, "Der Wettstreit zwischen Malerei und Skulptur" in *Ars et Scriptura*, edited by Hannah Baader (et al.) (Berlin: 2001), 93–106; Stefan Morét, "Der Paragone im Spiegel der Plastik", in *Benvenuto Cellini*, ed. Alessandro Nova and Anna Schreurs (Köln: 2003), 203–215.

11 Stoltz, *Das Bild-Druckverfahren*, 93–94.

THEORY OF PRINTMAKING IN THE EARLY MODERN AGE

either to sculpture (often in regards to the cutting of the plate), or to painting (often in regards to the painterly qualities of the impression), and in that way avoided an autonomous definition.

3   Printmaking Is Sculpture

The inscription *sculpsit* on prints, used occasionally instead of *fecit*, demonstrates the characterization of printmaking as sculpture. This can also be seen when woodcut or metalcut artists are referred to as *sculptor*, or in German *Formenschneider*, as can be seen in early 16th century text sources from northern Europe.[12] The link between woodcutting and sculpture seems obvious and almost natural. This is why the authors of some art treatises, such as Giovanni Baglione, made a hierarchical distinction between woodcutting and burin engraving, elevating woodcutting because of its difficulty and its evident relationship with wood sculpture by specifically using the term "carving" (*scolpire*). For example, Baglione writes about Giorgio Nuvolstella (*c*.1594–1624) whose "engravings in wood" ("*incise in legno*") for the Medici printing house were "very well carved" ("*assai bene scolpite*").[13] Furthermore, regarding Leonardo Parasole's (*b*. 1570) woodcuts, Baglione remarks: "(...) for this he gained praise, for the reason that the cut in wood is more difficult and risky than in copper".[14]

For Renaissance writers on printmaking it is obvious that the origin of copperplate printmaking derives from burin engraving, an ancient part of metalworking such as goldsmithery and bronzesmithery. Pomponius Gauricus (1482–1530) describes burin engraving in his treatise *De Sculptura* of 1504 as a part of chased work on cast bronze; and, long before the advent of printmaking, a similar description was made by Teophilus Presbyter in his *De diversis artibus*, written in the 12th century.[15] The art of printmaking through engraving is therefore generally referred to as "the art of the burin". However,

---

12   Tilmann Falk, "Formschneider—Formschnitt", *Reallexikon zur deutschen Kunstgeschichte*, 110 (2004), 190–224.

13   Baglione writes: "*Incise per la Stamperia Medicea molte historie di Santi Padri, da Antonio Tempesta disegnate; & in legno, per vero dire, sono assai bene scolpite.*" Giovanni Baglione, *Vite de' Pittori, Scultori et Architetti* (Rome: 1642), *Intagliatori*, 394.

14   Baglione writes: "(...) *alla memoria hora mi si presenta Lionardo Parasole Norcino, il quale in legno le sue opere formava, & acquistonne lode, per essere in ragione di taglio più difficile, e più pericoloso quello di legno, che del rame.*" Giovanni Baglione, *Vite de' Pittori, Scultori et Architetti* (Rome: 1642), *Intagliatori*, 396. If not specified, all translations in English derive from the author.

15   Pomponius Gauricus writes: "(...) engraving is a carving by pressing (...)": "(...) diaglyphice, quando insculpitur ad impressuram (...)." Pomponius Gauricus, *De Sculptura* (Napoli: 1504), *c*.6 (Chemiké), § 7. See Pomponio Gaurico, *De Sculptura*, trans. and

burin engraving (whether for printmaking, goldsmithery or bronzesmithery) always creates a two-dimensional image on a plate. This is quite unlike chasing, which creates relief out of the metal's surface through introducing concave or convex forms. The question therefore arises of whether printmaking was referred to as "sculpture" only because it is based on engraving, using the common tool with sculpture or goldsmithery, which means the burin.[16] For this particular problem Evelyn's treatise on printmaking, significantly entitled *Sculptura*, is enlightening.

The treatise begins with a chapter about the definition of sculpture, for which Evelyn uses ancient rhetorical and grammatical texts such as Quintilian and Diomedes as well as Gauricus' *De Sculptura*. His etymological and technical investigation discusses the Greek and Latin terms for "dig", such as *scáptein*, *sculpo* and *scalpo*, and *caelum* for chisel, and differentiates between the techniques of chasing, graving and casting. He comes to the conclusion that the activity in "plastic" art forms, for example in clay or wax, cannot be called sculpture, because "sculpture" follows the principal of cutting into a surface and taking out material, as is true of engraving in copper.[17] In this context, Evelyn cites the first sentence of Vasari's "Introduction to Sculpture":

> By this then it will not be difficult for any to define what the Art it self is; whither consider'd in the most general and comprehensive acceptation; or, as it concernes that of Chalcography chiefly, and such as have most Affinity with it; since (as well as the rest) it may be describ'd to be an Art which takes away all that is superfluous of the Subject matter, reducing it to that Forme or Body, which was design'd in the Idea of the Artist. And this as sufficiently Universal.[18]

---

ed. Paolo Cutolo (Napoli: 1999), 238–241. See also Teophilus Presbyter, *De diversis artibus*, 3, c.XI.

16 Significantly, in the Italian language for example, the term "*intagliare*" persists, which actually means "cutting", "carving" and "engraving" at the same time. The term "*incidere*" is used in texts for printmaking in the sense of "engraving" but often used also with the same significance as "*intagliare*" for woodcut (see citation from Baglione above, note 13). Baldinucci's first Italian art dictionary from 1681, demonstrates the prevalence of "*intagliare*", the word "*incidere*" is only shortly explained as "cutting". See Filippo Baldinucci, *Vocabolario toscano dell'arte del disegno* (Firenze: 1681). See also Zingarelli, *Vocabulario della lingua italiana*, ad vocem "incisione" and "intaglio".

17 Evelyn, *Sculptura*, chapter 1, in: John Evelyn, *Evelyn's Sculptura*, ed. C. F. Bell (Oxford: 1906), 6–7.

18 *Ibid.*, 6–7. Vasari wrote in his *Vite*: "The sculpture is an art which, by removing the superfluous from the material, it reduces it to that form of body, which is designed in the idea of the artifice" ("*La Scultura è una Arte, che levando il superfluo dalla materia suggetta, la riduce a quella forma di corpo, che nella idea dello Artefice è disegnata.*"). Vasari, *Vite*, vol. 1, "Introduzione alle tre arti del disegno", *Della Scultura*, chapter 8, 32.

THEORY OF PRINTMAKING IN THE EARLY MODERN AGE

Evelyn's text makes it clear that printmaking is a sculptural activity, because it cuts out material and by that it is also an activity that forms a body, in the sense of a three-dimensional object. Of course, such a firm vision of printmaking as sculpture creates a gap between the plate and the image printed from it.[19] The opposite is the case when printmaking is evaluated in relation to painting, where the printed image is seen as the only and actual work of art; sometimes as if the plate had not existed at all.[20]

4   Printmaking Is Painting

There is no author who defines printmaking as painting as determinedly as Karel van Mander. This becomes evident in several chapters of his *Schilder-Boeck* from 1604, in particular those on Dürer, Lucas van Leyden (1488–89/94–1533) and Hendrick Goltzius (1558–1617). For Van Mander, printmaking is a part of painting, or even painting itself. He writes about Van Leyden:

> Amongst the many spirits subtle and versatile in our art of painting who have excelled since the spring-time of their lives (…) I do not know one who can compare [with] the naturally gifted Lucas van Leijden, (…) who seems to have been born with the art of painting and drawing and with brush and burin in hand.[21]

In this sentence, which is one of several passages in the *Schilder-Boeck* where printmaking is broadly defined as painting, the brush is attributed to painting and the burin to drawing. Almost forty years earlier, Vasari defined the printed image as *disegno stampato*, and concretely as "an image that appears

---

19   Nonetheless, Evelyn also discusses the printed image in the following chapters of his treatise.

20   For instance, describing how Annibale Carracci seems to have made the print directly on paper, Bellori writes: "these papers were cut by acid water and refinished with a burin" (*"Queste carte intagliate all acqua, sono ritoccate al bulino ..."*). Giovanni Pietro Bellori, *Vite de' pittori, scultori e architteti moderni* (Roma: 1672), 88.

21   Translation from: Karel van Mander, *The Lives of the Illustrious Netherlandish and German Painters*, vol. 1, translated and edited Hessel Miedema (Dornspijk: 1994), 105 (*"Onder veel behendighe edel gheesten in onse Schilder-const, die van in den Lenten tijt huns levens uytmuntich zijn gheweest (…), en weet ick geenen, die te ghelijcken is by onsen voorgenomen natuerlijck begracyden Lucas van Leyden, welcken met Pinceel, en Graefijser in de handt, en met de Schilder en Teycken-const schijnt gheboren is gheweest"*). Van Mander, *Schilder-Boek*, 211V.

by printing and comes out like a drawing with pen and ink".[22] Within the theory of art, therefore, the printed image appears to have occupied an ambivalent position between the concepts of painting and drawing. The contrast between drawing and painting as diverging artistic practices emerged through an increasing appreciation of drawing, which became valued as the source of artistic conception, evidence of the artist's intellect and virtuosity, and also assumed an important position in art collections.[23] Nevertheless, drawing was still mainly regarded in the early modern age as an intermediary stage towards a completed work.[24] This is the crucial point about the printed image, which is a completed work having preliminary stages in drawings and printed proofs, but it works with the image language of drawing, which is the line.

However, the printed image, as an image of lines, simultaneously requires to be seen as a painting, in terms of a coherent representation of nature, space, bodies, light and shadow or narrative.[25] This requirement is strongly present, for example, in Vasari's appreciation of Lucas van Leyden's prints in the second edition of his *Vite*, where he observes that Van Leyden's way of representing nearness and distances in landscape prints may even surpass painting.[26] This text was to be repeated many times, for example by Van Mander in his *Schilder-Boeck* and by Baldinucci in his *Cominciamento* from 1686.[27]

Van Mander resolves the ambivalent position of the printed image between drawing and painting in several ways. He emphasizes that the image (painting or printed image) follows two main principles: it endeavours to be a perfect creation and composition, which is drawing, or rather design; and it pays attention to a balanced overall appearance in the distribution of light and shadow and tonalities, which is painting. For instance, Van Mander writes about the prints of Dürer:

---

22   ("(...) *il che non solo le faceva apparire stampate ma venivano come disegnate di penna*.") Vasari, *Vite*, 2, chapter "Marcantonio Bolognese", 295. See Stoltz, *Disegno* versus *disegno stampato*, 17; idem, *Das Bild-Druckverfahren*, 103–4.

23   For Vasari's discussion about the importance of drawings collections see: Stoltz, *Disegno* versus *disegno stampato*, 12–14.

24   Evelyn underlines that even a finished or virtuous drawing is still a stage towards the completed work: "(...) when all is done, it is still but a drawing, which indeed conduces to the making of profitable things, but is it self none." Evelyn, *Sculptura*, chapter 5, 113.

25   Cf. different view and discussion by Anne Bloemacher, "Von der Virtuosität bis zum System. Marcantonio Raimondi und das Scheitern des malerischen Kupferstiches", in *Technische Innovationen*, edited by Magdalena Bushart and Henrike Haug (Köln (et al.): 2015), 189–204.

26   Stoltz, *Disegno* versus *disegno stampato*, 15.

27   See Vasari, *Vite*, vol. 2, c. "Marcantonio Bolognese", 299, Van Mander, *Schilder-Boek*, chapter "Lucas van Leyden", 212r, Baldinucci, *Cominciamento*, chapter "Luca di Leida", 14.

THEORY OF PRINTMAKING IN THE EARLY MODERN AGE

> It is mostly admirable how he brought about or discovered so many particulars of our art (...), as much in the good effect of his poses, his compositions, as in the smoothness and beauty of the draperies—as can be seen in some of his last images of Mary in which one sees a distinguished majesty of pose and large lighted areas next to superb shadows and harmonious darks in rich draperies.[28]

Van Mander writes here about "our art", regarding art in general. Therefore, the praise of "smoothness" considers both the painted and the printed image. Both can evoke a balanced overall appearance.

This parallel view of a painted or printed image derives from Van Mander's definition of drawing. In his treatise, he uses the general term *teyckenkonst*, which is not only fundamental to any kind of art but comprises creating an image in several steps, beginning with line, composing figures and other elements, and following by modelling light, shadows and tonalities.[29] The last phase, colouring, is not an essential one, even though it is important for giving the picture vivacity and, above all, nearness to nature.[30] Van Mander sees also the continuum between drawing and painting, which is also shown by his argument that many types of art exist in between drawing and colouring, such as pastel drawing. Van Mander remarks about pastel drawing: "Here fame can be surely gained. Hence, the art of drawing is the father of painting, and no other things can be more similar to each other".[31]

In his treatises, some years before Van Mander's, Giovanni Paolo Lomazzo defines any kind of art as the production of an image, sculpture included, and directs attention towards the impact and potential of images. He writes: "(...) I say painting and sculpture are subordinated to but one and the same art. (...) Both of them gain equally to present beauty, decor, movement and the

---

28 Cited from Karel van Mander, *The Lives*, 90. The word "particulars from art" is meant by Van Mander as "characteristics", "aspects of art" (eyghenschappen). *"Het is seer te verwonderen, hoe hy soo veel eyghenschappen onser Const (...), soo wel in welstandt der actien, ordinantien, als van vlackheyt der lakenen en schoonheyt, als in eenige zijner lester Mary-beelden te sien is, daer men siet een schoon heerlijckheyt der stellinghe, groote vlacke daghen, en daer neffens treflijcke schaduwen, en eenparige diepselen, in de rijcklijcke lakenen."* Van Mander, *Schilder-Boeck*, c. "Albert Durer", 208r.

29 See the whole introduction, the "Grondt" in Van Mander's *Schilder-Boeck*.

30 Van Mander, *Schilder-Boeck, Grondt*, c.2, §15, 9v.

31 *"Hier mede can eere worden verworven/Want ist Teycken-const van Schilderen Vader,/ Geen dingh malcander can gheljiken nader."* Karel van Mander, *Schilder-Boek, Grondt*, chapter 2 §21, 10r.

surroundings (...)".[32] Some lines later Lomazzo emphasizes: "(...) there is no specific difference in the production of a portrait of a king in stone, wood or metal, or on a plate or with the brush or the chisel, because all these differences are only material ones."[33] Lomazzo therefore defines all kinds of art as one art, and this art, for him, is *pittura*.[34] Against this background, Lomazzo goes on to integrate the printed image in his discussion of the fundamental rules of images, such as proportion, light and shadow, and the creation of narrative.[35]

5 Printmaking Is Goldsmithery

The definition of printmaking in Renaissance art literature depends on a view of art, whereby the principal protagonists or antagonists are commonly sculpture and painting. Yet, Benvenuto Cellini, one of the most thoughtful early writers on the principles of art, has a particular view of printmaking. He assigns the technique of etching (*acqua forte*) to sculpture when discussing bronze and marble sculpture in his book *Due Trattati* of 1568, describing how the acid water is to be prepared.[36] But Cellini focuses most of his attention on burin engraving, which he defines as deriving from pen and ink drawing, the most difficult graphic discipline.[37] He writes: "(...) there are only few of them who drew excellently in pen and ink, and through this manner of drawing the engraving

---

32   "*Dico dunque, che la pittura & scoltura si contengono sotto una medesima arte (...). (...) l'una come l'altra egualmente s'affatica di rappresentare la belezza, il decoro, il moto & i contorni de le cose (...)*." Lomazzo, *Trattato*, 7–8.

33   "(...) *cosi non è differenza spec(i)fica fare il ritratto del Rè in pietra o in legno o in metallo, o in tauola, o con penello, o con scarpello, perche tutte queste differenze sono materiali.*" Lomazzo, *Trattato*, 8.

34   Lomazzo, *Trattato*, 1–12.

35   See e.g., Lomazzo praising the execution of hair by painters, sculptors including Dürer and Lucas van Leyden and other printmakers regarding the discussion about presentation of nature: Lomazzo, *Trattato*, book 2, chapter 21, 182.

36   Benvenuto Cellini, *Due trattati*, book 2, 43v.

37   Cellini's arguments are quite common. In the art literature, in the early modern age, drawing with pen was considered the most difficult graphic discipline, because of the fact to present objects or landscape etc., only with the line; the burin engraving was considered the equivalent to the pen drawing, and at the same time a more difficult printed graphic art in comparison to etching which was considered more "free" or "vigorous" than burin engraving but not to have "neat" image and especially "neat" lines. See for example Vasari, *Vite* (1568), vol. 2, 297 or Bosse, *Traicté*, 3 and Evelyn, *Sculptura*, book 1, chapter 5 (Bell 1906), 108, 110–112.

THEORY OF PRINTMAKING IN THE EARLY MODERN AGE

of plates in copper with the burin has been founded (...)."[38] Subsequently, he praises the art of engraving and names Dürer as one of the "most excellent" engravers.[39]

Cellini's high opinion of printmaking, however, was not founded on its relationship to drawing or sculpture. Rather, he valued it most as part of goldsmithery, which he considered as the fourth main art form under *disegno*, together with architecture, painting and sculpture. He even considered goldsmithery the equal or principal art above sculpture and painting defining it as a universal art that contains the principles of the other three.[40] Consequently, a goldsmith is able to do any other art. Cellini names several artists who became famous through their practice of goldsmithery, including some printmakers: Raimondi, Dürer and Schongauer. He affirms:

> No less praiseworthy are the very noble Florentine minds, and also some goldsmiths from the north of the Alps, who dedicated themselves to this art with enormous ability; among them was Martin Schongauer (...). The excellent Albrecht Dürer surpassed Martin Schongauer (...). Even Marcantonio Raimondi and Marco da Ravenna, also goldsmiths, competed in the art of engraving with Alberto [Albrecht Dürer], and for this they deserved great honour.[41]

For Cellini, goldsmithery is a universal art because it combines the creation of a sculptural form (by making concave or convex forms out of the metal) and a picture (by graving on the surface of the metal). In modern terms, a goldsmithery object combines two- and three-dimensionality.[42] When discussing

---

38 "(...) & pochi sono quegli che eccellentemente habbiano disegnato ben di penna, & mediante tal maniera di disegni s'è ritrovato l'intagliar le stampe col Bulino in Rame (...)." Cellini, *Due Trattati*, book 2, 6or.

39 "(...) fra' quali intagliatori il più eccellente, cosi per cagione della finezza dell'intaglio, come per la vivacità & fierezza del disegno, è stato Alberto Durero (...)."Cellini, *Due Trattati*, book 2, 6or.

40 See Marco Collareta, "Benvenuto Cellini ed il destino dell' oreficeria", in *Benvenuto Cellini*, ed. Alessandro Nova and Anna Schreurs (Köln: 2003), 161–169.

41 "*Non manco son degni di lode di questi mobilissimi ingegni Fiorentini, alcuni orefici oltramontani che con grandissima diligenza hanno operato in quest'arte, fra' quali fu Martino Fiammingo (...) Lasciossi addietro (...) Martino Fiammingo l'eccellentissimo Alberto Durero (...). Furono in questi tempi Antonio da Bologna & Marco da Ravenna pur orefici i quali gareggiarono nell'Intagliare con Alberto, & ne riportarono gran lode.*" Cellini, *Due Tratttati*, book, 1, 2r.

42 See above all Cellini's discussion about a clasp he made for Pope Clement VII. See Cellini, *Due Tratttati*, book, 1, 2ov.

pen drawing and prints from burin engraving, Cellini emphasizes that both are equivalent to goldsmithery. While praising the prints by Dürer, Cellini stresses that the perfect realization of a pen and ink drawing can be achieved in the printed image from an engraved plate. Additionally, he explains that, in contrast to chalk drawing, pen and ink drawing should be considered the highest level of drawing because it creates a three-dimensional appearance (*rilievo*, "relief") solely though the surfaces omitted between the lines. Cellini concludes with the observation that therefore *rilievo* (in this context in the meaning of the actual three-dimensionality and the appearance of it) must be the most important element of art. In contrast, colouring in painting only adds the colours of nature. According to Cellini, the main purpose of printmaking is to show *rilievo*, in the same way as in pen and ink drawing:

> therefore I say (...) the true drawing is nothing other than a shadow of *rilievo*. Therefore, one can say that *rilievo* is the father of drawing, and painting actually a coloured drawing with the same colours that nature shows.[43]

6   Printmaking Is ... Printmaking

Cellini belongs to the group of authors that does not fully consider the two-fold nature of printmaking or its entire procedure. The first author to do this is Vasari. Vasari describes printmaking in his *Introduction to the Arts* as being located within different arts, which are "something between sculpture and painting" including *tausìa*, enamel over bas-relief, *niello*, engraving and woodcut.[44] Vasari explains that engraving was developed from the technique of printing an image from the *niello*-plate during the process of *niello*, which later progressed to printing a picture from an engraved metal plate onto paper. He emphasizes not only the derivation of copperplate printmaking from goldsmithery, but above all that it is the printing of the plate afterwards that turns printmaking into a new artform. In this way, Vasari formulates the key link between the plate and the printed image:

> From this graving by the burin are derived the copper plates from which we see today so many impressions throughout all Italy of both Italian and

---

43   "*adunque* (...) *dico* (...) *il vero disegno non esser altro che l'ombra del rilievo, & perciò si può dire il rilievo essere il padre del disegno, & la Pittura essere veramente un disegno colorito con gl'istessi colori che dimostra la natura*" Cellini, *Due Tratttati*, book, 2, 60r–60v.

44   See Vasari, *Vite*, 1, "Introduzione alle tre arti del disegno", (Della Pittura) c.33–35, 63–66.

German origin. Just as impressions in clay were taken from silver plaques before they were filled with niello, and casts pulled from these in sulphur, in the same manner the printers found out the method of striking off the sheets from copper plates with the press, as we have seen printing done in our own days.[45]

A historical text about northern printmakers, which has only recently been studied, is even more explicit than Vasari in its definition of engraving as a two-part art form made by cutting into a plate and taking an impression on paper.[46] A chapter from a book about German history and geography, *Teutscher Nation Herligkeit*, this was written by Matthias Quad von Kinckelbach and published in 1609.[47] For Quad, the art of printmaking derives from letterpress printing. He writes:

The impression on paper derives from book-impression, and an impression [from the engraved plate] visualizes how much art, mind and subtleness was done on the plate, therefore the copper engraving derives from the invention of impression.[48]

---

45 Cited from Robert, H. Getscher, *An Annotated and Illustrated Version of Giorgio Vasari's History of Italian and Northern Prints*, 1 (Lewiston: 2003), 111. Niello is an ornamental technique in goldsmithery in which on metal, mostly silver objects the engraved parts are filled with a black liquid called *"nigellus"* (Latin: "black"), containing sulphur and lead, in order to create an image on the metal surface. This practice derives from the antique and was common in the medieval art. "Niello" can also indicate a print taken out of such engraved and black filled metal object. Such prints are mostly made in the 15th and 16th century. Correctly these prints should be named niello-prints."*Da questo intaglio di bulino son derivate le stampe di rame, onde tante carte e Italiane e Tedesche veggiamo hoggi per tutta Italia, che si come negli argenti s'improntava, anzi che fussero ripieni di niello, di terra & si buttava di zolfo, cosi gli Stampatori trovarono il modo del fare le carte su le Stampe di rame col torculo, come hoggi habbiam veduto da essi imprimersi.*" Vasari, *Vite* (ed. 1568), 1, "Introduzione" (Della Pittura), c.33, 64.

46 Jasper Kettner, "Die Aufwertung der Kunstschneider. Druckgraphik als Skulptur bei Matthias Quad von Kinckelbach und Paul Behaim", in *Druckgraphik zwischen Reproduktion und Invention*, ed. Markus A. Castor (et al.) (Berlin and Munich: 2010), 241–248.

47 Matthias Quad von Kinckelbach (Matthias Quad, 1557–1631), *Teutscher Nation Herligkeitt: Ein außführliche beschreibung des gegenwertigen, alten, vnd vhralten Standts Germaniae* (...), (Cologne: 1609). For this author see Thomas Cramer and Christian Klemm, *Bibliothek der Kunstliteratur*, 1 (*Renaissance und Barock*) (Frankfurt: 1995), 781–792.

48 "*Dieweil aber der abtruck uffs Papier scheinet aus dem Buchtruck entsprossen zu sein, und der abtruck am klaresten fur augen legen kann, was fur kunst, verstandt und subtilitet in der formen gebraucht seie, so wirdt die erfindung des Kupferschnits gemeinlich fur die erfindung des abtruckens genommen.*" Quad v. Kinckelbach, *Teutscher Nation Herligkeit*, 425.

Even though Quad recognizes the importance of the cut made on the copper-plate, he does not simply allocate printmaking to sculpture as some scholars did previously.[49] In his text, printmaking is just printmaking. Quad's text is a rare case. Later texts that give a full and precise definition of printmaking, such as those of André Félibien (1619–1695) and Joachim Sandrart (1606–1688) at the end of the 17th century, still locate printmaking as part of either sculpture or painting. In early modern art literature, printmaking largely remains "something in between".[50]

7 Excursus: Printmaking and Reproduction

In his definition of printmaking, Quad chose to use the word "*Abtruck*" which, more than impression ("*Druck*"), signifies "replica" (of the image from the engraved plate). As is well known, the role of printmaking as a reproductive medium is one of the most debated issues in art historical literature on subject.[51] However, outside of this discussion, it is equally important to look at the role actually given to printmaking in the 16th and 17th centuries.

The designation of printmaking as "reproductive" does not exist in the art literature of the early modern age. The only terms used for a printed image that presents an existing art-object (painting, sculpture or drawing) are simply: "made from" or "copy".[52] Furthermore, already the early texts on prints recall the concept of the printing as making public, divulgation of an image, independently of the fact if the image copy another work or is designed by the engraver himself. Vasari defines the printed image as a medium through which an artist can demonstrate his inventions, and disseminate his work to the

---

49 Cf. Kettner, "Die Aufwertung der Kunstschneider", 242.
50 André Félibien (1619–1695) discusses the principles of printmaking in his general book about art in the part "sculpture", see André Félibien, *Des principes de l'architecture, de la sculpture, de la peinture, et des autres arts* (Paris: 1676), book 2, chapter 10, 382–388. Joachim Sandrart (1606–1688) discusses printmaking mainly as sculpture but discusses *chiaro-scuro* woodcut and *mezzotinto* engraving in the part about painting, probably for the "painterly" effects both techniques present on the printed paper. See Sandrart, *Teusche Akademie der Edlen Bau-, Bild, und Mahlerey-Künste*, 1. (Nuremberg: 1675), book 2, chapter 6, 49–52, and book 3, chapter 16, 100–103.
51 For one of the more recent and abundant discussions about printmaking and reproduction see *Druckgraphik zwischen Reproduktion und Invention*, edited by Markus A. Castor (et al.) (Berlin and Munich: 2010).
52 Baldinucci for example uses concretely the word "*copia*" for prints after works from other artists. See in this article note 63.

THEORY OF PRINTMAKING IN THE EARLY MODERN AGE

public, as a writer does with the publication of a printed book.[53] For example, Vasari writes in relation to Mantegna:

> He bequeathed to painters the difficult foreshortening of figures from below upwards, a difficult and ingenious invention; and the way of engraving figures on copper for printing, a singularly true convenience, by which the world has been able to see not only the Bacchanalia, the Battle of Marine Monsters, the Deposition from the Cross, (…), works by Mantegna himself, but also the manners of all the craftsmen who have ever lived.[54]

This concept of printmaking's role in publishing an artist's "inventions" was repeated in most 16th and 17th century texts about printing.[55] The common expressions for "making public" with a print, which were principally used in the Italian texts, are *"mandare fuori"* ("sending out") or *"andare fuori"* ("going out").[56]

Vasari does not suggest any hierarchical distinction in artistic value between "reproductive" prints and those made after an artist's "own" invention. This kind of judgement would be increasingly expressed in 17th century treatises, beginning with Baglione's *Vite* mentioned above. Thus, the concept emerged of what is now usually formulated as the *peintre-graveur*, a term established by Adam von Bartsch (1757–1821) at the beginning of the 19th century. That is a painter who "also" works with printing in contrast to an artist who is "only" a

---

53   See Stoltz, *Disegno versus disegno stampato*, 8–12.

54   Cited from Getscher *An Annotated and Illustrated Version of Giorgio Vasari's*, 1, 120–121. *"Lasciò costui alla pittura la difficultà degli scórti delle figure al di sotto in su, invenzione difficile e capricciosa, et il modo dello intagliare in rame le stampe delle figure: comodità singularissima veramente, per la quale ha potuto vedere il mondo non solamente la Baccanaria, la Battaglia de' mostri marini, il Deposto di croce, (…),—opere di esso Mantegna—, ma le maniere ancora di tutti gli artefici che sono stati."* Vasari, *Vite* (ed. 1550), chapted "Andrea Mantegna", cited from Rosanna Bettarini and Paola Barocchi, ed., *Giorgio Vasari. Le Vite*, 3 (Florence: 1971), 555–556. This part is changed in the second edition, cf. Vasari, *Vite*, vol. 1, chapter "Andrea Mantegna", 492, and Bettarini and Barocchi, op. cit, *ibid.*

55   Vasari also emphasizes this in the second edition of his *Vite*, especially regarding the collaboration between Marcantonio and Rafael. See the chapter about Rafael and Marcantonio Raimondi, Vasari, *Vite*, 2, 78–79, 297, 299–301.

56   Vasari writes about the woodcuts from Titian: *"L'anno appresso 1508 mandò fuori Tiziano in istampa di legno il Trionfo della Fede (…)"*. Vasari, *Vite*, 2, 157. Baglione, *Vite*, 392 wrote for example about Francesco Villamena: "(…) he was a particularly good copper burin engraver, and several papers of him, that went out in prints, can show it (…)" ("(…) *particolarmente fu bravo intagliatore di bulino in rame, e ne fanno fede diverse carte, che del suo vanno fuori in stampa (…)*").

printmaker.[57] This concept was already formulated by Bellori and Félibien in the 17th century:[58]

Bellori's texts on printmaking, in his two treatises *Vite* and *Descrizione*, reveals the following hierarchy of prints: the highest works of art are prints both invented/created and executed by the artist; they are followed by prints executed by painters and masters after inventions by other masters; and finally prints executed by so-called "professional printmakers" after inventions by other artists.[59] Nevertheless, Bellori is highly interested in prints creating images of other artists' work, because he sees the importance of printmaking's ability to conserve the history of art, acting as a document in an almost legal way. Bellori writes in his *Descrizione*:[60]

> In order to give the required fame to the Painter, and the glory to the art of this present century, it [the rendering of paintings] has to be similar, it must correspond to the images with its examples, so, beside copies, drawings and prints (impressions of the plates), they [the paintings] can also remain impressed with their colours and lines by the letters [of a text].[61]

Lastly, Félibien, summarising all the above-mentioned aspects of the "reproductive" function of printmaking, writes in his *Principes* of 1676 that it is the art of reproducing in general which makes the work of art eternal. This is best facilitated through the art of engraving on copper and on wood: "With engraving it is possible to bring forth an endless quantity of images of one drawing, in which it is possible to see the thought of an artist, which had formerly only been known from the work that came directly from his hands."[62] For the "art of

---

57   Or a printmaker of a high quality. Adam von Bartsch, *Le peintre-gravuer* (Vienna: 1802).

58   Félibien writes that for "painters" who also work as or with "printmakers" the engraving is much harder to execute than for "professional printmakers": "*Ce qui est cause les Peintres qui font graver eux-mesmes leurs Ouvrages, travaillent souvent à former les premiers traits des Figures pour conserver la force, & la beauté du dessein.*" Félibien, *Principes*, II, X, 386. Bellori names Agostino Carracci in the title of the chapter about him as: "painter engraver": "Vita di Agostino Carracci pittore intagliatore", Bellori, *Vite*, 99.

59   See Bellori's critique of 'ordinary' "*intagliatori*" in comparison with Agostino Carracci. Bellori, *Vite*, 109–110.

60   Bellori, *Vite*; idem, *Descrizzione delle imagini dipinte da Raffaele d'Urbino* (Roma: 1695).

61   "*Laonde stimai dovuto alla fama del Pittore, ed alla gloria dell'Arte, e del presente secolo rassomigliare, e riscontrare le medesime Imagini col loro esempio, perche oltre le copie, li disegni, e le impressioni delle stampe, rimanghino impresse ancora ne' colori, e lineamenti delle lettere.*" Bellori, *Descrizione*, 2.

62   "*Un des plus grands avantages que l'Art de Portraire ait recu, pour eterniser ses Ouvrages, est la Gravuere sur le Bois, & sur le Curve, par le moyen de laquelle, on tire an grand nombre d'Estampes, qui multiplient presque à l'infiny un mesme Dessin, & sont voir en differens lieux*

THEORY OF PRINTMAKING IN THE EARLY MODERN AGE

reproducing" Félibien uses the term *portraire*, which he explains as the general act of doing something that is similar to another thing.

With the standardisation of "professional printmakers" and *peintre-graveurs* at the end of the 17th century, authors like Félibien and Baldinucci began to distinguish between "imitation" ("*portraire*") as a general artistic act (which can range between the partial or full replication of an object) and "reproduction" (which is a specific function of imitation), Baldinucci writes that, by imitating the work of other masters, prints "communicate" and "render" their work visible all over the world.[63] This discussion about imitation and the function of reproduction also brings up the question of "relativity", concerning the distinction between the "original" and the "copy".[64] Baldinucci argues in particular about the problem of defining a work of art as an "original" or a "copy" when, for example, a pupil copies a master's painting and the master himself subsequently adds changes to it. However, he emphasizes the overall importance of copies of all kinds, in painting, drawing or casting, and particularly praises printmaking.[65] For Baldinucci, any copy in the sense of "reproduction" takes the art object "off the walls" and allows it to be shared more widely, leading to the general improvement of art.[66]

8   Conclusion

Early modern authors formulated various and complex views on the potential of printmaking, and the examples given above demonstrate that the modern word "reproduction" was understood in a different way: What we call "reproductive" images were used to share artists' inventions and, occasionally, improve upon them. As Bellori, Félibien and Baldinucci emphasize, it was printmaking's potential to preserve and fix art history that made it so important. Here, the two-fold nature of printmaking discussed by previous authors

---

la pansée d'un Ouvrier, qui auparavant n'estoit connuë que par le seul travail qui fortoit de ses mains." Félibien, *Principes*, lib. 2, c.10, 382, ibidem, ad vocem "*portraire*", 707.

63   "(...) l'opere più degne de' valorosi Maestri d'ogni Città, e Provincia in ciò, che tali opere e per invenzione, e per disegno s'ammira, eccellentemente imitando, e contraffacendo e quelle eziandio a piccola, ma godibile proporzione riducendo, rendele comunicabili a tutto 'l Mondo." Baldinucci, *Cominciamento*, j.

64   See Félibien's *Entretiens* from 1676 and Baldinucci's published letter to Vincenzo Capponi from 1681: André Félibien, *Entretiens sur le vies et sur les ouvrage de plus excellens peintres ancient et modernes*, vol. 3 (Paris: 1705), 215–221; Filippo Baldinucci, *Lettera di Filippo Baldinucci nella quale risponde ad alcuni quesiti in materie di pittura* (Roma: 1687).

65   Baldinucci, *Lettera*, 14.

66   Ibidem, 14–15.

including Vasari plays a relevant role: the copper plate is not only a matrix to distribute an image, but also a medium used to preserve it. This echoes the concept described by Pliny the Elder who, in his *Naturalis historia*, praises the eternity of metal art referring to the antique *usus* of inscribing law on bronze plates.[67]

This brief overview of early modern printmaking theory has aimed to demonstrate that a developing and conceptual understanding of printmaking existed in the 16th and 17th centuries. Each author's definition of printmaking depended on key factors, firstly, whether they focused more the plate or the printed image and, secondly, on their overall view of art and their position in the *paragone* between sculpture and painting. Lastly, the problem of the two- or three-dimensionality of the art object played a role in the definition of printmaking, as Cellini's consideration of printmaking as *rilievo* demonstrates. Of course, all the authors discussed in this essay knew how printmaking was done, but only a few authors, such as Quad, managed a precise definition of printmaking encompassing its two-fold nature as plate and as impression.

Select Bibliography

Primary Sources

Baglione, Giovanni, *Vite de' Pittori, Scultori et Architetti dal ponteficato di Gregorio XIII del 1572 in fino a'tempi di Papa Urbano Ottavo nel 1642* (Rome: 1642).

Bellori, Giovanni Pietro, *Vite de' pittori, scultori e architteti moderni* (Rome: 1672).

Bellori, Giovanni Pietro, *Descrizzione delle imagini dipinte da Raffaele d'Urbino* (Rome: 1695).

Bosse, Abraham, *Traicté des manières de graver en taille douce sur l'airin* (Paris: 1645).

Baldinucci, Filippo, *Lettera di Filippo Baldinucci Fiorentino nella quale risponde ad alcuni quesiti in materie di pittura* (Rome: 1687).

Baldinucci, Filippo, *Cominciamento e progresso dell'arte dell'intagliare in Rame* (Florence: 1686).

Cellini, Benvenuto, *Due trattati, uno intorno alle otto principali arti dell'oreficeria, l'altro in materia dell'arte della scultura* (Florence: 1568).

Erasmus van Roterdam, *De recta Latini Graecique sermonis pronuntiatione Des. Erasmi dialogus* (Paris: 1528).

---

67 "Usus aeris ad perpetuitatem monimentorum iam pridem tralatus est tabulis aeris, in quibus publicae constitutiones inciduntur." Plinus, *Naturalis historia*, XXXIV, 99.

Evelyn, John, *Sculptura: or the History and art of Chalcography and Engraving in Copper* (London: 1662).

Félibien, André, *Des principes de l'architecture, de la sculpture, de la peinture, et des autres arts qui en dependent* (Paris: 1676).

Félibien, André, *Entretiens sur le vies et sur les ouvrage de plus excellens peintres ancient et modernes* 5 vols (Paris: 1672–1705).

Lomazzo, Giovanni Paolo, *Trattato dell'arte de la pittura, scoltura et architettura* (Milan: 1584).

Lomazzo, Giovanni Paolo, *Idea del tempio della pittura* (Milan: 1590).

Mander, Karel van, *Het Schilder-Boeck waer in Voor eerst de leerlustighe Iueght den grondt der Edel Vry Schilderconst in Verscheyden deelen Wort Voorghedraghen* (Haarlem: 1604).

Presbyter, Teophilus, *De diversis artibus*, 3, c.XI.

Quad von Kinckelbach, Matthias, *Teutscher Nation Herligkeitt: Ein außfuhrliche beschreibung des gegenwertigen, alten, vnd vhralten Standts Germaniae* (...) (Cologne: 1609).

Sandrart, Joachim von, *Teusche Akademie der Edlen Bau-, Bild, und Mahlerey-Künste* 3 vols (Nuremberg: 1675–1680).

Vasari, Giorgio, *Le vite de' più eccellenti architetti, pittori, et scultori italiani, da Cimabue insino a' tempi nostri* (Florence: 1550).

Vasari, Giorgio, *Le vite de' più eccellenti pittori, scultori, e architettori* 3 vols (Florence: 1568).

Secondary Sources

Barocchi, Paola and Rosanna Bettarini, ed. *Giorgio Vasari. Le vite de' più eccellenti pittori, scultori e architettori nelle redazioni del 1550 e 1568* 6 vols (Florence: 1966–1969).

Bell, C. F. (ed.), *Evelyn's Sculptura. With the Unpublished Second Part* (Oxford: 1906).

Bohunovsky-Bärnthaler, Irmgard, editor, *Streit. Domäne der Kultur* (Klagenfurt: 2006).

Cramer, Thomas and Klemm, Christian (editors), *Renaissance und Barock*, in *Bibliothek der Kunstliteratur in vier Bänden*, 1, edited by, Gottfried Boehm u. Norbert Miller (Frankfurt: 1995).

Cutolo, Paolo (ed.), *Pomponio Gaurico. De Sculptura*, trans. Paolo Cutolo (Naples: 1999).

Miedema, Hessel (ed.), *Karel van Mander. The Lives of the Illustrious Netherlandish and German Painters*, translated by Hessel Miedema 6 vols (Dornspijk: 1994–1999).

Secondary Literature

Baader, Hannah, et al., ed., *Ars et Scriptura* (Berlin: 2001).

Barocchi, Paola, "Der Wettstreit zwischen Malerei und Skulptur" in *Ars et Scriptura*, ed. Hannah Baader (et al.) (Berlin: 2001), 93–106.

Bartsch, Adam von, *Le Peintre Graveur*, 21 vols (Vienna: 1802–1821).

Bloemacher, Anne "Von der Virtuosität bis zum System. Marcantonio Raimondi und das Scheitern des malerischen Kupfstiches", in *Technische Innovationen und künstlerisches Wissen in der Frühen Neuzeit*, ed. by Magdalena Bushart and Henrike Haug (Cologne: 2015), 189–204.

Castor, Markus A. (ed.), *Druckgraphik zwischen Reproduktion und Invention* (Berlin and Munich: 2010).

Collareta, Marco, "Benvenuto Cellini ed il destino dell' oreficeria", in *Benvenuto Cellini. Kunst und Kunsttheorie im 16. Jahrhundert*, ed. Alessandro Nova and Anna Schreurs (Cologne: 2003), 161–169.

Falk, Tilmann, "Formschneider—Formschnitt", *Reallexikon zur deutschen Kunstgeschichte*, 110 (2004): 190–224.

Gramaccini, Norberto and Hans Jakob Meier, *Die Kunst der Interpretation. Italienische Reproduktionsgraphik 1485–1600* (Berlin and Munich: 2009).

Getscher, Robert H., *An Annotated and Illustrated Version of Giorgio Vasari's History of Italian and Northern Prints from his Lives of the Artist (1550 & 1568)* 2 vols (Lewiston: 2003).

Kettner, Jasper, "Die Aufwertung der Kunstschneider. Druckgraphik als Skulptur bei Matthias Quad von Kinckelbach und Paul Behaim", in *Druckgraphik zwischen Reproduktion und Invention*, ed. Markus A. Castor (et al.) (Berlin and Munich: 2010), 241–248.

Morét, Stefan, "Der Paragone im Spiegel der Plastik", in *Benvenuto Cellini. Kunst und Kunsttheorie im 16. Jahrhundert*, ed. Alessandro Nova and Anna Schreurs (Cologne: 2003), 203–215.

Nova, Alessandro and Anna Schreurs, editors, *Benvenuto Cellini. Kunst und Kunsttheorie im 16. Jahrhundert* (Cologne: 2003).

Stoltz, Barbara, "Das Bild-Druckverfahren in der frühen Neuzeit", *Marburger Jahrbuch für Kunstwissenschaft* 39 (2012), 93–117.

Stoltz, Barbara, "*Disegno* versus *Disegno stampato*: printmaking theory in Vasari's *Vite* (1550–1568)", *Journal of Art Historiography* 7, December (2012) (e-journal), 1–20.

Stoltz, Barbara, "Ars Nova? Die Neue Kunst? Die Bedeutung der Druckgraphik in der Kunstliteratur des 15. und des frühen 16. Jahrhunderts", *Ars Nova. Frühe Kupferstiche aus Italien*, ed. Gudula Metze (Petersberg: 2013), 19–29.

Stoltz, *Die Kunst des Schneidens und die gedruckte Zeichnung: Theorie der Druckgraphik in der Kunstliteratur des 16. und 17. Jahrhunderts* (Merzhausen 2023 and Heidelberg 2023: https://doi.org/10.11588/arthistoricum.489).

Wyss, Beat, "Der Paragone. Spielregeln des Kunstsystems" in *Streit. Domäne der Kultur*, ed. Irmgard Bohunovsky-Bärnthaler (Klagenfurt: 2006), 31–55.

CHAPTER 3

Poussin and the Theory of Hatching

Ben Thomas

In spite of the evidence that he made abundant use of them, the celebrated French painter Nicolas Poussin (1594–1665) seems to have had an ambivalent attitude towards prints. Writing to Hilaire Pader (1607–1677) in 1654, to thank him for sending a manuscript of his *Peinture parlante*, Poussin explained that sadly he was unable to reciprocate because "they have not engraved any of my works, about which I am not particularly bothered".[1] A year later, in a letter to his patron, Paul Fréart de Chantelou (1609–1694), Poussin complained of the engraver François de Poilly (1623–1693): "Poilly does not understand chiaroscuro" ("*Poilly … n'entend pas le clair et l'obscur*").[2] An earlier letter to the Roman patron and collector Cassiano dal Pozzo (1588–1657), written from Paris in 1642, reveals Poussin complaining about being prevented from working on paintings by being employed on "bagatelles" such as drawings for engraved frontispieces of books.[3]

This essay aims to assess whether Poussin's apparent negativity towards prints is indicative simply of a lack of interest in them, or symptomatic of a broader set of concerns about copying and translatability: an insistence, in other words, on the singularity of his art. For example, when he returned to Rome in 1642, Poussin coordinated a campaign of copying artworks and antiquities on behalf of Chantelou. While acknowledging the utility of copies for this purpose, Poussin's concerns about their fidelity to the originals gave rise to his decision to paint a new series of the *Seven Sacraments* for Chantelou, instead of just making copies of the original set that he completed for Cassiano

---

1 Pierre du Colombier (ed.), *Lettres de Poussin* (Paris: 1929), no. 162, Nicolas Poussin to Hilaire Pader, from Rome, 30 January 1654, 287: "*Au demurant je suis bien marri de ne vous pouvoir envoyer réciproquement quelque chose du mien, comme vous le désirez: l'on n'a rien gravé de mes ouvrages, dont je ne suis pas beaucoup fâché*".

2 *Lettres de Poussin*, no. 167, Nicolas Poussin to Paul Fréart de Chantelou, from Rome, 26 December 1655, 295–96: "*Je serai trompé si Poilly fait quelque chose de bon autour de votre Vierge car il n'entend pas le clair et l'obscur. Il est aussi rassis et taillant en ce qu'il fait et sans garbe*". Poilly's print is: Georges Wildenstein, "Les graveurs de Poussin", *Gazette des Beaux-Arts*, 64 (1955): no. 50.

3 *Lettres de Poussin*, no. 48, Nicolas Poussin to Cassiano dal Pozzo, 4 April 1642, 68.

© KONINKLIJKE BRILL BV, LEIDEN, 2024 | DOI:10.1163/9789004703834_005

dal Pozzo in 1640.[4] With regard to prints, Poussin seems to have been preoccupied with their capacity to accommodate two of his principal aesthetic concerns: stylistic decorum and tonal precision. Could the subtleties of his art, and the nuanced poetical and theological content for which painting was his vehicle, survive their translation into what William M. Ivins (1881–1961), in his *Prints and Visual Communication* (1953), described as "a syntax of the laying of lines for an average purpose".[5]

Perhaps this point can best be illustrated by an example of a print, made after Poussin's death, reproducing one of his paintings now in the Hermitage collection: the engraving with etching of *Esther before Ahasuerus* (1680) signed "F. de Poilly" published in Paris. Given the mediocre level of workmanship, which compares unfavourably with another etching after this painting by Jean Pesne (1623–1700), this print is unlikely to have been executed by the François de Poilly, whose handling of *chiaroscuro* Poussin criticised in 1655, but is more likely to have been executed by another member of this extensive family of French printmakers and publishers.[6] As the text from the Book of Esther (13, 9–10) inscribed on the print in both French and Latin explains, the narrative hinges around a moment of emotional transformation manifested in the painting by a physical change of colour: the Jewish Queen faints before King Ahasuerus, her complexion becoming pallid, and his anger at her unauthorised presence before his throne consequently turns to protective concern ("*... la couleur de son teint se changeant en une pasleure elle laissa tomber sa teste sur la fille qui la soutenoit*"). While this dramatic metamorphosis is made clear in the print's inscription, it is far less evident in the burin work, where Esther's pallor is barely distinguished from the faces of the surrounding handmaidens who support the falling Queen in a group reminiscent of the fainting Virgin in Raphael's *Borghese Entombment* (1507). The sole difference is that Esther is figured using fewer cross hatchings and slightly more stipple work.

The basic "syntax" deployed by 17th-century printmakers of engraved lines of varying thickness and direction, cross hatching, flicks and dots, was adequate to the purpose of producing "repeatable pictorial statements", to use Ivins' phrase, and to some extent it was standardized through training and in practice. However, this practice remained unsystematic from a theoretical point of view. As we shall see, several texts about prints written by members of Poussin's circle express a shared anxiety about the accuracy of copies, and an

---

4   *Lettres de Poussin*, no. 79, Nicolas Poussin to Chantelou, from Rome, 12 January 1644, no. 79, 136–39.
5   William M. Ivins, Jr, *Prints and Visual Communication* (Cambridge MA and London: 1978), 68.
6   Wildenstein, 136 and 26.

POUSSIN AND THE THEORY OF HATCHING   77

awareness of the actual or potential difference between the style of the artist reproduced in a print, and the style of the engraver executing it. Underlying these concerns are the significant, and at the time relatively novel, assumptions that prints should reproduce paintings in as accurate and unmediated a manner as possible and, consequently, that they would create the potential for a new type of art history based on prints rather than written descriptions of artworks.

1   Poussin and Prints

While the infrequent remarks cited above should not be interpreted as constituting anything so extreme as a rejection of printmaking, Poussin was certainly less personally engaged with the reproduction of his designs in print than several of his contemporaries. Painters like Simon Vouet (1590–1649) and Pietro da Cortona (1596–1669), for example, took a close interest in the reproduction of their work, sustaining long-term professional relationships with individual printmakers. As is well known, Peter Paul Rubens (1577–1640), after initially exploring the possibility of employing engravers from the school of Hendrick Goltzius (1558–1617), cultivated his own team of specialist printmakers like Paulus Pontius (1603–1658) and Schelte à Bolswert (1586–1659), whose distinctive style of engraving was developed to interpret the tonal qualities of the master's painting. In the case of the printmaker Lucas Vorsterman (1595–1675), the engraver came to resent the subordination of his talent to the painter, and Rubens in turn complained that "he [Vorsterman] contends that it is his engraving alone and his illustrious name that give the prints [after my designs] any value".[7]

While Vorsterman's claim was no doubt excessive, it was certainly the case that the production of numerous good quality prints contributed to the fame and reputation of Rubens, and of his celebrated pupil Anthony van Dyck (1599–1641). The lack of comparable print reproductions for Poussin's paintings, which were largely made for private collectors, was keenly felt by his patrons and supporters. This situation began to be addressed in the latter part of Poussin's life, with the publication of a set of etchings after the *Seven Sacraments* in Rome, alongside a series of other prints etched after Poussin's paintings by Pietro del Pò (1610–1692). In Paris, printmakers like François Poilly, Jean Pesne, Guillaume Chasteau (1635–1683) and others, also began a

---

7   Ruth Saunders Magurn (ed.), *The Letters of Peter Paul Rubens* (Cambridge MA 1955), 47, Peter Paul Rubens to Pieter van Veen, 1622, 87.

campaign of reproducing paintings in French collections. This development had the support of Poussin's patrons, and by implication of the artist himself. Such late 17th and early 18th-century prints undoubtedly helped to establish the artist's *oeuvre* and cement his posthumous fame.

During his lifetime, however, Poussin was also directly involved in the production of illustrative prints for two book projects, and a third book reproduced a suite of his original drawings. One of the book projects Poussin contributed to was the *Hesperides; sive De malorum aureorum cultura et usu libri quator* (Rome, 1646). Written by the Jesuit scholar Giovan Battista Ferrari (1584–1685), and published by Hermann Scheuss, *Hesperides* is a hybrid text. It combines exhaustive analysis of the myth of Hercules and the Apples of the Hesperides (the hero's eleventh labour in which he tricked the giant Atlas into liberating Hera's apples, which were guarded in a northern garden by Atlas's daughters, the Hesperides, by temporarily relieving Atlas of his task of holding the world upon his shoulders) with the author's specialism in botany through a scrupulous study of citrus fruits. The illustrations to the text similarly combine scientifically accurate renditions of varieties of oranges and lemons, with reproductions of antique representations of the story of Hercules and the Hesperides. *Hesperides* is an excellent example of how in the scientific and artistic circles supported in Rome by the Barberini family the interpretation of myth, the archaeological study of the visual culture of antiquity, natural science and the creative work of artists were all connected.

A preparatory drawing for the project by Poussin exists in the Louvre. Dating to about 1640, the *Nymphs of Lake Garda offering Lemons to the River God Benalus* is a highly schematic study in pen and wash.[8] It provides the overall composition and blocks out bold chiaroscuro contrasts in painterly washes, but it gives hardly any guidance to the engraver, Cornelis Bloemart (1608–1692), in terms of the deployment of line. A comparison with Andrea Sacchi's (1599–1661) drawing of *Harmonilius transformed into a Lemon Tree*, also for the *Hesperides* and also in the Louvre, brings out just how unhelpful Poussin's drawing was in this respect (although the existence of copies and variants after Poussin's design suggest that the Louvre drawing may be a first sketch and that at least one other preparatory drawing has been lost).[9]

---

8 Paris, Louvre, inv. 32442, provenance Everard Jabach. See: Pierre Rosenberg and Louis-Antoine Prat, *Nicolas Poussin 1594–1665*, exhibition catalogue (Paris: 1995), 308, no. 105.

9 For example, see Bloemart's engraving after Sacchi of the *Metamorphosis of Harmonilus into a Lemon Tree*, for which there is a preparatory drawing in the Louvre (inv. 3821r), which has the same orientation as the print.

Bloemart's engraving, therefore, was a triumph of interpretative translation, almost a metamorphosis—and it was for this talent that Filippo Baldinucci (1624–1697) praised Bloemart's technical ability, particularly the sweetness and evenness of his engraving (*"una tale dolcezza ed egualità della taglia"*), and his ability to imitate the particular style of the painter he was reproducing. In fact, it was precisely these qualities that prompted Pietro da Cortona to abandon his working relationship with the engraver François Spierre (1639–1681) and to work with Bloemart instead.[10]

It is significant that the engravings John Evelyn (1620–1706) singled out for praise in *Hesperides* were those that demonstrated how *chiaroscuro* could be effectively rendered, and how even colouristic effects could be suggested in a monochrome medium; achieving "a certain splendor, and beauty in the touches of the Burin, so as the very Union and colouring itself may be conceiv'd without any force upon the imagination, as we have before observed ... in what Greuter, Bloemart, and some others have done after Monsieur Poussin, Guido Rheni, Corton &c".[11] Evelyn was particularly admiring of Bloemart's work for the *Hesperides*, which had "given ample Testimony how great his abilities are; for certainly, he has in some of these stamps arrived to the utmost perfection of the *Bolino*, though some Workmen will hardly allow him this *Elogie*".[12]

The possibility of doing art history through images opened up by reliable reproductive prints such as those engraved by Bloemart in the *Hesperides*, or to put it in *seicento* terms, the potential for *figure* to supplant *discourse*, was one that, no matter how attractive it was to seventeenth-century critics like Baldinucci and, as we will later see, Roland Fréart de Chambray (1606–1676), always brought with it the anxiety of how exactly the tonal values of painting could be translated into the linear syntax of engraving.[13] The more prints were pressed into constituting a history of painting, the more necessity there was for a consistent and rational approach to engraving to be developed; in other words, for a theory of hatching.

---

10   Filippo Baldinucci, *Cominciamento e progresso dell'arte dell'intagliare in rame ...* (Florence: 1686), 64.

11   John Evelyn, *Sculptura* (London: 1662), 127.

12   *Ibid.*, 78.

13   Sarah Hyde and Katie Scott (ed.), *Prints (Re)presenting Poussin* (London and Manchester: 1994), 3: Here it is concluded that "the translation of oil paintings into patterns of line or dots in black ink on white paper cannot avoid change or distortion", and that De Piles' desire for a style-free form of engraving producing unmediated reproductions is an impossible project.

2 Poussin's Critique of Mellan

Poussin was directly involved in the production of prints for a book project on one other occasion; when he produced drawings for three frontispieces engraved by Claude Mellan (1598–1688) for editions of Horace, Virgil and the Bible published in Paris by the *Imprimerie Royale du Louvre* during the early 1640s.[14] The prints produced in Paris did not have the same elegant execution that Bloemart provided for the *Hesperides*, which proved so sympathetic to the work of the artist-designer. On the contrary, they are products of one of the most distinctive printmakers of the 17th century. The sober force of Mellan's engraving "with a single cut" (*d'une seule taille*) endows the frontispieces that Poussin designed with a somewhat "tragic" style. The distinctive quality of Mellan's engravings thus brings to mind Poussin's letter to his patron Chantelou in 1647 paraphrasing Gioseffe Zarlino (1517–1590) on the musical modes: "the good poets used great care and marvellous artifice in order to fit the words to the verses and to dispose the feet in accordance with the usage of speech as Virgil did throughout his poem".[15] So there may have been an appropriate decorum in the pairing of Poussin's drawing with Mellan's engraving in the production of three visual statements epitomising the cultural legacy of Roman poetry and Biblical history, where the severe elegance of the engraved line matched the elevated content which it conveyed. This did not, however, prevent Poussin from complaining about both Mellan and the distracting project of book illustration in his correspondence with patrons.

Writing to his patron Paul Fréart de Chantelou on 30 August 1641, Poussin provided a brief explanation of the iconography of the design for his frontispiece to the Bible later engraved by Mellan: "the winged figure represents History, whose left-handed gesture will be reversed by the printing process; the veiled figure represents Prophecy, and the sphinx above the book she is holding represents 'the obscurity of enigmatic things'; finally, the central figure is

---

14 Maxime Préaud et al, *L'oeil d'or: Claude Mellan 1598–1688*, exhibition catalogue (Paris: 1988), 143–149, nos. 188–190: for a discussion of the fractious relationship between Mellan and Poussin, and for the view that "*Poussin était par principe hostile à l'interprétation gravées de ses oeuvres*". Roger-Armand Weigert, "La Gravure et la renommée de Poussin" in *Nicolas Poussin* (Paris: 1960), 277–82.

15 See Anthony Blunt, *Nicolas Poussin* (London: 1995), 226 for Poussin's reliance on Gioseffe Zarlino, *Istituzioni harmoniche* (1553). Baldinucci credits Mellan with being "*inventore di quella sorta di'intaglio a bulino, che noi diciamo ad una taglia sola, perchè senza intersecazione di line trovò modo di far rilevare le sue figure con chiaro scuro, e mezza tinta …*". Filippo Baldinucci, *Cominciamento e progresso dell'arte dell'intagliare in rame …* (Florence: 1686), vii.

POUSSIN AND THE THEORY OF HATCHING 81

the Eternal Father, the author and motor of all good things".[16] Although brief, these remarks demonstrate Poussin's commitment to interpretative writing as the appropriate response to his art and to the complementary processes of reading text and image together. During March and April 1642, Poussin complained to Chantelou about the slow progress on the frontispieces, suggesting that Mellan was blaming him for the delay in finishing the books. He felt overwhelmed with a confusing multiplicity of projects, including the "*frontispices de livres*", and he told Chantelou frankly that "my nature constrains me to seek out and love well-ordered things, fleeing confusion which is as inimical to me as light is to dark shadows".[17] Although these remarks principally demonstrate the artist's dislike of collaboration, given Poussin's key concern with the parallel process of reading text and image, or the ekphrastic approach to iconography, they can also be seen to reveal something of his attitude to printmaking.

Some twenty-three years later, Gian Lorenzo Bernini's (1598–1680) visit to France prompted some further reflections on Poussin's collaboration with Mellan. On 10 October 1665, Chantelou recorded a conversation he had with Bernini concerning Mellan's engraving technique in his diary. According to Chantelou, "there were others better at his [Mellan's] profession" and he told Bernini that he had "never thought much of his work, for he was too preoccupied with a good line". Bernini, who had worked with Mellan earlier in his career when he provided a design of *David strangling the Lion* for the engraved title-page of Maffeo Barberini's (1568–1644) *Poemata* (1631), disagreed, replying that:

> He had seen some wonderful engraving by him [Mellan], notably some of Signor Poussin's works, of which he mentioned one of Eternal Wisdom. I told the Cavaliere that M. Poussin, like myself, considered his drawings poorly engraved, as he only tried to give a good line ["*n'ayant songé qu'à ne faire qu'un trait à sa gravure*"] and never attempted to render light and shade nor the half-tones; this was all the easier as M. Poussin's works were extraordinarily finished, considering how shaky his hand was; M. Mellan only produced a sort of shell with no half-tones or shadows for fear of

---

16   *Lettres de Poussin*, no. 32, 44–46: "*La figure ailée représente l'histoire; elle écrit de la main gauche afin que la planche la remette à droit; l'autre figure voilée représente la prophétie; sur le livre qu'elle tient sera écrit: 'Biblia Regia'. Le sphinx qui est dessus ne représente autre que l'obscurité des choses énigmatiques. Celle qui est au milieu représente le père éternel auteur et moteur de toutes les choses bonnes.*"

17   *Lettres de Poussin*: letters to Chantelou, 20 March 1642, no. 46, 64–66; and 7 April 1642, no. 49, 70–72: "*Vous m'excuserez, Monsieur, si je parle si librement. Mon nature me contraint de chercher et aimer les choses bien ordonnés, fuyant la confusion qui m'est aussi contraire et ennemie comme est la lumière des obscures ténèbres.*"

hiding the outline ["*de corrompre ses beaux traits*"]. The Cavaliere said that he thought it fine and well engraved. I said that there were many in France who engraved better.[18]

From this account, it seems that Poussin was not convinced by Mellan's belief that if you could not achieve the right effect with the first cut of the burin, then a second would not improve the situation, as the engraver Domenico Tempesti recalled ("*dice che quello che non fa esprimere l'effetto della cosa con la prima taglia non lo fa nemeno con la seconda*").[19] On the contrary, he felt that Mellan's distinctive style of engraving "*d'une seule taille*" failed to render fully the tonal effects of his designs. Not for the first time in the history of art we discover a disagreement between a painter and a sculptor: whilst clarity of contour and the decisive cut hollowing out form appealed to Bernini, the lack of tonal gradation, and a missing sense of chiaroscuro disappointed Poussin.

The appreciation of tonal unity within painting also lay behind Roger de Piles' (1635–1709) later view that a good engraver "must not, if possible, put anything of himself into his work. He must simply ensure that the print achieves the same effect ... as the painting it seeks to imitate".[20] In his *Dialogue sur le Coloris* (1673), De Piles criticized prints that "seem lifeless" through neglecting painting's tonal properties and "instead of creating an Esteem for the Originals ... tend only to dishonour them. Not that it is always necessary to imitate the Bodies of the Colours by the Degrees of the *Claro-Obscuro*; but there often happens occasions when it must be indispensably done".[21] De Piles'

---

18 Paul Fréart de Chantelou, *Diary of the Cavaliere Bernini's Visit to France*, Anthony Blunt (ed.), Margery Corbett (trans.) (Princeton: 1985), 280: "*Je lui ai dit que M. Poussin, aussi bien que moi, avait trouvé ses dessins faiblement gravés, n'ayant songé qu'à ne faire qu'un trait à sa gravure, au lieu de penser à imiter les ombres et les lumières, et les demi-teintes, ce qui était fort aisé, pour ce que les dessins de M. Poussin étaient extraordinairement achevés, vu sa mauvaise main, qu'il n'avait donné à ces estampes que l'écorce sans demi-teintes et sans ombres, au degré qu'il eût fallu, et cela peur de corrompre ses beaux traits. Le Cavalier a reparti que cela lui avait semblé bien gravé et beau*". For Mellan's title-page after Bernini see: Préaud, *L'oeil d'or: Claude Mellan 1598–1688*, 43, n. 27.

19 Furio de Denaro (ed.), *Domenico Tempesti: I discorsi sopra l'intaglio* (Florence: 1994), 140.

20 Hyde and Scott, *Prints (Re)presenting Poussin*, 3.

21 Roger de Piles, *Dialogue sur le Coloris* (Paris: 1699), 67: "*Cependant les oppositions qui se trouvent dans les Tableaux par les differens tons de Couleurs, contribuant extrêmement à leur donner de la force, il n'est pas étonnant que leurs Estampes paroissent fades, & que bien loin de donner de l'estime pour les Originaux, elles ne servent qu'à les deshonorer. Ce n'est pas qu'il soit toujours necessaire d'imiter les corps des Couleurs par les degrez du Clair-Obscur; mais il se trouve souvent des occasions où il le faut faire indispensablement.*" English translation from *Dialogue upon Colouring. Translated from the Original French of Monsieur du Pile ... by Mr Ozell* (London: 1711), 41. On Roger de Piles, see: *Bernard Teyssèdre, Roger de Piles et les Débats sur le Coloris au siècle de Louis XIV* (Paris: 1957).

POUSSIN AND THE THEORY OF HATCHING

remarks on the need for a form of reproductive engraving that can imitate a painting's tonal unity without the distraction of the engraver's style, and unmediated by the visual syntax of hatched lines, seem to anticipate the "paradoxical" technique of mezzotint heralded by Evelyn, although this was not a printmaking technique that De Piles appears to have known.

3 Chambray's Critique of Ekphrasis

In 1651, a suite of Poussin's drawings were reproduced in print to illustrate the treatise on painting by Leonardo da Vinci (1452–1519) published by Roland Fréart de Chambray.[22] According to Chambray, the prints illustrating his translation of the treatise into French illuminated the obscurity of Leonardo's notes. Without them, the text would have been "without anything to recommend it, and almost useless". Poussin's contribution made him, in effect, the book's second author after Leonardo.[23] The manuscript of Leonardo's treatise, together with Poussin's drawings, had been made available to Chambray by the antiquarian Cassiano dal Pozzo in Rome in 1640. Chambray had been in Rome, together with his brother Chantelou, in order to persuade Poussin to return to France and enter the King's service. Interestingly, in a letter written to the printmaker Abraham Bosse (1604–1676), probably dating around 1653 and first published by Bosse in 1660, Poussin distanced himself from the prints that were later made after his drawings, criticising the landscapes that were added to them by the engraver Charles Errard (1606–1689) and stating that "everything good in this book could be written in large letters on a single sheet of paper".[24]

Chambray returned to the significance of the prints illustrating the Leonardo treatise in his 1662 publication, *L'Idée de la Perfection de la Peinture*. Here, he commented that Leonardo's notes on painting could not have been made public without the existence of the art of engraving and the printing press, and that this was a great advantage that the 17th century had over antiquity. In this text, Chambray advocated an idealist commitment to universal aesthetic principles. He believed that the correct rules of painting—invention, proportion, colour, motion and composition—could be demonstrated by direct visual comparison, and that the artist whose works served "as so many Demonstrations

---

22   Roland Fréart de Chambray, *Traité de la Peinture de Leonard de Vinci donné au public et traduit d'Italiens en François par R. F. S. D. C.* (Paris: 1651), dedication to Nicolas Poussin, iii.

23   *Ibid.*, [unpaginated dedication].

24   *Lettres de Poussin*, no. 161, Nicolas Poussin to Abraham Bosse, 1653, 285: "*Tout ce qu'il y a de bon en ce livre se peut écrire sur une feuille de papier en grosses lettres ...*".

of the absolute necessity of exactly observing the Principles which we have established in this Treatise" was Raphael. By contrast, Michelangelo's example encouraged every licentious and capricious deviation from true principles. In order to follow this argument visually, the reader was advised to have alongside him four prints after Raphael—three by Marcantonio Raimondi, Giorgio Ghisi's (1520–1582) engraving *School of Athens* (1550), and one of Michelangelo's *Last Judgement*.[25] The use of prints as integral to the process of art criticism is emphasised in Chambray's text, and forms part of an attack on "ekphrastic" writing about the visual arts. In particular, Chambray scornfully condemned the mistakes in Vasari's account of Raphael's frescoes in the Vatican and the interpretative manoeuvres of his "amphibiological discourse": a good print would have removed the possibility of error and replaced the need for interpretation.[26]

Ironically, Vasari's "mistakes" in his descriptions of Raphael's frescoes derive from his use of prints, as Bellori would later point out.[27] Moreover, when Chambray conducted an "ocular demonstration" based on Marcantonio's *Judgement of Paris* after Raphael, he fell into error: treating it as given that Raphael had used single point perspective, he located the vanishing point of the composition in the eye of Paris. However, as Bosse pointed out later, Chambray's analysis is incorrect as there are four or five vanishing points within Raphael's composition, which he based on an antique relief in the Villa Medici in Rome.

Marcantonio's mythological print after Raphael's design of the *Judgement of Paris* was therefore required to carry quite a critical burden by Chambray: an engraving created in the early years of the 16th century to disseminate Raphael's *disegno* was now being pressed anachronistically into service to demonstrate the enduring and universal principles of *painting*. When prints were required to do such important theoretical work, questions of technical quality and reproductive reliability became urgent. Bad handling of the burin could disfigure a masterpiece and falling into the hands of a poor printmaker could

---

25   These prints, described by Chambray in the unpaginated preface to *L'Idée de la Perfection de la Peinture* (Paris: 1662), are *The Massacre of the Innocents* (Bartsch, XIV, 21, 20), *The Judgment of Paris* (Bartsch, XIV, 197, 245), *The Descent from the Cross* (Bartsch, XIV, 37, 32) by Marcantonio Raimondi, and *The School of Athens* by Giorgio Ghisi and published by Hieronymous Cock in 1550 (Bartsch, XV, 394, 24). It is not clear which print after Michelangelo's *Last Judgement* Chambray is referring to.

26   Evelyn, *Sculptura*, 110.

27   This was something that Giovan Pietro Bellori, a defender of the ekphrastic approach to visual analysis, would later point out. Giovan Pietro Bellori, *Descrizzione delle Imagini Dipinte da Raffaelle d'Urbino nelle Camere del Palazzo Apostolico Vaticano* (Rome: 1695), 15.

POUSSIN AND THE THEORY OF HATCHING 85

damage the reputation of any painter: as Chambray remarked, "what a misfortune it is for a painter to fall into the hands of a bad engraver".[28] It could be argued that Poussin's complaints about Errard's prints in the Leonardo treatise published by Chambray demonstrate his basic agreement with this sentiment.

4   The Theory of Hatching

The Dutch painter Gérard de Lairesse (1640–1711), writing in the early 1700s, provides a useful summary of debates concerning engraving techniques that had occurred throughout the preceding century: in particular about the various systems employed for representing forms through networks of lines cut into the copper plate with the burin. In his *Het Groot Schilderboek* (1707), Lairesse pointed out the failings of etchers and engravers in two important areas: firstly, the lack of correspondence between the shape and direction of their hatched strokes and the perspective of the scenes they represented, and secondly the lack of any relation between hatchings and the material properties and textures of the things represented in their prints. An undifferentiated use of engraved lines of uniform quality led to a failure to describe spatial diminution properly, an inability to distinguish between different tonal values, and it produced prints that felt airless and wooden. If the engraver were to relate the thickness, spacing and direction of his cuts to the things represented—rather than to the established conventions of previous printmakers—then "the course of hatching" would "yield great pleasure to the eye because it makes everything appear in its nature and quality".[29]

Lairesse remarked "it is very strange to me, in the old prints, that the masters have in nothing represented the natural qualities but etched everything after one manner", not distinguishing between thin and thick strokes of the burin or needle, but only employing an unsystematic form of cross-hatching.[30] Lairesse called for greater systematic rigour in engraving, for a rational deployment of cuts, in effect for a theory of hatching: "It is certain, that engraving as well as painting, is founded as much on theory as on practice, and that both depend on established and positive rules, which, if orderly followed, will make a man a

---

28   Chambray, *L'Idée de la Perfection de la Peinture*, 21: "*quel malheur c'est à un Peintre de tomber entre les mains d'un mauvais Graveur*".

29   Gérard de Lairesse, *A Treatise on the Art of Painting in all its branches* ..., W. M. Craig (ed.) (London: 1817), II, 257.

30   Ibid., 267.

master: why then, are they not made public, for the information of the curious in what they want to know?"[31]

A similar set of criticisms was made in 1649 by Abraham Bosse in the chapter on engraving in his *Sentimens sur la distinction des diverses manières de peinture, dessein & gravure*. According to Bosse, the engravings by Marcantonio Raimondi after designs by Raphael, which were used by Chambray in his analysis of the rules of painting, showed him to be an exact imitator of the originals from which he was working, but also to be lacking freedom in his handling of the burin, and beauty in the arrangement of his hatchings. Marcantonio also failed to convey distance by varying the strength of his strokes, making everything appear as if it was in the same plane because of the uniform force of his execution.[32]

Bosse's critical remarks on different manners of engraving, and the particular engravers he chose to praise, create a vivid sense of what he admired by way of technique: Bosse's taste in prints, it seems, had been formed by Italian printmakers like Agostino Carracci (1557–1602) and Francesco Villamena (1564–1624) working in a style fundamentally indebted to the example of Cornelis Cort (1533–1578), and by the northern school of engravers founded by Hendrick Goltzius. "*Liberté*", "*egalité*" and "*netteté*" were the qualities that Bosse admired in engraving technique, and which contributed to "*une belle conduite des hacheures*". However, Bosse was at pains to make it clear at the outset that excellence in technique did not necessarily make for a good print. Many practitioners and connoisseurs will esteem those prints on the basis of its design ("*dont le trait ou dessein est bon*"), preferring a badly engraved print after a good design to one whose only merit is its execution.

Good painters and good engravers do not always coincide historically or geographically, and so many of the printmakers whose style of engraving Bosse admired had worked after inferior designs. For this reason, Bosse argued that Marcantonio's prints after Raphael were to be preferred to Dürer's prints after his own designs, even though the latter's technique was incomparable. Similarly, Bosse regretted the fact that the Sadelers had not been alive at the time of Raphael so that they, rather than Marcantonio, could have reproduced his works. Overall, the true print connoisseur would prefer to see good design

---

31   Ibid., 263.

32   Abraham Bosse, *Sentimens sur la distinction des diverses manières de peinture, dessein & gravure* (Paris: 1649), 75–76: "*Ledit Marc Antoine a tesmoigné par ses Oeuvres qu'il estoit fort exact imitateur de ses Originaux, mais non pas de rechercher une grande liberté de burin, & beauté en l'ordre & arrengement des hacheures, fortifement & affoiblissement d'icelles, suivant le pres & le loin à l'égard du Tableau ou section, ains au contraire tout y paroist d'une mesme force, que est à dire comme si tout estoit en un mesme plan ...*".

combined with good technique. To this end, Bosse hoped that the many excellent contemporary engravers in Italy, Flanders, Holland and especially in Paris, would be inspired to engrave after the works of Raphael, Poussin "and other excellent painters of the same quality" (*"du mesme Goust"*). Here, Bosse shared with Chambray the growing desire for good prints after Poussin's works.

Bosse is careful not to name any living engravers, but his awareness of the range of different styles of engraving practiced by his contemporaries is evident from a remarkable passage in which he allowed engravers greater stylistic latitude than painters so long as their work tends towards the same end.[33] This conclusion reflects both the arbitrariness of the engraver's visual syntax of lines and dots, and also the persistence of divergent approaches to printmaking. One engraver, for example, might execute his work employing only a single order of engraved lines, which swell and diminish in thickness to convey dark and light as necessary (*"une taille ou hacheure seule"*). Another will achieve the same effect by adding a second order of cuts across this first *"taille"*: in other words, by using cross hatchings. Yet another will multiply cross hatchings, and combine them with small flicks of the burin and dots in order to soften and blend together shades and half-shades. Others might simply employ a greater or lesser massing of flicks and dots, without using lines, to convey forms through stippling. As long as these different styles of engraving are well executed and achieve the same overall translation of the original then they are equally permissible.[34]

The apparent relativism of this conclusion is somewhat unusual for Bosse, who as a teacher of perspective in the recently founded Academy took a consistently strict position on the necessity that artists followed precepts based on a

---

33   Ibid., 79: *"Pour ledit Art de la Graveure, il ne doit estre assujetty ainsi que celuy de la Peinture, à n'avoir point de maniere, dautant que les oeuvres d'iceluy, peuvent quoy qu'elles tendent à une mesme fin, estre faites de diverse sortes ...".*

34   Ibid., 79: *"l'on sçait que chaque Graveur peut conduire ou mener des hacheures de divers sens, & en plus grand nombre qu'une autre, car l'un exprimera son Ouvrage par une taille ou hacheure seule, en grossissant les traits plus ou moins selon la necessité; l'autre fera le mesme par deux hacheures l'une sur l'autre; Un autre fera la mesme chose par un grand nombre, & mesme y adjoustant en divers endroits, de petits traits, & des points, pour attendrir, noyer ou perdre ensemble, les Ombres, Teintes & demies Teintes; Et finalement d'autres executeront ces mesmes choses par petites hacheures ou traits, & par un nombre de poinctillemens meslez parmy; & bien souvent le tout par plusieurs points, gros & menus, pressez & eslargis, selon l'occasion; Or ces choses estant bien executées, il est asseuré qu'elles arriveront à une mesme fin, qui est de bien exprimer la forme des corps & partie contenuës en leur Original."* A similar set of opinions about the existence of a variety of engraving techniques, and how to arrive at the best possible practice, can be found in Domenico Tempesti's *I discorsi sopra l'intaglio*, where he also records the maxims on engraving of his master Robert Nanteuil: Denaro, *Domenico Tempesti*.

rational and natural order. Significantly, he immediately qualified his remarks on the variety of modes of engraving by stating that certain manners are more appropriate than others and that one engraver might "render his work more correct and complete by means of a single hatching, than another who uses a great number".[35] Bosse then defended the method of engraving employed by Mellan, using *"une seule hacheure"* against scornful criticism based on a few negligently executed prints, stating that marvellous effects could be achieved by this manner, which was "extremely agreeable to the eye", and not just because of the strong visual effect of contrasting areas of black and white created by this method.[36]

The technique of employing only a single order of lines without cross-hatchings, known as *"le taille simple"*, where tonal values are evoked by varying the thickness, depth and spacing of these cuts so that they swell and taper, had been pioneered on a small scale by the etcher Jacques Callot (1592–1635). According to André Félibien (1619–1695), Callot had been inspired by the chiaroscuro pavements in Siena cathedral to develop an approach to printmaking that at its most developed would famously result in Mellan's *Head of Christ* or *Sudarium* (1649), composed simply of a single line spiralling outwards from the tip of Christ's nose. As Goldstein has aptly remarked, the technique of this print seems almost as miraculous as the divine image it represents: "Mellan's one-line technique is such a wonder seemingly 'not made by hand', as though originating in a growth process such as is found in nature, in the 'thing itself', and that thereby functions as such a medium for the divine".[37] Bosse was strongly influenced by both printmakers, adopting the hard-ground etching methods of Callot, and using a specially adapted tool called the *"echoppe"* to make his etched strokes imitate the engraved lines of the burin, and he even collaborated with Mellan on a number of plates following his return to Paris around 1637. An example of their collaboration is the charming portrait of the Englishman James Howell (1594–1666) leaning against a tree from 1641. Mellan engraved the head, hand and collar, whilst Bosse etched the rest of the plate employing a swelling Mellan-esque line in the shading of Howell's cloak and trousers. The print was used as a frontispiece to the French edition of Howell's book on forestry, *Dendrologie*, published in 1641. Bosse employed the *"taille*

---

35 Ibid., 79–80: "... *Car il y a tel qui rendra son Ouvrage plus correct & complet par une seule hacheure, qu'un autre par un grand nombre*".

36 A. Hyatt Mayor vividly describes Mellan's "curving, swelling parallels without crosshatching, all sparkling as limpidly as sunlight under the water of an aquarium" in *Prints and People: A Social History of Printed Pictures* (New York: 1981), no. 289.

37 Carl Goldstein, *Print Culture in Early Modern France: Abraham Bosse and the Purposes of Print* (Cambridge: 2012), 86.

simple" technique in a systematic way in only a few of his own prints because he experienced technical difficulties in adapting the method to the etching process. However, it is significant that he used it in prints dedicated to disseminating information about the art of printmaking, including the well-known prints *Les Graveurs en taille douce* (1643) and *Comme on imprime les planches de taille douce* (1642).[38]

Given Bosse's concerns about the arbitrary nature of engraving technique, the lack of method in the distribution of hatchings, and his preference for the geometrical clarity of the "taille simple", the publication of a "certain" method to guide the engraver's cutting of strokes based on perspective in his *Moyen Universel de pratiquer la perspective* of 1653 was a major breakthrough. Bosse was approached by the engraver Robert Nanteuil (1623–1678), who wanted to consult him on how to manage the distribution of hatchings in his prints. Together with Nanteuil, therefore, Bosse hit on the idea of employing a frame strung with an evenly spaced grid like a racket (*"une forme de raquette treillissée de fils ou cordes"*) that cast a network of shadows onto the object the artist wanted to represent, whether the smooth ball or the complex surface of the antique bust shown in the diagram Bosse provided, for as he points out, a diagram is always more apt than a written description ("figure" is preferable to "discourse").[39] When lit, the strings would project a shadowy pattern of curving but regular lines over the swellings and concavities of, say, the passage between cheek, chin and neck. Following these shadows the printmaker could achieve a greater sense of relief with lines cut into copper with a burin, or marked onto the wax etching ground with the *"echoppe"*.

While draughtsmen had used similar grids before to draw objects in perspective—as in Albrecht Dürer's (1471–1528) woodcut of an artist doing just this with a steeply foreshortened female nude in his book *Underweysung der Messung* of 1525—this is the first instance of such a device being used as part of the process of printmaking. The use of shadows to determine the patterns of etched or engraved lines even endowed the print with a form of

---

38   Abraham Bosse, *Traicté des manières de graver* ... (Paris: 1645), 2–3: "*Pour moi, j'advouë que la plus grande difficulté que j'ay rencontrées en la graveure à l'eau forte, est d'y faire des hacheures tournantes, grosses, & deliées au besoin comme le burin les fait ...*". See: Marianne Le Blanc, *D'Acide et d'Encre: Abraham Bosse (1604?–1676) et son siècle en perspectives* (Paris: 2004), 68. Also Evelyn's comment in *Sculptura*, 90: "especially those of his latter manner, performed in single and masterly strokes, without decussations and cross hatchings, in emulation of the graver".

39   Abraham Bosse, *Moyen Universel de pratiquer la perspective sur les tableaux ou surfaces irrégulières* (Paris: 1653), 37–38. On Nanteuil's collaboration with Bosse, and his knowledge of Mellan, see: Audrey Adamczak, *Robert Nanteuil, ca. 1623–1678* (Paris: 2011), 37–40.

indexicality, placing it somewhere between a drawing and a photograph. The relatively arbitrary visual syntax of dots and cross hatchings could now be replaced with a "natural" approach that had the clarity of Mellan's single swelling line and the authority of real presence.[40] The racket, however, had limitations: it was best applied to the rendering of particular objects and was less helpful in addressing the problem of perspective depth in a print across a larger composition. Also, as Evelyn pointed out, most prints were translations of already two-dimensional drawings rather than images worked from three-dimensional reality, and he reported in 1662 that Bosse's "racket" had not been widely adopted by printmakers. He did, however, reproduce Bosse's diagram in his *Sculptura*, naming the method "perspective parallelism"; the other illustration to his book being more famously Prince Rupert's "specimen" of the paradoxical and secret new method of mezzotint.

5 Conclusion: Poussin's Ideas in the Context of Prints

On 4 February 1663, Poussin asked Chantelou to send him Chambray's *Idea of Perfect Painting*.[41] It was this text attacking ekphrasis and promoting the use of prints in its place which prompted Poussin's moving letter evoking the *Golden Bough* of Virgil. Poussin wrote to Chambray in 1665, stating that "[The subject matter] must be chosen so as to be capable of taking on the most excellent form. The painter must begin with disposition, then ornament, decorum, beauty, grace, vivacity, *costume, vraisemblance*, and judgement in every part. These last qualities spring from the talent of the painter and cannot be learned. They are like Virgil's Golden Bough which none can find or pick, unless he is guided by destiny".[42] As Bellori records Poussin noting "the idea of beauty does not descend into matter that is not prepared as thoroughly as possible".[43] Evidently, Mellan's style of engraving "*d'une seule taille*" was an insufficient vehicle for the idea of beauty according to Poussin. Bellori recorded in the epistolary preface to his *Lives* that he had been advised to follow his ekphrastic style of description of works of art by Poussin himself, building on

---

40   Ivins, *Prints and Visual Communication*, 66.

41   *Lettres de Poussin*, 174, 304: "*Ce me sera comble d'obligations si vous m'envoyez le livre de monsieur de Chambray touchant l'art de la peinture*".

42   Nicolas Poussin to M. de Chambray, 1 March 1665, in Blunt, *Nicolas Poussin*, 372: "*Ces dernières parties sont du Peintre et ne se peuvent aprendre. Cest le Rameau d'or de Virgile que nul ne peut trouver ny ceuillir sil n'est conduit par la Fatalité*".

43   Giovan Pietro Bellori, *Le vite de' pittori, scultori et architetti moderni*, ed. E. Borea, Turin: 1976, 481.

an exposition of the over-all conception of a work by paying careful attention to how each particular figure acted out its role in the scheme.[44] Yet Bellori also acknowledged himself a "mere translator", risking obscurity through thick description, and potentially reducing the "delight of painting ... which resides in sight". As figure and discourse continued their symbiotic dance around the "idea of perfect painting", the print's theoretical status was perhaps never more keenly debated.

Select Bibliography

Primary Sources

Baldinucci, Filippo, *Cominciamento e progresso dell'arte dell'intagliare in Rame* (Florence: 1686).

Bellori, Giovanni Pietro, *Descrizzione delle imagini dipinte da Raffaele d'Urbino* (Rome: 1695).

Bosse, Abraham, *Traicté des manières de graver en taille douce sur l'airan* (Paris: 1645).

Bosse, Abraham, *Sentimens sur la distinction des diverses manières de peinture, dessein & gravure* (Paris: 1649).

Bosse, Abraham, *Moyen Universel de pratiquer la perspective sur les tableaux ou surfaces irrégulières* (Paris: 1653).

de Chambray, Roland Fréart, *Traité de la Peinture de Leonard de Vinci donné au public et traduit d'Italiens en François par R. F. S. D. C.* (Paris: 1651).

de Chambray, Roland Fréart, *L'Idée de la Perfection de la Peinture* (Paris, 1662).

Evelyn, John, *Sculptura: or the History and art of Chalcography and Engraving in Copper* (London: 1662).

Secondary Sources

Adamczak, Audrey, *Robert Nanteuil, c.1623–1678* (Paris: 2011).

Blunt, Anthony, *Nicolas Poussin* (London: 1995).

de Chantelou, Paul Fréart, *Diary of the Cavaliere Bernini's Visit to France*, edited by Anthony Blunt, translated by Margery Corbett (Princeton: 1985).

du Colombier, Pierre (ed.), *Lettres de Poussin* (Paris: 1929).

de Denaro, Furio, edited by, *Domenico Tempesti: I discorsi sopra l'intaglio* (Florence: 1994).

---

44   Ibid., 8: "... *poiché havendo già descritto, l'immagini di Rafaelle nelle camere Vaticane, nell'impiegarmi dopo a scriver le vite, fu consiglio di Nicolò Pussino che io proseguissi nel modo istesso, e che oltre l'inventione universale, io sodisfacessi al concetto, e moto di ciascheduna particolar figura, & all'attioni che accompagnano gli affetti*".

Goldstein, Carl, *Print Culture in Early Modern France: Abraham Bosse and the Purposes of Print* (Cambridge: 2012).

Hyde, Sarah and Katie Scott (ed.), Prints (Re)presenting Poussin (London and Manchester: 1994).

Ivins, William M., Jr, *Prints and Visual Communication* (Cambridge MA and London: 1969).

de Lairesse, Gérard, *A Treatise on the Art of Painting in all its branches*, edited by W. M. Craig (London: 1817).

Le Blanc, Marianne, *D'Acide et d'Encre: Abraham Bosse (1604?–1676) et son siècle en perspectives* (Paris: 2004).

Préaud, Maxime, et al., *L'oeil d'or: Claude Mellan 1598–1688* (Paris: 1988).

Rosenberg, Pierre and Louis-Antoine Prat, *Nicolas Poussin 1594–1665* (Paris: 1995).

Saunders Magurn, Ruth (ed.), The Letters of Peter Paul Rubens (Cambridge MA 1955).

Teyssèdre, Bernard, *Roger de Piles et les Débats sur le Coloris au siècle de Louis XIV* (Paris: 1957).

Wildenstein, Georges, 'Les graveurs de Poussin', *Gazette des Beaux-Arts*, 64 (1955): 77–371.

CHAPTER 4

Paul Sandby and Reproductive Printmaking

Ann V. Gunn

∴

The illiberal reflections, which, by ignorant pretenders to the art, have been cast upon the engravers, hardly merit an answer, and particularly, when not mentioned under proper restrictions; namely, that they deserve not the name of artists, but are to be considered as mere copyists.[1]

∴

Thus wrote Joseph Strutt (1749–1802) in 1785, in defence of reproductive engravers and opposing views such as that expressed by William Gilpin (1724–1804) in his 1768 *Essay on Prints*, in which he wrote that: "Mere engravers, in general, are little better than mere mechanics."[2] Strutt continued by comparing the engraver's work in reproducing the work of artists to that of the literary translator: "What the poet has to do with respect to the idiom of the language, the engraver has also to perform in his translation, for so it may be called, of the original picture upon the copper."

The discussion about the merits of reproductive prints was tied up both with the art politics of the day and aesthetic arguments. The 1760s were singularly turbulent years in the London art world, with various factions vying for royal favour and arguing over the establishment and running, firstly, of the Society of Artists and, subsequently, of the Royal Academy. Strutt was continuing a discussion about the status of engravers in relation to that of artists which had come to a head in 1768 when the Royal Academy was founded. Unlike many academies on the continent, the new establishment originally excluded engravers from membership.[3] In their desire to promote their

---

1   Joseph Strutt, *A Biographical Dictionary containing an historical account of all the engravers, from the earliest period of the art of engraving to the present time* (London: 1785), 5.
2   William Gilpin, *Essay on Prints* (London: 1768), 53–54. Interestingly, this comment was removed in later editions of the book.
3   When the rules were amended, printmakers were only admitted as Associate Engravers with minimal rights.

© KONINKLIJKE BRILL BV, LEIDEN, 2024 | DOI:10.1163/9789004703834_006

own professional standing, the founder members (which included William Chambers (1723–1796), Sir Joshua Reynolds (1723–1792) and Benjamin West (1738–1920)) specified that academicians should be "Painters, Sculptors, or Architects", thus effectively downgrading the status of engravers, much to the vexation of the latter.[4] The Scottish engraver Robert Strange (1721–1792) believed this exclusion was aimed at him personally, and gave his version of events in *An inquiry into the rise and establishment of the Royal Academy of Arts* (1775), exclaiming that it was "Amazing that men, who pretended to promote the fine arts, and reflect honour upon the King, could have the effrontery to present the public with a regulation equally contradictory and unjust."[5] This exclusion was made at the risk of alienating a workforce of skilled printmakers on whom artists relied for the dissemination of their work, which Strange also pointed out:

> What idea can the reader form [of] a set of men, who ... were on this occasion so insensible of what could not but affect their own reputations? I appeal to their understandings, whether perpetuating the merit of their works to posterity ... must not, in a great measure, depend upon the perfection of engraving, an art, which they meant to disgrace by this exclusion?[6]

Until the advent of public exhibitions, first with the Society of Artists from 1760 and then from 1769 with those held annually by the Royal Academy, artists had no way of reaching a wider public except through the medium of the engraved copy.[7] At this time, the bulk of the English print trade consisted of reproductions of works of art in another medium. As Richard Godfrey notes, "Throughout the 18th century, reproductive prints must outnumber those which were designed and executed by a single hand in a proportion of at

---

4   Sidney C. Hutchison, *The History of the Royal Academy 1768–1986* (London: 1986), Appendix A, *The Instrument of Foundation*, 245. Two engravers were among the first members, but Richard Yeo was elected as a sculptor and Francesco Bartolozzi as a painter.

5   Robert Strange, *An inquiry into the rise and establishment of the Royal Academy of Arts. To which is prefixed, A Letter to the Earl of Bute* (London: 1775), 112–113.

6   Strange, *An inquiry*, 120–121.

7   As Alexander and Godfrey have noted, highlighting the importance of prints in disseminating knowledge of works of art, "in the early years of the eighteenth century it was primarily through prints that the English public and English artists knew painting. Foreign travel was open only to a very small minority ... [and] there were no art galleries open to the public" David Alexander and Richard T. Godfrey, *Painters and Engraving: the Reproductive Print from Hogarth to Wilkie*, exhibition catalogue (New Haven: 1980), 1.

least fifty to one."[8] Publications ranged from large format *de luxe* fine plates for the connoisseur and the print collector down to cheap and topical prints aimed at the more popular market. Subjects encompassed copies of old master paintings and drawings, reproductions of contemporary portraits, views and events. Portrait and landscape painters joined up with specialist mezzotint scrapers or line engravers to promote and advertise their work. A good print by a sought-after engraver could make a painter's reputation. As Thomas Jones (1742–1803) recalled in his memoirs, after William Woollett's (1735–1785) success with his copy of Richard Wilson's (1714–1782) *Niobe* in 1761, the young Jones hoped he could get Woollett to engrave one of his landscapes:

> I began to flatter my self with hopes that my Reputation would be established, and spread abroad through the Medium of that celebrated Engraver, as my Master, Wilson, had in some degree, even his fame extended by the admirable Prints of this Artist after his Pictures.[9]

Paul Sandby (1731–1809) was a founder member of the Royal Academy. He is best known as a watercolour artist, but printmaking was a core part of his artistic practice throughout his career.[10] It is intriguing to speculate what he might have made of this treatment of engravers, many of whom were friends with whom he had worked over the years. There is no documentary evidence which might indicate his views, so we must rely on circumstantial evidence to provide a clue. While most of the 370 or so prints he made from the late 1740s to the 1780s were his own original prints, he also contributed to the huge market in reproductive prints, both before and after the establishment of the Royal Academy and the controversial exclusion of engravers from membership, so he had a vested interest in the issue. Sandby's main contributions to this thriving market were three sets of line etchings and engravings from the 1750s and early 1760s, and three sets of aquatints published in the 1770s and 1780s.[11] The early works were *Eight Views in Windsor Great Park* (1754–58) after Thomas Sandby (1723–1798), illustrations to Tasso's *Jerusalem Delivered* (*c.*1757–60) after paintings by John Collins (*c.*1725–58/9), and *Six Remarkable Views in the Provinces of New York, New Jersey, and Pennsylvania* (1761–68) after drawings by Governor

---

8   Richard T. Godfrey, *Printmaking in Britain* (Oxford: 1978), 43.

9   Thomas Jones, "The Memoirs of Thomas Jones" edited by Adolph Paul Oppé, *Walpole Society*, 32, 1946, 19.

10 All references to his prints are from Ann V. Gunn, *The Prints of Paul Sandby, (1731–1809), a Catalogue Raisonné* (Turnhout: 2015).

11 See Gunn, *Catalogue Raisonné*, cat. nos. 146–150, 152–154, 169–173, 244–259, 266–277, 278–281.

Thomas Pownall (1722–1805). The aquatint series were *Views in and around Naples* (1777–78) after paintings by Pietro Fabris (fl. 1756–84), Jean Baptiste Lallemand (1716–1803) and Charles Louis Clérisseau (1721–1820); *Ionian Antiquities* (1779–80) after William Pars (1742–82), and scenes of the *Roman Carnival* (1780–81) after David Allan (1744–96). Moreover, from the early 1770s Sandby's own landscape watercolours were reproduced by other printmakers and publishers for the growing market of amateur artists, antiquarians, travellers and collectors of more modest means. The remainder of this essay will discuss what can be deduced from these projects about Sandby's attitude as an artist to the issue of reproductive printmaking and the profession of engraver in England during the second half of the 18th century.

Paul Sandby began his training as a draughtsman for the military survey of Scotland after the 1745 Jacobite uprising. He spent four years in Scotland travelling with the survey parties and working up drawings into the finished map of the country. He returned to England in 1751 and embarked on his artistic career. By the early 1760s he was well-established as a landscape painter. He exhibited at the Society of Artists from the first exhibition in 1760, becoming a director of the organisation probably around 1765 and, as has been noted, he was a founder member of the Royal Academy in 1768. In the same year, he was appointed Drawing Master at the Military Academy at Woolwich. In 1772, Sandby moved out of the Soho area of London to a new house at St George's Row opposite Hyde Park where he lived and worked for the rest of his life.

In his biography of the artist, Thomas Paul Sandby (fl. 1797–1828, d. 1832) describes how while in Edinburgh, becoming "acquainted with Mr. Bell, an engraver in that city, he [Sandby] got some insight into his mode of etching, and himself etched a number of scenes in the neighbourhood, which were done on the spot, upon the copper."[12] This was almost certainly Andrew Bell (1726–1809) who was apprenticed to Richard Cooper senior (1701–1764), so it may be that Sandby also had instruction from Cooper. Bell went on to become the co-founder and first illustrator of the *Encyclopaedia Britannica*. Establishing himself in London from 1751, Sandby, while building up his career as an artist, also continued printmaking, publishing landscapes, a set of *Cries of London*, and two sets of anonymous satirical prints aimed at Hogarth. While Sandby's earliest prints were his own original etchings, his careful interpretation and meticulous copying of surveyors' drawings and protractions into the large-scale fair copy of the map learnt through his work with the Military Survey were valuable skills that he could transfer to his reproductive printmaking.

---

12   Thomas Paul Sandby, "Memoirs of the Late Paul Sandby Esq. R. A.", *Monthly Magazine, or, British Register*, 31, June 1811, 437–38.

PAUL SANDBY AND REPRODUCTIVE PRINTMAKING

Had his career path as a landscape painter foundered, Sandby could probably have made a living in this field.

It is perhaps significant that Sandby chose to herald his arrival on the London art scene with a series of original prints of *Views in Scotland*, published in 1751, which targeted both Scottish and English buyers.[13] The prints were advertized in Scotland on 26 February 1752 in the *Caledonian Mercury*:

> This Day is published, and sold by G. HAMILTON and J. BALFOUR Booksellers, [...] Price 6 Shillings, Six VIEWS in SCOTLAND drawn upon the spot by PAUL SANBY [*sic*] and beautifully engraved.[14]

The following week they were advertised for sale in London, with Sandby's name in prominent capital letters:

> All drawn on the Spot, and engraved by PAUL SANDBY. Sold by W. Sandby, Bookseller, at the Ship, over-against St Dunstan's Church in Fleet-street; and Gavin Hamilton, Bookseller, in Edinburgh.[15]

The prints demonstrated his grasp of different landscape styles, some being straightforwardly topographical, others more picturesque and atmospheric (Figs. 4.1 and 4.2). They also displayed his technical skills as a printmaker and showed he was qualified to join other, more established engravers in the various projects on which he later collaborated.

The first of Sandby's collaborative projects was the series of *Eight Views of Windsor Great Park*.[16] These were engraved after drawings by his brother, Thomas Sandby who was working for the Duke of Cumberland (1721–1765). They showed the grand scheme of improvements undertaken by the Duke in his roles as Ranger of Windsor Great Park and Warden of Windsor Forest. They were advertised as available by subscription in 1754:

> Decemr 1754 PROPOSAL for engraving by Subscription Eight Views in WINDSOR GREAT PARK belonging to HIS ROYAL HIGHNESS the DUKE From Drawings taken on the Spot by T. Sandby Draughtsman to

---

13   Gunn, *Catalogue Raisonné*, cat. nos. 129–135. The set was sold in Edinburgh by Gavin Hamilton and in London by William Sandby. It was republished in 1753 by Robert Sayer who added two further plates.

14   *Caledonian Mercury*, 25 February 1752.

15   *General Advertiser*, Friday 6 March 1752. The bookseller and publisher William Sandby was a cousin of the artist.

16   Gunn, *Catalogue Raisonné*, cat. no. 146a–150.

FIGURE 4.1   Paul Sandby, *East View of Edinburgh Castle*, 1753, etching

FIGURE 4.2   Paul Sandby, *South View of Bothwell Castle*, 1751 and 1753, etching

HIS ROYAL HIGHNESS ...... Each Plate to be 23 Inches by 13, 3–4ths To be Engraved by Mr Vivares, Mr Paul Sandby &c and Printed on the best French Paper. The Price to Subscriber will be Two Guineas, one to be paid at the time of Subscribing, the other on delivery of the Prints which now in hand, and will be finished with all convenient expedition, after which the Price will be advanced.

They were finally announced as ready for subscribers in 1758.[17]

The subscription advertisement highlights certain characteristics which this enterprise shared with Sandby's later projects, both in the medium of line engraving and, subsequently, aquatint. They were all clearly aimed at the top end of the market. They were substantial and handsome prints which could be framed for display, and impressions survive which have been carefully hand-painted in watercolour (Fig. 4.3).[18] The subscription notices often emphasized the quality of the work and materials. All the plates for these series were large, measuring half a meter wide or more.[19] The Windsor subscription specified that they would use "the best French Paper".

> To the connoisseur, the quality of the paper made an immeasurable difference to the appearance of prints. The best copperplate paper was made in the Auvergne and this was used to an increasing extent in England for fine prints ... The largest French paper (68×101 cm) known as *grand aigle* from its double-headed eagle watermark, was employed for the finest large prints.[20]

Sandby used high quality French paper for most of his prints. While English, Italian and Dutch paper was also available, paper made in the Auvergne was considered the best quality for intaglio printing. The rags from which it was made were rotted before pulping into fibres; this "gives better rendering of the lines and tones of the print."[21] The paper was strong and lightly sized; and

---

17   *General Evening Post*, 27–29 April 1758.
18   For example, Paul Sandby after Governor Pownall, *A View of the Falls of the Passaic*, hand-coloured etching Yale Mellon Center for British Art, Inv. no. B1994.4.544.
19   The Windsor prints were 58.0 cm wide; the Tasso illustrations were 54.0 cm wide and the American views measured 53.0 cm.
20   Timothy Clayton, *The English Print 1688–1802* (London and New Haven: 1997), 21.
21   Ad Stijnman, *Engraving and Etching 1400–2000: A History of the Development of Manual Intaglio Printmaking Process* (London and Houten: 2012), 259.

FIGURE 4.3   Paul Sandby after Thomas Pownall, *A View of the Falls on the Passaick, or second River, in the Province of New Jersey*, 1761, hand coloured etching and engraving

its whiteness was due to the purity of the water used in the manufacturing process.[22] Although James Whatman II was developing and refining paper-making in England, Sandby continued to use French paper for his prints into the 1780s.[23] For the *Ionian Antiquities* aquatints (1779–80), which Sandby made for the discerning members of the Society of Dilettanti, he used the largest Auvergne size, *grand aigle*, with the double-headed eagle watermark.[24]

Their high quality was reflected in the price charged for the sets of prints. Whereas Sandby's six *Views in Scotland* sold for six shillings (about £25.00 in modern currency), the Windsor prints cost 2 guineas (about £190.00 in modern currency) for eight prints, a price which went up after the subscription.[25] The six Tasso prints (*c*.1757–60) were one guinea, and the aquatint *Views of Naples* (1777–78) were three guineas, which drew the comment that they were "very

22   Clayton, *The English* Print, 21.
23   See, Theresa Fairbanks Harris, and Scott Wilcox, et al., *Papermaking and the Art of Watercolor in Eighteenth-Century Britain: Paul Sandby and the Whatman Paper Mill*, exhibition catalogue (New Haven and London: 2006).
24   Gunn, *Catalogue Raisonné*, 96.
25   http://www.nationalarchives.gov.uk/currency/ accessed 26.1.17. A guinea was £1 and one shilling.

PAUL SANDBY AND REPRODUCTIVE PRINTMAKING

pretty but dear price—three guineas".[26] The four *Roman Carnival* (1780–81) aquatints were even more expensive; David Allan wrote of his drawings "which Sandby bought from me in London […] he has executed them charmingly in aquatinta prints at 4 guineas the set. They take well and he will make money of them."[27]

Another shared characteristic of Sandby's work in print was that all his projects were undertaken in partnership with family or friends, and sometimes in order to help a colleague. The Windsor prints were a family project, while the Tasso prints were published after the death of the painter John Collins, and apparently sold to help his widow Elizabeth. Many of the prints were collaborative works by Sandby and his friend Edward Rooker, where Sandby did the initial etching and Rooker completed the plate with the more finished engraving process. The Carnival aquatints were made after Sandby bought eleven of David Allan's paintings when the young artist was struggling to get established. The *Ionian Antiquities* project was initiated by Sandby's friend and patron, the Hon. Charles Greville (1749–1809).[28] And the Naples views brought the work of Pietro Fabris to the public's attention, whose patron was Greville's uncle, Sir William Hamilton (1730–1803).[29]

It may be that these close personal ties allowed Sandby to choose which roles he took on, particularly when it came to reproductive projects. For instance, Thomas is credited on the Windsor prints as the original artist, but it is fairly certain that Paul provided the figures as well as engraving the plates. Sketches that have been confidently attributed to Paul exist for many of the figure groups that appear in two of the Windsor prints he engraved, *The Great Bridge over the Virginia River* (Fig. 4.4) and *View from the North side of the Virginia River near the Manour Lodge*.[30]

---

26   Frederick Robinson to his brother Thomas Robinson, 2nd Baron Grantham, Ambassador at Madrid. Bedford and Luton Archives and Record Service. L30/14/333/345 16 February 1779. The equivalent of 3 guineas today would be about £200, so each aquatint print cost the equivalent of about £17.00 (see http://www.nationalarchives.gov.uk /currency/results.asp#mid).

27   David Allan to Sir William Hamilton dated Nov 6th, 1780, written from Hopetoun House. Hopetoun Papers Trust at Hopetoun House (Bundle 3482). I am very grateful to Dr Peter Burman and Mindy Lynch for checking the original letter, which was mis-transcribed in Thomas Crouther Gordon's, *David Allan, the Scottish Hogarth* (Alva: 1951), 32, as "a guinea."

28   Ann V. Gunn 'Views in and Near Naples: Aquatints by Paul Sandby and Archibald Robertson', *The British Art Journal*, 14, no. 1 (2013), 33–43.

29   Ann V. Gunn, 'Paul Sandby, William Pars and the Society of Dilettanti', *Burlington Magazine*, 152, no. 1285 (2010), 219–27.

30   See Gunn, *Catalogue Raisonné*, 25.

FIGURE 4.4 Paul Sandby after Thomas Sandby, *The Great Bridge over the Virginia River*, 1754–58, etching and engraving

The third plate for the Windsor series, *The cascade and grotto*, which Paul Sandby made with Edward Rooker, initiated a long-term collaborative friendship, in which Sandby took on the role of etcher and Rooker of engraver. Reproductive prints were usually made with a combination of etching and engraving, a practice Gilpin approved of:

> As engraving therefore and etching have their respective advantages and deficiencies, artists have endeavoured to unite their powers, and correct the faults of each, by joining the freedom of the one, with the strength of the other. In most of our modern prints, the plate is first etched, and afterwards strengthened, and finished by the engraver. And when this is well done, it has a happy effect.[31]

Etching, where the line is drawn with a needle through a waxy resist, allowed for a free and expressive line, while the engraved line, cut into the metal with a burin, produced a strong and controlled finish.

The remaining five plates in the Windsor series were etched and engraved by some of the best-known printmakers of the day. Francis Vivares (1709–80) engraved two, and Pierre Charles Canot (c.1710–77/78), James Mason (c.1723–1805) and William Austin (1721–1820) engraved one each. However,

---

31   William Gilpin, *Essay on Prints*, 51.

PAUL SANDBY AND REPRODUCTIVE PRINTMAKING

only Paul Sandby and Vivares were mentioned by name in the subscription list. Vivares was an influential figure and something of a pioneer of landscape engraving in England, and his name would be known to the subscribers. He also seems to have been a friend of the Sandby brothers, and he sold Paul's *Cries of London* (1760) in his shop in Newport Street.

The project to publish Tasso's *Jerusalem Delivered* was initiated by the artist, John Collins himself.[32] On Saturday 15 January 1757, an advertisement appeared:

> Mr. Collins proposes to publish by Subscription, six Prints now engraving by Mr. Rooker, Mr. Wood, Mr. Cannot, Mr. Walker, from his original Design of those Scenes painted by him for grand Representations of the Enchanted Forest, or Jerusalem delivered, taken from Tasso. These Representations was [*sic*] exhibited by the King of France's Command in April 1754, in the Theatre of the Royal Palace of the Thuilleries [*sic*]. The Grandeur and Expence [*sic*] of this Spectacle was suspected to exceed any Thing of the Kind ever shewn in Europe; the Action and Machinery were conducted by the Chevalier Servandoni, as were the Paintings by Mr. Collins, Price One Guinea, Subscriptions are taken in by Mr. Collins, at the Golden Head in Long Acre, near St. Martin's Lane; where the Original Designs are to be seen.[33]

Interestingly, Sandby's name does not appear in the advertisement alongside the names of the professional engravers. He must have been brought in by Edward Rooker, and together they worked on three of the six plates, once more combining their skills of etching and engraving. Collins and Rooker both worked in London theatres, so this may be how they met. The images Sandby worked on were *The magicians marching off after the success of their incantations*; *The forest as enchanted*; and *A morning scene of the forest with Rinaldo on the bank of the enchanted river*, all set in deep forest scenery. Sandby's interest in the depiction of trees is a well-known feature of his work and is on full display in Collins' theatrical scenes of Tasso's magical forest (Fig. 4.5).

---

32 See Gunn, *Catalogue Raisonné*, 29.

33 *Public Advertiser*, London, Saturday 15 January 1757. See also *London Evening Post*, 10–12 May 1757, a follow-up advertisement announcing the publication of 'Proposals for Publishing by Subscription' of the set of prints.

FIGURE 4.5   Paul Sandby and Edward Rooker after John Collins, *A Morning Scene of the Forest with Rinaldo on the Bank of the Enchanted River* c.1757–60, etching and engraving

Sandby's contribution to the series of *Six Remarkable Views in the Provinces of New York, New Jersey, and Pennsylvania* was based on drawings by Governor Thomas Pownall (1722–1805) (See fig. 4.3). It was first published in May 1761 by Thomas Jefferys (c.1719–1771), Geographer to the King, who specialized in maps. The other printmakers for the series were Paul Benazech (1730?–98), a former pupil of Vivares, William Elliot (1727–66), and James Peake (1729–c.1782). Some of Pownall's sketches were first painted by Sandby and then etched and engraved from these more finished works. The series was enlarged and republished as *Scenographia Americana* in 1768 and included two more prints etched by Sandby, who exhibited one of the American prints at the 1761 Society of Artists exhibition: "No. 224, A View in North America, a print by Mr Sandby." This was the only time he exhibited a print there. In 1763, Francis Cotes (1726–70) exhibited a portrait of Sandby which was then reproduced in mezzotint by the Irish engraver Edward Fisher (1722–1781/2) in the same year. The print carries the inscription "*Ruralium Prospectuum Pictor*" (painter of rural prospects). It seems that, by this point, Sandby was distancing himself from the engravers and asserting his artistic status as a landscape painter, first and foremost. He did not return to reproductive printmaking until he made his pioneering aquatints in the 1770s.

Historically, almost all discoveries and advances in print technology have been driven by the desire to find new ways to reproduce and replicate images. Mezzotint was found to be a suitable way to reproduce oil paintings, but was not appropriate for the tonal effects of wash and watercolour. Many printmakers throughout Europe experimented with techniques for this purpose, and several came up with versions of aquatint. The story of Sandby's acquisition of the 'secret' of aquatint from P. P. Burdett (*c*.1735–1793) has been told elsewhere.[34] However, it is important to note that when Burdett was trying to interest possible patrons in his technique, he stressed its qualities for reproducing "every touch & manner" of an artist's drawing. Sandby, on the other hand, enjoyed the medium for its own sake. In September 1775, he wrote to his friend John Clerk of Eldin (1728–1812):

> I own no hobby horse in the world woud [*sic*] suit me eaqual [*sic*] to this, indeed I have rid so closely these 4 month past I have scarcely done anything else, the work is so delightful and easy to me now in the execution I do it with the same ease but with more pleasure than on paper.
> Your much obliged and most humble servt P. Sandby.[35]

The aquatint method he developed was the spirit ground, where rosin is dissolved in alcohol and poured over the plate, rather than the more durable but less regular dust ground. Sandby's ground was fragile and gave fewer impressions before needing new grounds or other reinforcement.[36] He also

---

34   Ann V. Gunn, 'Sandby, Greville and Burdett, and the "Secret" of Aquatint', *Print Quarterly*, 29, no. 2 (2012), 178–80.

35   Letter from Sandby to Clerk of Eldin, London. Reference sourcce available on National Art Library website, see https://nal-vam.on.worldcat.org/search/detail/1008300031?query String=MSL%2F1932%2F1563&clusterResults=false&groupVariantRecords=false, 8 September 1775. London, Victoria and Albert Museum, National Art Library, MSL/1932/1563.

36   There is no record of how many impressions Sandby took from his aquatint plates, but the number of surviving prints from his first Welsh series in different states with alterations

made his images with the sugar-lift technique, which reproduces the actual brush strokes of the artist, rather than the stopping out method which gave broader washes of tone. Sandby approached aquatint as a painter-etcher, producing his own originals, rather than as an engraver copying the work of others.

Sandby also realized aquatint's potential to reproduce watercolour washes and he undertook three projects which demonstrated its capabilities and its commercial applications. These were the *Views in and around Naples* after Pietro Fabris, Jean Baptiste Lallemand, and Charles Louis Clérisseau; *Ionian Antiquities* after watercolours by William Pars; and scenes of the *Roman Carnival* after David Allan. Unlike the earlier engraved series, there are no newspaper advertisements for these prints. Sandby published them himself, perhaps to retain quality control over their production. His own early series, the *Four Views of Warwick Castle* and the first set of Welsh views, were originally published by John Boydell (1720–1804), but Sandby took the publishing of the Welsh set back into his own hands and subsequently published all his prints himself. For the *Views in and around Naples*, he did collaborate both in production and publication. His partner was Archibald Robertson (act. 1765, d. 1804), a print-seller, stationer and drawing master with a shop in Savile Row Passage. They published fifteen prints together in 1777, but thereafter the collaboration ceased and they published further prints separately. This is almost certainly a quality control issue as Robertson was no artist, nor even a very competent copyist (Figs. 4.6 and 4.7).[37]

The project to make aquatint copies after the work of William Pars originated from the intervention of Charles Greville.[38] As the patron who paid Burdett for his aquatint method, Greville took a personal interest in the use and development of the medium. Pars was the official draughtsman on the expedition to Greece and the Ionian regions of Asia Minor, funded by the Society of Dilettanti, which took place from 1764 to 1766. Some images from the tour were reproduced as engravings and published as *Ionian Antiquities* in 1769, but the Society had not yet published the complete collection of material. In May 1776, soon after his election to the Society, and only months after

---

in the sky indicates that the more delicate tones broke down quite quickly. See Gunn, *Catalogue Raisonné*, cat. nos. 196–208.

37   See Ann. V. Gunn, 'Views in and Near Naples', 33–43.

38   See Ann V. Gunn, 'Paul Sandby, William Pars and the Society of Dilettanti', 219–27.

FIGURE 4.6 Paul Sandby after Pietro Fabris, *View of Arco Felice*, 1777, aquatint

FIGURE 4.7 Archibald Robertson after Pietro Fabris, *A View of the Ruins of the Temple of Bacchus*, 1777, aquatint

Sandby's first aquatints had appeared, Greville proposed that that Pars' views, which "have for some years been confined to a Portfolio & have been of little use to the curious or to the world [should be] delivered to an able artist for that purpose on his engaging to make the Prints of the same".[39] Twelve views were published in 1779 and 1780. Aquatint proved to be the perfect medium to reproduce Pars' delicate washes, though the views were later also engraved, allowing for a much larger print run.

Sandby's final project as a reproductive printmaker was the series of scenes from the *Roman Carnival* after drawings by the Scottish artist David Allan (Fig. 4.8). Allan, newly arrived in London after ten years in Italy, was having a hard time getting established. In 1778, he showed five of his Carnival drawings at the Royal Academy. Edward Edwards (1738–1806) later recalled that

> There are also four prints, which were executed in aqua tinta by Mr. Paul Sandby, from drawings made by Mr. Allen while at Rome, which represent the Sports and Employments of the People during the Carnival, in the Corso. Several of the figures introduced in them, are portraits of persons well known to the English who visited Rome between the years 1770 and 1780.[40]

Sandby surely saw these prints as a commercial opportunity to appeal to any of the young gentlemen who had made the Grand Tour.

Sandby's aquatint reproductions of the works of Fabris and others demonstrate again his fidelity and accuracy in copying their wash drawings and watercolour paintings. Although none of the works by Fabris have yet come to light, the watercolours by Pars are in the British Museum and some of Allan's original Roman drawings are in the Royal Collection.[41] Sandby managed to copy accurately but also transmit the other artists' style, both in the case of Pars's serene classical landscapes and of Allan's lively, slightly caricatured figures. Hopefully Strutt would have approved of these prints, having described what is expected of a reproductive engraver:

---

39 London, Library of the Society of Antiquaries, Society of Dilettanti archives, Letter Book, May 1776, 221.

40 Edward Edwards, *Anecdotes of Painters who have resided in or been born in England with critical remarks on their production* (London: 1808), 229.

41 Royal Collection Trust, RCIN 913351-RCIN 913360.

FIGURE 4.8   Paul Sandby after David Allan, *The Opening of the Carnival at Rome*, 1780–81, aquatint

However he may suppose himself arrived at a superior degree of excellence, it will be greatly to his discredit, as an engraver, if he forgets to pay that attention to the picture he copies, which is due to its author; and instead of giving us the style of the painter, exhibits one of his own.[42]

Sandby's investment in the new technique of aquatint may have brought him back into the circle of engravers, who wanted extended copyright protection for their work.[43] Copyright for prints was first introduced in England in 1735. It was instigated by William Hogarth (1697–1764), George Lambert (1700–1765), Isaac Ware (1704–1766), architect and translator of Palladio's work into English, the engravers John Pine (1690–1756), George Vertue (1684–1756), Joseph Goupy (1689–1769), and Gerard Vandergucht (1696/97–1776); and the poet and lawyer William Huggins (1696–1761) who gave legal advice.[44] However, it only covered

---

42   Strutt, *Biographical Dictionary*, 4.
43   David Hunter, "Copyright Protection for Engravings and Maps in Eighteenth-Century Britain", *The Transactions of the Bibliographical Society Library* (London: 1987), s6-IX (2), 128–47.
44   *The Case of Designers, Engravers, Etchers, &c, Stated in a Letter to a Member of Parliament*, cited in Hunter "Copyright Protection", 130.

engravings that were original works of art, rather than reproductions. In 1767, this protection was extended in a new Act to cover all etchers and engravers of all subjects—portraits, conversation pieces, landscape, architecture, maps, charts or plans—and to those who caused to be engraved or etched "any print taken from any picture, drawing, model, or sculpture either ancient or modern".[45] The period of protection was also lengthened to 28 years. Copyright was vested in the owner of the plate, so it was in Sandby's interest to keep the plates in his possession when he began to publish his aquatints. In 1777, Paul Sandby was one of eleven printmakers who petitioned Parliament for a further amendment to prevent forgeries:

> It has become a Practice for inferior Artists to engrave ordinary Prints, and to affix thereto the Names of Artists known and esteemed by the Public, in order to give to the same a Credit with the Public, by which fraudulent Practice the Reputation of the Painter, and the Fortune and Reputation of the Engraver, suffer essentially, as there is not Penalty inflicted by the former Acts on Persons guilty of such Forgeries.[46]

Sandby's friend and patron, Greville, who was the Member of Parliament for Warwick, introduced the Bill to the House of Lords. The petitioners were William Woollett, Francis Bartolozzi (1727–1815), Thomas Watson (1750–1781), John Boydell, Peter Mazell (fl. 1761–1797), Thomas Major (1720–1799), William Wynne Ryland (1738–1783), Pierre Charles Canot, Francis Vivares, Paul Sandby, and William Byrne (1743–1805). In the Petition they identified themselves as "Artists and Designers, and Engravers, of original Prints, on behalf of themselves and others", and together comprised the leading printmakers of the day.[47] The *Prints Copyright Act, 1777* provided protection against anyone engraving, or in any other way copying, commissioning, printing, publishing or selling a copy of a print "without the express Consent of the Proprietor".[48] In spite of their treatment by the Royal Academy, reproductive printmakers were clearly esteemed enough by collectors for it to be worthwhile for forgers to attach their names to spurious works. Through the petition, Sandby was no

---

45 Hunter, "Copyright Protection", 143, n. 59 citing Act of 7 Geo. III. *c*.38, Statutes at Large, xxvii, 412–13.

46 Hunter, "Copyright Protection", 144.

47 17 Geo. III, 17 Feb. 1777, *Journals of the House of Commons* (London: 1803) vol. 36, 191.

48 17 Geo. III *c*.57, Hunter, "Copyright Protection", 145, n. 66 citing Statutes at Large, xxxi, 471.

PAUL SANDBY AND REPRODUCTIVE PRINTMAKING

doubt aligning himself professionally with printmakers in order to protect his aquatint publications.

Any concerns Sandby may have had about the status of printmakers as copyists, or about forgeries of his work, did not extend to legitimate copies after his paintings. From the early 1770s, Sandby became for a while "the most widely known and imitated landscape artist in England."[49] Although we have no documentary evidence about Sandby's part in various schemes, we must assume his acquiescence from the sheer volume of paintings that were reproduced in print and the use of his name in the marketing of them. In 1774, the publisher George Kearsley launched the *Copperplate Magazine, or Monthly Treasure for the Admirers of the Imitative Arts*, which included three prints per issue (a portrait, an historical subject, and a landscape view). The advantage of prints as reproductions was presented as a key selling point:

> The greatest advantage that sculpture has ever received for rendering its works universal, and transmitting them to posterity, is that of engraving upon copper, by which means a number of prints are taken off, that multiply a design almost to Infinity, and the Author's ingenuity is conveyed to every part of the globe, which before could be known only from a view of his single original production.[50]

Sandby's name was also used as a marketing hook. After the third issue, the landscape views in the magazine were solely provided by Paul Sandby and prints were made by Rooker and William Watts. They were marketed through newspaper advertisements such as this:

> The connoisseurs in the polite arts have now an opportunity of gratifying their taste upon very moderate terms; In the Copper-plate Magazine published this day, here is a most elegant engraving of Mr. Rooker's, from an original drawing of Mr. Paul Sandby's. [...] The work having met with uncommon encouragement, the Proprietors intend to give an engraving from a drawing of Mr. Sanby's [*sic*] in every succeeding number, that for the future their perspective views and landscapes may be equal in

---

49   Bruce Robertson, *Paul Sandby and the Early Development of English Watercolor*, PhD dissertation, Yale, 1987, 320.

50   *Morning Chronicle and London Advertiser*, Wednesday 27 July 1774.

elegance to their heads and historical subject, which have been so universally approved.[51]

This publication was followed by the *Virtuosi's Museum*, issued in monthly numbers from February 1778 to January 1781. It was aimed at "the admirer of the ingenious art of sculpture" who wished to make "a beautiful addition ... to the furniture of their apartment, for less than the value of a masquerade ticket!"[52]

Sandby worked on his own aquatint publications at the same time as he was producing copies after other artists and providing the images for Kearsley's publications. Many of the views provided for Kearsley were the country seats of the nobility, subjects he did not use for his aquatints (Fig. 4.9). For these, he preserved more elevated subjects—mountainous landscapes and ancient Norman castles. His preoccupations as a landscape artist are mirrored in his aquatints, largely because many of his prints are based on sketches and paintings he made earlier in his career. For example, Sandby's first aquatints in 1775 and 1776 of views in Wales are based on drawings and paintings he made during two tours of the country, in 1771 and 1773, so they could in some ways be seen as reproductions. But the landscape aquatints were widely admired for their pictorial qualities. In his 1778 *Tour of Wales*, Thomas Pennant (1726–1798) recommended them to any readers "that wish to anticipate the views in the intended progress [who] may satisfy themselves by the purchase of the late publications of the admirable Mr. PAUL SANDBY, in whose labours fidelity and elegance are united."[53] Richard Gough (1735–1809) also recognized the close relationship between Sandby's drawings and aquatints when he wrote that:

> Paul Sandby proposes to publish by subscription, at two guineas, six prints, from the original drawings in water-colours, to be executed in imitation of the drawings, in their various colours, in a new method, called Aqua Tinta.[54]

However, Sandby's obvious delight in the medium for its own sake (conveyed in his letter to John Clerk quoted above), shows he was using aquatint as an alternative means of artistic expression, rather than a manner of reproducing drawings alone. Not only did the sugar-lift process replicate his brushstrokes;

---

51   *London Chronicle or Universal Evening Post*, 4–6 October 1774.

52   For a more in-depth discussion of the print market, collecting and Kearsley's schemes in relation to Sandby, see Gunn, *Catalogue Raisonné*, 57–70.

53   Thomas Pennant, *Tours in Wales*, 3 vols. (London: 1778), v.

54   Richard Gough, in the entries on Kent in *Anecdotes of British Topography* (London: 1780), 2nd edition published as *British Topography*, Vol. 1, 471.

PAUL SANDBY AND REPRODUCTIVE PRINTMAKING

FIGURE 4.9 William Watts after Paul Sandby, *Duchess of Athol's Seat near Charlton in Kent*, 1777, engraving

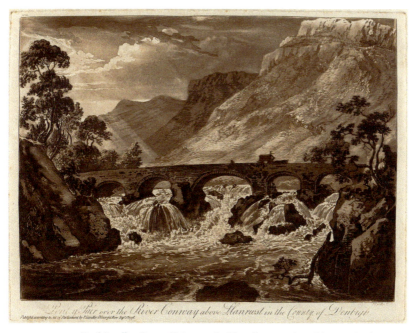

FIGURE 4.10 Paul Sandby, *Pont-y-Pair over the River Conway above Llanrwst in the County of Denbigh*, 1776, aquatint

the whole process also echoed his technique of painting in watercolour and gouache. A description he later wrote explaining the aquatint process sounds very similar to the way a watercolour painting was made:

> I suppose the design to be already etched, [...] I have sometimes nearly compleated [*sic*] a plate with one ground, which is the best way when it can be done. In that case I first stop out the parts I wish to remain white and bite in the blue of the sky and a faint general tint over the rest. I then lay in all the broad masses, and form the cloud with mixture of treacle, etc., and varnish the whole, then bite it long enough for the clouds and tints of that sort, then proceed with shadowing and making smaller touches in trees, etc., varnish it again, thus repeating it like making a drawing in Indian ink, till the whole is done.[55]

A comparison with the description of Sandby's painting method, written by his friend Colonel Gravatt (1771–1851), reveals the similarity of technique. He explains how Sandby:

> painted the whole of the paper over with azure ... he then sketched the design ... he proceeded to shadow the picture exactly as is done in forming transparent drawings ... the middle tint, with which he covered the whole place of the foliage, without regarding the lights, leaving them for the opaque colours.[56]

While the aquatint technique went on to become the medium of choice for the reproduction of watercolours, Sandby's sugar-lift method, which so faithfully reproduced his brush marks, was not a technique suited to the reproductive print trade. Sandby used it for his own artistic purposes, but also recognized its potential as a new means of reproducing watercolour paintings. He may have withdrawn himself from the practice of reproductive engraving as his artistic career took off, but he seems to have been keenly aware of its importance in promoting an artist's reputation, not least his own.

---

55 "A Mode of Imitating Drawings on Copper Plates discovered by P. Sandby R. A., in the year 1775, to which he gave the Name of Aquatinta", British Library, Add. Mss 36994 ff 117–119. See Gunn, *Catalogue Raisonné*, 81.

56 Excerpt from the diary of Col. William Gravatt, October 25 1802. Cited in William A. Sandby, *Thomas and Paul Sandby, Royal Academicians* (London: 1892), 117–119.

Select Bibliography

Manuscript Collections

Bedford and Luton Archives and Record Service. L30/14/333/345 16 February 1779: Frederick Robinson to his brother Thomas Robinson, 2nd Baron Grantham, Ambassador at Madrid.

British Library, Add. Mss 36994 ff 117–119: "A Mode of Imitating Drawings on Copper Plates discovered by P. Sandby R. A., in the year 1775, to which he gave the Name of Aquatinta".

London, Library of the Society of Antiquaries, Society of Dilettanti archives, Letter Book, p. 221, May 1776.

National Art Library, MSL/1932/1563: Letter from Sandby to Clerk of Eldin, London, 8 September 1775. London, Victoria and Albert Museum.

Primary Sources

Edwards, Edward, *Anecdotes of Painters who have resided in or been born in England with critical remarks on their production London* (London: 1808).

Gilpin, William, *An Essay on Prints, containing Remarks upon the Principles of picturesque Beauty, the different kinds of prints, and the characters of the most noted Masters* (London: 1768).

Jones, Thomas, "The Memoirs of Thomas Jones" ed. Adolph Paul Oppé, *Walpole Society*, vol. 32 (1946).

Sandby, Thomas Paul, "Memoirs of the Late Paul Sandby Esq. R. A.", *Monthly Magazine, or, British Register*, vol. 31 (June 1811), 437–41.

Caledonian Mercury, 25 February 1752.

General Advertiser, Friday 6 March 1752.

General Evening Post, 27–29 April 1758.

London Evening Post, 10–12 May 1757.

London Chronicle or Universal Evening Post, 4–6 October 1774.

Morning Chronicle and London Advertiser, Wednesday 27 July 1774.

Public Advertiser, London, Saturday 15 January 1757.

The Case of Designers, Engravers, Etchers, &c, Stated in a Letter to a Member of Parliament, cited in David Hunter, "Copyright Protection for Engravings and Maps in Eighteenth-Century Britain", *The Transactions of the Bibliographical Society Library*, vol. s6-IX, no. 2 (1987), 130.

Secondary Sources

Alexander, David, and Richard T. Godfrey, editors. *Painters and Engraving: the Reproductive Print from Hogarth to Wilkie*, exhibition catalogue (New Haven: 1980).

Clayton, Timothy, *The English Print 1688–1802* (London and New Haven: 1997).

Godfrey, Richard, *Printmaking in Britain* (Oxford: 1978).

Gordon, Thomas Crouther, *David Allan, the Scottish Hogarth* (Alva: 1951).

Gunn, Ann V., *The Prints of Paul Sandby, (1731–1809), a Catalogue Raisonné* (Turnhout: 2015).

Gunn, Ann V., "Views in and Near Naples: Aquatints by Paul Sandby and Archibald Robertson", *The British Art Journal*, 14, no. 1 (2013), 33–43.

Gunn, Ann V., "Paul Sandby, William Pars and the Society of Dilettanti", *Burlington Magazine*, 152, no. 1285 (2010), 219–227.

Gunn, Ann V., "Sandby, Greville and Burdett, and the 'Secret' of Aquatint", *Print Quarterly*, 29, no. 2 (2012), 178–80.

Hopkinson, Martin, 'The Burdett–Banks Correspondence', *Print Quarterly*, 24, no. 3 (2007), 269–270.

Hunter, David, 'Copyright Protection for Engravings and Maps in Eighteenth-Century Britain', *The Transactions of the Bibliographical Society Library*, s6-IX, no. 2 (1987), 128–47.

Robertson, Bruce, *Paul Sandby and the Early Development of English Watercolor*, PhD dissertation (Yale: 1987).

Sandby, William A., *Thomas and Paul Sandby, Royal Academicians* (London: 1892).

Strange, Robert, *An inquiry into the rise and establishment of the Royal Academy of Arts. To which is prefixed, A Letter to the Earl of Bute* (London: 1775).

Strutt, Joseph, *A Biographical Dictionary containing an historical account of all the engravers, from the earliest period of the art of engraving to the present time* (London: 1785).

Online Sources

http://www.nationalarchives.gov.uk/currency/.

CHAPTER 5

Not for the Feeble of Mind! Color-printed Illustrations in European Medical Literature, 1500–1850

Ad Stijnman

This essay discusses early modern European medical illustrations printed in color that are held in the Herzog August Library in Wolfenbüttel (HAB),[1] in comparison with single-sheet artistic prints housed in the collection of the Herzog Anton Ulrich-Museum printroom (HAUM) in nearby Braunschweig (Germany).[2] Placing this study of medical illustrations in a larger context shows that researching color prints means making a selection on the basis of materiality, in this case color inks and particular printing processes, before studying further aspects of each object such as iconographical, social, economical, medical, religious, or military themes. It shows how in a process-led approach any studies should start from the art work itself as a material object relating it to ideas of its maker(s) during production, considering that eventually printing in colors was decided by printers and or publishers.[3] Color-printed medical figures provide a good example, because engravers were commissioned by publishers to produce illustrations for the books and journals they issued, while in some cases illustrations were made by the authors themselves. Such an interdisciplinary, process-led approach shows the coherence of areas that seem disparate from an iconographical, social or other perspective.

The Herzog August Bibliothek and the Herzog Anton Ulrich-Museum share a common history, both are formed from collections gathered in the ducal library in Wolfenbüttel. Provenances of color-printed materials in both

---

1 With many thanks to Elizabeth Savage for discussions, ideas and further support in the compilation of this essay.

2 Visual materials in the archives of the library are observed, but not discussed here. More in general, color-printed or stamped fabric, parchment or leather objects are not included here either. I gratefully acknowledge the financial support of the Land Niedersachsen for my fellowships in 2015, 2016 and 2017 in the framework of the *Kupferstichkabinett-Online* project of the HAB and the HAUM from which this essay is developed. I much appreciate the permissions given me to liberally peruse the collections of both Library and Museum.

3 See further Ad Stijnman, "Thoughts on art history from the perspective of the maker", *Art in Print* 6 (2016), 3 (Sept./Oct.), 16–17.

© KONINKLIJKE BRILL BV, LEIDEN, 2024 | DOI:10.1163/9789004703834_007

collections go back to the 15th century and together they offer an overview of international developments in fine art prints and book illustrations.

The institutions, physically only twelve kilometers in distance, collaborated in the compilation of an online print database, *Virtuelles Kuperstichkabinett* (VKK), from 2007.[4] The database is one of a kind because it combines descriptions of single sheet prints, book illustrations, printed ephemera (such as *ex libris*, visiting cards, almanacs, etc.) and artistic drawings. As a result, this reunites materials that have traditionally been divided or placed into different kinds of collections, and thus into different fields of research.

The conceptual divide between libraries and print rooms, and thereby the disciplinary division between art and book history and art history, is an artificial one that materialized in Europe in the course of the 18th century with the founding of the first print rooms. Printed medical imagery can be found in libraries, print rooms and map rooms. It is commonly studied from a medical perspective, not so much from a bibliographic, art historic or cartographic aspect. Presumably bibliographers, art historians and cartographers were not concerned with, or considered themselves not educated enough in the field of medicine.

Before the establishment of the Braunschweig print room in 1765, most of the ducal collections were kept under one roof, if not on one shelf.[5] Then, from 1766 to 1928 numbers of prints and drawings were moved from the library to the print room repeatedly, separating artistic prints from—in our case—imagery in medical publications.[6] Otherwise both institutions continued expanding their collections. The HAUM, for example, acquired medical color prints and the HAB artists books. The VKK database allows these materials to be joined together by theme of category, as well as facilitating detailed cross-category searches by printmaking process. For example, once entered into the system, color prints can be easily selected by a general search for *Farbdruck* (color printing), with options for further selection criteria.

---

4   http://www.virtuelles-kupferstichkabinett.de (accessed 1 July 2024); https://de.wikipedia.org /wiki/Virtuelles_Kupferstichkabinett (accessed 1 July 2024).

5   Contemporaneous catalogues and interior depictions of the ducal library make clear that prints were usually bound as books and stacked on book shelves similarly, which is the situation in the HAB still. Materials were lent by members of the ducal family, staff to the court, but also local citizens, as registered in the 'lending books' (*Ausleihbücher*); Mechtild Raabe, *Leser und Lektüre im 17. Jahrhundert: die Ausleihbücher der Herzog August Bibliothek Wolfenbüttel 1664–1713*, 3 vols (Munich: 1998).

6   For a history of the print collections in HAB and HAUM see: Hole Rößler, "Von gesammelter Grafik zur Graphischen Sammlung", in Peter Burschel et al. (eds.), *Die Herzog August Bibliothek: eine Sammlungsgeschichte* (Wolfenbüttel: in progress for 2025).

1 Color in Printing and Printmaking

Understanding color printmaking has two issues; firstly, the lack of research into 'color' in prints in general and, secondly, the fact that previous scholarship has typically been divided between art history and book history. Concerning color, art history has prized single-sheet 16th-century *chiaroscuro* woodcuts and later 18th-century intaglio color prints.[7] Book history has focused on the first steps of printing text in black, red and blue in the second half of the 15th century, as well as color-printed illustrations in books produced and published by Erhard Ratdoldt (1442–1528). Research into color printing in cartography has been limited to occasional references to some early modern color-printed maps, with the idea that it only took off with the introduction of color lithography from 1820.[8] However, these disciplines remain largely concerned with printing in black inks on white supports.[9] The exhibition and accompanying scholarly volume *Anatomie de la couleur* (Paris, Bibliothèque Nationale de France: 1996) was the first time that color-printed anatomical figures were considered across the disciplines of art and book history, centered around the well-known anatomical publications of the eighteenth-century Gautier-Dagoty family.[10]

Scholarship on the history of medicine often discusses anatomical images, far less pathological depictions or other health related areas. Only few studies exist on *color*-printed medical figures, despite the prevalent use of color printing in this field.[11] It may be for reason that colour-printed materials were

---

7   For discussions on this theme see Ad Stijnman and Elizabeth Savage, *Printing Colour 1400–1700: History, Techniques, Functions and Receptions* (Leiden: 2015).

8   Karen Severud Cook, "From False Starts to Firm Beginnings: Early Colour Printing of Geological Maps", *Imago Mundi* (1995), 155–72. A first overview of over 50 early modern colour printed maps and plans was presented by the present author at the International Conference for the History of Cartography (ICHC 2019) as *Maps and Plans Printed in Colour before 1820* (Amsterdam: 15 July 2019, unpublished).

9   Recipes for black relief and intaglio ink are different. The oily binding medium (the oil varnish) for relief printing ink always contains resin and a constituent that expedites the drying of the ink (the dryer), while the black colourant used is always pure carbon (lampblack). Oil varnish for black intaglio ink does not contain a resin or a dryer, while for the black colourant charred animal or vegetable blacks were used.

10 Florian Rodari, *Anatomie de la couleur: l'invention de l'estampe en couleurs*, exhibition catatalogue (Paris, Lausanne: 1996).

11 Ludwig Choulant, *Geschichte und Bibliographie der anatomischen Abbildung nach ihrer Beziehung auf anatomische Wissenschaft und bildende Kunst* (1852; repr. Niederwalluf bei Wiesbaden: 1971), 105–11; Robert Herrkinger and Marielene Putscher, *Geschichte der medizinischen Abbildung*, 2 vols (Munich: 1967–72); Monique Kornell, *Flesh and Bones: The Art of Anatomy*, with contributions by Thisbe Gensler, Naoko Takahatake and Erin Travers, exhibition catalogue (Los Angeles: 2022); Domencio Bertoloni Meli, *Visualizing Disease:*

not catalogued and therefore could not be found by researchers. They referred therefore to works by known artists who had also produced medical colour prints, such as the Gautiers. Otherwise they were dependent on coincidental finds and references.

Working from this basis, the aim of my fellowships in the museum in Braunschweig and the library in Wolfenbüttel was to collect materials printed in color for an exhibition on the history of European color prints from the 15th to the mid-19th century, to be held in both institutions in 2019–20.[12] The overall idea was to research the relationship between color printing processes and the style and function of both book illustrations and single sheet prints, with further comparison to other color-printed materials. Evolving from this, the specific research discussed in the present essay concerns analyzing medical book illustrations in comparison to illustrations in other scholarly areas, including fine art single-leaf colour prints, produced between around 1500 and 1850.

2   Color Prints

The first colour printed medical illustration appeared in the 2nd (Italian) edition of the *Fasciculo di medicina* by Johannes de Ketham (Venice: 1493, opposite fol. 65r). The design of the figure is printed from a woodcut inked in black, the colors are presumably applied with oil-based printing inks through stencils. More medical colour prints would appear in the centuries to follow, with their numbers increasing from the middle of the 18th century. Various printmaking and colour printing techniques were used, often reflecting technical developments in the graphic media or the intended function of these medical diagrams.

The basic early modern processes were relief printmaking (woodcut, metalcut, wood engraving), intaglio printmaking (engraving, etching, mezzotint, aquatint) and from *c*.1800 lithography (crayon, pen).[13] Color printing is independent from printmaking techniques and can be used with any technique.[14] Five main processes can be discerned, any of which may be combined with any

---

     The Art and History of Pathological Illustrations (Chicago, London: 2017); K. B. Roberts and J. D. W. Tomlinson, *The Fabric of the Body: European Traditions of Anatomical Illustration* (Oxford: 1992), 521–33.

12   The project was eventually cancelled.

13   Ad Stijnman and Elizabeth Savage, "Materials and Techniques for Early Colour Printing," in Stijnman and Savage (ed.), *Printing Colour 1400–1700*, 11–22, at 11–12.

14   Stijnman and Savage, "Materials and Techniques," 13–15.

other, both in relief and intaglio or combined (etching printed over woodcut, etc.), and any color impression may be further hand-colored to enhance or add tinges. As follows:

1. One matrix inked monochromatic with one color (not black), including white ink on a dark support, and gold or silver ink.[15]
2. One matrix inked with two or more colors (so called *à la poupée* inking, including black). The first unquestionable example is an initial 'D' inked in relief in blue and red, dating from 1457.[16] However, it only became common with the activity of Johannes Teyler's (1648–1709?) workshop for intaglio printmaking in Holland in the late 17th century that produced thousands of *à la poupée* prints in up to ten different colors per impression.[17] À *la poupée* inking was regularly used for medical imagery in the 18th century.
3. Frisket printing: One matrix inked in one colour (usually black), covered with a mask (frisket) for the parts that should stay blank, and printed on a support; next the matrix was cleaned, inked in a second color (usually red), covered with a mask for the parts that are already printed and printed on the same support again. Frisket printing was carried out on a common press, of which the frisket was a mechanical part of, and used for text and decoration in black and red.[18]

---

15   For printing with one color see: Antony Griffiths, "White Ink", *Print Quarterly*, 8 (1991), 3 (Sep.), 286–90; Jun Nakamura, "On Hercules Segers's 'Printed Paintings'," in *Printing Colour 1400–1700*, ed. Stijnman and Savage, 189–195, at 190–92; Ad Stijnman, "White Ink", *Print Quarterly*, 9 (1992), 2 (June), 181–83; Ad Stijnman, "Another Clair-obscur Etching", *Print Quarterly* 10 (1993), 1, 58–59; Ad Stijnman, *Engraving and Etching 1400–2000: A History of the Development of Manual Intaglio Printmaking Processes* (London and Houten: 2012), 277–80; Ad Stijnman, "Hercules Segers's Printmaking Techniques," in *Hercules Segers: Painter, Etcher*, ed. Huigen Leeflang and Pieter Roelofs (Amsterdam: 2017), 62–77, at 73. For the use of gold and silver inks see: Elizabeth Savage, "Jost de Negker's Woodcut Charles V (1519): An Undescribed Example of Gold Printing," *Art in Print*, 5, no. 2 (2015, July/Aug.), 9–15; Elizabeth Savage curated an exhibition of 16th-century prints with gold ink in the British Museum, 25 November 2015–27 January 2016.
16   *Johannes Teyler and Dutch Colour Printing c.1700*, comp. Ad Stijnman, ed. Simon Turner (The new Hollstein Dutch & Flemish etchings, engravings and woodcuts: 1450–1700), 4 pts (Ouderkerk aan den IJssel: 2017), pt. I, xxv. The red inked rubrication in some copies of the first version of part I of Johann Gutenberg's (1395/1400–1468) *Latin Bible* may have been printed together with the black text, but this is uncertain.
17   *Johannes Teyler and Dutch Colour Printing c.1700*, comp. Stijnman, ed. Turner.
18   For Elizabeth Savage's census of frisket sheets used in bicolour printing see: http://www.bibsocamer.org/wp-content/uploads/Upper-Red-Frisket-Sheets.pdf (accessed 1 March 2023).

4. Two or more matrices printed next to each other; each inked in its own color, including black but not all black, either printed one after the other or joined together as a kind of puzzle; known as 'compound plate printing' for relief techniques and 'jigsaw plate printing' for intaglio techniques; first examples are the bicolored initials in books printed and published by Johann Fust (*c*.1400–1466) and Peter Schöffer (*c*.1425–1503) from 1457.[19]

5. Two or more matrices printed 'in register' over each other (each inked in its own color, including black but not all black); over-printing a woodcut key block in black with a woodcut for the red elements became standard for title pages from around 1520 until *c*.1800.[20] Color relief printing with multiple overprinting blocks began in 1485 and developed into 'chiaroscuro' printing from 1510. It continued until the second quarter of the 17th century, when it was used only once in medical literature, as discussed below.

The early 18th century saw a major change in color printing and a stronger connection with medical figures following Jacob Christoff Le Blon's (1667–1741) invention of the three-color printing system in Amsterdam around 1708–10, a process which he intended for the reproduction of old master paintings as can be seen in his later output.[21] The trichromatic system involved overprinting three mezzotint plates in blue, yellow and red in this order in register following process 5 discussed above. In 1718, Le Blon moved to London where he further developed the technique by adding a fourth mezzotint plate inked in black overprinted by the three others; the black impression enhanced shades, making the production process more efficient. Occasionally he printed an extra engraved plate with details such as hairs inked in white on top of all earlier impressions. Four-color printing is the principle of the current CMYK color system used in offset printing, photocopiers and digital printers.[22]

---

19 Mayumi Ikeda, "The Fust and Schöffer Office and the Printing of the Two-Colour Initials in the 1457 Mainz Psalter," *Printing colour 1400–1700*, ed. Ad Stijnman and Elizabeth Savage, 65–75.

20 Elizabeth Savage, "A Printer's Art: The Development and Influence of Colour Printmaking in the German Lands, c.1476–c.1600", in *Printing Colour 1400–1700: History, Techniques, Functions and Receptions*, ed. Ad Stijnman and Elizabeth Savage (Leiden: 2015) (Library of the Written World; 41/The Handpress World; 32), 93–102, at 95.

21 *Jacob Christoff le Blon and the Start of Trichromatic Printing*, comp. Ad Stijnman, ed. Simon Turner (Ouderkerk aan den IJssel: 2020) (The New Hollstein Dutch & Flemish Etchings, Engravings and Woodcuts 1450–1700).

22 CMYK stands for Cyan Magenta Yellow + Key (for black).

NOT FOR THE FEEBLE OF MIND!

In England, Le Blon came upon a new idea when he used the three-color printing method to illustrate a dissection of human male genitalia for the third edition of William Cockburn's *The Symptoms, Nature, Cause and Cure of a Gonorrhea* (London: 1719). In this print the colors were super-imposed with a fourth plate with engraved lettering inked in black.[23] In March 1721 Le Blon offered a subscription to an anatomical work, supported by Royal physician Nathanael St. André (1680–1776), with twelve of his colour prints of the same quality as his anatomical print of 1719.[24] Jan L'Admiral (1698–1773), Le Blon's apprentice and employee in London, worked in the same trichromatic manner for seven anatomical images in the period 1737–41 (Fig. 5.1).[25] In 1736, Le Blon moved to Paris, acquired a French royal privilege for his process and from 1738 ran a printshop, in which year Jacques-Fabien Gautier-Dagoty (1716–85) worked six weeks for him from 24 April to 8 June.[26] In his subsequent independent work Gautier-Dagoty used Le Blon's new technique, usually with an additional black plate first for darkening shades, but also over-printing three-colour impressions with plates with engraved lettering inked in black. He started with 25 reproductions after oil paintings, like Le Blon had done, but from 1746 he mainly applied it for illustrating anatomical texts. Gautier-Dagoty's use of color printing was sometimes on an impressive scale, with his largest prints measuring 130 cm high (Fig. 5.2).

After its introduction in Paris printshops, the four-color system was adopted by French engravers for the production of the most fashionable color prints. Their skills, in combination with those of Parisian toolmakers, printers and publishers, created the best quality color prints on the European market in the second half of the 18th century. In these high end works the mezzotint rocker

---

23 The British Library and the British Museum, Department of Prints and Drawings both hold single-leaf copies of the print, still in its original blue paper wrapper with a key to the letters on the print in both French and Latin printed in letterpress in black, entitled on fol. [2]r: *Préparation Anatomique des parties de l'homme, servant à la generation, faite sur les découverts les plus modernes. Apparatus Anatomicus G. Cockburni Libello, super Gonorhoeâ virulentâ, inserviens*; BL, Department of Manuscripts, C 70 I 9 (2); BM, 1928,0310.101. Another copy in the print room of the Rijksmuseum, Amsterdam, has the key printed separately on white paper: RP-P-1910-1582. The whereabouts of a fourth copy formerly in a private collection are unknown.

24 "[Note by the editor]," *Mercure de France* (1721, June/July), 115–16. The process was cancelled in 1726 when Sankt André fell victim to the Mary Toft hoax and lost his position.

25 Only the plate going with L'Admiral's first anatomical colour print has lettering and some details printed from a fourth etched plate inked in black; Bernard Siegfried Albinus, *Dissertatio de arteriis et venis intestinorum hominis* (Leiden, Amsterdam: 1736).

26 "Réponse de M. [Antoine Gauthier] de Montdorge, aux informations de M. Rémond de Sainte Albine, au sujet de la contestation entre deux élèves de feu M. le Blond, sur l'art d'imprimer les tableaux," *Mercure de France* (1749, July), 173–79.

FIGURE 5.1
Jan L'Admiral, *Preparations of the Skin and Nail of a Black Woman*, 1737, mezzotint

FIGURE 5.2
Jacques-Fabien Gautier-Dagoty, *Muscles of the Back: Partial Dissection of a Seated Woman, Showing the Bones and Muscles of the Back and Shoulder*, 1746, mezzotint

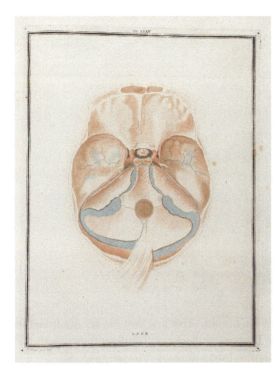

FIGURE 5.3
Angelique Briçeau, *Les Fosses du Cerveau et du Cervelet Recourvertes de la Dure-Mere*, 1786, etching with crayon engraving

was replaced by roulettes, small steel wheels with irregular toothed threads set in a handle, with which engravers could create fine-grained hues that appear like watercolor washes (Fig. 5.3).

3   Colour Printed Medical Illustrations

Before 1600, color in medical illustrations was limited to red and black ink on white paper, with red being used to depict fire, blood and anything decorative (Fig. 5.4). The four prints in Gaspare Aselli's (1581–1625) book on the lymphatic system (of a dog), the *De Lactibus* (1627) are a landmark in color book illustrations, although for unknown reasons he did not produce another book illustrated in a similar manner.[27] The images are in *chiaroscuro*, each printed

---

27   Gaspare Aselli, *De lactibus, sive lacteis venis, quarto vasorum mesaraicorum genere* (Milan: 1627); see http://diglib.hab.de/?grafik=mb-355-00001; http://diglib.hab.de/?grafik=mb-355-00002; http://diglib.hab.de/?grafik=mb-355-00003, http://diglib.hab.de/?grafik=mb-355-00004 (all accessed 1 July 2024).

FIGURE 5.4
Amputation of the Right Lower Leg of a Man, 1559, woodcut

from three woodblocks, one for each color. The first two blocks are inked in light red-brown and red-brown to show the organs. The third block with the outlines, hatching and background is inked in black. The white of the paper is used to render the lymphatic vessels saved from the light-brown inked block, and only occasionally for highlights as is more common in *chiaroscuro* prints (Fig. 5.5). In fine art *chiaroscuro* prints, complementary tones and whites are applied to render volume, rather than as actual colors as in the illustrations to Aselli's *De Lactibus*. The lymphatic fluid being colorless or off-white, the natural color of the paper provided Aselli with a contrasting hue necessary to communicate the appearance and location of lymphatic vessels to his medical colleagues.

With knowledge of anatomy growing in the later 17th century, more books on medicine were published, which were eagerly sought by anatomists and physicians. Consequently, the new color processes of Teyler and Le Blon, although originally intended for fine art prints, were also used for anatomical figures. Illustrations were created on an epistemological base and color was included to help the reader identify different anatomical elements, such as bones, muscles and organs. Color coding systems were also developed to show different functions of organs, such as arteries in red and veins in blue. From the later 18th century, color was furthermore employed for the depiction of morbid symptoms in studies on pathology.

White as a printed color in medical images was used by the French medical doctor Charles Billard (1800–32) in his *Traité des maladies des enfans* on children's diseases (1828), the result of autopsies of 700 corpses of dead children

FIGURE 5.5
Lymphatic System of the Liver of a Dog, 1627, woodcut

from the Paris foundling-hospital. The volume has a separate *Atlas* with two etchings printed with white ink on black-coated paper and eight etchings inked *à la poupée* in black and brown and then colored by hand (Fig. 5.6). Of the white inked plates, Billard stated: "I thought it necessary to paint the figure on a black base, to render well the shape and the white color of the morbid secretion that constitutes the mould".[28] In the captions accompanying other plates, the choice of colors and hues is also mentioned, with brown

---

28   Charles Billard, *Traité des maladies des enfans nouveaux-nés et a la mamelle* (Paris etc.: 1828) together with an *Atlas d'anatomie pathologique, pour servir à l'histoire des maladies des enfans*, 1 vol. in 2 parts (captions, plates), *Atlas*, pl. 5: "*Planche première. Muguet de l'oesophage et de l'estomac.J'ai cru devoir peindre ces figures sur un fond noir, afin de bien faire ressortir la forme et al couleur blanche de la secrétion morbide, qui constitue le muguet.*"; 'muguet' concerns a kind of mould that infects the body. The titlepage also states Billard painted or drew his own illustrations, which were then printed in color and further hand-colored under direction of Mr Duménil (*Les planches, exécutées sur les dessins de l'auteur, ont été gravées, imprimées en couleur et retouchées au pinceau avec le plus*

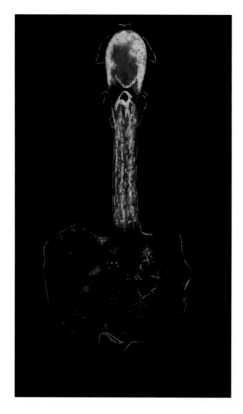

FIGURE 5.6
Stassel after Charles Billard, *Muguet de l'Estomac et de l'OEsophage*, 1828, etching

printing inks creating a base tone for human skin and internal tissue, while further details are often rendered through coloring the impressions by hand. The German translation of Billard's volume followed the original text in detail, although digressions were summarized or left out, while otherwise the latest information on the topic was added.[29] This volume was only illustrated with copies after Billard's two figures in white on black, , technically similar to produce, the others instead being described in greater detail. Meaningful enough, these two white inked plates were copied, because, as the editors stated on p. vi, the reader should not miss the depictions of this "destructive orphanage disease".[30]

   grand soin sous la direction de M. Duménil). I am grateful to Katharina Maehler for drawing my attention to this volume.

29 Charles Billard's *Krankheiten der Neugebornen und Säuglinge, nach den neuesten klinischen und pathologisch-anatomischen im Hospital der Findelkinder zu Paris gemachten Beobachtungen*, ed. Meißner, Friedrich Ludwig (Leipzig: 1829), v–vi.

30 Meißner, *Billard's Krankheiten*, vi, "und endlich haben wir mehrere Kupfertafeln, die das Werk zu kostspielig machen und keinesweg unentbehrlich sind, weggelassen und durch genaue Beschreibungen die bildliche Darstellung zu ersetzen gesucht. Was jedoch die

NOT FOR THE FEEBLE OF MIND!

4   Publishers and Engravers

Publishers and authors of medical and scientific theses often financed the production of their own works in the 18th and early-19th centuries and therefore decided on the illustrations; meaning that authors often chose whether or not to use color. A typical example is Emanuel Luz's (*fl.* 1799) thesis *Dissertatio inauguralis medica* of 1799 on surgery in the abdomen, with a particular focus on preventing damage to the epigastric artery, illustrated with two figures.[31] Tab. I is compiled of two plates printed in register. The author states that the function of the different colors is that the red impression has the image and part of the lettering for the German explanation, while the complementary black impression has lettering only for the Latin explanation.

Surprisingly, names of engravers recorded on medical illustrations are seldom found in the well-known art historical reference dictionaries of printmakers, *Benezit, Thieme-Becker* and *Allgemeines Künstler Lexikon.* The known exceptions are Jan L'Admiral (1698–1773) and Jacques-Fabien Gautier-Dagoty (1716–85), mentioned above. Between twelve and sixteen years after his London apprenticeship, L'Admiral produced prints made in Le Blon's trichromatic process (see fig. 5.1). He created two illustrations for pamphlets on anatomy by Bernard Siegfried Albinus (1697–1770), dated 1736 and 1737, and three for pamphlets by Frederick Ruysch (1638–1731) dated 1738, a sixth one of 1741 was based on Le Blon's print of dissected male human genitalia.[32] Additionally, he created an anatomical single-leaf print representing a dissected human heart, over-printing four plates in register, inked in blue, yellow and red (from two plates, one mezzotint and one etching) respectively.[33]

---

    wichtigsten Kupfertafeln betrifft, nämlich die Darstellungen des Soors (Muguet), dieser verheerende Findelhauskrankheit, über welche schon vor einigen Jahren Heyfelder unter dem Namen Schämmchen eine ziemlich genaue Beschreibung geliefert hat, so haben wir Sorge getragen, daß der Leser sie nicht vermisse."

31   Emanuel Luz, *Dissertatio inauguralis medica exhibens momenta quaedam circa herniotomian praecipue circa evitandam arteriae epigastricae laesionem* [*etc.*] (Tübingen: 1799), 35, concerning the black and red of Tab. I *Quae litteris germanicis hac in explicatione natantur, litteras significant in icone rubro colore expressas; quae latinis litteris exprimuntur, literas notant in icone nigras,* and see Tab. I and II.

32   *Hollstein's Dutch and Flemish Etchings, Engravings and Woodcuts: 1450–1700,* 72 vols. (Amsterdam: 1949–2010), vol. X, 1, nos. 1–6; *Jacob Christoff le Blon and the Start of Trichromatic Printing,* catalogue of Jan L'Admiral, nos. 8–14.

33   Rodari, *Anatomie de la couleur,* nos. 63–68; Nicolaas Gerhardus Van Huffel, *Coloritto: bijdrage tot de geschiedenis van de kunst om in drie kleuren te drukken, met een herdruk van het boekje van J. C. Le Blon* [*Paris 1756*] (Amsterdam: 1916), loose plates.

Only trial proofs exist and it is unknown what text it may have been intended to illustrate.[34]

Gautier-Dagoty had worked for Le Blon in Paris for only six weeks in 1736.[35] This was enough, however, to acquaint him with Le Blon's trichromatic process, from which he developed his own variants. He first used the process for 25 fine art prints made in the period 1736–43, reproducing oil paintings of various subjects such as still lifes, portraits, flowers, landscapes and religious images.[36] Gautier-Dagoty subsequently became a prolific publisher of volumes on human anatomy in cooperation with French anatomists using the same color printing process (see Fig. 5.2). He also issued the scientific journal *Observations sur l'histoire naturelle, sur la physique et sur la peinture* published between 1752–55, with articles on medical subjects illustrated with his color-printed mezzotints. Every year three parts in quarto format (26 cm high) with multiple illustrations were issued. Simultaneously a smaller format (18 cm high) appeared with only one illustration per part. Both in the title (*Avec des planches imprimées en couleur*), and on page 4 of the introduction (*Avis*) of the first volume (*Les Planches colorées de l'Histoire Naturelle feront la baze de cette entreprise*), color printing is emphasized. Gautier-Dagoty also sold the color plates separately, indicating that there was a market for these works.[37]

However, the journal was apparently not very successful. Gautier edited it from 1752–55, his eldest son Jean-Baptiste André (1745–83) took over to continue publication in 1756, and in 1757 it was issued by Pissot, Lambert & Cailleau.[38] Also working as a printmaker and publisher, Jean-Baptiste André

---

34   Rijksmuseum, Amsterdam, inv. nos. RP-P-1961-507–518.

35   Gautier was asked to help Le Blon on 24 April 1738 but he quit on 8 June 1738; Jacques-Fabien Gautier-Dagoty, "Lettre à M. de Boze, de l'Académie Françoise, & Honoraire de l'Académie de peinture & sculpture, Garde des médailles & pierreries du Cabinet du Roi, &c," in *Mercure de France* (1749, July), 158–72, at 164.

36   "Extrait des Registres du Conseil d'Etat," in *Mercure de France* (1741, Dec.), 2924–29; "Tableaux imprimés," in *Mercure de France* (1742, August), 1838–43.

37   Jacques-Fabien Gautier-Dagoty (ed.), *Observations sur l'histoire naturelle, sur la physique et sur la peinture* (Paris: 1752–55), vol. 1, pt. I, titlepage: *Les planches en couleur se distribuent séparement chez M. Gautier, Pensionnaire du Roy, rue de la Harpe*; the same on titlepages of later issues of the journal. The HAB keeps the journal, Na 4 ° 31 (1.1752–6.1755), Na 4 ° 31a (1756); the HAUM keeps a number of single-leaf impressions, inv. nos. Vasel 2583 (1–22).

38   The journal's title changed per publisher, as follows:—*Observations sur l'histoire naturelle, sur la physique et sur la peinture*, Paris: Delaguette, 1752–55;—*Observations périodiques sur la physique, l'histoire naturelle, et les Beaux Arts*, July 1756–December 1757, Paris: Cailleau & Gautier Fils, [for 1756]; next Toussaint (François Vincent), Gautier[-Dagoty] (= Jacques-Fabien) & Gautier[-Dagoty] (= Jean-Baptiste);—*Observations périodiques, sur la physique, l'histoire naturelle, et les Arts, ou Journal de sciences et arts*, Paris: Pissot, Lambert & Cailleau, [1757].

NOT FOR THE FEEBLE OF MIND! 131

employed the same technique as his father to produce anatomical prints and a series of portraits in color. Gautier-Dagoty's other sons applied his graphic process, too.[39] Arnaud-Éloi (1741–*c*.80/83) stayed closest to his father's subject manner specializing in anatomical illustrations with further scientific illustrations; Eduard (1745–83), who made botanical prints, was the most artistically talented of the family and is better known for his reproductions after paintings; Louis-Charles (1746–after 1787) also produced botanical works and at least one portrait; and Fabien (1747–82) worked on scientific illustrations.

Other engravers of medical illustrations are often better known for their artistic prints and only rarely for their medical works. Elisha Kirkall (*c*.1682–1742), for example, is known for his early English artistic color prints, less for his botanical works, but not for his medical illustrations in color.[40] William Stukeley was author of a text *Of the Spleen* (1722–23) and designer of the two plates that were etched by Kirkall.[41] Plate 1 of the volume titled *Schema Arteriarum, Abdominalium, Tabula Prima*, is signed in the lower margin *Stukeley delin / E. Kirkall sculp.* and is inked in red, indicating the arteries. Plate 2 shows the veins and is titled *Schema Venae Portae, Tabulae Secunda*, is signed in the lower margin *Stukeley delin., E. Kirkall scu.* and is inked in blue, now discolored to green due to the yellowing of the oily binding medium in the ink.

Three printmakers known solely for anatomical works who are listed in dictionaries of artists are Johann Friedrich Schröter (1770–1836), Alexandre Briceau (*fl.* 1786) and Angélique Allais (née Briceau) (*fl.* 1789–94). The Thieme-Becker reference to Johann Friedrich Schröter is minimal, describing him as *Illustrator medizin. Werke.*[42] Schröter was the engraver who copied Billard's white ink prints described above. Father and daughter Alexandre Briceau and Angélique Allais (Briceau) were among the top of French crayon engravers of the late

---

39   His daughter Marguerite (1764–?) is not known to have been active as printmaker. For an overview of the activities of the Gautier family see *Allgemeines Lexikon der bildenden Künstler von der Antike bis zur Gegenwart*, ed. Ulrich Thieme and Felix Becker, (1907–50), vol. 13, 290–94; *Allgemeines Künstler Lexikon*, vol. 1 (...) (Berlin, Munich: 1992 (...)), vol. 50, 303–06; Rodari, *Anatomie de la couleur*, 140–43.

40   Simon Turner, "Elisha Kirkall and his Proposals for Printing in Chiaroscuro, Natural Colours and Tints, 1720–1740", in Margaret Morgan Grasselli and Elizabeth Savage (eds.), *Printing Colour 1700–1830: Histories, Techniques, Functions and Receptions* (forthcoming), Chapter 4.

41   William Stukeley, *Of the Spleen, its description and history, uses and diseases, particularly the vapors, with their remedy: Being a lecture read at the Royal College of Physicians* (London: 1722), *To which is added some anatomical observations in the dissection of an elephant* (London: 1723).

42   Th-B, 30, 295.

18th century, producing very refined works by over-printing two to four plates in register, depending on the requirements of the design. They illustrated Félix Vicq-d'Azyr's (1748–94) volumes on the anatomy of the human brain (see Fig. 5.3).[43] The plates signed *Briceau sculp.* are likely all by Alexandre Briceau as those of his daughter are signed *Mlle Briceau del. et sculp.*

The artist Johann Stephan Capieux (1748–1813) studied medicine and science from 1771, before focusing on precise drawings and etchings of anatomical and scientific subjects from 1775, for which he became renowned. He is one of the few engravers specialising in medical and scientific illustrations in color.[44]

Interestingly, it is not uncommon to find authors supplying the drawings for the figures in their own works and even preparing the printing plates. Billard and Stukeley have already been mentioned as producing the illustrations to their texts. Similarly, the author Karl Friedrich Senff (*fl.* 1802) designed and etched his own figures, printed in monochromatic brown, for his publication on embryonal skeletons *Nonnulla de incremento ossium embryonum* published in (Halle: 1802). The title page states his role as author (*autore Car. Frid. Senff*) and the addresses of the two figures acknowledge that he drew and etched them (*Senff del. et fec.*). Georg Karl Heinrich Sander's (*fl.* 1827) selection of medical cases titled *Praelectionum et chirurgicarum et physicarum* (Braunschweig: 1827) was illustrated with two lithographs drawn by the author from life (*G. C. H. Sander ad nat. pinx.*).[45] Working in lithography, the author could draw directly on the stone as easily as on paper, with the further preparation and printing in red-brown ink done by a professional lithographic printer.

In the case of Ralph Fawcett Ainsworth's (1811–1890) dissertation on a disease of the male genitalia *De corneis humani corporis excrescentiis* (Berlin: 1836), the address records that the illustration, etched and printed in monochromatic brown with some hand-coloring in red and yellow, was drawn after nature by his colleague the medical doctor Robert Froriep (*Dr. Robert Froriep ad nat. pinx.*). Froriep also illustrated from nature his own publications, such as on eye diseases *Dissertatio medica de corneitide scrofulosa* (*etc.*) (1830), where

---

43   AKL, 14, 199: '*Zus. mit der Tochter illustrierte B. den "Traité d'Anatomie et de Physiologie"* (...) *von Vicq d'Azyr'.* Félix Vicq-d'Azyr, *Traité d'anatomie et de physiologie: avec des planches coloriées représentant au naturel les divers organes de l'Homme et des Animaux*, 2 vols (Paris: 1786).

44   AKL 16, 242; Th-B 5, 539: *Seine farbigen Radierungen nach Pflanzen, Mineralien, Muskeln etc.zeichnen sich durch große Akkuratesse und Lebenswahrheit aus*, being his best known work.

45   Tab. I and II are lithographs printed in red-brown and colored by hand; Tab. III is an etching inked in black.

it states on the titlepage that he is the author (*auctor Robertus Froriep*) and in the address of the plate that he drew the designs for the plates (*Dr. R. Froriep ad naturam pinx.*). Similarly, the doctor Frans Heinrich Martens (1778–1805) illustrated his publication about a patient with a harelip and badly grown hands and feet the *Ueber eine sehr complicirte Hasenscharte* (Leipzig: 1804). On the titlepage it states that Martens depicted and described his observations and he signed the illustrations as drawn and etched after nature.[46] In the introduction (*Vorrede*), the author explains that he drew his own etching plates to show everything described in the text precisely, which is how he believes figures should be drawn or else the text should not be illustrated. While Martens does not claim artistic perfection, calling himself a dilettante, he states how he aimed to produce clear figures that are true to scale in his illustrations.[47]

5 Influence of Iconographical Traditions on the Appearance of Medical Illustrations

In the 15th and 16th centuries, although medical illustrations gradually became more functional, they still compared visually with iconographical traditions of the time. Even the revolutionary anatomical figures by Andreas Vesalius (1514–64) in his *De humani corporis fabrica* (Basel: 1543) were shown in dramatic poses and placed in landscapes. Black-and-red printed images on white paper, for medical illustrations first introduced in the 16th century, remained the main manner of color printing for medical figures until the beginning of the 18th century (see Fig. 5.4). Due to a growing knowledge of anatomy during the Enlightenment, images were created more and more on an epistemological base and, after 1700, color was introduced to show the difference between arteries (always in red) and veins (in another color until blue became

---

46   Franz Heinrich Martens, *Ueber eine sehr complicirte Hasenscharte oder einen sogenannten Wolfsrachen: mit einer an demselben Subjekte befindlichen merkwürdigen Misstaltung der Hände und Füsse, operirt von Johann Gottlob Eckoldt* (Leipzig: 1804), titlep., "*abgebildet und beschrieben von Franz Heinrich Martens*", "*n. d. Nat. gez. u. gest. v. Dr. Martens*".

47   Martens, *Ueber eine sehr complicirte Hasenscharte*, 4: the above translates Martens statement more freely ("*Die dieser Schrift hinzugefügten Abbildungen zeigen alles, was im Texte beschrieben ist, dem Auge ganz genau, und ich denke, dass in jedem Falle entweder solche, oder gar keine Abbildungen geliefert werden müssen. Zwar will ich damit keinesweges behaupten, dass diese Tafeln den höchsten Grad artistischer Volkommenheit erreicht haben, denn, da ich bloss Dilettant bin, darf niemand dies von mir erwarten; aber ich glaube, sie sind ganz deutlich, und das ist denn ihr vorzüglichstes Verdienst, worauf es hier ankommt, weshalb ich auch die natürlich Grösse fast ganz beybehalten habe.*").

standard in the 19th century) (see Fig. 5.1). Color became a necessity for reproducing morbid symptoms of smallpox, skin infections (Fig. 5.7), venereal diseases (Fig. 5.8) etc., as well as the depiction of curing aids such as medical plants, new processes of vaccination, and new medical treatments. By then iconographical traditions were followed only in so far as concerned the rules of perspective and the rendering of volumes. In the first half of the 18th century, medical color prints created on aesthetical principles were still made (see Fig. 5.2) but after the middle of the century they had become realistic and systematic.

6 The Function of Color-printed Medical Illustrations in Relation to Art Prints

With single sheet fine art prints, color printing is more aesthetical, with different shades being introduced by the engraver, printer and publisher to create a wider variety of tones and effects and to make an image more pleasing to the eye. Illustrations in scholarly literature became more functional, often offering naturalistic depictions which, with some antecedents, is aided from the 18th century by the use of color. Reference to color in library catalogues

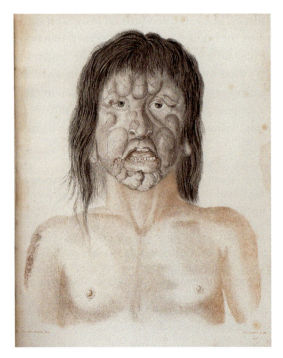

FIGURE 5.7
Themoteo Antonio and
I. L. Sailliar, *Symptoms of Skin Disease Caused by Mites*, 1807, etching

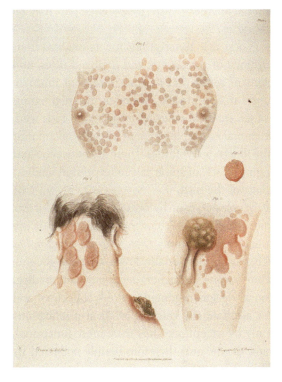

FIGURE 5.8
James S. Stewart, *Symptoms of Syphilis*, 1814, dotting

usually solely concerns printing red text on titlepages, often making it difficult to search for color-printed illustrations in early modern books and resulting in them being little studied. The only way of retrieving color figures therefore is by perusing volume after volume, as the present author did.

The project from which this essay stems focused largely on medical and scientific literature as these genres frequently utilized printed color. Research for the project revealed many hundreds of color-printed title pages and book illustrations in medical literature, the majority produced from the middle of the 18th century in the collections of the HAB. This is because the holdings incorporate book collections of several former medical societies from the region.[48] With some exceptions, the greater part of this material is unique and not found in other print rooms or library catalogues, such as medical theses

---

48 *Lexikon zur Geschichte und Gegenwart der Herzog-August-Bibliothek Wolfenbüttel: Paul Raabe zum 29.2.92*, ed. Georg Ruppelt and Sabine Solf (Wiesbaden: 1992), 110.

compiled for obtaining an academic degree.[49] Otherwise a large part may be lost, or simply not collected by libraries.[50]

The HAB catalogue has over 15,000 title descriptions for its medical literature. By deducting title descriptions of microfilms and digitized titles, and considering that title descriptions of series and journals represent multiple volumes, there is a total of around 16,000 physical volumes, of which about a third are illustrated. A total of 128 medical volumes from before 1850 were found to use color printing, which makes for 0.8 per cent of the total amount consulted or 2.4 per cent of all the illustrated volumes. There are between 1 and 50 color prints per volume, bringing a total of some 700 color-printed medical book illustrations in the collections of the HAB.

Out of the about 10,000 scientific volumes from before 1850 consulted for this project, 55 incorporate 1,350 color prints, of which over a thousand alone are found in Johann Wilhelm Weinmann's four-volume *Phytanthoza-Iconographia* (*etc.*) (Regensburg: 1737–45). This is proportionally lower than in general, because books on natural history were in higher demand than medical books.[51] They are often luxuriously designed, aimed at book collectors, and consequently illustrations were aesthetically refined. Medical publications reached that aesthetical level only by exception. They were more functional, with subject matter less pleasing to see, and therefore mainly collected by medical practitioners and societies. By comparison, any devotional or religious literature published between Ratdolt's books with color prints of around 1500 and the introduction of chromolithography in 1838 is only rarely illustrated with colour prints.

To compare this with fine art color prints, some 100,000 early modern works in the HAUM were checked, out of which over 1,200 color impressions were found. The majority of these date from the 18th century when they were acquired, with only limited later acquisitions, and reflects the interest of the ducal family in modern art and fashion of the period. The question in how far the percentage of color prints deviates from those in other contemporary print collections remains open.

---

49   For comparison the present author studied the holdings of numerous libraries and print-rooms in Europe, Japan and the USA.

50   The present author studied the holdings of numerous libraries and print rooms in Europe, Japan and the USA. Discussed works are best found in libraries specialised in medicine, natural history and science.

51   See the publications on books on natural history compiled by Claus Nissen (1901–1975) from 1930 onwards.

7 Conclusion

Medical literature from before 1850 is well represented in the HAB holdings, because of acquisitions of medical works, and volumes on natural history and science from this period are underrepresented. The book illustrations in the HAB and the single-leaf prints in the HAUM together warrant a sufficiently large body of objects for a process-led study of color printing in Europe in the handpress period. Important also is that most books and prints were acquired at the time of publication and kept ever since, although divided between two institutes, forming a joint fund of research. This is different from institutes founded in the modern period that aim to collect materials from widely divergent provenances to create an historical overview and do not aim at the interests of a coherent social group.

Summarising, taking the collections of HAB and HAUM as one source, the number of European colour printed medical images covers the historical production of its kind. Enough color prints in other disciplines are available for comparison of the use of colour prints in different fields, applied printmaking techniques, and aesthetic appearances of prints.

Select Bibliography

Primary Sources

Ainsworth, Ralph Fawsett, *De corneis humani corporis excrescentiis adiecta cornu praeputialis observatione* [*etc.*] (Berlin: 1836).

Albinus, Bernard Siegfried, *Dissertatio de arteriis et venis intestinorum hominis* (Leiden, Amsterdam: 1736).

Aselli, Gaspare, *De lactibus, sive lacteis venis, quarto vasorum mesaraicorum genere* (Milan: 1627).

Bertoloni Meli, Domencio, *Visualizing Disease: The Art and History of Pathological Illustrations* (Chicago, London: 2017).

Billard, Charles, *Traité des maladies des enfans nouveaux-nés et a la mamelle* (Paris, London and Brussels: 1828).

Billard, Charles, *Atlas d'anatomie pathologique, pour servir à l'histoire des maladies des enfans*, 1 vol. in 2 parts (Paris, London and Brussels: 1828).

Billard, Charles, *Krankheiten der Neugebornen und Säuglinge, nach den neuesten klinischen und pathologisch-anatomischen im Hospital der Findelkinder zu Paris gemachten Beobachtungen*, ed. Friedrich Ludwig Meißner (Leipzig: 1829).

Choulant, Ludwig, *Geschichte und Bibliographie der anatomischen Abbildung nach ihrer Beziehung auf anatomische Wissenschaft und bildende Kunst* (1852; repr. Niederwalluf bei Wiesbaden: 1971).

"Extrait des Registres du Conseil d'Etat", in *Mercure de France* (1741, Dec.), 2924–29.

Froriep, Robert, *Dissertatio medica de corneitide scrofulosa (etc.)* (Jena: 1830).

Gautier-Dagoty, Jacques-Fabien, 'Lettre à M. de Boze, de l'Académie Françoise, & Honoraire de l'Académie de peinture & sculpture, Garde des médailles & pierreries du Cabinet du Roi, &c', in *Mercure de France* (1749, July), 158–72.

Gautier-Dagoty, Jacques-Fabien (ed.), *Observations sur l'histoire naturelle, sur la physique et sur la peinture* (Paris: 1752–55).

Gautier-Dagoty, Jacques-Fabien (ed.), *Observations périodiques sur la physique, l'histoire naturelle et les arts* (Paris: 1756).

Herrkinger, Robert, and Marielene Putscher, *Geschichte der medizinischen Abbildung*, 2 vols (Munich: 1967–72).

Kornell, Monique, *Flesh and Bones: The Art of Anatomy*, with contributions by Thisbe Gensler, Naoko Takahatake and Erin Travers, exhibition catalogue (Los Angeles: 2022).

Luz, Emanuel, *Dissertatio inauguralis medica exhibens momenta quaedam circa herniotomian praecipue circa evitandam arteriae epigastricae laesionem [etc.]* (Tübingen: 1799).

Martens, Franz Heinrich, *Ueber eine sehr complicirte Hasenscharte oder einen sogenannten Wolfsrachen: mit einer an demselben Subjekte befindlichen merkwürdigen Misstaltung der Hände und Füsse, operirt von Johann Gottlob Eckoldt* (Leipzig: 1804).

Observations périodiques, sur la physique, l'histoire naturelle, et les Arts, ou Journal de sciences et arts (Paris: 1757).

"Réponse de M. [Antoine Gauthier] de Montdorge, aux informations de M. Rémond de Sainte Albine, au sujet de la contestation entre deux élèves de feu M. le Blond, sur l'art d'imprimer les tableaux," *Mercure de France* (1749, July), 173–79.

Sander, Georg Karl Heinrich, *Praelectionum et chirurgicarum et physicarum selectus quas in Societate Physico-Medica Brunsvicensi Habuit [etc.]* (Brunswick: 1827).

Senff, Karl Friedrich, *Nonnulla de incremento ossium embryonum in primis graviditatis temporibus* (Halle: 1802).

Stukeley, William, *Of the Spleen, its description and history, uses and diseases, particularly the vapors, with their remedy: Being a lecture read at the Royal College of Physicians* (London: 1723), *To which is added some anatomical observations in the dissection of an elephant* (London: 1723).

"Tableaux imprimés", in *Mercure de France* (1742, August), 1838–43.

Vesalius, Andreas, *De humani corporis fabrica libri septem* (Basel: 1543).

Vicq-d'Azyr, Félix, *Traité d'anatomie et de physiologie: avec des planches coloriées représentant au naturel les divers organes de l'Homme et des Animaux*, 2 vols (Paris: 1786).

Secondary Sources

Allgemeines Künstler Lexikon, vol. 1 (Berlin, Munich: 1992).

Allgemeines Lexikon der bildenden Künstler von der Antike bis zur Gegenwart, ed. Ulrich Thieme and Felix Becker, 37 vols. (1907–50, repr. Leipzig: 1999).

NOT FOR THE FEEBLE OF MIND!

Griffiths, Antony, "White Ink", *Print Quarterly*, 8, no. 3 (1991), 286–90.

Hollstein's Dutch and Flemish Etchings, Engravings and Woodcuts: 1450–1700, 72 vols (Amsterdam: 1949–2010).

Ikeda, Mayumi, "The Fust and Schöffer Office and the Printing of the Two-Colour Initials in the 1457 mainz Psalter", in *Printing Colour 1400–1700: History, Techniques, Functions and Receptions* ed. Ad Stijnman and Elizabeth Savage (Leyden, Boston: 2015), 65–75.

Nakamura, Jun, "On Hercules Segers's 'Printed Paintings'", in *Printing Colour 1400–1700: History, Techniques, Functions and Receptions* ed. Ad Stijnman and Elizabeth Savage (Leyden, Boston: 2015), 189–195.

Raabe, Mechtild, *Leser und Lektüre im 17. Jahrhundert: die Ausleihbücher der Herzog August Bibliothek Wolfenbüttel 1664–1713*, 3 vols (Munich: 1998).

Roberts, K. B. and J. D. W. Tomlinson, *The Fabric of the Body: European Traditions of Anatomical Illustration* (Oxford: 1992).

Rodari, Florian (ed.), *Anatomie de la couleur: l'invention de l'estampe en couleurs*, exhibition catalogue (Paris, Lausanne: 1996).

Savage, Elizabeth, "Jost de Negker's Woodcut Charles V (1519): An Undescribed Example of Gold Printing", *Art in Print*, 5, no. 2 (2015, July/Aug), 9–15.

Savage, Elizabeth, "Colour Printing in Relief before c.1700: A Technical Story", in *Printing Colour 1400–1700: History, Techniques, Functions and Receptions*, ed. Ad Stijnman and Elizabeth Savage (Leyden, Boston: 2015), 23–41.

Savage, Elizabeth, "A Printer's Art: The Development and Influence of Colour Printmaking in the German Lands, c.1476–c.1600", in *Printing Colour 1400–1700: History, Techniques, Functions and Receptions*, ed. Ad Stijnman and Elizabeth Savage (Leyden, Boston: 2015), 93–102.

Savage, Elizabeth, "Proto-*à la poupée* Printing in Relief: An Initial 'D' in the Rylands Mainz Psalter, 1457," (unpublished manuscript).

Stijnman, Ad, "White Ink", *Print Quarterly*, 9, no. 2 (1992), 181–83.

Stijnman, Ad, "Another Clair-obscur Etching", *Print Quarterly*, 10, no. 1 (1993), 58–59.

Stijnman, Ad, *Engraving and Etching 1400–2000: A History of the Development of Manual Intaglio Printmaking Processes* (London and Houten: 2012).

Stijnman, Ad and Elizabeth Savage, "Materials and Techniques for Early Colour Printing", in Ad Stijnman and Elizabeth Savage (ed.), *Printing Colour 1400–1700: History, Techniques, Functions and Receptions* (Leiden: 2015), 11–22.

Stijnman, Ad and Elizabeth Savage, *Printing Colour 1400–1700: History, Techniques, Functions and Receptions* (Leiden: 2015).

Stijnman, Ad, "Thoughts on art history from the perspective of the maker," in *Art in Print*, vol. 6, no. 3 (2016), 16–17.

Stijnman, Ad, "Hercules Segers's Printmaking Techniques", in *Hercules Segers: Painter, Etcher*, exhibition catalogue, ed. Huigen Leeflang and Pieter Roelofs (Amsterdam: 2017), 62–77.

Stijnman, Ad, *Johannes Teyler and Dutch Colour Prints c.1700*, ed. Simon Turner (The new Hollstein Dutch & Flemish etchings, engravings and woodcuts: 1450–1700) (Ouderkerk aan den IJssel: 2017).

Van Huffel, Nicolaas Gerhardus, *Coloritto: bijdrage tot de geschiedenis van de kunst om in drie kleuren te drukken, met een herdruk van het boekje van J. C. Le Blon [Paris 1756]* (Amsterdam: 1916).

PART 2

The Reception of Print: Circulation and Use

∴

CHAPTER 6

Multiplied Madonnas—Strategies of Commercializing Raphael in Print

Anne Bloemacher

The collaboration of Raphael (1483–1520) and Marcantonio Raimondi (early 1480s–before 1534), of celebrated painter and engraver, has been well studied in existing scholarship. However, many questions about the mechanics of the partnership still remain unsolved.[1] While the selection of Raphael designs to be developed into engravings by Marcantonio was likely not coincidental, we still know little about this process and why specific inventions were chosen to be published and these often differ so considerably from their sources. This also raises the question of what can be deduced from the prints themselves regarding their audiences.

Virtually no contemporary written sources on the partnership between Raphael and Marcantonio survive. To answer the above questions, the extant materials in the form of prints, paintings and drawings have to be analysed carefully. This essay focusses on prints in relation to Raphael's *Madonna di Foligno* (Figs. 6.1, 6.2 and 6.3). The aim is to show that the differences between the drawings and paintings made by Raphael and the engravings made after them were not the product of mere coincidence.[2] Raimondi did not simply receive unused or discarded drawings from Raphael's workshop upon which he based his prints. On the contrary, Raphael took an active part in the business of print.[3] The following discussion will take the case study of prints

---

1 For a thorough analysis of the literature see Anne Bloemacher, *Raffael und Raimondi. Produktion und Intention der frühen Druckgraphik nach Raphael* (Berlin and Munich: 2016), 10–16; Edward H. Wouk, "Introduction: Marcantonio Raimondi, Raphael and the image multipled", in *Raphael, Raimondi and the image multiplied*, ed. Edward H. Wouk and David Morris, exhibition catalogue (Manchester: 2016), 10–11.

2 For the assumption that Raphael and Raimondi did not cooperate (for various reasons) see Paul Kristeller, "Marcantons Beziehung zu Raffael", *Jahrbuch der Königlich-Preussischen Kunstsammlungen*, 4 (1907), 199–229, especially 220; Arthur Mayger Hind, *Marcantonio and Italian engravers and etchers of the Sixteenth Century* (London: 1912), 4; Arthur E. Popham and Johannes Wilde, *The Italian drawings of the XV and XVI centuries in the collection of His Majesty the King at Windsor Castle* (London: 1949), Cat. 793, 310–311.

3 Several scholars have already argued for Raphael pursuing printmaking after his inventions, to show his competence or as an extra source of income; Patricia Emison, "Marcantonio's

---

© KONINKLIJKE BRILL BV, LEIDEN, 2024 | DOI:10.1163/9789004703834_008

FIGURE 6.1 Marcantonio Raimondi, *Madonna on Clouds* (*B.52*), engraving, 250 × 177 mm, Metropolitan Museum of Art, New York, Purchase Joseph Pulitzer Bequest, 1917, inv. 17.50.79

FIGURE 6.2　Marcantonio Raimondi, *Madonna on Clouds* (B.53), engraving, 246 × 149 mm, Rijksmuseum, Amsterdam, inv. RP-P-OB-11.750

of the *Madonna of Foligno* to consider the processes and purposes of prints produced through the Raphael Raimondi partnership. Changes introduced to the engraving, specifically the reduction of the composition to solely the central figures of Madonna and Child, will first be considered in relation to adapting the invention to its intended audience of pilgrims to Rome for whom the central religious subject was of universal importance. In a what I call "re-iconisation" of subject matter, Marian devotion is combined with specific reference to the miracle that occurred in Santa Maria in Aracoeli. The second part of the paper analyses prints by Giovanni Antonio da Brescia made after Raimondi's engravings, again for a different audience to Marcantonio's as can be established in light of their quality and inscriptions. The essay will conclude by using visual evidence to question the traditional assumption that Giovanni Antonio da Brescia, like Raimondi, worked directly with Raphael.

Three engraved versions of the *Madonna on Clouds* after Raphael's *Madonna di Foligno* are attributed to Raimondi, numbered B.47, B.52 and B.53 by Adam von Bartsch (Figs. 6.1, 6.2, and 6.4).[4] This essay will consider B.52 and B.53 first, due to their stronger ties to the final *Madonna di Foligno* painting and their interrelation to each other. It will then address B.47 in relation to a drawing depicting an earlier stage in Raphael's inventive process behind the painting.

The two engravings B.52 and B.53 show Mary, seated on a bank of clouds, with the Christ Child about to climb down from her lap and holding her veil with both hands. His gaze is focused on something outside of the picture plane below, which appears to have inspired his movement. Mary supports her son, completely absorbed in his action. In his *Lives*, Giorgio Vasari [1511–1574] already connected these engravings to Raphael's painting of the *Madonna di Foligno* (Fig. 6.3), the altarpiece Raphael produced in 1511 or 1512

Massacre of the Innocents", *Print Quarterly*, 1, no. 4 (1984), 257–267, here 258; Patricia Emison, *Invention and the Italian Renaissance Print, Mantegna to Parmigianino*. Ph.D. Dissertation, Columbia University (New York, NY: 1985), 142; Patricia Emison, "Raphael's Multiples", *The Cambridge Companion to Raphael*, ed. Marcia B. Hall (Cambridge: 2005), 186–206, especially 206; Konrad Oberhuber, "Raffaello e l'incisione", in *Raffaello in Vaticano*, exhibition catalogue ed. Fabrizio Mancinelli (Milan: 1984), 332–342, especially 334. Oberhuber speaks of an outright collaboration also in regard of an artistic exchange while Emison postulates that Raimondi's interest in working with Raphael was mainly commercial. Research is still divided on the subject of Raimondi's and Raphael's co-production. For a summary of the vast literature on the topic see Bloemacher, *Raffael und Marcantonio Raimondi*, 10–17.

4   Marcantonio Raimondi, *Madonna on Clouds* (B.52), engraving, 250 × 177 mm, Metropolitan Museum of Art, New York, Purchase Joseph Pulitzer Bequest, 1917, inv. 17.50.79; Marcantonio Raimondi, *Madonna on Clouds* (B.53), engraving, 246 × 149 mm, Rijksmuseum, Amsterdam, inv. RP-P-OB-11.750.

FIGURE 6.3
Raphael, *Madonna di Foligno*, 1511/12, oil on canvas, transferred from wood, 301,5 × 198,5 cm, Pinacoteca Vaticana, Città del Vaticano, inv. 329

for the high altar of the Roman church Santa Maria in Aracoeli.[5] The altarpiece's donor was Sigismondo Conti (1432–1512) from Foligno, private secretary (*segretario domestico*) and later political secretary (*segretario politico*) of Pope Julius II [1443–1513]. Conti would eventually be buried close to the altar in the same church.[6]

---

5 Raphael, *Madonna di Foligno*, 1511–12, Oil on canvas, transferred from wood, 301.5 × 198.5 cm, Pinacoteca Vaticana, Città del Vaticano, inv. 329. Vasari mentions under Raimondi's prints "half a folio with Our Lady, which Raphael painted in S. Maria in Aracoeli" ("[…] *et in un mezzo foglio la nostra Donna che Raffaello aveva dipinta nella tavola d'Aracelí*"); Paola Barocchi and Rosanna Bettarini (Ed.), *Giorgio Vasari. Le vite de' più eccellenti pittori, scultori e architettori nelle redazioni del 1550 e 1568* (Florence: 1966–1969), vol. 5, 10.

6 The commission of the altarpiece showing Conti as patron is connected to his death on 23 February 1512. For a discussion of the panel's location in Santa Maria in Aracoeli and for its dating see Jürg Meyer zur Capellen, *Raphael. A critical catalogue of his paintings. T. II. The Roman religious Paintings ca. 1508–1520* (Landshut: 2005), 100, and Arnold Nesselrath in Andreas Henning and Arnold Nesselrath (Ed.), Exh. Cat. *Raffael, Dürer und Grünewald malen die Madonna* (6.9.2011–8.1.2012, Gemäldegalerie Alte Meister, Staatliche Kunstsammlungen Dresden). (Munich: 2011), 40–42.

Albeit in reverse, Raimondi faithfully reproduces the Virgin and Child group from Raphael's altarpiece in both of his engravings, whose subtle differences will be analysed in more detail later on. Yet, the saints, donor and putto who figure in the earthly sphere of the altarpiece and cover the lower half of the panel, are not integrated into Raimondi's prints. On the basis of this and in light of what can be deduced from other instances of the two artist's collaboration, it is most probable that Raimondi received a drawing from Raphael's workshop on which to base his engraving, which only showed the central group of Mother and Child.[7] No extant drawings related to the project are known.

What prompted the publication of this print, likely based on a preparatory drawing, which crops the image to the figures rather than reproducing the whole composition of Raphael's finished altarpiece? Very likely the answer lies in the prints' intended audience and function. While scholars have convincingly established that Raimondi's most famous engravings after Raphael, such as the *Massacre of the Innocents*, the *Judgement of Paris* and the *Parnassus*, were produced for an elite circle, the smaller prints of devotional character, like the *Madonna of the Clouds*, and those of lower quality, appear to have been intended for a larger audience.[8]

---

7 Vasari states that Raphael gave drawings to Raimondi to be engraved. Vasari, *Le Vite*, vol. 5, 10. That Raimondi worked with drawings by Raphael or his workshop has never been questioned. It has only been discussed how he came into possession of these drawings. Michael Bury has elucidated that quite generally, if an artist was not a so-called 'peintre-graveur' who made prints himself, the printmaker worked after drawings, not after paintings or frescoes, at least before ca. 1530; Michael Bury, *The Print in Italy, 1550–1620* (London: 2010), 10. See also: Lidia Bianchi, "La Fortuna di Raffaello nell'Incisione", *Raffaello: L'opera, le fonte, la fortuna*, ed. Mario Salmi, vol. 2 (Novara: 1969), 652: Giulio Bonasone's (*c.*1498–after 1574) print after Raphael's *Saint Cecilia* is the first truly 'reproductive' print. Oberhuber, Landau and Parshall argue as well that only the generation of engravers after Raimondi, such as Gian Giacopo Caraglio (*c.*1500–1570) and Bonasone, began to work after executed paintings, inaugurating the so-called 'reproductive engraving'; Oberhuber, "Raffaello e l'incisione", 333–342, especially 340; David Landau and Peter Parshall, *The Renaissance Print 1470–1550* (New Haven and London: 1994), 121.

8 Marcantonio Raimondi, *The Massacre of the Innocents* (B.18 and B.20), engraving, 283 × 434 mm; Marcantonio Raimondi, *Parnassus* (B.247), engraving, 359 × 472 mm, lettered: RAPHAEL PINXIT IN VATICANO, signed with the monogram "MAF"; Marcantonio Raimondi, *Judgement of Paris* (B.245), engraving, 292 × 433 mm, signed "MAF" and "RAPH. URBI INVEN". For the *Parnassus* print being intended for an elite circle see Lisa Pon, *Raphael, Dürer, and Marcantonio Raimondi. Copying and the Italian Renaissance Print* (New Haven and London: 2004), 94. David Landau and Peter Parshall have established the high regard for prints after Raphael in the early 16th century: large prints of a high quality such as the *Massacre of the Innocents*, *Parnassus* or the *Judgement of Paris* were quite expensive, already a small print by Raimondi after Raphael would have been 26 times more expensive than a simple woodcut; Landau and Parshall, *The Renaissance Print*, 353. Concerning the different audiences

MULTIPLIED MADONNAS

According to Peter Partner, pilgrims and visitors to Rome numbered around 100,000 each year, generating a continual flow of potential customers for prints. This was in addition to the Papal Court and its administration of about 1700 people, large households of cardinals (of which there were between 25 and 30, each housing around 150 people), convents and other ecclesiastical institutions, as well as other inhabitants of the city, who formed a constant group of buyers.[9] Engravings of religious subjects made up half of Raphael's and Raimondi's production in print.[10] This differs considerably from Raimondi's time in Bologna, where he primarily made engravings of mythological and allegorical subjects.[11] The prevalence of religious subjects among the Raphael/Raimondi engravings is even more evident when second versions and repetitions are included. Seventeen of Raphael and Raimondi's religious engravings exist in one or more versions, whereas there are only five re-editions of engravings representing profane subjects.[12] For the large clientele of pilgrims and visitors to the Holy City, prints with religious subjects were clearly of greater commercial interest than more erudite compositions.

The commercial potential of religious prints in Rome in the opening decades of the 16th century helps us understand why Raimondi's engraving shows only

     of Raimondi's and Raphael's prints in more detail Anne Bloemacher, "Die Idee als Ware. Marcantonio Raimondis Kupferstiche nach Raffael", *Luxusgegenstände und Kunstwerke vom Mittelalter bis zur Gegenwart. Produktion—Handel—Formen der Aneignung* (Irseer Schriften. Studien zur Wirtschafts-, Kultur- und Mentalitätsgeschichte, Bd. 8), ed. Christoph Jeggle, Andreas Tacke, Markwart Herzog (Konstanz and Munich: 2015), 155–184.

9   In middle of the 16th century about 100,000 people were living in Rome. This number could quadruple for religious feast days. The number of priests, monks and nuns comprised about 3000 in the beginning of the century. Peter Partner, *Renaissance Rome 1500–1559. A Portrait of a Society* (Berkeley: 1976), 52–54.

10   65 of the 149 prints after Raphael show religious subjects, 48 mythological ones, 17 antique history and 19 allegories (series such as the "Twelve Apostles" counting as one), including Ugo da Carpi's woodcuts.

11   Konrad Oberhuber, "Marcantonio Raimondi", *Bologna e l'umanesimo 1490–1510*, exhibition catalogue, ed. Marzia Faietti and Konrad Oberhuber (Bologna: 1988), 51–210; Marzia Faietti, "Intorno a Marcantonio", in *Bologna e l'Umanesimo*, exhibition catalogue ed. Marzia Faietti and Konrad Oberhuber, 213–236; Bernice Davidson hinted at Raimondi's "academic humanist background" already in her PhD thesis in 1954, yet did not elaborate on that topic as Oberhuber and Faietti would in their 1988 exhibition catalogue cited above (including many analyses of Raimondi's early prints); Bernice Davidson, *Marcantonio Raimondi, The engravings of his Roman Period*. Ph.D. thesis Harvard University, Cambridge, MA, 195 (unpublished), 41.

12   Adam von Bartsch coined the term "repetition" for cases in which one artist copies a print by another without trying to suppress his own style and technique (which would be a "copy" for Bartsch); Bartsch, *Peintre-Graveur*, 24–25.

the Madonna and Child from Raphael's altarpiece. The engraving was very likely intended to be sold and used as a private devotional picture, and the specific references to the donor in the altarpiece (such as his portrait and landscape from his native Foligno) would therefore have been of minor interest to a prospective buyer. In contrast, the central religious subject of the Madonna and Child was of universal importance. In the particular case of the *Madonna di Foligno,* the Virgin and Child furthermore embody an important event said to be connected to the Church where the altarpiece hung. According to the *Golden Legend,* Mary with Christ on her lap in a Mandorla formed by angels and in front of a sun disc appeared to Emperor Augustus [63 BC–14 AD] on the Roman Capitol on the day of Christ's birth in the 1st century AD. Voragine recounts that she spoke the words: "This is the altar in heaven" (*"Haec est aracoeli"*).[13] To commemorate this epiphany, Augustus had an altar erected in the Capitol on the exact spot of this miraculous vision to honour the Virgin. In the 6th century AD, the church of Santa Maria in Aracoeli was built on the site of the altar. For pilgrims visiting the church, Raphael's altarpiece provided a convincing visualisation of the miraculous event that had taken place on the site. Raimondi's engraving thus offered the visitor the opportunity to buy an object which combined Marian devotion and a specific reference to the miracle that occurred at Santa Maria in Aracoeli.

As mentioned above, engravings such as the *Madonna on clouds* were not intended to showcase Raphael's design in the same way as, for example, the *Parnassus* (Fig. 6.6), which is explicitly marked as Raphael's invention by the inscription.[14] Raphael painted the fresco *Parnassus* in the *Stanza della Segnatura* of the Apostolic Palace in 1511. It shows Apollo playing his lyre on Mount Parnassus surrounded by poets and muses in an idyllic setting. There are some curious differences between the fresco and the later print (*c.*1517) in which some poets are missing, while a number of putti are added. Lisa Pon has convincingly argued that the print was made for members of the Papal Court, as Pope Leo X, like his predecessor and patron of the fresco Julius II, had established himself as Apollo reborn.[15] Details including the additional putti with laurels would have addressed this intended audience, suggesting that they might also be crowned for their achievements like the poets depicted on Mount Parnassus.[16] Moreover, differences between the actual architecture

---

13   Arnold Nesselrath, "La Madonna di Foligno", *Raffaello a Milano. La Madonna di Foligno,* exhibition catalogue, ed. Valeria Merlini and Daniele Storti (Milan: 2013), 63–73.

14   The inscription reads *"RAPHAEL PINXIT IN VATICANO"* and the print is signed with the monogram "MAF" for Marcantonio Raimondi. It is therefore explicitly stated that Raphael invented the composition and Raimondi made the print.

15   Pon, *Raphael, Dürer, and Marcantonio Raimondi,* 88.

16   Pon, *Raphael, Dürer, and Marcantonio Raimondi,* 90.

FIGURE 6.4 Marcantonio Raimondi, *Madonna on Clouds* (B.47), engraving, 176 × 134 mm, Metropolitan Museum of Art, New York, The Elisha Whittelsey Collection, The Elisha Whittelsey Fund, 1949, inv. 49.97.17

in the *Stanza* and the depiction of the window in the engraving invite the audience to compare print and painting. The curious inscription performs a similar function. Only a specific audience, one that had access to the *Stanza della Segnatura*, would understand the full range of references in this print.[17] By

---

17 Pon, *Raphael, Dürer, and Marcantonio Raimondi*, 93 and 94.

comparing print and fresco they would have the opportunity to see Raphael's idea for the *Parnassus* without the compromises dictated by the window in the room. Raimondi's *Parnassus* was therefore a witty product made for a select number of *cognoscenti*. The engravings of the *Madonna and Child*, in contrast, were made for the faithful masses—who all the same could appreciate a good quality print.

The core concern of the *Madonna on Clouds* engravings was what could be called the *re-iconisation* of subject matter; the retrieval or recovery of the iconic from the painting's wider narrative. This does not exclude the possibility that a lot of pilgrims knew that the *Madonna di Foligno* had been painted by the famous Raphael.[18] It was one of the artist's few paintings which could be seen publicly in Rome.[19] However, an engraving recreating this venerated Madonna was likely to have sold especially well because of its holy subject matter as well as its being based on the composition of a celebrated artist.[20]

The engraving's commercial success is underlined by the fact that there are two versions. The existence of two plates with almost the same motif suggests a re-edition of the print after the first plate wore out.[21] A comparative analysis of the two versions will help to establish the chronology of the two prints and, moreover, how Raphael may have intervened to ensure that the second edition of the engraving improved upon the first.

Both of Raimondi's engraved versions of Raphael's composition are approximately the same size and appear quite similar at first glance, yet they differ in several important details. In B.52 (Fig. 6.1), Mary holds the child with her right hand at his thigh; in B.53 (Fig. 6.2), she grabs him under his arm. In both engravings, Mary holds the Christ Child with her left hand at his belly. While four of her fingers are visible in B.52, we can only see two in B.53. In B.52, some

---

18   By 1512, the year in which the *Madonna di Foligno* was painted, Raphael had reached the position of a court artist at the Vatican. He emerged increasingly with credit from the papal commissions he had been receiving since 1508; Meyer zur Capellen, *Raffael*, 59.

19   Most probably Raphael's panel adorned the high altar of the church, the altar in Conti's chapel being too small for such a large scale altarpiece, see: Christa Gardner von Teuffel, "Raffaels römische Altarbilder: Aufstellung und Bestimmung", *Zeitschrift für Kunstgeschichte*, 50 (1987), 1–45, especially 8ff., Sibel De Blauw, "Das Hochaltarretabel in Rom bis zum frühen 16. Jahrhundert. Das Altarbild als Kategorie der liturgischen Anlage", *Mededelingen van het Nederlands Instituut te Rome*, 55 (1996), 83–110, here 96ff. and Meyer zur Capellen, *Raffael*, 100.

20   This is underlined by the second version of this engraving and very weak prints of the plate, see for further discussion Bloemacher, *Raffael und Raimondi*, 187–189.

21   Innis H. Shoemaker, "Marcantonio and his Sources. A Survey of His Style and Engraving Techniques", in *The engravings of Marcantonio Raimondi*, exhibition catalogue, ed. Innis H. Shoemaker and Elizabeth Broun (Lawrence: 1981), 3–18, 11.

MULTIPLIED MADONNAS 153

strands of Mary's curly hair have fallen loose from her veil and are waving in the wind. In B.53, her hair is straight and almost completely covered by her headdress, which also falls in a smoother fashion. In B.52, Mary and the Christ Child are framed by an *aureole*, which does not occur in B.53. In B.53, Mary's halo is rendered at an angle due to the turning of her head, while in B.52, her halo is rendered frontally. On the whole, in B.52 the rendering of the body covered by the garments is elegantly done. In comparison, the rendering of the figures in B.53 is more awkward, for example the unnatural position of Mary's upper arm and her lower left leg. There are also subtle differences between the prints in the formations and shapes of the clouds.

Adam von Bartsch considered B.53 a repetition of B.52.[22] On the contrary, Konrad Oberhuber dates B.53 earlier, to Raimondi's first years in Rome around 1512–13 where he used the fine, delicate technique seen here, while B.52 shows Raimondi's later, mature style.[23] Oberhuber's proposed chronology of the states is more convincing; stylistic evidence such as the sculptural rendering of the hair also suggests a date for B.52 of around 1515–16.[24] Raimondi made clear improvements in his ability to render the body and drapery during his time in Rome.

The figure group in the earlier print, B.53, is closer to Raphael's painting than in B.52. In B.53 and the painting, Mary holds Christ under his left arm. The modification from B.53 to B.52 thus signifies a deliberate change of the composition, possibly even correcting what could be seen as mistakes in perspective and the modelling of body parts. The way Mary holds Jesus in the painting and the first engraving, B.53, shows Raphael and Marcantonio striving to capture the natural pose of a mother holding her restless child by the arm. In B.52, however, the Madonna's gesture of holding the child at his thigh eliminates the somewhat unclear and unflattering placing of hands and arms in the earlier composition. The compositional clarification in B.52 is supported by the slightly different position of Christ's arms grabbing the veil: his right arm is held higher and further away from his left arm, creating a better effect of the figure receding into space. Mother and child appear more dynamic in B.52,

---

22   Bartsch, *Le Peintre-Graveur*, vol. 14 (Vienna: 1813), 58.

23   Oberhuber, "Raffaello e l'incisione", 333–342, especially 336. The empty-tablet-signature on B.52 supports a dating to 1515, because Raimondi used this signature only after the mid of the second decade of the 16th century (see: Anne Bloemacher, "Raphael and Marcantonio Raimondi—the empty tablet as a plurivalent sign", *Chicago Art Journal* 2008, 20–41, especially 26).

24   The different rendering of the hair also appears in the two versions of Raimondi's *Massacre of the Innocents* which were made contemporaneously to the versions of the *Madonna on clouds*.

yet at the same time more dignified and centered, with the child's movement to the left being counter-balanced by the strands of the Virgin's hair flying to the right.

The most likely source for the development of the composition in B.52 is Raphael himself. As is evidenced by all of Raimondi's prints after Raphael's drawings, Raimondi never made independent changes to figures or figural groups, only to backgrounds and surroundings.[25] Raphael must therefore have reworked details of his own composition at a later date, and most probably in preparation for the print's re-edition. The same pattern has also been shown in other examples of Raphael's collaboration with Raimondi, for example the *Massacre of the Innocents* and the *Pietà*.[26] This makes it almost certain that Raphael took an active role in the printing business and cared deeply about how his inventions were represented in engravings and woodcuts, even long after they were first issued.

One further engraving of a *Madonna on clouds* by Raimondi exists, numbered B.47 by Bartsch (Fig. 6.4).[27] As the composition differs so considerably from B.52 and B.53, it has not been integrated into the above discussion. It shows Mary and Jesus on a bank of clouds high above a roughly outlined landscape. As opposed to the *Madonna di Foligno* painting and the engravings B.52 and B.53, Christ is standing to the left of his mother. He leans into her legs and is supported by her affectionately. Technically and stylistically, the engraving can be dated to Raimondi's first years in Rome, about 1510–11.[28] We can deduce this from the fine, delicate hatching which has also prompted us to date B.53 to Raimondi's early Roman years. Moreover, the drawing which Raimondi used must have been an idea for the composition of the *Madonna di Foligno*, before Raphael decided to place the Christ Child on Mary's lap. Thus, on compositional and technical grounds the print may even have been produced before the engraving B.53 which is closer to the painting.

Some years later, around 1515 to 1520, Giovanni Antonio da Brescia (*act. c.*1485–*c.*1523) took Raimondi's early engraving of the *Madonna on clouds*,

---

25   An analysis of extant *modelli* by Raphael and his workshop and the prints which were based on them (*c.*40—in some cases it is not entirely clear if the drawings are copies after the original drawings or copies with deviations after the prints), makes this obvious. See in further detail Bloemacher, *Raphael and Raimondi*, Appendix D. For a discussion of the term *modello* see *ibid.*, 53.

26   Bloemacher, *Raffael und Raimondi*, 182–186.

27   Marcantonio Raimondi, *Madonna on Clouds* (B.47), engraving, 176 × 134 mm, Metropolitan Museum of Art, New York, The Elisha Whittlesey Collection, The Elisha Whittlesey Fund, 1949, inv. 49.97.17.

28   Shoemaker and Broun, *The engravings of Marcantonio Raimondi*, 115, fn. 1.

FIGURE 6.5 Giovanni Antonio da Brescia, *Madonna on Clouds*, engraving, 158 × 110 mm, Paris, Bibliothèque Nationale, inv. Reserve EA-31(B, 3) –Boite Ecu

156   BLOEMACHER

B.47, as a model for his own version of the print (Fig. 6.5).[29] Significantly, he did
not rely on the prints B.52 and B.53, which at that time were more up-to-date
and certainly more popular (as we have seen, there already had been a need
to produce a re-edition of the print). Giovanni's engraving is not a copy in
the strict sense. In his smaller print, he adopts the group of Mary and Jesus
from Raimondi's print, but modifies the rest of the composition, creating a
completely different image.[30] Mary and Christ are transferred to the upper
two-thirds of the plate. Below, Giovanni introduces an inscription in Italian
which refers to a Latin prayer printed below. The prayer promises that everyone in Bologna who says it once daily will be protected from the plague: "This
prayer is given by an unnamed preacher saint to the people of Bologna against
the plague. He says that every person who says once a day in honour of the
immaculate conception the said prayer, will never die of the plague" ("*Questa
oratiôe esta denôtiata da uno sâto bô pdicatore / al populo ð bologna côtra peste
el dice cħ[e] qualûque psona / cħ[i] una volta el giorno î honore ð la îmaculata
côceptiôe dira / la dita oratiôe nô potr[a] mai morir di morbo*"). The inscription
continues: "Those who cannot read shall carry the prayer close to their bodies. Its power will hold good for Florence, Siena, Cortona and Volterra as well"

---

29   There is a quite extensive corpus of engravings attributed to Giovanni Antonio da
      Brescia (27 prints signed with "*IO.AN.BX*" plus a varying quantity of unsigned works
      which come close to this nucleus), but not much known about his life and career. Three
      of the prints with signature are also dated. Giovanni Antonio must have belonged
      to the circle of engravers around Mantegna in Mantua. Later on, he engraved after
      Benedetto Montagna and Dürer. From the portrait of Leo x., who became pope in 1513,
      it is deduced that he worked in Rome in the second decade of the 16th century. See:
      Jay A. Levenson, Konrad Oberhuber and Jacquelyn Sheehan, *Early Italian Engravings
      from the National Gallery of Art* (Washington DC: 1973), 235–37; Mark J. Zucker, *Early
      Italian Masters*. Vol. 25 (Commentary). Formerly Volume 13 (part 2). *The Illustrated
      Bartsch*, ed. Walter L. Strauss (New York: 1984), 315; Arthur M. Hind, *Early Italian
      Engraving* [London 1938–1948] Reprint Nendeln (Liechtenstein: 1970), vol. 5, 35;
      Gudula Metze, "Giovanni Antonio da Brescia", *Ars Nova. Frühe Kupferstiche aus Italien.
      Katalog der italienischen Kupferstiche von den Anfängen bis um 1530 in der Sammlung
      des Dresdener Kupferstich-Kabinetts*, exhibition catalogue, ed. Gudula Metze (Petersberg:
      2013), 148.
30   Giovanni Antonio da Brescia, *Madonna and Child on clouds*, engraving, 158 × 110 mm. The
      engraving is not signed, yet Hind argues for an attribution to Giovanni Antonio da Brescia:
      The type on the print is the same compared to signed engravings, such as *Abraham and
      Melchisedek* after Raphael; Hind, *Early Italian Engraving*, 47 and cat. no. 21. Zucker is con-
      vinced by Hinds attribution: he argues that the engraving's technique would be typical for
      Giovanni's later works and the prints should be dated to 1515–1520; Zucker, *Early Italian
      Masters*, 332.

FIGURE 6.6   Marcantonio Raimondi, *Parnassus*, engraving, 359 × 472 mm, Metropolitan Museum of Art, New York Gift of Henry Walters, 1917, inv. 17.37.150

("*chi nô sa legere / la porti adosso e qsto e sperimetato a fireza siena Cortona e voltera*").[31]

In Giovanni Antonio's engraving, Raphael's composition is significantly cropped. The figures' legs are cut off above the knees and concealed by clouds in order to leave space for the inscription. The smaller size of the engraving made it cheaper and allowed its owner to carry it close to his or her body more conveniently, as the inscription recommended. To Giovanni Antonio, the most

---

31   The inscription in the upper left reads: "*S / Ambrosi*[*us*] *Hec ç V*[*ir*]*ga î qua / nec nodus origina- / lis nec cortex ve- / nialis culpe fuit*". It alludes to Sermo 28 of St. Ambrose: "*Hec est virga, in qua nec nodus originalis nec cortex venialis culpe fuit*" (Migne, P. L. 17, Sp. 664). Ambrose was an advocate of Mary's eternal virginity. Therefore, the quote fits the depiction of Mary with Christ child and enforces the cultic character of the print. Below the Madonna is written the text already quoted above in the running text, which is followed by the word "*oratiô*" (prayer). The prayer is eventually printed below in Latin: "*Stella celi extirpauit q*[*uem*] *lactauit dominom mor- / tis pestç quâ platauit prim*[*us*] *parçs hominv / ipsa stella nvc dignet*[*ur*] *sidera pescç quorû / bella plebç scîdût dire mortis ulcç amç*"; cf. Hind, *Early Italian Engraving*, 47. Considering the Italian inscription elucidating that the prayer was recommended to the people of Bologna by a holy preacher against the plague, Ambrosio's quote makes even more sense: he was an important patron saint of the city of Bologna.

important feature of Raimondi's engraving was the motif of Mary and the Christ child and not the refined technique Raimondi used to render Raphael's invention adequately. His engraving is a low-priced product, likely produced on a much larger scale, which aims at a different sort of customer than Raimondi: still the faithful, to whom the religious function of the image was central—yet those with less money and without a direct connection to the original site of both Raphael's painting and the miraculous apparition. The Italian inscription of Giovanni's print only requires a minimum of education and the engraver increased the potential number of buyers by including all those who could not read Latin with his vernacular inscriptions.

The explanatory text below the Madonna in Giovanni Antonio's print, which includes a prayer against the plague given to the Bolognese people by a good and holy priest, suggests that it was intended primarily for distribution in that city. A Bolognese market is also alluded to by the mention of Saint Ambrosius, one of the city's patron saints, in the upper left of the engraving. The inscription below the saint's name also quotes Sermon 28, which identifies Ambrosius as an advocate of Mary's virginity and is perfectly in line with the depiction of the epiphany of the Madonna and Child. The inscription therefore performs a double function: it alludes to Bologna, and it strengthens the cultic character of the image in terms of Marian devotion. In Bologna, most of the customers buying the print would not have known Raphael's painting in Rome and therefore would have been unaware of how closely, or not, Giovanni Antonio was following the altarpiece in his print.

Giovanni Antonio's adaption of Raimondi's engravings in this case and others such as the *Quos Ego* and *Sibyls and Angels* raises the question of whether he was ever part of Raimondi's workshop himself.[32] The likely answer is no. Giovanni Antonio rather seems to have been a follower who tried to participate in the lucrative production that Raimondi and Raphael set up without being authorized to do so and without direct access to Raphael's drawings.[33] He therefore had to rely on prints after Raphael's designs already in circulation by Raimondi and his workshop. Yet his output shows that there was apparently a market for such one-removed copies in Rome and elsewhere.[34]

This analysis of the prints of *Madonna on Clouds* shows that, on the basis of Raphael's invention, a number of different products were generated in print.

---

32   For the other cases see Bloemacher, *Raffael und Raimondi*, 246–258.

33   Oberhuber was the first to hypothesize that Giovanni Antonio da Brescia might have tried to rival Raimondi by engraving some of Raphael's works. Yet Oberhuber did not comment on this hypothesis in further detail; Oberhuber, "Raffaello e l'incisione", 337.

34   The first hypothesis must be credited to Arthur M. Hind; Hind, *Early Italian Engraving*, 47.

Raimondi's three versions for the Roman market focus on the group of Mary and the Christ Child and omit the saints and the donor present in Raphael's painting. Contemplating the print, the buyer does not see the latter adoring the Madonna, but she appears to them directly. The iconic content is thus extracted from the composition, having more relevance and a greater impact on the beholder. Yet it is not only the image's content that counts: an aesthetically ambitious product was created as the direct result of the designer and print-maker working closely together to produce high-quality, marketable engravings. After having transferred a first drawing for the composition to Raimondi to engrave (B.47), Raphael felt the need to publish another version when he changed his design by dynamicizing the child's movement (B.53). This print seems to have been commercially successful as another version was published some time later in which Raphael improved details of his composition (B.52). On a completely different level is Giovanni Antonio da Brescia's print. The printmaker uses Raimondi's engraving as his model, but without the pretense or desire to produce a print that reflects the artistry of Raphael's or Raimondi's work. Giovanni Antonio rather created a low-cost devotional object upon which the text was more important than the image. Thus, we can conclude that variations in quality in prints after Raphael are due to the extent of his collaboration and direct involvement in the process, including the exchange of drawings, but also, significantly, they result from the target-audience of the products. Audience played a defining role in determining their character.

Select Bibliography

Secondary Sources

Bartsch, Adam von, *Le Peintre Graveur*, 21 vols (Vienna: 1802–1821).

Bianchi, Lidia, "La Fortuna di Raffaello nell'Incisione", in *Raffaello: L'opera, le fonte, la fortuna*, ed. Mario Salmi, 2 vols (Novara: 1969).

De Blauw, Sibel, "Das Hochaltarretabel in Rom bis zum frühen 16. Jahrhundert. Das Altarbild als Kategorie der liturgischen Anlage", *Mededelingen van het Nederlands Instituut te Rome*, 55 (1996), 83–110.

Bloemacher, Anne, "Raphael and Marcantonio Raimondi—the empty tablet as a plurivalent sign", *Chicago Art Journal*, 18, 2008, 20–41.

Bloemacher, Anne, "Die Idee als Ware. Marcantonio Raimondis Kupferstiche nach Raffael", *Luxusgegenstände und Kunstwerke vom Mittelalter bis zur Gegenwart. Produktion—Handel—Formen der Aneignung* (Irseer Schriften. Studien zur Wirtschafts-, Kultur- und Mentalitätsgeschichte, Bd. 8), ed. Christoph Jeggle, Andreas Tacke, Markwart Herzog (Konstanz and Munich: 2015), 155–184.

Bloemacher, Anne, *Raffael und Raimondi. Produktion und Intention der frühen Druck-graphik nach Raphael* (Berlin and Munich: 2016).

Bury, Michael, *The Print in Italy, 1550–1620*, exhibition catalogue (London: 2010).

Campbell, Caroline, Dagmar Korbacher, Neville Rowley, and Sarah Vowles, *Mantegna and Bellini: A Renaissance Family*, exhibition catalogue (London: 2018).

Canova, Andrea, "Mantegna Invenit" in *Mantegna 1431–1506*, ed. Giovanni Agosti, and Dominique Thiébaut (Milan: 2008), 243–295.

Canova, Andrea, 'Gian Marco Cavalli incisore per Andrea Mantegna e altre notizie sull'oreficeria e la tipografia a Mantova nel XV secolo', *Italia medioevale e umanistica*, XLII, 2001, 149–181.

Canova, Andrea, 'Andrea Mantegna e Gian Marco Cavalli: nuovi documenti mantovani', *Italia medioevale e umanistica*, XLIII, 2002, 201–229.

Davidson, Bernice, *Marcantonio Raimondi, The engravings of his Roman Period*. Ph.D. thesis Harvard University (Cambridge, MA.: 1954) (unpublished).

Emison, Patricia, "Marcantonio's Massacre of the Innocents", *Print Quarterly*, 1, no. 4 (1984), 257–267.

Emison, Patricia, *Invention and the Italian Renaissance Print, Mantegna to Parmigianino*. Ph.D. Dissertation, Columbia University (New York, NY: 1985).

Emison, Patricia, "Raphael's Multiples", *The Cambridge Companion to Raphael*, ed. Marcia B. Hall (Cambridge: 2005), 186–206.

Faietti, Marzia, "Intorno a Marcantonio", in *Bologna e l'umanesimo 1490–1510*, exhibition catalogue, ed. Marzia Faietti and Konrad Oberhuber (Bologna: 1988), 213–236.

Faietti, Marzia and Konrad Oberhuber, ed., *Bologna e l'umanesimo 1490–1510*, exhibition catalogue (Bologna: 1988).

Gardner von Teuffel, Christa, "Raffaels römische Altarbilder: Aufstellung und Bestimmung", *Zeitschrift für Kunstgeschichte*, 50 (1987), 1–45.

Hind, Arthur Mayger, *Marcantonio and Italian engravers and etchers of the Sixteenth Century* (London: 1912).

Hind, Arthur Mayger, *Early Italian Engraving* [London 1938–1948] Reprint Nendeln (Liechtenstein: 1970), 7 vols.

Kristeller, Paul, "Marcantons Beziehung zu Raffael", *Jahrbuch der Königlich-Preussischen Kunstsammlungen*, 4 (1907), 199–229.

Landau, David and Peter Parshall, *The Renaissance Print 1470–1550* (New Haven and London: 1994).

Levenson, Jay A., Konrad Oberhuber and Jacquelyn Sheehan, *Early Italian Engravings from the National Gallery of Art* (Washington DC: 1973).

Mancinelli, Fabrizio, ed., *Raffaello in Vaticano*, exhibition catalogue (Milan: 1984).

Merlini, Valeria, and Daniele Storti, ed., *Raffaello a Milano. La Madonna di Foligno*, exhibition catalogue (Milan: 2013).

Metze, Gudula, ed., *Ars Nova. Frühe Kupferstiche aus Italien. Katalog der italienischen Kupferstiche von den Anfängen bis um 1530 in der Sammlung des Dresdener Kupferstich-Kabinetts*, exhibition catalogue (Petersberg: 2013).

Meyer zur Capellen, Jürg, *Raphael. A critical catalogue of his paintings. T. II. The Roman religious Paintings ca. 1508–1520* (Landshut: 2005).

Nesselrath, Arnold, "La Madonna di Foligno", *Raffaello a Milano. La Madonna di Foligno*, exhibition catalogue, ed. Valeria Merlini and Daniele Storti (Milan: 2013), 63–73.

Oberhuber, Konrad, "Raffaello e l'incisione", in *Raffaello in Vaticano*, exhibition catalogue, ed. Fabrizio Mancinelli (Milan: 1984), 332–342.

Oberhuber, Konrad, "Marcantonio Raimondi", in *Bologna e l'umanesimo 1490–1510*, exhibition catalogue, ed. Marzia Faietti and Konrad Oberhuber (Bologna: 1988), 51–210.

Partner, Peter, *Renaissance Rome 1500–1559. A Portrait of a Society* (Berkeley: 1976).

Pon, Lisa, *Raphael, Dürer, and Marcantonio Raimondi. Copying and the Italian Renaissance Print* (New Haven and London: 2004).

Popham, Arthur E., and Johannes Wilde, *The Italian drawings of the XV and XVI centuries in the collection of His Majesty the King at Windsor Castle* (London: 1949).

Shoemaker, Innis H., "Marcantonio and his Sources. A Survey of His Style and Engraving Techniques", in *The engravings of Marcantonio Raimondi*, exhibition catalogue, ed. Innis H. Shoemaker and Elizabeth Broun (Lawrence: 1981), 3–18.

Shoemaker, Innis H. and Elizabeth Broun ed., *The engravings of Marcantonio Raimondi*, exhibition catalogue (Lawrence: 1981).

Wouk, Edward H., "Introduction: Marcantonio Raimondi, Raphael and the image multiplied", in *Raphael, Raimondi and the image multiplied*, exhibition catalogue, ed. Edward H. Wouk and David Morris (Manchester: 2016), 10–11.

Wouk, Edward H., and David Morris (ed.), *Raphael, Raimondi and the image multiplied*, exhibition catalogue (Manchester: 2016).

Zucker, Mark J., *Early Italian Masters*, vol. 25 (Commentary). Formerly Volume 13 (part 2). The Illustrated Bartsch, ed. Walter L. Strauss (New York: 1984).

CHAPTER 7

Copying Motifs and Reworking Printing Plates as Part of the French Royal Propaganda in the First Half of the 17th Century

Małgorzata Biłozór-Salwa

The importance of printed materials such as leaflets, brochures, pamphlets, and small books for the dissemination of ideas and the shaping of attitudes can be linked to the Reformation in Germany (1517–1555).[1] The deliberate use of mass-scale printing (and above all printed images) for propaganda purposes was first seen in German-speaking lands in the first half of the 16th century. Most of this propaganda concerned the promotion of works by Martin Luther (1483–1546).[2] Alongside Luther's ideas, the production of printed propaganda spread rapidly through Europe. Thanks to a growing mass of "popular" prints produced for commercial sale, large audiences could now be reached in a short time. In France, this was discovered in spectacular style when, on the night of the 17th of October 1534, Paris and the surrounding towns were "flooded" by huge quantities of Protestant broadsheets (*placards*). Known as *L'Affaire des Placards*, the event has been regarded as the symbolic beginning of the Reformation in France.[3]

More than half a century later, the power of prints was skilfully exploited by the French King Henry IV (1553–1610), who used print to fashion a public image of a brave and victorious ruler in the face of religious and political turmoil.[4] It was during Henry's reign that a special type of "popular" print,

---

1 Wolfgang Brückner, *Populäre Druckgraphik Europas. Deutchland von 15. biz zum 20 Jahrhundert* (Munich: 1969), 41–67.
2 Mark U. Jr. Edwards, *Printing, Propaganda, and Martin Luther* (Minneapolis: 2005), 1–13.
3 Francis Higman, "Le livre et les propagandes religieuses Le levain de l'Évangile", in: *Histoire de l'édition française. Le livre conquérant du Moyen-Âge au milieu du XVIIᵉᵐᵉ siècle*, edited by Roger Chartier, Henri-Jean Martin, vol. 1 (Paris: 1982), 309; David El Kenz, "La propagande et le problème de sa réception, d'après les mémoires-journaux de Pierre de L'Estoile", *Cahiers d'histoire. Revue d'histoire critique* 90–91 (2003), 30.
4 José Lothe, "Images d'actualité éditées à Paris sous le règne d'Henri IV", in *L'estampe au Grand Siècle. Études offertes à Maxime Préaud*, ed. Peter Fuhring, Barbara Brejon de Lavergnée et al. (Paris: 2010), 57; Margaret M. McGowan, "The French Royal Entry in the Renaissance: The Status of Printed Text", *French Ceremonial Entries in the Sixteenth Century: Event, Image, Text*, ed. Nicolas Russell, Hélène Visentin (Toronto: 2007), 33–50.

© KONINKLIJKE BRILL BV, LEIDEN, 2024 | DOI:10.1163/9789004703834_009

COPYING MOTIFS AND REWORKING PRINTING PLATES 163

combining text and image, was developed. Broadsheets called *images d'actualité*, or *occasionnels* set pictures above letterpress text on a single sheet of paper. They covered news of important events such as skirmishes, battles, triumphal entries and captured cities, as well as reporting upon celebrations related to the monarchy such as royal christenings, coronations and marriages.

Broadsheets, as well as single-sheet printed images without text (*images volantes*), targeted everyone with their ideological messages, not just the educated classes. The evidence for this is twofold. Firstly, thanks to printed images, even the illiterate could engage with the content of propaganda. Secondly, the contemporary practice of reading was not limited to private reading as it is today. Published directives, proclamations, announcements and descriptions of important events were broadcast to wide audiences by being read out in public. Broadsheets were also frequently designed in such a way that it was the large image, occupying the top half of the page, which first attracted attention and encouraged the viewer to read the description below, if they could. The development and increasing production of such prints in France can be associated with the rules of Henry IV and his son Louis XIII (1601–1643).

When the Protestant King Henry IV ascended the throne in 1589, he had to face the Catholic League which controlled the vast majority of the Parisian market of print-publishers. As a result, most printed materials addressing religion and the monarchy attacked both Protestantism and the King. In 1594, having recanted his own Protestantism after years of religious wars, Henry ordered the burning of all the printed images related to the Catholic League, which remained hostile to him.[5] Being deeply aware of the persuasive power of printed images, the King's propagandists produced a vast quantity of engraved portraits depicting Henry as a valiant absolute ruler. The same imagery of the king also appeared on medals, coins and occasional triumphal arches, but it was printed materials that most effectively disseminated the propagandistic message.[6]

After the 1610 assassination of Henry IV by a religious fanatic, Queen Marie de' Medici (1575–1642) became Regent for their young son Louis XIII. She continued to make use of Henry IV's propaganda machine. An excellent example

---

5 Roger Chartier, "Stratégies éditoriales et lectures populaires, 1530–1660," in: *Histoire de l'édition française. Le livre conquérant du Moyen-Âge au milieu du XVII ᵉᵐᵉ siècle*, edited by Roger Chartier, Henri-Jean Martin, vol. 1 (Paris: 1982), 595.

6 Corrado Vibanti, "Henry IV, the Gallic Hercules," *Journal of the Warburg and Courtauld Institutes*, 30 (1967), 176–197; Marie-Claude Canova-Green, "Warrior King or King of War? Louis XIII's Entries into his Bonnes Villes (1620–1629)," in *Ceremonial Entries in Early Modern Europe. The Iconography of Power*, ed. J. R. Mulryne, Maria Ines Aliverti, Anna Maria Testaverde (Routledge: 2016), 77–98.

is the series of official publications that were produced to celebrate the double marriage she arranged between Louis XIII and Anne of Austria (1601–1666), and Philip IV (1605–1665), the future King of Spain, and Elizabeth of France (1602–1644). The so-called "Spanish marriages", which took place in 1615, were intended to guarantee a political alliance between France and Spain, two of the most powerful European monarchies and traditional rivals. The fact that the children were far too young for marriage when the alliance was first made in 1612 did not prevent the Queen Mother from celebrating it in a three-day carrousel at the Place Royale in Paris. An essential element was the publications that disseminated news of the French royal festivities (and diplomatic triumph) across Europe. The Lvov-born, Parisian draughtsman and printmaker Jan Ziarnko, also known as Jean le Grain (*act.* 1598–1629) was one of the printmakers involved in this propagandistic process, producing two prints representing the *Carrousel at the Place Royale* in 1612. The first one is a spectacular etching for the broadsheet, the second, as a smaller version was used as a book illustration.[7] Ziarnko is also the author of numerous other etchings for broadsheets that became instruments of printed propaganda. Later printmakers exploited the persuasive function of these prints by Ziarnko through altering his plates to suit the needs of successive rulers. The remainder of this essay will address four instances in which Ziarnko's plates were reworked and modified.

Louis XIII's coming of age was publicly announced on the day of the King's thirteenth birthday, the 27th of September 1614. This brought the Regency of Marie de' Medici to an official end, although she remained the *de facto* ruler of France. Under pressure from the nobles in the camp of her staunchest opponent Henri, Prince of Condé (1588–1646), the Queen Mother decided to call an assembly of the Estates-General following Louis' birthday. The assembly had served as an advisory body to the monarch from the 14th century onwards and comprised of representatives of the three estates (the clergy, the nobility, and the Third Estate—the commoners or the rest of society). Marie hoped that calling it would help to reinforce the young King's, and thus her own, position against rival factions at court.[8] Crucially, the fanfare surrounding the event

---

7   Jan Ziarnko, *Carrousel at the Place Royale*, 1612, etching; Stanisława Sawicka, "Jan Ziarnko peintre-graveur polonais et son activité a Paris au premier quart du XVIIe siècle", in *La France et la Pologne dans leurs relation artistiques* 2–3 (1938), 101–257; Małgorzata Biłozór-Salwa, "Paryski Karuzel 1612 roku, czyli skały tryskające winem, grające góry i tańczące konie na usługach propagandy władzy," *Rocznik Biblioteki Narodowej*, 44 (2014), 113–358; Małgorzata Biłozór-Salwa, *Jan Ziarnko czy Jean le Grain? Twórczość lwoskiego artysty w XII-wiecznym Paryżu* (Warszawa: 2021), 51–58, 182–184, no. 7–8.

8   Joseph H. Shennan, *The Bourbons: the history of a dynasty* (London: 2009), 66–67.

COPYING MOTIFS AND REWORKING PRINTING PLATES   165

also provided a timely opportunity to publicize and promote the monarchy's strength in print.[9]

One of the most famous illustrations of the assembly was a broadsheet called *The Assembly of the Estates-General in 1614*, published the same year by Jean Le Clerc IV (*fl.* 1560–1622) (Fig. 7.1). It consisted of an etching of the assembly by Ziarnko incorporating both a dedication addressed to the Queen Mother by Jean-Baptiste Du Val and an inscription detailing the characters portrayed in the print. The text of the dedication shows that the print was intended to strengthen not only Louis's position, but also that of the Queen Mother. The author praised Marie's qualities as a ruler and reminded the audience that she was the wife of Henry IV, the greatest king on earth.

On its surface, the print appears to accurately relate the events of the historical assembly. The great hall of the palace Hôtel du Petit Bourbon in Paris, where the assembly took place, is depicted from above.[10] Inside, Ziarnko carefully delineates the representatives of all three estates and, in fine detail in the centre of the composition, there is a group of courtiers attending to the enthroned King and Queen Mother. However, on closer inspection, the broadsheet bears the very distinct qualities of a propaganda poster. In the top part of the print there are symbolic figures of Peace and Justice and the royal escutcheons of Bourbon and Navarre illuminated by divine light, which enrich the scene and glorify the king and monarchy in general. Visible in the lower part of the etching, geniuses support the crowned coat of arms of Marie de' Medici and form a kind of allegorical pendant to the main image, celebrating the Queen Mother's political triumph.

As we have seen, the Queen Mother played a significant role in the preparations for an assembly of the Estates-General. She managed to delay its opening until the end of the Regency, so that the King could appear to be acting as a mature and autonomous ruler. The delay had also allowed the young monarch to carry out a number of state visits to major provincial towns. In less than two months, Louis XIII and his mother had visited Blois, Tours, Poitiers, Angers and Nantes.[11] Each time, the arrival of the ruler was a spectacle and a manifestation of royal power. He entered the city in solemn procession, passing through

---

9   The same approach was used by the Queen for the celebrations of the so-called "Spanish marriages" (*les mariages espagnols*) in 1612. Biłozór-Salwa, "Paryski Karuzel 1612", 113–358.

10   Jan Ziarnko, *Assembly of the Estates-General in 1614*, etching published by Jean Le Clerc, 1614; Sawicka, "Jan Ziarnko", 162, No. 10; Biłozór-Salwa, *Jan Ziarnko*, 51–58, 58–63, no. 13.

11   Hélène Duccini, *Faire voir, faire croire. L'opinion publique sous Louis XIII* (Seyssel: 2003), 157.

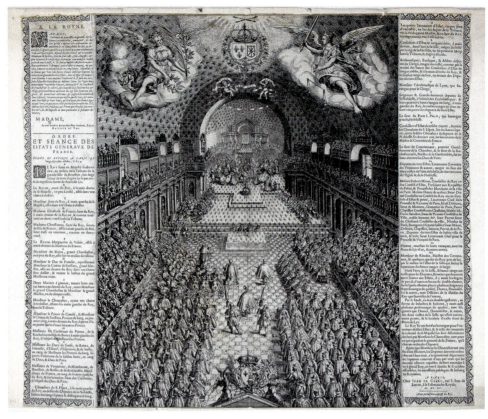

FIGURE 7.1 Jan Ziarnko, *The Assembly of the Estates-General in 1614*, state II, 1615, etching and engraving

triumphal arches and other ephemeral decorations.[12] The ideological program, expressed through painted and sculpted ornament, as well as speeches and performed songs, was a tribute to the King. Louis was extolled and addressed as the successor to his late father's achievements. Thereby a language of symbols and a set of motifs originally developed for the needs of Henry IV were recycled for his young son.

An inscription on Ziarnko's etching testifies to the continuity between the iconographic program of the royal travels and the assembly of the representatives of the Estates-General. For instance, a legend placed on the sash supported by the putti, located at the top centre of the composition, states: "For a long time, looking at the world with kindness".[13] This is a direct reference to the

12 Alison Sounders, *The Seventeenth-century French Emblem: A Study in Diversity* (Geneva: 2000), 257–258.
13 *"Oculus orbi diu bonus"*.

COPYING MOTIFS AND REWORKING PRINTING PLATES   167

ideological program of the triumphal arch through which Louis XIII entered Angers on the 8th of August 1614.[14] The archway featured two Latin anagrams of the King's name. The first—"Louis Bourbon. You are the only sun in an uncertain world"—compared the king to the sun shining over France, illuminating the kingdom with his care and kindness.[15] The second was identical with the inscription on Ziarnko's etching: "Louis Bourbon. For a long time you look at the world with kindness".[16] Thus, the position of the monarch was symbolically reinforced before the opening of the assembly of the Estates-General.

Every element of Ziarnko's etching of the assembly of the Estates-General performed a carefully considered function, which was tied to the needs of monarchy at the time of its original publication. Later printmakers who returned to and retouched various aspects of his plate took equal care to update the plate to reflect a changing political environment. At present, two states of the Ziarnko's etching related to two consecutive editions of the broadsheet are known. A year after it was first published, changes were made to three key areas of the plate (Fig. 7.2.a). The first concerned the table visible in the centre of the composition, where ten Secretaries were originally seated (a group marked with the letter Q). During the reworking of the plate, their number was reduced to four. An immediate result of this was that the composition gained in clarity, as the eye of the viewer was now more clearly directed towards the King seated in a niche. From a subject matter point of view, however, leaving the Secretaries sitting on only one side of the presidential table also created an impression of confrontation with the rest of the assembly. The table became a barrier separating the King from the representatives of the estates.

Another change that increased the sense of conflict between the monarch and the representatives is the alteration of the figure of Robert Miron (1569–1641). Marked with letters "Bb" on the plate, Miron was the leader of merchants, so a representative of the Third Estate. Initially, Ziarnko showed him standing next to Pierre V de Roncherolle, baron du Pont S. Pierre (*d.* 1627), who is shown speaking on behalf of the nobility. The second state of the plate was reworked to show Miron kneeling (Fig. 7.2.b). Thus the image of the

---

14   The exact description of the ceremony and the occasional monuments can be found in Jehan Louvet's diary published in 1855. Jehan Louvet, "Journal ou Récit véritable de tout ce qui est advenu digne de mémoire tant en la ville d'Angers, pays d'Anjou et autres lieux (depuis l'an 1560–jusqu'à l'an 1634)," *Revue de l'Anjou et de Maine et Loire*, 1, no. 4 (1855), 129–192.

15   "*Ludovicus Borbonius. Tu sol unus orbi dubio*". Louvet, "Journal ou Récit," 133. My thanks to Isabela Wiencek-Sielska for her assistance with translating the Latin quotations.

16   "*Ludovicus Borbonius. Oculus orbi diu bonus*". Louvet, "Journal ou Récit," 133.

FIGURE 7.2.A
Jan Ziarnko, *The Assembly of the Estates-General in 1614* (detail), state I, 1614, etching

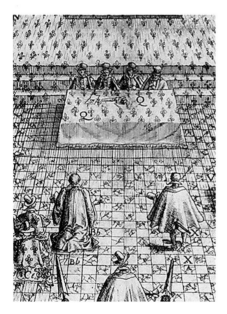

FIGURE 7.2.B
Jan Ziarnko, *The Assembly of the Estates-General in 1614* (detail), state II, 1615, etching and engraving

COPYING MOTIFS AND REWORKING PRINTING PLATES 169

representative of the Third Estate was changed so that he now addressed the monarch as a person of a distinctly lower social status.[17]

The nature of these corrections, made one year after the event, indicates that the plate was purposely manipulated, on behalf of the monarchy, in accordance with current political goals. In the first state, the table was a common point of connection between all the secretaries sitting around it. This reflects the ambition of the King and Queen Mother, at the time of calling the estates general, of stressing their unity against rival factions at court, led by the Prince of Condé. The altered composition instead emphasizes the powerful position of the monarch and underlines the distance between him and the representatives of the estates, especially from the Third Estate. This reflects the ensuing political dispute, which played out in the assembly against the monarchy's wishes and was the subject of a great number of occasional prints and pamphlets.[18] All the Estates united against the King to fight for the abolition of the King's tax and the suppression of corruption in public institutions. The King, however, remained absolute and would countenance no concessions. Hélène Duccini describes the publications that appeared in France during the period 1614–1615 in relation to the Estates-General as "the war of words" (*guerre des mots*).[19] As the example of Ziarnko's etching shows, it was also a war of images. In the end, attempts to empower the estates and reform existing social divisions resulted in complete failure, and the King's position as God's anointed ruler was strengthened.

The final change made to Ziarnko's etching was the addition of a man in court clothes, standing directly behind the enthroned ruler on his right, between the monarch and the Queen. This placement emphasizes the extremely privileged position of the man and could also suggest his strong influence on the King and Queen Mother. Given his influence, it is a fair assumption that this figure is intended to represent the Queen's favourite, the nobleman and politician Concino Concini, from 1613 known as the Marshal d'Ancre (1575–1617).[20] His power was a result of his profound influence on the Queen, and this led the

---

17 Bussey, Georges Moir, and Thomas Gaspey, *The pictorial history of France and the French people* (London: 1843), vol. 2, 326.

18 Jeffrey K. Sawyer, *Printed Poison. Pamphlet Propaganda, Faction Politics, and the Public Sphere in Early Seventeenth-Century France* (Oxford: 1990), 107–111.

19 Duccini, *Faire voir*, 191–267.

20 Sawicka, "Jan Ziarnko", 177; Małgorzata Biłozór-Salwa, "The Monogram of the Virgin Mary (1605) by Jan Ziarnko as Maria de Medici's Watchword", in *Polish Emblems*, vol. 1 (2016), http://polishemblems.uw.edu.pl/index.php/en/news-uk/43-news-text-2, access: 1.06.2016. Although it is intriguing that the facial features of the mysterious man in the print match those of Concini, it is not possible to definitively confirm this hypothesis.

representatives of the Estates-General to demand his removal. As Ziarnko's broadsheet reflects the interests of the Queen Mother and her circle so directly, it was, in all likelihood, both produced and altered on the orders of someone in its immediate confines. The original appearance of the image was changed to suit the political climate of the times, in accordance with the position of the monarchy. Although in technical terms the changes were minor, they carried a clear propaganda message.

A similar compositional interference, though somewhat more intrusive, can be observed in another of Ziarnko's works. His etching documenting the *Assembly of Notables in Rouen* (Fig. 7.3) was created as an illustration to another broadside by Le Clerc IV.[21] Similarly to the Estates-General, the Assembly of Notables functioned as an advisory body to the King, but was subjected to him to a much greater extent. In 1617, the Assembly of Notables was convened in order to calm the public mood as, in the spring of that year, the general discontent with the activities of Concini had led to riots skilfully incited by the Prince of Condé and Concini's house was ransacked by the angry mob.[22] Eventually, the young King, on the advice of his courtiers, decided to definitively solve the problem of Marie's ambitious favourite as part of a wider scheme to gradually remove his mother from power. Concini was duly assassinated, and the sixteen-year-old monarch broke away from the influence of his mother's circle.[23] Calling the Assembly of Notables was a political act undertaken to confirm the King's independent power. The opening ceremony took place on Monday the 4th of December in Rouen in the presence of the King, while the debates were presided over by his younger brother, the nine-year-old Gaston Jean-Baptiste, duc d'Orléans (1608–1660).

Ziarnko's print depicting the assembly uses a similar viewpoint to the *Assembly of the Estates-General*, looking down on the scene from above. However, the complex symbolic motifs of the former print were abandoned. The only symbol now present is the crowned coat of arms of France and Navarre at the bottom of the picture. The top of the composition features the

---

21 The original title of the broadsheet reads *Ordre tenu en la premiere seance de l'Assemblee des Notables Rouen and tenue au Mois de Decembre* 1617. Sawicka, "Jan Ziarnko," 167–168, No 18; Biłozór-Salwa, *Jan Ziarnko*, 51–58, 182–184, no. 7–8.

22 Ziarnko executed an etching for the broadsheet commemorating this event, Jan Ziarnko, *Hunting Foxes and Thieves*, 1617, etching; Sawicka, "Jan Ziarnko", 165, No 14; Biłozór-Salwa, *Jan Ziarnko*, 201, no. 18.

23 The death and desecration of Concini's body were also immortalized by Ziarnko. Jan Ziarnko, *Satire on Concino Concini'c life and death*, 1617, etching; Sawicka, "Jan Ziarnko", 165–166, No 15; Biłozór-Salwa, *Jan Ziarnko*, 202–203, No. 19–20.

COPYING MOTIFS AND REWORKING PRINTING PLATES 171

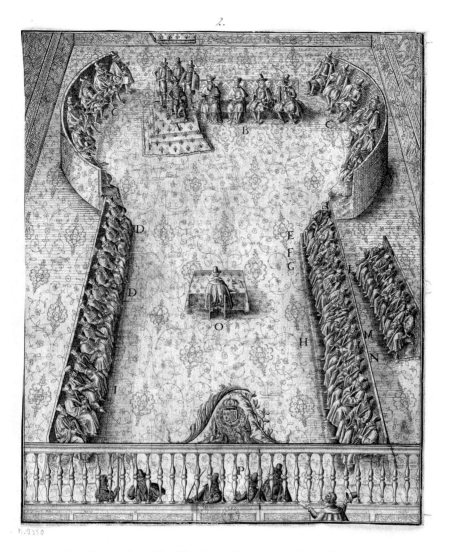

FIGURE 7.3 Jan Ziarnko, *Assembly of Notables in Rouen*, state I, 1617, etching

King's brother, with his closest advisers, presiding over the meeting. On either side of him, notables are seated on benches.

In the catalogue raisonée of Ziarnko's *oeuvre*, Stanisława Sawicka identifies three states of this print, which were used in successive editions of the broadsheet.[24] She pinpoints the exact modifications introduced at each occasion. The alterations made to the second state, especially to the right section

---

24   Sawicka, "Jan Ziarnko", 168, no. 18; Biłozór-Salwa, *Jan Ziarnko*, 204–206, no. 21–22.

of the composition, mostly relate to changes in the seating arrangement of the notables and can easily escape the attention of the viewer (Fig. 7.4). For example, the bench in the second row on the right was modified and the number of notables sitting on it changed from six to four. Somewhat more difficult to miss are the changes to the immediate surroundings of the royal brother, visible in the proof of the third state, and reflected in the legend of the poster. In the first two states, the majesty of the Prince was expressed by placing his throne under a canopy on a two-step platform. Later changes in the third state burnished out this platform. The canopy, emphasizing his splendour, was also removed. The low-ranking tutor to the Prince, Mr. Demansan, disappeared, while the figure of the Master of Ceremonies, Charles Perrochel (*act.* 1597–1629), was added behind Cardinal Jacques du Perron (1556–1618), seated on the Prince's left.

All these changes to the plate were related to the shifting social or political status of the individuals portrayed. The effort invested in repositioning characters in the print also demonstrates the important role such details clearly played in printed propaganda. Equally notable is that Ziarnko, who must have known the rules of perspective, completely abandoned them in this instance.[25] All the individuals depicted in the immediate vicinity of the Prince, including the representatives facing the viewer and sitting on the semi-circular benches, were therefore significantly enlarged in relation to others.

A short introductory text by the publisher, placed underneath the etching, explains some of the problems Ziarnko encountered, which resulted in the need to make a rapid series of changes to the plate. The reader is told that the broadsheet was made on the 11th of December, so only two days after the event took place. Furthermore, the publisher states that in the first week after the opening ceremony nothing much was achieved by the representatives, except for the negotiating the seating arrangements of the delegates and their agenda. It is therefore probable that the correct seating of the representatives, which *de facto* defined their social position, changed during the first week of the assembly.

The examples discussed above clearly demonstrate how important it was for royal propaganda, and for Queen Marie de' Medici in particular, to disseminate appropriate information about important events. During her regency state celebrations were organised in such a way that as to allow as many people

---

25   Ziarnko's interest in the issue of perspective was reflected by his treatise on the creation of conic anamorphoses. Małgorzata Biłozór-Salwa, "Teoria tworzenia anamorfoz", *Rocznik Historii Sztuki*, 39 (2014): 43–53; Ada Pałka, "Jan Ziarnko's Anamorphic Print A Pair of Lovers Embracing," *Print Quarterly*, 32, no. 1 (2015), 3–13; Małgorzata Biłozór-Salwa, "Anamorphosis as a Tool for Presenting Erotic Subjects: Some Remarks on Jan Ziarnko's Lovers," in *"The most Noble of the Senses". Anamorphosis, Trompe-L'Oeil, and Other Optical Illusions in Early Modern Art*, ed. Lilian H. Zirpolo (Ramsey: 2016), 29–48.

COPYING MOTIFS AND REWORKING PRINTING PLATES   173

FIGURE 7.4 Jan Ziarnko, *Assembly of Notables in Rouen*, state III, 1617, etching and engraving

as possible to participate in them. This is evidenced by the number of state visits to provincial French towns in 1614 and by the Carousel organized in the city space in 1612 for the first time. Previously, this genre of royal performances had been held exclusively in royal palaces. What is more, the magnificence of these events was to be testified not only by eyewitnesses, but also through printed descriptions and images. Printed materials reached a much wider audience, both outside Paris and abroad. Easily transportable prints spread rapidly, and thanks to them so did the royal propaganda. Additionally, these images were sometimes immediately copied as it was the case of *Carrousel at the Place Royale* repeated in contemporary German etchings.[26]

The practice of making compositional changes on the plates of existing etchings was widely practiced for a number of reasons. Printmakers corrected errors, modified compositions, responded to the needs of clients or, as in the celebrated case of Rembrandt van Rijn, searched for the best artistic effect.[27] Another type of alteration was often made to Ziarnko's works, for a purpose completely different to that of the original prints and which reflected publishing practices of the time. At the beginning of the 17th century, printing plates and blocks typically belonged to publishers. After their death, they became the property of their heirs along with the entire printing house. Often, publishers conducted an exchange or traded plates, so that they could expand their stock of published material at a relatively low cost.[28] Changes to plates were regularly made following such a change of ownership, to indicate the new publisher's details, for instance. The reworking of plates was also linked to their restoration, if any damage occurred during the printing process and engravers frequently deepened the lines to extend the life span of a plate. In general, however, they tried not to change the original appearance of the print. One such etching by Ziarnko, in which the new publisher only added an inscription, without making any changes to the original composition, is *The Story of the Turnip presented to Louis XI* (before 1629).[29] The print illustrates an anecdote described by Erasmus of Rotterdam in *Colloquia Familiaris* about a poor peasant who gave the king an extraordinary turnip. As a reward he received a pair of gold bellows. Seeing this, one of the courtiers wanted to receive a higher

---

26 Dietrich Meier, *Fireworks in Paris*, 1612, etching and Anonymous, *Fireworks in Paris*, 1612, etching, Biłozór-Salwa *Jan Ziarnko*, 182–183, no. 7.

27 Ad Stijnman, *Engraving and Etching 1400–2000. A History of Development of Manual Intaglio Printing Processes* (London and Houten: 2012), 152–153.

28 Marianne Grivel, *Le Commerce de l'estampe a Paris au XVIIᵉ siècle* (Geneva: 1986), 74–82.

29 Jan Ziarnko, *The Story of the Turnip presented to Louis XI*, before 1629, etching, Sawicka, "Jan Ziarnko", 175–176, No. 34; Biłozór-Salwa, *Jan Ziarnko*, 240–241, no. 42.

reward and offered the king a beautiful horse. In return he received a turnip.[30] In the 1640s the plate for the print was in the possession of Jacques Lagniet, who ordered a new inscription explaining the illustrated story.

In several instances, new editions of Ziarnko's etchings were published only after the composition had been changed considerably. The earliest of these prints has not been attributed to the artist in previous scholarship and can be found in the *Almanac for the year 1617*, published by the little-known Parisian publisher Bonaventure Mezoulle (*act.* 1605–1617). At the beginning of the 17th century, almanacs enjoyed great popularity in France. They included the days of the week throughout the year and all the church holidays. They were also supplemented by a variety of information on the phases of the moon, the powerful influence of certain planets, as well as all kinds of calculations and predictions for the future.[31] A special type of almanac was also developed in France, similar in form to *placards*. Such poster-like almanacs incorporated a printed calendar and an engraved frame. As these publications reached large audiences, almanacs were excellent disseminators of ideas.[32]

An etching made by Ziarnko for the *Almanac for the year 1617* was prophetic in character (Fig. 7.5).[33] In the centre of the composition, the young Louis XIII appears on a rampant horse, wielding a sword. Behind him is a host of armed men, trampling the fallen, and chasing the fleeing hordes of Turks. The image alludes to the now largely forgotten idea of organizing a pan-European crusade against the Turks. From 1616, the French monk Père Joseph (Leclerc du Tremblay) (1577–1638) promoted the idea of combining the major forces of the Christian world under the leadership of the French King.[34] His task was to recapture Jerusalem and expel the Turks from Europe. Père Joseph, a close collaborator of Cardinal Richelieu (1585–1642) called *eminence grise*, had a large influence on French foreign policy. He failed, however, to make the crusade a reality. In 1616, the 15-year-old Louis XIII had no actual experience of war. So, when making his etching for the almanac, Ziarnko drew on Henry IV's legacy instead. He made a clear reference to the rich iconography of the valiant Henry IV in the image, who was often portrayed on a rampant horse. Above the

---

30   Jan Ziolkowski, *The Medieval Latin Past of Wonderful Lies* (Michigan: 2009), 176.

31   Hervé Drévillon, *Lire et écrire l'avenir. L'astrologie dans la France du Grand Siècle (1610–1715)* (Seyssel: 1996) 145–150.

32   In the second half of the 17th century such elaborate almanacs were an important element in the fabrication of Louis XIV's image. Peter Burke, *Fabrication of Louis XIV* (London: 1992), 29.

33   Biłozór-Salwa, *Jan Ziarnko*, 113–116, 197–198, no. 16.

34   Pierre Benoist, "Le père Joseph, l'empire Ottoman et la Méditerranée au début du XVIIe siècle," *Cahiers de la Méditerranée*, vol. 71 (2005), 189.

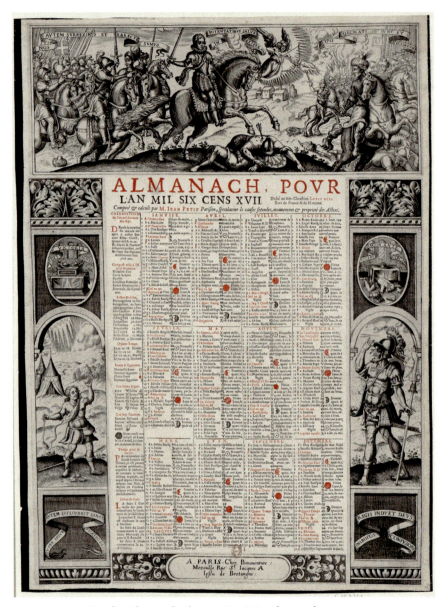

FIGURE 7.5 Jan Ziarnko, *Almanac for the year 1617*, 1616, etching and engraving

COPYING MOTIFS AND REWORKING PRINTING PLATES 177

monarch's head is an angel shooting arrows of fire. The motif recalls the vision of the salvation of Israel, described in the Old Testament's Book of Zechariah.[35] The angel also symbolizes divine blessing and acts as guarantor of the success of the whole undertaking.

Ziarnko's print showing the defeat of the Turks is placed at the top of the sheet of paper, above the tables of the almanac. He also made two decorative vignettes, positioned on both sides of the folio, which form a decorative border. The two vignettes, which should be read together, illustrate the dynamic battle between David and Goliath. Thus, a story of the triumph of good over evil drawn from the Old Testament is used to supplement to the concept of an almanac which presents a prophecy of Christian victory over the Turks. Ziarnko's etching does not refer to a real event, but to a vision of the future: with the King as the most important ruler of the Christian world who commands the joint Christian armies against their common enemy, following in the footsteps of his late father Henry IV, who was a brave and victorious leader, too.

Eleven years later, Ziarnko's plate for the almanac was reused by the renowned Parisian publisher, Michel de Mathonière (1573–1640) for the illustrated broadside *The victory over the English troops by the royal army* (Fig. 7.6).[36] At that time, Louis XIII's military career was truly flourishing, as he led numerous clashes against the French Huguenots. *The victory over the English troops* was an excellent opportunity to celebrate and spread the news of the glory of the French royal army. That is why Mathonière reused Ziarnko's almanac image in a broadside praising the royal exploits in a poetic manner. The retouched etching was printed on the same sheet as the description of the battle, which recalled descriptions from Pierre Corneille's (1606–1684) tragic comedy in *Le Cid*.[37] Although the overall composition of Ziarnko's image corresponded only slightly to the textual description of the battle, the later printmaker made sure all the key details matched. He completely transformed upper part of the image. Lances, banners with inscriptions, and the angel leading the Christian army were all burnished out. In their place, he depicted the sea with the ships of the British fleet. The facial features of the king are also changed to resemble those of the Jean Caylar d'Anduze de Saint-Bonnet, Marshal de Toiras (1585–1636). As a new inscription on the plate states, the

---

35 Za. 8:13–15.

36 *The victory over the English troops by the royal army*, broadsheet with Jan Ziarnko's etching reworked, edited by Michel de Mathonière, 1627; Paris, Bibliothèque Nationale de France, Reserve Fol-QB-201 (24) [Hennin 2121].

37 Duccini, *Faire voir*, 413.

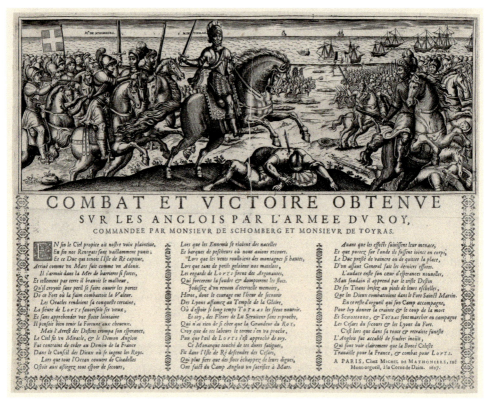

FIGURE 7.6 *The victory over the English troops by the royal army*, broadsheet with Jan Ziarnko's etching reworked, edited by Michel de Mathonière, 1627, etching and engraving

Marshal de Toiras, together with Marshal Henri de Schomberg (1575–1632), led the battle. The author of later these changes took great care to remove all visual references to the Turk. He transformed the headgear of the commander of the Turkish troops into a European helmet; the turban lying on the ground was transformed into a stone, and another one was removed altogether. Through this relatively minor reworking of the plate, the character of the entire print was transformed.

Reusing readymade plates reduced the cost of printing and also accelerated the process of production considerably. The speed of publication was of great importance for publications of the *Images d'actualité* type. The quick reaction of publishers was essential in shaping the public image of rulers who took the throne suddenly, as a result of unforeseen circumstances. For instance, the unexpected death of Henry IV, apart from its political consequences, had a real impact on the situation of Parisian artists. In the spring of 1610, numerous

COPYING MOTIFS AND REWORKING PRINTING PLATES

artists, poets, musicians, but also engravers and publishers, were working on the preparations of the solemn entry of Marie de' Medici following her coronation on the 13th of May.[38] Due to the death of her husband this never became reality, and the joyful celebrations were replaced by mourning ceremonies. In such rapidly changing circumstances, publishers who reacted quickly made great material gains. Winning the favour of the new ruler brought opportunities to obtain prestigious commissions and privileges.

It is telling that prints showing the Dauphin as King were already being sold in Paris on the 17th of May, only two days after the nine-year-old Louis XIII became King.[39] On the 22nd of May, two experienced publishers, Jean Le Clerc IV and Robert III Estienne (*fl.* 1572–1629) presented to the child-king (*roi-enfant*) an exceptional piece of work. It was a broadsheet comprising a copperplate engraving showing an equestrian portrait of Louis XIII executed by Jan van Halbeeck (*d.* 1630), and a sonnet praising the new king composed by Estienne. The whole broadsheet was embellished with a highly decorative border, made with woodcut illustrations originally published as designs for lace. According to Maxime Préaud, the sheet is an excellent example of "the art of using up leftovers".[40] To produce this decorative broadside, old wood blocks were used, together with a new engraving. It is possible that the engraving was created a little earlier, as the portrait of the Prince. Nevertheless, it clearly referred back to official portraits of Henry IV.

The strategy of adopting the iconographic models of previous rulers for those of their successors was widespread. Besides broadsheets and ceremonial portraits, it was a common feature of early-modern maps. The idea of using a city map for propaganda purposes was exploited for the first time in France by Henry IV, and then by Marie de' Medici as Queen Mother.[41] It was most probably Marie de' Medici or someone from her entourage who commissioned in 1616 a barely known map of Paris etched by Ziarnko (Fig. 7.7). It measures 674 × 494 mm and is composed of four sheets printed on separate

---

38   Marie de Medici was crowned Queen of France on the 13th of May 1610 in the Basilica of Saint-Denis near Paris. A ceremonial entry of the Queen to the city was planned for the 16th of May. It never took place as on the 14th of May Henry IV was assassinated.

39   Philippe Rouillard, "Van Halbeeck et vieilles dentelles," in *L'estampe au Grand Siècle. Études offertes à Maxime Préaud*, ed. Peter Fuhring, Barbara Brejon de Lavergnée et al. (Paris: 2010), 67–78.

40   "*L'art d'accommoder les restes*", Rouillard, "Van Halbeeck", 77.

41   This map is discussed in detail in an essay written for the British Library project *Picturing Places*: Małgorzata Biłozór-Salwa, *The printed map as a tool of political struggle: Paris is well worth a ... map.* [https://www.bl.uk/picturing-places/articles/the-printed-map -as-a-tool-of-political-struggle-paris-is-well-worth-a-map access 1.06.2017]; Biłozór-Salwa, *Jan Ziarnko*, 78–81, 199–201, no. 17.

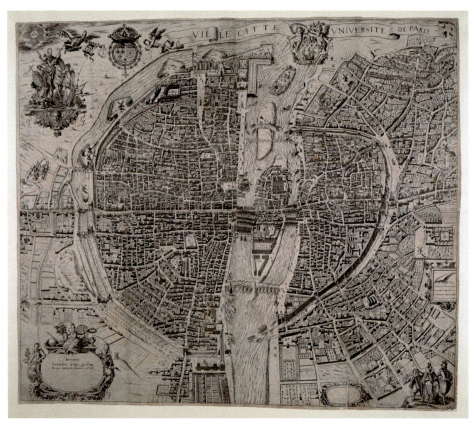

FIGURE 7.7 Jan Ziarnko, *Map of Paris*, 1616, etching

plates. Although it showed an up-to-date view of the city, the composition referred to 16th-century maps and offered a bird's eye view of the capital seen from the North.[42] Ziarnko further enhanced his map with a group of burghers, decorative cartouches, and two allegoric groups including portraits of Henry IV and Marie de' Medici. An equestrian portrait of Henry IV, accompanied by personifications of Faith and Law, is in the upper left-hand corner (Fig. 7.8). Accompanied by a personification of Fame blowing a trumpet, this vignette is a compilation of motifs borrowed directly from the ideological program found in famous Quesnel's and Vassallieu's maps of 1609. Characteristically, Ziarnko incorporated three female figures in contemporary attire in the

42 The most famous print of this type was the lost *Plan de Saint-Victor* (c.1552) ascribed to Jacques Androuet Du Cerceau (1510–1585) copied in 1756–1757 by Guillaume Dheulland. Jean Boutièr, *Les Plans de Paris des origines (1493) à la fin du XVIIIe siècle: étude, carto-bibliographie et catalogue colectif* (Paris: 2007), 88–89, 287–289.

FIGURE 7.8 *Portrait of Henry IV*—detail from Jan Ziarnko, *Map of Paris*, 1616, etching

lower right-hand corner of the print. This image, which has presented some difficulties in interpretation to researchers, should be read as an allegorical portrait of Marie de' Medici as patron of the arts and sciences. The Queen, wearing a crown, is flanked by the personifications of Science and of Knowledge and shown surrounded by scientific instruments (Fig. 7.9).

The portrait of Marie de' Medici is taken from the obverse of a commemorative medal minted in 1613 that celebrated the ceremonial laying of the cornerstone for the first modern aqueduct in Paris. Although the new pumping station, which lay near to Paris Rungis, was mainly built to provide water for the private gardens and fountains of the Queen, it also supplied a number of public wells. The motif was chosen to illustrate a project for which Parisians could be grateful to their Queen. Like her late husband, the aqueduct project showed that Marie cared about the development of the city. Notably, the map shows not so much a portrait of Henry IV, but his statue. His likeness clearly refers to the past. In contrast, the portrait of Marie is a contemporary portrait. Thus, only the Queen relates to the present and the future. Her government will provide prosperity and development of the arts and sciences. The presence of both king and his consort emphasizes that Marie de' Medici is continuing the rule of her husband.

FIGURE 7.9 *Portrait of Maria de Medici*—detail from Jan Ziarnko, *Map of Paris*, 1616, etching

Drawing royal portraits directly onto the space of the map can be considered as a clear demonstration of power and possession. More than this, in this case it functions as a manifestation of the control of the capital city.[43] Ziarnko's map was created in 1616, which has been described by Jean-François Dubost, as the

---

43 John Brian Harley, Paul Laxton, *The New Nature of Maps: Essays in the History of Cartography* (London: 2001), 75.

COPYING MOTIFS AND REWORKING PRINTING PLATES   183

year of Marie de' Medici's real political autonomy.[44] As a Queen Mother she constantly increased her influence on royal politics. It was not a coincidence that, in response, the Prince of Condé attempted to retrospectively dissolve the marriage of Henry and Marie in 1616. The Queen took drastic decision to imprison him, a prince of the blood, and his attempt to discredit her, and even to deny Louis XIII's right to the throne of France, failed.[45] Nevertheless, the court intrigues led to conflict and an open struggle for power between mother and son. In 1617, as already mentioned, Louis XIII took up government and his mother was forced to leave Paris in exile to Château de Blois.

While discussing Zianko's map, reference should be made to another print. In 1615, the German etcher Mattheus Merian (1593–1650) completed a remarkable map of Paris (985 × 375 mm). The view of the city was enhanced with official portraits of Louis XIII and Quenn Mother. Interestingly, the latter is often mistakenly identified as Anne of Austria.[46] Both maps can be considered as glorifying monarchs. However, it is a map by Ziarnko that openly praises the Queen Mother's virtues, making her unappealing not as a mother but as a ruler. However, after the expultion of Marie de Medici from Paris, Ziarnko's map became outdated and even undesirable in the new political environment.

The plates for Ziarnko's map were reused by the Parisian publisher Nicolas Berey (1610–1665) in 1648. For the second time, it became an instrument of political propaganda. After Louis XIII died in 1643, the crown was inherited by his minor son Louis XIV. Riots broke out in Paris four years later against the absolutist government of the Minister Jules Mazarin (1602–1661) in the parliamentary Fronde. It was at this point that Berey revised the old Ziarnko plates to record the slight changes that had happened in the urban space during the thirty years since the first state of the map was printed. He also discarded all the elements referring to previous rulers and instead inserted an oval portrait of the young Louis XIV to substitute that of Henry IV. The map thus announced the new King's dominance over the rebellious city (Fig. 7.10).[47] An unprecedented increase in the production of maps during Louis XIV's reign indicates how often they were used as instruments of propaganda. At the same time, old plates were still being modified and reused. Ziarnko's map was used repeatedly for the purpose of re-fashioning Louis XIV's image: it was reissued in 1666 and again in 1668–1669.[48] Before each new edition, the portrait of the monarch was

---

44   Jean-François Dubost, *Marie de Médicis, la rein dévoilée* (Paris: 2009), 504.
45   Dubost, *Marie de Médicis*, 504–508.
46   Sue Werlsh Reed, *French Prints from the Age of the Musketeers* (Boston: 1998), 46–47.
47   Harley, Laxton, *The New Nature of Maps*, 75.
48   Boutièr, *Les Plans de Paris*, 138–139, no. 75.

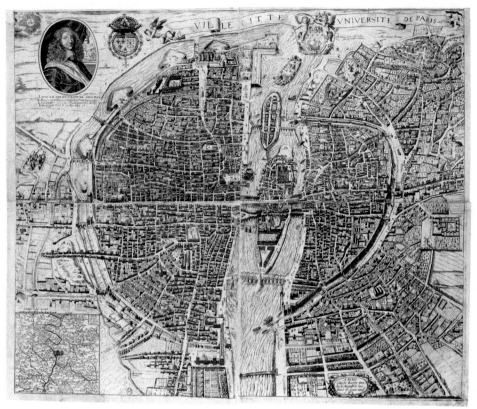

FIGURE 7.10 *Map of Paris*, Jan Ziarnko's etching reworked, edited by Nicolas Berey, 1693, etching and engraving

updated to match his current appearance. This type of approach has been used before. In 1618, in Amsterdam, Willem Janszoon Blaeu (1578–1638) published a view of Paris with the equestrian statues of Louis XIII and Anne of Austria in the foreground. Before the new edition of the view was published around 1630, the face of the ruler was modified. It no longer showed a youth but rather a grown-up man with a beard.[49]

Although the French did not yet use the term "propaganda" in the 16th and 17th centuries, they were keenly aware of the power of printed information. Thus, French rulers and the printmakers who worked for them carefully and skilfully manipulated their image in print, frequently returning to the same iconographic motifs.[50] In France, emphasizing the continuity of power

---

49 Boutièr, *Les Plans de Paris*, 125, no. 52.
50 Sawyer, *Printed Poison*, 15.

was very important, since the motto of the monarchy from the 16th century onwards stated that "the king never dies".[51] Marie de' Medici, Louis XIII, and later his son Louis XIV, all evoked themes and images devised in the 16th century for the needs of Henry IV. By stressing this continuity, they reinforced their own position, as well as that of the French monarchy in general. They also used the same instruments: printed broadsheets, almanacs and maps. Ziarnko worked across all these categories of printed media. His etchings clearly demonstrate how iconographic models were adapted to suit the political needs of each ruler.

Translated by Katarzyna Krzyżagórska-Pisarek

Select Bibliography

Benoist, Pierre, "Le père Joseph, l'empire Ottoman et la Méditerranée au début du XVIIᵉ siècle," *Cahiers de la Méditerranée*, 71 (2005), 185–202.

Biłozór-Salwa, Małgorzata, "Teoria tworzenia anamorfoz", *Rocznik Historii Sztuki*, 39 (2013): 43–53.

Biłozór-Salwa, Małgorzata, "Paryski Karuzel 1612 roku, czyli skały tryskające winem, grające góry i tańczące konie na usługach propagandy władzy", *Rocznik Biblioteki Narodowej*, 44 (2014), 113–358.

Biłozór-Salwa, Małgorzata, "Anamorphosis as a Tool for Presenting Erotic Subjects: Some Remarks on Jan Ziarnko's Lovers", *"The most Noble of the Senses". Anamorphosis, Trompe-L'Oeil, and Other Optical Illusions in Early Modern Art*, ed. Lilian H. Zirpolo (Ramsey: 2016), 29–48.

Biłozór-Salwa, Małgorzata, "The Monogram of the Virgin Mary (1605) by Jan Ziarnko as Maria de Medici's Watchword", in *Polish Emblems*, 1 (2016), http://polishemblems .uw.edu.pl/index.php/en/news-uk/43-news-text-2, accessed June 2017.

Biłozór-Salwa, Małgorzata, *The printed map as a tool of political struggle: Paris is well worth a ... map*. https://www.bl.uk/picturing-places/articles/the-printed-map-as-a -tool-of-political-struggle-paris-is-well-worth-a-map, accessed June 2017.

Boutièr, Jean, *Les Plans de Paris des origines (1493) à la fin du XVIIIᵉ siècle: étude, carto-bibliographie et catalogue colectif* (Paris: 2007).

Brückner, Wolfgang, *Populäre Druckgraphik Europas. Deutchland von 15. biz zum 20 Jahrhundert* (Munich: 1969).

Burke, Peter, *Fabrication of Louis XIV* (London: 1992).

---

51 "*Le roi ne meurt jamais*", Ralph E. Giesey, *The Royal Funeral in Renaissance France* (Genava: 1960), 177–183.

Bussey, Georges Moir and Thomas Gaspey, *The pictorial history of France and the French people*, 2 vols (London: 1843).

Canova-Green, Marie-Claude, "Warrior King or King of War? Louis XIII's Entries into his Bonnes Villes (1620–1629)", in *Ceremonial Entries in Early Modern Europe. The Iconography of Power*, ed. J. R. Mulryne, Maria Ines Aliverti and Anna Maria Testaverde (Routledge: 2016), 77–98.

Chartier, Roger, "Pamphlets et gazettes", in *Histoire de l'édition française. Le livre conquérant du Moyen-Âge au milieu du XVIIeme siècle*, ed. Roger Chartier, Henri-Jean Martin, vol. 1 (Paris: 1982), 405–425.

Chartier, Roger, "Stratégies éditoriales et lectures populaires, 1530–1660", in *Histoire de l'édition française. Le livre conquérant du Moyen-Âge au milieu du XVIIeme siècle*, ed. Roger Chartier, Henri-Jean Martin, vol. 1 (Paris: 1982), 585–603.

Chartier, Roger, and Henri-Jean Martin (ed.), *Histoire de l'édition française. Le livre conquérant du Moyen-Âge au milieu du XVIIeme siècle*, vol. 1 (Paris: 1982).

Drévillon, Hervé, *Lire et écrir l'avenir. L'astrologie dans la France du Grand Siècle (1610–1715)* (Seyssel: 1996).

Dubost, Jean-François, *Marie de Médicis, la rein dévoilée* (Paris: 2009).

Duccini, Hélène, *Faire voir, faire croire. L'opinion publique sous Louis XIII* (Seyssel: 2003).

Edwards, Mark U. Jr., *Printing, Propaganda, and Martin Luther* (Minneapolis: 2005).

Giesey, Ralph E., *The Royal Funeral in Renaissance France* (Genava: 1960).

Grivel, Marianne, *Le Commerce de l'estampe a Paris au XVIIe siècle* (Geneva: 1986).

Harley, John Brian, and Laxton, Paul, *The New Nature of Maps: Essays in the History of Cartography* (London: 2001).

Higman, Francis, "Le livre et les propagandes religieuses Le levain de l'Évangile", in *Histoire de l'édition française. Le livre conquérant du Moyen-Âge au milieu du XVIIeme siècle*, ed. Roger Chartier, Henri-Jean Martin, vol. 1 (Paris: 1982), 305–321.

Kenz, David El, "La propagande et le problème de sa réception, d'après les mémoires-journaux de Pierre de L'Estoile", *Cahiers d'histoire. Revue d'histoire critique*, 90–91 (2003), 19–32.

Lothe, José, "Images d'actualité éditées à Paris sous le règne d'Henri IV," in *L'estampe au Grand Siècle. Études offertes à Maxime Préaud*, ed. Peter Fuhring, Barbara Brejon de Lavergnée et al. (Paris: 2010), 55–65.

Louvet, Jehan, "Journal ou Récit véritable de tout ce qui est advenu digne de mémoire tant en la ville d'Angers, pays d'Anjou et autres lieux (depuis l'an 1560–jusqu'à l'an 1634)," *Revue de l'Anjou et de Maine et Loire*, 1, no. 4 (1855).

McGowan, Margaret M., "The French Royal Entry in the Renaissance: The Status of Printed Text", *French Ceremonial Entries in the Sixteenth Century: Event, Image, Text*, ed. Nicolas Russell, Hélène Visentin (Toronto: 2007), 33–50.

Pałka, Ada, "Jan Ziarnko's Anamorphic Print A Pair of Lovers Embracing", *Print Quarterly*, 32, no. 1 (2015), 3–13.

Rouillard, Philippe, "Van Halbeeck et vieilles dentelles," in *L'estampe au Grand Siècle. Études offertes à Maxime Préaud*, ed. Peter Fuhring, Barbara Brejon de Lavergnée et al. (Paris: 2010), 67–78.

Sawicka, Stanisława, "Jan Ziarnko peintre-graveur polonais et son activité a Paris au premier quart du XVIIe siècle", in *La France et la Pologne dans leurs relation artistiques*, 2–3 (1938), 101–257.

Sawyer, Jeffrey K., *Printed Poison. Pamphlet Propaganda, Faction Politics, and the Public Sphere in Early Seventeenth-Century France* (Oxford: 1990).

Shennan, Joseph H., *The Bourbons: the history of a dynasty* (London: 2009).

Sounders, Alison, *The Seventeenth-century French Emblem: A Study in Diversity* (Geneva: 2000).

Stijnman, Ad, *Engraving and Etching 1400–2000: A History of the Development of Manual Intaglio Printmaking Processes* (London and Houten: 2012).

Vibanti, Corrado, "Henry IV, the Gallic Hercules", *Journal of the Warburg and Courtauld Institutes*, 30 (1967), 176–197.

Ziolkowski, Jan, *The Medieval Latin Past of Wonderful Lies* (Michigan 2009).

CHAPTER 8

Displaying Gift-Giving: Thesis Prints in the Spanish Netherlands

Gwendoline de Mûelenaere

In the 17th and 18th centuries, *pro gradu* disputations led to the publication of engraved broadsheets or booklets summarizing thesis conclusions.[1] The *disputatio*, an oral exercise aimed at developing skills in eloquence and argumentation, was an important learning practice at institutions of higher education and a form of examination that concluded bachelors, masters and doctors degrees in Philosophy, Law, Medicine and Theology.[2] The broadsides produced for these occasions were used to announce the public disputation, to provide a visual program to the spectators during the event, and afterwards constituted a *souvenir* of the ceremony. Thesis prints were initially decorated with coats of arms and dedications to academic, ecclesiastical or political figures. From the early 17th century, however, they evolved progressively into large-sized and abundantly illustrated frontispieces, intended to glorify the applicant's patrons.[3]

This essay focuses on the circulation of thesis prints produced in the Southern Low Countries (mainly the universities of Louvain and Douai and the Jesuit schools established in those cities) and explores how this circulation

---

1 See Gwendoline de Mûelenaere, *Early Modern Thesis Prints in the Southern Netherlands: An Iconological Analysis of the Relationships between Art, Science and Power*, Brill's Studies on Art, Art History, and Intellectual History 60 (Leiden/Boston: 2022); Maddalena Malni Pascoletti, *Ex universa philosophia: Stampe barocche con le tesi dei Gesuiti di Gorizia*, exhibition catalogue (Monfalcone: 1992); Véronique Meyer, *L'illustration des thèses à Paris dans la seconde moitié du XVIIe siècle: Peintres, graveurs, éditeurs*, Commission des travaux historiques de la ville de Paris (Paris: 2002); Louise Rice, "Jesuit Thesis Prints and the Festive Academic Defence at the Collegio Romano", in *The Jesuits: Cultures, Sciences, and the Arts, 1540–1773*, ed. John W. O'Malley (Toronto: 1999), 148–69.

2 On the *disputatio*, see Olga Weijers, *In Search of the Truth: A History of Disputation Techniques from Antiquity to Early Modern Times* (Turnhout: 2013).

3 Originally meaning the main façade of a building, the word "frontispiece" came to denote the opening image of a book, containing its title and other bibliographical indications. The term was sometimes used to refer to large-format thesis broadsides, even if they were autonomous plates.

© KONINKLIJKE BRILL BV, LEIDEN, 2024 | DOI:10.1163/9789004703834_010

DISPLAYING GIFT-GIVING

influenced their iconography.[4] Such broadsides were not intended for the open print-market; they were mainly designed and issued to be given to members of the social and intellectual elite. The act of gift-giving is expressed in the written dedication to the patron printed alongside the scientific conclusions on the thesis print. It is also visually staged through a *mise en abyme*, a device in which the broadside depicts its own presentation to the student's sponsor. These visual and textual constructions aid our understanding of the functioning and intentions of thesis engravings in the sociopolitical context of courtly patronage permeating teaching institutions during the 17th century.

1   Displaying Gift-Giving: the Device of *Mise en Abyme*

At first, thesis prints did not enter commercial channels. They were intended to be posted in college halls, distributed to an audience during the defense, or sent to relatives and friends. In addition, more luxurious editions printed on satin were meant to be given personally to a dedicatee. From the beginning, the conclusions were accompanied by dedications to rich or powerful patrons. This practice of dedication epitomizes the relationship of patronage (existing or wanted) between a student and his sponsor, which governed the production and circulation of these works in the early modern period.[5]

The dedication is part of a gift-and-return-gift-system in which connections of power can be made and strengthened.[6] This gesture, although it is presented as a material and symbolic gift, should be understood as an instrument of exchange between student and protector, in which the former expected advantages from the latter in return for the dedication.[7] The value of these prints as works of art explains why so many of them survived after the *disputatio*, which was by nature an ephemeral event. Large thesis broadsheets of wealthy candidates were often commissioned from famous painters, such as Peter Paul

---

4   The Old University of Louvain was founded in 1425 and closed in 1797. The University of Douai, established by Paul IV's papal bull in 1559 and opened in 1562, was transferred to the jurisdiction of the King of France in 1668, following the conquest of the territory by Louis XIV.

5   Roger Chartier, "Patronage et dédicace", *Culture écrite et société: L'ordre des livres* (Paris: 1996), 81–106.

6   Isabelle Diu, "Enjeux de pouvoir dans la République des Lettres. Préfaces et dédicaces d'Erasme pour ses éditions et traductions d'œuvres classiques et patristiques," in *Le pouvoir des livres à la Renaissance*, ed. Dominique de Courcelles (Paris: 1998), 65–76. For further discussion on the subject, see the seminal works of Marcel Mauss, in particular: *The Gift. Forms and Functions of Exchange in Archaic Societies*, trans. Ian Cunnison (London: 1966).

7   Roger Chartier, "Patronage et dédicace," 101–102; Sharon Kettering, "Gift-Giving and Patronage in Early Modern France," *French History* vol. 2, no. 2 (1988): 131–151.

Rubens (1577–1640) and his followers Antoon Sallaert (1580/85–1650), Cornelis Schut (1597–1655), Abraham van Diepenbeeck (1596–1675), and Erasmus Quellinus (1607–1678).[8] These expensive engravings were later sought by collectors for their high quality, aesthetic originality, and rarity. The prints could also be exchanged among scholars who wanted to establish or strengthen relationships and to encourage scientific discussions.[9]

Numerous figurative scenes surround the scientific conclusions in thesis prints. Among them, a device frequently displayed in Flemish thesis engravings is the depiction of the gift-giving of the broadsheet itself.[10] The applicant is featured presenting to his patron a miniature copy of his thesis broadside or booklet. It is sometimes repeated a second time within itself, and the process can continue toward the infinitesimally small: even if the engraver stopped after one or two repetitions, it is enough to suggest the possibility of endless, diminishing recurrences.[11] Such staging of the offering replicates the composition *ad infinitum* and functions as a pictorial *mise en abyme* of the dedication.[12] This reflexive process proposes a visualization of the academic exchange inside the thesis and emphasizes the act of gift-giving expressed in

---

8   On one of Rubens's thesis prints, the Austroseraphic Heavens, see "Chapter 5: The Transatlantic Thesis Disputation" in Aaron M. Hyman, *Rubens in Repeat: The Logic of the Copy in Colonial Latin America* (Los Angeles: 2021), 217–256.

9   It is for instance the case of a thesis print designed by Abraham Van Diepenbeeck for Théodore d'Immerseel (1633–1654) in 1652. The painter Daniel Seghers (1590–1661), coadjutor brother of the Society of Jesus, wanted to put André Tacquet (1612–1660), the professor who presided over the dispute, in contact with Christiaan Huygens (1629–1695). Seghers sent three copies of the thesis program to the Dutch scientist, who received them on 28 October 1652. Huygens replied to Seghers on November 4, 1652, and then began a regular correspondence with Tacquet over mathematical topics. See Henri Bosmans, "Tacquet (André)," in *Biographie nationale de Belgique*, t. 24 (Brussels: 1929), col. 443.

10   The practice of gift-giving is also represented in thesis frontispieces of French, Italian and German production. For examples see: Sibylle Appuhn-Radtke, *Das Thesenblatt im Hochbarock* (Weissenhorn: 1988), cat. no. 46; Bénédicte Gady, *L'ascension de Charles Le Brun: Liens sociaux et production artistique* (Paris: 2010), fig. 136; Géza Galavics, "Thesenblätter ungarischer Studenten in Wien im 17. Jahrhundert: Künstlerische und pädagogische Strategien," in *Die Jesuiten in Wien. Zur Kunst- und Kulturgeschichte der österreichischen Ordensprovinz der "Gesellschaft Jesu" im 17. und 18. Jahrhundert*, ed. Herbert Karner and Werner Telesko, Veröffentlichungen der Kommission für Kunstgeschichte 5 (Vienna: 2003), cat. no. 3–4; Annalisa Pezzo, *Le tesi a stampa a Siena nei secoli XVI e XVII: Catalogo degli opuscoli della Biblioteca comunale degli Intronati*, Biblioteca di Redos 1 (Milan: 2011), cat. no. 69; Bernhard Schemmel and Wolfgang Seitz, *Die graphischen Thesen- und Promotionsblätter in Bamberg* (Wiesbaden: 2001), cat. no. 96.

11   John J. White, "The Semiotics of the *Mise-en-Abyme*", *The Motivated Sign*, edited by Olga Fischer and Max Nänny, Iconicity in Language and Literature 2 (Amsterdam: 2001), 36–38.

12   Lucien Dällenbach, *Le récit spéculaire. Essai sur la mise en abyme* (Paris: 1977), 62.

DISPLAYING GIFT-GIVING 191

FIGURE 8.1 Richard Collin after Abraham van Diepenbeeck, *Young Man Offering his Thesis*, c.1675, engraving

the dedication. It is therefore an eloquent example of the praiseful function assigned to thesis broadsheets.

The device of *mise en abyme ad infinitum* can be observed in a print designed by Abraham van Diepenbeeck and engraved by Richard Collin (1626–c.1697) (Fig. 8.1). The miniature scene occupies the upper part of the thesis page presented by the candidate while the textual summary is depicted by lines and dots below. It can be deduced from the representation that the image was initially joined by a scientific text but was separated from it later.[13] The dedicatee is joined by Minerva and Prudence. Terrestrial and celestial globes and books on the ground further indicate the erudite nature of the event.

These prints-within-prints could take the form of a frontispiece, opening the written section of the booklet with the detailed conclusions; of a rectangular

---

13 David Steadman nevertheless suggests that the page containing the conclusions was never produced, for economic reasons (David W. Steadman, *Abraham van Diepenbeeck: Seventeenth-Century Flemish Painter*, Studies in Baroque Art History 5 (Ann Arbor: 1982), 37–38). There is no material evidence that the print of the Rijksmuseum has been cut down, which would confirm Steadman's hypothesis.

figurative frame surrounding the scientific text sketched in the broadside; or of a *velum* or large panel bringing together the entire composition. The candidate's representation usually followed a more or less standard pattern; his face can show individualized features, but their general attitude is subject to *decorum*. The young man is often shown walking towards his benefactor, bending down or kneeling as a mark of respect, while he holds out a *velum* or an open leaflet. By contrast, the dedicatee's image is more elaborate; he is represented wearing contemporary or classical clothes, in a head-and-shoulder portrait medallion or as a full-length or equestrian figure, and his identity is often used as a source of inspiration for the general iconography of the engraving.[14] Devices including stages, staircases, steps or a mound of soil tend to be used to emphasize the distance separating the dedicatee from the candidate. The spatial left-right disposition is respected, observing the traditional precedence of the dextral over the sinistral that prevailed in Western art.[15]

Another broadside designed by Abraham van Diepenbeeck (possibly after Rubens) and engraved by Schelte A. Bolswert (1586–1659) reproduces in a schematic way its own page setup, generating an image-within-the-image (Fig. 8.2).[16] The philosophical conclusions, defended in Douai on the 22nd of August 1628 by the Polish Jesuit Gabriel Kilian de Bobrek Ligeza, are inscribed in the lower part of the poster. The discussed subjects are preceded by a cartouche naming the patron, Sigismund III King of Poland and Sweden (1566–1632), and by a Latin address in his honor. The engraved frame is made of eight figurative

---

14   Ann Diels, *"Uit de schaduw van Rubens": Prentkunst naar Antwerpse historieschilders*, exhibition catalogue (Brussels: 2009), 45–46.

15   Christine Dubois, "L'image 'abymée'", *Images Re-vues*, 2, no. 8 (2006), [http://images revues.revues.org/304] (accessed December 21, 2014): § 8–9. See also Hugo Van der Velden, "Diptych Altarpiece and the Principle of Dextrality," in *Essays in Context. Unfolding the Netherlandish Diptych*, edited by John Oliver Hand and Ron Spronk (Cambridge: 2006), 124–155.

16   At least four copies of this broadside are known. The copy held at the British Museum (inv. 1858,0417.1259) contains in the lower corners of the top part the inscriptions: "S. Bolswert fc." and "P. P. Rub. inv.". The others only bear the signature "S. Bolswert fc." (Brussels, Royal Library of Belgium, inv. SI 28107; Amsterdam, Rijksmuseum, inv. RP-P-OB-67.556; Cambridge, Fitzwilliam Museum, inv. PDP, 23.K.4-202). However, this engraving is not mentioned in the volume of the *Corpus Rubenianum* dedicated to Rubens's frontispieces (J. Richard Judson and Carl Van de Velde, *Book Illustrations and Title-Pages*, Corpus Rubenianum Ludwig Burchard, vol. 21, London: 1978). According to Max Rooses, "One of these theses bear the name of Abraham van Diepenbeeck as designer [...]. None of them can justify an attribution to Rubens" (*L'oeuvre de P. P. Rubens. Histoire et description de ses tableaux et dessins*, vol. 5 (Antwerp: 1892), 39–40). It is possible that van Diepenbeeck conceived the composition after an invention by Rubens, as is the case for a broadsheet of 1636, *Neptune and Minerva* (Judson and Van de Velde, *Book Illustrations and Title-Pages*, vol. 1, no. 86).

FIGURE 8.2 Schelte a Bolswert after Abraham van Diepenbeeck (and Peter Paul Rubens?), *Thesis Dedicated to Sigismund III Vasa, King of Poland*, 1628, engraving

scenes depicting the history of Poland, as well as a portrait of Gabriel Kilian de Bobrek Ligeza. The student, joined by embodiments of Science and War, gives his thesis print to his monarch portrayed in the top section of the print.[17] Sigismund III sits on a throne bearing the motto *More Maiorum* ("after the custom of our ancestors"). He is surrounded by allegorical figures holding coats of arms, who can be identified as the personifications of Russia holding a crown; Poland as Minerva, Sweden (crowned), and an Ottoman woman, who offers a laurel branch while pointing to her broken weapons.

The Polish candidate, studying in Douai within the framework of a *peregrinatio academica*, took advantage of his public defense to glorify Sigismund III.[18] The iconography presents the latter as a worthy heir of the Jagellonian dynasty, a strong advocate for the Catholic faith, and a sovereign successful in his military conquests (although the reality was significantly different).[19] The intended function of praising is visually conveyed through the embedded image showing the gift-giving, as well as the allegorical, heraldic, and emblematic language. Among these different languages of a symbolic nature, the emblems occasionally inserted in thesis broadsides or thesis booklets can be compared to the *mise en abyme* method. Jesuit emblematics, codified within the pedagogical program of the *Ratio studiorum* (1599), often focuses on the forms and functions of the pictorial *imago*—the visual image.[20] Construed by the order's members of produced for the order, such emblems were used as a signifying instrument reflecting on the status of the *imago*. A similar deferral of meaning is involved in embedded images in Jesuit and university thesis prints.

In the example cited above, the work of art takes itself as a subject and is therefore reflexive. It combines the dimension of reflexivity with an embedding relation, resulting in an engraving-within-the-engraving. According to Bernard Vouilloux, this structure is typically a process of sampling and exemplification, since it draws the viewer's attention to the embedded image, identical to the

---

17   The figure of Sigismund III is copied from a painting dated *c.*1626, now attributed to Pieter Soutman (formerly Rubens), in the Alte Pinakothek, Munich (inv. 948).

18   About the *peregrinatio academica*, see Dominique Julia and Jacques Revel, *Les universités européennes du XVIᵉ au XVIIIᵉ siècle. Histoire sociale des populations étudiantes*, vol. 2, *France* (Paris: 1986–1998), 33–105.

19   Sigismund's eviction from the Swedish throne started the Polish-Swedish war (1626–29), which rekindled the ancient rivalry with Muscovy. This conflict is closely related to the campaigns the ruler led against the Turks and the Tatars. Norman Davies, *God's Playground: A History of Poland*, vol. 1, *The Origins to 1795* (Oxford: 1985), 447.

20   Walter S. Melion, "Introduction: The Jesuit Engagement with the Status and Functions of the Visual Image", in *Jesuit Image Theory*, ed. Wietse de Boer, Karl A. E. Enenkel, and Walter S. Melion, Intersections 45 (Leiden: 2016), 6–8.

one that surrounds it.[21] The phenomenon of reduplication (i.e. the evocation of the work in the work itself), which is at play in thesis prints, is one of the numerous forms of *mises en abyme* that flourished particularly in 17th-century art, along with extensions of the representation using embedded mirrors or references to prior works (in *Kunstkammers*, gallery paintings, or the painter in his studio).[22]

2 Narrativizing the Reception: the Tradition of Dedication Images

It is helpful here to consider the expression of *mise en abyme* and the theories it has produced. The phrase was first used by the French author André Gide in 1893 to outline self-reflexive embeddings in artistic fields.[23] It is adapted from a technical term in heraldry, the *abîme*, which is the heart of the coat of arms. This concept was gradually applied by scholars to various realms: graphic arts, literature, theater, film, advertising, and has developed multiple meanings in modern criticism, art-historical and semiotic discourses. Lucien Dällenbach (*Le récit spéculaire*, 1977) describes this structure as "any enclave keeping up a relation of similarity with the work that contains it"; it appears as a mode of *reflection*, a method for the work to return to itself, having the faculty of conjuring up its formal structure, and hence of informing the reader about the meaning of the whole.[24]

Dällenbach distinguishes *mises en abyme ad infinitum* from "simple" or "specular" reflections. The latter consists of a reduplication of the narrative or the representation within itself by means of mirrors. In pictorial works of art, the process compensates for the limitation of the viewer's look and reveals details that would otherwise be excluded from his field of vision. The well-known examples quoted by Gide are *The Arnolfini portrait* (1434) by Jan Van Eyck (*c*.1390–1441), *The diptych of Maarten Van Niewenhoven* (1487) by Hans Memling (*c*.1430–1494) and *The Moneylender and his wife* (1514) by Quentin Metsys (1466–1530), as well as *Las Meninas* (1656) by Diego Velázquez (1599–1660).[25]

---

21 Bernard Vouilloux, *L'œuvre en souffrance: Entre poétique et esthétique*, L'extrême contemporain (Paris: 2004), 160.

22 André Chastel, *Le tableau dans le tableau, suivi de La figure dans l'encadrement de la porte chez Velasquez*, Champs arts (Paris: 2012), 13 and 35; Dubois, "L'image 'abymée'," 1.

23 André Gide, *Journal 1889–1939*, Bibliothèque de la Pléiade 54 (Paris: 1948), 41.

24 Dällenbach, *Le récit spéculaire*, 15–18, and pictorial examples: 19–22.

25 Ibid., 19–20 and 34–38.

Mises en abyme ad infinitum, for their part, presuppose a faithful repetition of the subject endlessly, at least theoretically, each iteration reducing the image's size. This visual experience is also known as the "Droste effect", named after the design on the boxes of the Dutch brand Droste cocoa powder, introduced in 1904. The advert shows a nurse carrying a tray with a box displaying a smaller picture of her holding the same object, which in turn bears a reduced picture of her carrying the same tray, and so on (Fig. 8.3).[26] This clever compositional formula strategy proved very popular in advertising at the beginning of the 20th century. The device can also be described as an optical feedback, a potential infinite regression, an unending loop, a recursive sequence, and as a self-similar object. The relation between the "reflected" and the "reflecting" is of a literal nature when the embedded image is identical (or rather almost identical) to all or part of the embedding image, as is the case for self-portraits of painters in action, which juxtapose the "original" (the painter while painting) and its painted representation (his depicted portrait).[27]

The *mise en abyme* is a "privileged image", as André Chastel describes, "because it defines itself in relation to the form or origin of the very work in which it appears".[28] This technique of showing a small-scale model of its own structure would be an occurrence of absolute iconic replication (except for size). The device also explains the production scenario of the work of art, and here the act of reception, by stimulating the imagination of the audience. The *mise en abyme* leads to confusion in the articulation of levels, normally separated, of the narrative and of the narrated events, and "because of the complexities of the multi-layered process of *semiosis* involved, it demands substantial interpretive creativity on the viewer's part".[29] But, in exchange, the device provides a reflection, formal and intellectual, on the materiality of the work of art and on its process of creating.[30]

The reflexivity implied by the phenomenon of images-within-images attests to the increasing artistic self-awareness in the medieval and early modern periods, which first developed in Italy around 1300. From the 14th century in Europe, an increasing number of paintings on panel, frescoes, sculpted

---

26   Corine Schleif, "Kneeling on the Threshold: Donors Negotiating Realms Betwixt and Between," in *Thresholds of Medieval Visual Culture: Liminal Spaces*, ed. Elina Gertsman and Jill Stevenson (Woodbridge: 2012), 209–211.

27   Vouilloux, *L'œuvre en souffrance*, 138. The embedding process can also be metaphorized, such as *mises en abyme* in which the embedding function is assumed, metaphorically, in the representational space, by the depiction of doors, windows and niches. See: Victor Stoichita, *L'instauration du tableau: Métapeinture à l'aube des temps modernes* (Geneva: 1999), 53–99.

28   Chastel, *Le tableau dans le tableau*, 12.

29   White, "The Semiotics of the *Mise-en-Abyme*", 37, 45 and 50.

30   Dubois, "L'image 'abymée'", 1.

DISPLAYING GIFT-GIVING 197

FIGURE 8.3 *Advertisement for Droste Cocoa Powder*, after 1904

capitals, mosaics, stained-glass windows and manuscript illuminations included embedded images, themselves belonging to various mediums.[31] The compositional device continued to grow in early modern paintings, appearing predominantly in the theme of Saint Luke portraying the Virgin Mary, in self-portraits of artists, and in studio compositions. Victor Stoichita has demonstrated, in his book *The Self-Aware Image* (1997), that metapainting (paintings that visually reflect on the nature of paintings), was a key factor in establishing the modern condition of art. Lorenzo Pericolo includes within this "epiphenomenon of the self-assertion of the early modern painting" "the whole gamut of pictorial devices through which painting stages its fictiveness. Incorporating a painting—or an image with an equivalent status—as an object of representation is a means to achieve this goal."[32]

Self-representation highlights the status of the image and *artificium* of the work and affirms its artistic value. It plays a "corporate intention", an advertising role in favor of its own style.[33] To this end, the formula provides the opportunity to visualize the account of some key events in the life of the object, among which are its own creation and donation. In the first case, the emphasis is put on the pictorial gesture. In the second case, self-references are used to strengthen the symbolism of gift-giving by visually stressing the act of donation of the work.[34] According to Stuart Whatling, "to depict upon an object a scene showing the origin and the purpose of its own existence reifies its foundation-myth in a manner that makes it inseparable from the object itself".[35] It leaves a stronger mark on people's minds than traditional inscriptions would do.

Scenes of artistic donations spread widely in medieval art, in particular in byzantine iconography.[36] Many examples of self-referential offerings can be found in varied artistic mediums, and from the 9th century onwards, dedication

---

31 Peter Bokody, *Images-within-Images in Italian Painting (1250–1350)* (Farnham: 2015), 3–5.

32 Lorenzo Pericolo, "What is Metapainting? *The Self-Aware Image* Twenty Years Later", in *The Self-Aware Image: An Insight into Early Modern Metapainting*, edited by Victor Stoichita (London: 2015), 11–13. This book was first published in 1993 under the title *L'instauration du tableau* (see note 27).

33 Chastel, *Le tableau dans le tableau*, 39; Victor Stoichita, "L'effet Don Quichotte. Le problème de la frontière esthétique dans l'œuvre de Murillo," in *Cadre, seuil, limite. La question de la frontière dans la théorie de l'art*, ed. Thierry Lenain and Rudy Steinmetz, Essais (Brussels: 2010), 89.

34 Stuart Whatling, "Putting Mise-En-Abyme in its (Medieval) Place", lecture at the workshop *Medieval Mise-En-Abyme: The Object Depicted within Itself*, online articles of the Courtauld Institute, February 2009, accessed March 17, 2014, 1–10 [http://www.courtauld.ac.uk/researchforum/projects/medievalarttheory/documents/Mise-en-abyme.pdf].

35 Ibid., 2.

36 On this practice in medieval art, see Schleif, "Kneeling on the Threshold," 195–216.

images were increasingly produced in *scriptoria*.[37] For instance, manuscript illuminations often show representations of the codex in which they are contained, following a relatively standard iconographic repertoire. The genre continued beyond the 13th century, but it progressively lost its spiritual dimension, becoming less an affirmation of piety than a tool serving personal ambitions. This is the case in the presentation miniature decorating the frontispiece of the *Chroniques de Hainaut* (c.1447–1448), attributed to Rogier van der Weyden (1399/1400–1464) (Fig. 8.4). In this miniature, Simon Nockart, who sponsored the French translation of this history of the county, is depicted while giving the volume to Philip the Good (1396–1467).[38]

FIGURE 8.4 Attributed to Rogier Van der Weyden, Frontispiece to the *Chroniques de Hainaut* dedicated to Philip the Good, 1447–1448, presentation miniature

37 Noémi Colin, *Le pouvoir en images: l'acte de dédicace dans l'iconographie occidentale du VIe au début du XIIIe siècle*, doctoral dissertation (Université de Paris X-Nanterre: 2007), 11.
38 The translation project of the *Chroniques de Hainaut* was under the patronage of Simon Nockart, high official of Hainaut and advisor to Philip the Good (Pascal Schandel, "Les images de dédicace à la cour des ducs de Bourgogne. Ressources et enjeux d'un genre", in *Miniatures flamandes, 1404–1482*, edited by Bernard Bousmanne and Thierry Delcourt, exhibition catalogue (Paris: 2011), 75–77).

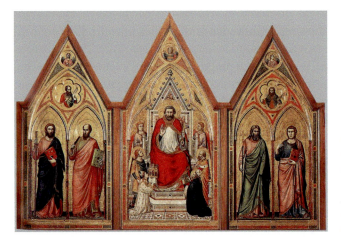

FIGURE 8.5
Giotto di Bondone and workshop, *The Stefaneschi Altarpiece* (verso), c.1320, tempera on pane

Even though the phenomenon of self-reference, whether alluding to a gifting scene or not, is common in Western art, the identical depiction of an image within itself is much rarer. The abyssal form of self-representation is not a mere representation-within-the-representation showing a generic work of art, but it gains an additional degree of significance since it indicates that specific picture.[39] A unique instance of *mise en abyme ad infinitum* in medieval painting is the *Stefaneschi triptych*, commissioned by Cardinal Giacomo Gaetani Stefaneschi (c.1260–1343) as an altarpiece for one of the altars in St. Peters, Rome, and executed by Giotto di Bondone (1266/1267–1337) around 1320 (Fig. 8.5).[40] The patron is portrayed in the central panel donating the altarpiece to Saint Peter. The miniature copy of the altarpiece shows an even smaller version of the composition, represented by a simple golden mark (Fig. 8.6). Giotto used the device of infinite regression to include the patron twice within the altarpiece and emphasize his role as donor.[41]

The more unusual *mise en abyme* of the presentation scene occurs in a very similar fashion in the iconography of 17th-century thesis broadsides. In a thesis poster dedicated to Leopold I (1640–1705), the reduplication has the same intention of strengthening the artistic value of the composition, and thus functions as an advertisement in favor of the engraved work (Fig. 8.7). This thesis print was executed in 1663 by two artists from Liège, Bertholet

---

39 Bénédicte Gady, "La gravure dans la gravure: Exercices visuels et sémantiques", in *L'estampe au Grand siècle: Études offertes à Maxime Préaud*, ed. Peter Fuhring, Barbara Brejon de Lavergnée and Marianne Grivel, Matériaux pour l'histoire 9 (Paris: 2010), 452.
40 The altarpiece is now housed in the Pinacoteca Vaticana, Rome.
41 Bokody, *Images-within-Images in Italian Painting*, 14–15.

DISPLAYING GIFT-GIVING   201

FIGURE 8.6
Giotto di Bondone and workshop, *The Stefaneschi Altarpiece* (detail)

FIGURE 8.7   Michel Natalis after Bertholet Flémalle, *Thesis of Henri Hatzfeldt, Count of Gleichen*, 1663, engraving

Flémalle (1614–1675) and Michel Natalis (1611–1668) to celebrate the disputation in *Jurisprudentia* argued by Count Heinrich von Hatzfeldt (d. 1683), a German nobleman studying at the University of Louvain, under the supervision of Henri Loyens (1607–1686).[42] The homage paid to the Emperor, written on the stone pedestal in the lower part of the composition, is visually repeated through the representation of the broadside gift and reads "To the most powerful and invincible Caesar Leopold, most august Emperor" (*Potentissimo invictissimoque Leopoldo Caesari. Augustissime imperator*); "Here I am thrown down at [your] sacred feet and with me the entire family of Hatzfeld" (*Ecce me sacros advolutum ad pedes et Mecum totam Hatzfeldiorum familiam*). The image and the dedication explicitly refer to the war between the Holy Roman Empire and the Ottoman Empire from 1663 to August 1664: "Vanquisher of the Turks and defender of the Church of God" (*Turcorum debellator, defensorque Ecclesiae Dei*).

The small central panel, which reproduces the scene, underlines what is already visible: it stresses the political and religious stakes of the representation by repeating the motif of angels fighting the Turkish army and other dissidents, with the help of a cross, a lantern, a sword and lightning. The candidate positions his defense under the auspices of Leopold I and reiterates his tribute at the end of the Latin text.[43]

Such representations pertain to a conscious strategy of narrativizing gift-giving and its acceptance by the benefactor (implying the acceptance of commitment towards the giver in return). Through the device of self-reference, the act of donation is permanently recorded within the engraving. It claims the merit due to the work and its recipient, and calls to mind the generosity of the donor.[44] Those images not only affirm the student's status of authorship, but they also emphasize the dedicatee's role as a patron.[45] In this way, they create a reciprocal praise: the young candidate benefits from the moral authority and political power of the protector, while the student's knowledge has a positive impact on the dedicatee's reputation. The mediation between the two communication actors is achieved by the poster depicted within the print.

---

42 Pierre-Yves Kairis, *Bertholet Flémal (1614–1675): Le "Raphaël des Pays-Bas" au carrefour de Liège et de Paris* (Paris: 2015), 200–201, cat. no. G20.

43 "And I dedicate my theses of Universal Law very modestly [...] and I refer entirely to you [...]" (*Et meas Universi Iuris theses cum voto submississime [...] et ego me totum refero ad te [...]*).

44 Whatling, *Putting Mise-en-Abyme in its (Medieval) Place*, 2.

45 Although the student was presented as the author of the dissertation in thesis prints, he was not necessarily its actual producer. The thesis conclusions were not innovative theories written by the candidate, but they provided above all an occasion for the candidate to display his rhetoric skills. A thesis could also be a means for a professor to spread his ideas among patrons or other scholars through a laureate.

DISPLAYING GIFT-GIVING

3   Showing the Communication Exchange: Socio-Political Stakes

Although it occupies a minimal place in thesis compositions, the visual and semantic device of the *mise en abyme* plays a central narrative role since it repeats, in the pictorial representation, the written dedication.[46] Furthermore, the *mise en abyme* serves as metanarration in the sense that it shows to the audience the context of the broadside's reception.

Through the insertion of its miniature version, the conveyed message and the image of its oral communication coexist within a unique medium, enabling an optical journey between them. This visual experience is synchronic: during the defense, the message orally discussed by the candidate was at the same time heard, seen and read by the audience, by means of the poster. Therefore, the image-within-the-image reinforces the link between the viewer and the conclusions of the thesis, merging the contemplation of the figurative scene with the decoding of the text. Its self-referential nature introduces us into the communicational exchange, which has directed the conception of these documents.[47] Sender, receiver, context, contact, and code are depicted on the fringe of the message, showing the *modus operandi* of the reception situation to the reader. The conveyed information includes the academic positions to be argued, as well as the textual eulogy. The message has thus scientific and rhetorical implications as well as social and political stakes.

Two *atlantico* broadsides bear witness to this double form of donation, in words and in image, through an elaborate iconographic program.[48] The first one was engraved by Michel Natalis (1611–1668) after Cornelis Schut for a doctoral thesis in Law defended by two Austrian brothers in 1643 at the University of Louvain (Fig. 8.8). George Nicolaus (1623–1695) and Wolffgang Andreas (1626–1693), Barons of Rosenberg, are portrayed presenting an abridged version of the thesis poster to the Holy Roman Emperor Ferdinand III (1608–1657). The *velum* held shows the entire scene with remarkable accuracy, including a reduced copy of itself (Fig. 8.9). Conclusions are engraved on seven medallions presented by flying cherubs, while the written encomium ("they give, they declare, they dedicate", *dant, dicant, consecrant*) echoes the gesture of donation.

In the thesis print of the Barons of Rosenberg, the Holy Roman Emperor sits on a throne under a monumental canopy on the left half of the composition in front of a column topped with a Habsburg eagle. At the base of the column are

---

46   Gady, "La gravure dans la gravure", 452.

47   See Jean-Marie Klinkenberg, *Précis de sémiotique générale*, Culture et communication (Brussels: 1996), 33–44.

48   In bibliography, the term *atlantico* means a sheet or book of large dimensions.

FIGURE 8.8 Michel Natalis after Cornelis Schut, *Thesis Defended by George Nicolaus and Wolffgang Andreas, Barons of Rosenberg*, 1643, engraving

DISPLAYING GIFT-GIVING 205

FIGURE 8.9 Michel Natalis after Cornelis Schut, *Thesis Defended by George Nicolaus and Wolffgang Andreas, Barons of Rosenberg* (detail)

three chained figures, symbolizing the sinners defeated by the Catholic faith, while a snake-haired woman, embodying discord or heresy, is shown falling from the steps of the throne. On their left are putti depicted with scales, an olive branch, a sword, a compass and rule, a lead weight, and an open book, attributes referring to Peace, Justice, and the Liberal Arts. The laudatory iconographical program of the print follows the tradition of court culture and sponsorship pervading academic institutions at this time.

Two years later, in 1645, Claudius Count of Collalto (1627–1661) obtained his Law degree from the University of Louvain and dedicated his thesis to Archduke Ferdinand of Austria (1633–1654), the Emperor's eldest son.[49] The donation is depicted in the poster designed by Abraham van Diepenbeeck and produced by Paul Pontius for this specific event (Fig. 8.10).[50] The candidate, accompanied by the personifications of Justice and Faith, is shown holding ostentatiously a panel containing the *mise en abyme* of the broadside. Once again, the visualization of the dedicatory offering is added to the verbal eulogy, written in a large cartouche.[51] The repetition, in a smaller space, of all the elements of the representation attracts the viewer's curiosity and encourages him to enter the image in order to examine each of its components. The *mise en abyme* in the thesis prints of the Count of Collalto and the Barons of Rosenberg do not leave any doubt as to the laudatory nature of these two engravings.

One can discern at least three levels of embeddings in the *mise en abyme* device: first the defense, that includes the actual moment of dedication, which occurred in real life; then the broadsheet that depicts allegorically the act of thesis-giving in the printed composition; finally, the graphic representation of the broadside in miniature in this very image surrounding the scriptural area. This process pertains to the paradox of the frame that frames itself: the eye is

---

49 Claudius of Collalto was the son of Ramboldo of Collalto (1575–1630), an Italian commander at the service of the Holy Roman Empire during the Thirty Years' War and the War of the Mantuan Succession. After his studies, Claudius of Collalto pursued a career in diplomacy and the army.

50 Marc De Beyer, Patrick Ramade and Hans Vlieghe, *Dans la lumière de Rubens: Peintres baroques des Pays-Bas du Sud*, trans. Joke Muller and Milou Boon, exhibition catalogue (Paris: 2000), 64, 71; Friedrich W. Hollstein, *Dutch and Flemish Etchings, Engravings and Woodcuts, ca 1450–1700*, vol. 17, *Pauli-Rem* (Amsterdam: 1976), 163, no. 49; Steadman, *Abraham van Diepenbeeck*, 80.

51 "Count Claudius of Collalto and San Salvatore has accomplished his vow toward [by dedicating his work to]" the "august Prince Ferdinand of Austria as 4th of the three Ferdinand emperors, great-great-grandson of the first, grandson of the second and son of the third" ("*Augusto principi Ferdinando Austriaco Trium Ferdinandorum Caesarum primi secundi tertii abnepoti nepoti filio pro quarto votum posuit Claudius Comes de Collalto et S. Salvat ᵒʳ*").

FIGURE 8.10   Paul Pontius after Abraham van Diepenbeeck, *Thesis of Claudius, Count of Collalto*, 1645, engraving

caught by the engraved composition encouraging the viewer to imagine the image of the broadside multiplying over and over again to the infinitesimal.[52]

The optical route induced by the *mise en abyme* can also be made in the opposite direction, allowing the viewer to enter virtually the presentational space of the work of art at the time of the disputation. His imagination, stimulated by the model in the model, has an idealized vision of the student giving their broadside to their protector. So at each level of the self-referential structure, the graphic elements are both framed and framing representations. As figures, they structure the page area, and as borders, they involve a temporal dimension. In any case, the paradoxical mechanism of the engraving-within-the-engraving causes a disturbing experience as it questions the relations between illusion and reality.[53]

The spatial organization and the juxtaposition of visual and textual signs on one sheet are not exclusively typical of thesis broadsides. Other ephemeral prints such as almanacs and political handbills combine the power of images and texts in similar layouts. Those posters, pinned or plastered on walls, could also present *mises en abyme* that clarify their own context of distribution, like street vendors. This method is illustrated in an almanac for the year 1653 held at the Bibliothèque Nationale de France (Fig. 8.11).[54] The calendar, surrounded by two intaglio-printed pillars, occupies the lower part of the broadsheet. The upper part is populated by a crowd of individuals identifiable by their trade: musician, pastry chef, baker, seller of roast meat, painter, book seller, and solicitor. In the middle of the assembly, a man is facing the spectator and indicates the almanac itself, with the difference that the lower part includes the signature (*avec Privilege / Pierre Saincto(n) / excudit*) instead of the calendar. This staging shows that almanacs were sold by street vendors, like chapbooks or popular prints. The *mise en abyme* therefore fulfills the same mission in this engraved broadsheet as that intended in the thesis print, namely to shed light on its own circulation.

In the context of thesis prints, beyond a mere playful representation, the *mise en abyme ad infinitum* offers a metanarrative discourse by mentioning the context of existence of the work of art within itself. The visualization of the gift-giving clarifies the intentions of the laureate, stresses the role of patron of the dedicatee, and introduces a dimension of curiosity in order to attract the viewer's attention.

---

52 Louis Marin, "Le cadre de la représentation et quelques-unes de ses figures", *Les cahiers du Musée national d'art modern*, vol. 24 (1988): 77–78.

53 Chastel, *Le tableau dans le tableau*, 32, 60.

54 Maxime Préaud, "'Nous allons à l'an pire': à propos d'un almanach mural pour 1653 et de sa mise en abyme," *Nouvelles de l'estampe*, 245 (2013): 4–14.

FIGURE 8.11 Jean Frosne, *Nous Allons à l'An Pire*, 1653, engraving (upper part)

Select Bibliography

Primary Sources

Marolles, Michel de, *Catalogue de livres d'estampes et de figures en taille douce* (Paris: 1666).

Secondary Sources

Appuhn-Radtke, Sibylle, *Das Thesenblatt im Hochbarock* (Weissenhorn: 1988).
Bokody, Peter, *Images-within-Images in Italian Painting (1250–1350)* (Farnham: 2015).
Chartier, Roger, *Culture écrite et société: L'ordre des livres* (Paris: 1996).
Chastel, André, *Le tableau dans le tableau, suivi de La figure dans l'encadrement de la port chez Velasquez*, vol. 651 Champs arts (Paris: 2012).
Colin, Noémi, *Le pouvoir en images: l'acte de dédicace dans l'iconographie occidentale du VIe au début du XIIIe siècle*, doctoral dissertation (Université de Paris X-Nanterre: 2007).
Dällenbach, Lucien, *Le récit spéculaire. Essai sur la mise en abyme* (Paris: 1977).
Davies, Norman, *God's Playground: A History of Poland*, vol. 1, *The Origins to 1795* (Oxford: 1985).

De Beyer, Marc, Patrick Ramade and Hans Vlieghe, *Dans la lumière de Rubens: Peintres baroques des Pays-Bas du Sud*, trans. Joke Muller and Milou Boon, exhibition catalogue (Paris: 2000).

Diels, Ann, *"Uit de schaduw van Rubens": Prentkunst naar Antwerpse historieschilders*, exhibition catalogue (Brussels: 2009).

Diu, Isabelle, "Enjeux de pouvoir dans la République des Lettres. Préfaces et dédicaces d'Erasme pour ses éditions et traductions d'œuvres classiques et patristiques", in *Le pouvoir des livres à la Renaissance*, ed. Dominique de Courcelles (Paris: 1998), 65–76.

Dubois, Christine, "L'image 'abymée'", *Images Re-vues*, 2, no. 8 (2006), accessed December 21, 2014 [http://imagesrevues.revues.org/304].

Gady, Bénédicte, "La gravure dans la gravure: Exercices visuels et sémantiques", in *L'estampe au Grand siècle: Études offertes à Maxime Préaud*, ed. Peter Fuhring, Barbara Brejo de Lavergnée and Marianne Grivel, Matériaux pour l'histoire vol. 9 (Paris: 2010), 449–462.

Gady, Bénédicte, *L'ascension de Charles Le Brun: Liens sociaux et production artistique* (Paris: 2010).

Galavics, Géza, "Thesenblätter ungarischer Studenten in Wien im 17. Jahrhundert: Künstlerische und pädagogische Stragegien," in *Die Jesuiten in Wien. Zur Kunst- und Kulturgeschichte der österreichischen Ordensprovinz der "Gesellschaft Jesu" im 17. Und 18. Jahrhundert*, ed. Herbert Karner and Werner Telesko, Veröffentlichungen der Kommission für Kunstgeschichte, vol. 5 (Vienna: 2003), 113–130.

Gide, André, *Journal 1889–1939*, Bilbiothèque de la Pléiade, vol. 54 (Paris: 1948).

Hollstein, Friedrich W., *Dutch and Flemish Etchings, Engravings and Woodcuts, ca 1450–1700*, vol. 17, *Pauli-Rem* (Amsterdam: 1976).

Hyman, Aaron M., *Rubens in Repeat: The Logic of the Copy in Colonial Latin America* (Los Angeles: 2021).

Judson, J. Richard and Carl Van de Velde, *Book Illustrations and Title-Pages*, Corpus Rubenianum Ludwig Burchard, vol. 21 (London: 1978).

Julia, Dominique and Jacques Revel, *Les universités européennes du XVI*^{e} *au XVIII*^{e} *siècle. Histoire sociale des populations étudiantes*, vol. 2, *France* (Paris: 1986–1998).

Kairis, Pierre-Yves, *Bertholet Flémal (1614–1675): Le "Raphaël des Pays-Bas" au Carrefour de Liège et de Paris* (Paris: 2015).

Kettering, Sharon, "Gift-Giving and Patronage in Early Modern France", *French History*, 2, 2 (1988): 131–151.

Klinkenberg, Jean-Marie, *Précis de sémiotique Générale* (Brussels: 1996).

Malni Pascoletti, Maddalena, *Ex universa philosophia: Stampe barocche con le tesi dei Gesuiti di Gorizia*, exhibition catalogue (Monfalcone: 1992).

Marin, Louis, "Le cadre de la représentation et quelques-unes de ses figures", *Les cahiers du Musée national d'art moderne*, 24 (1988): 62–81.

Mauss, Marcel, *The Gift. Forms and Functions of Exchange in Archaic Societies*, trans. Ian Cunnison, London, 1966.

Melion, Walter S., "Introduction: The Jesuit Engagement with the Status and Functions of the Visual Image", in *Jesuit Image Theory*, ed. Karl Wietse de Boer, A. E. Enenkel, and Walter S. Melion, Intersections 45 (Leiden: 2016), 1–49.

Meyer, Véronique, *L'illustration des thèses à Paris dans la seconde moitié du XVIIᵉ siècle: Peintres, graveurs, éditeurs* (Paris: 2002).

de Mûelenaere, Gwendoline, *Early Modern Thesis Prints in the Southern Netherlands: An Iconological Analysis of the Relationships between Art, Science and Power*, Brill's Studies on Art, Art History, and Intellectual History, 60 (Leiden/Boston: 2022).

Morrissette, Bruce, "Un héritage d'André Gide: La duplication intérieure", *Comparative Literature Studies*, 8, no. 2 (1971), 125–142.

Pericolo, Lorenzo, "What is Metapainting? The Self-Aware Image Twenty Years Later," in *The Self-Aware Image: An Insight into Early Modern Metapainting*, ed. Victor Stoichita (London: 2015), 11–31.

Pezzo, Annalisa, *Le tesi a stampa a Siena nei secoli XVI e XVII: Catalogo degli opuscoli della Biblioteca comunale degli Intronati* (Milan: 2011).

Préaud, Maxime, "'Nous allons à l'an pire': à propos d'un almanach mural pour 1653 et de sa mise en abyme," *Nouvelles de l'estampe*, 245 (2013), 4–14.

Rice, Louise, "Jesuit Thesis Prints and the Festive Academic Defence at the Collegio Romano", in *The Jesuits: Cultures, Sciences, and the Arts, 1540–1773*, ed. John W. O'Malley (Toronto: 1999), 148–69.

Rooses, Max, *L'oeuvre de P. P. Rubens. Histoire et description de ses tableaux et dessins* (Antwerp: 1892).

Schandel, Pascal, "Les images de dédicace à la cour des ducs de Bourgogne. Ressources et enjeux d'un genre," in *Miniatures flamandes, 1404–1482*, ed. Bernard Bousmanne and Thierry Delcourt, exhibition catalogue (Paris: 2011), 66–80.

Schemmel, Bernhard and Wolfgang Seitz, *Die graphischen Thesen- und Promotionsblätter In Bamberg* (Wiesbaden: 2001).

Schleif, Corine, "Kneeling on the Threshold: Donors Negotiating Realms Betwixt and Between", in *Thresholds of Medieval Visual Culture: Liminal Spaces*, ed. Elina Gertsman and Jill Stevenson (Woodbridge: 2012), 195–216.

Steadman, David W., *Abraham van Diepenbeeck: Seventeenth-Century Flemish Painter* (Ann Arbor: 1982).

Stoichita, Victor, *L'instauration du tableau: Métapeinture à l'aube des temps modernes* (Geneva: 1999).

Stoichita, Victor, "L'effet Don Quichotte. Le problème de la frontière esthétique dans L'œuvre de Murillo", in *Cadre, seuil, limite. La question de la frontière dans la théorie de l'art*, ed. Thierry Lenain and Rudy Steinmetz, Essais (Brussels: 2010), 51–99.

Van der Velden, Hugo, "Diptych Altarpiece and the Principle of Dextrality," in *Essays in Context. Unfolding the Netherlandish Diptych*, ed. John Oliver Hand and Ron Spronk (Cambridge: 2006), 124–155.

Vouilloux, Bernard, *L'œuvre en souffrance: Entre poétique et esthétique*, L'extrême contemporain (Paris: 2004).

Weijers, Olga, *In Search of the Truth: A History of Disputation Techniques from Antiquity to Early Modern Times* (Turnhout: 2013).

Whatling, Stuart, "Putting Mise-En-Abyme in its (Medieval) Place," lecture at the workshop *Medieval Mise-En-Abyme: The Object Depicted within Itself*, online article of the Courtauld Institute, February 2009, accessed March 17, 2014, 1–10 [http://www.courtauld.ac.uk/researchforum/projects/medievalarttheory/documents/Mise-en-abyme.pdf].

White, John J., "The Semiotics of the *Mise-en-Abyme*," in *The Motivated Sign*, ed. Olga Fischer and Max Nänny (Amsterdam: 2001), 29–53.

CHAPTER 9

Jan Ponętowski's Print Albums in the Jagiellonian Library in Cracow: an Early Print Collection in Moravia and the Kingdom of Poland

Magdalena Herman

In 1592, Jan Ponętowski (*c.*1540–1598), a Polish nobleman and an Abbot in the Premonstratensian monastery in Hradisko near Olomouc, donated his collection of books, manuscripts, prints, paintings, tapestries, liturgical paraments, and other precious objects to the University of Cracow.[1] Most of this donation has been lost and is known only from Ponętowski's inventory, which was written on the 11th of May 1592.[2] However, his miter, crosier, many luxuriously bound books, and over 1,000 Netherlandish, Italian, German, and French prints bound in albums, pasted into books, or presented in the form of monumental friezes remain in the collections of the Jagiellonian Library and the Jagiellonian University Museum in Cracow.[3] Though on a slightly smaller scale, Ponętowski's print collection could be compared to the collections of Philip II of Spain (1527–1598) and Ferdinand II of Tyrol, Archduke of Austria (1529–1595).[4] The aim of this essay is to give an initial overview of the surviving Ponętowski's albums and bound print suites that were donated to the University of Cracow, explore their content, and, in doing so, to shed some light on this little-known early modern collector.

Jan Ponętowski was born into a family that had not yet significantly distinguished itself from other noble houses in Poland. The House of Ponętowski

---

1 The research for this essay was supported by the National Science Centre, Poland (grant no. 2016/21/N/HS2/02659). I would also like to express my sincere gratitude to Prof. Grażyna Jurkowlaniec for the immeasurable support and guidance she has provided throughout this study. The essay was originally submitted in 2017, with latest major corrections in 2020.

2 Cracow, Archiwum Uniwersytetu Jagiellońskiego, Akta pap. 16330; Piotr Hordyński, "Kolekcja Jana Ponętowskiego. Wstęp do opisu zawartości," *Biuletyn Biblioteki Jagiellońskiej* 66 (2016), 69–84; translation in Biuletyn Biblioteki Jagiellońskiej, Special Issue (2020): 137–152.

3 On Jan Ponętowski's mitre and crosier see: Jan Samek, "Pastorał i mitra z daru opata Jana Ponętowskiego w zbiorach Muzeum Uniwersytetu Jagiellońskiego," *Opuscula Musealia* 5 (1991): 85–93.

4 Peter Parshall, "The Print Collection of Ferdinand, Archduke of Tyrol," *Jahrbuch der Kunsthistorischen Sammlungen in Wien* 78 (1982): 139–184; Mark P. McDonald, "The Print Collection of Philip II at the Escorial," *Print Quarterly* 15, no. 1 (1998): 15–35.

© KONINKLIJKE BRILL BV, LEIDEN, 2024 | DOI:10.1163/9789004703834_011

came to importance due to the political actions undertaken by Jan's brother, Jakub Ponętowski (*d.* 1586), and through the offices held by Jan himself. Jan matriculated at the University of Cracow in 1569.[5] His biographer, Leszek Hajdukiewicz, conjectured that Jan Ponętowski traveled through Europe with his older brother Jakub in the service of Emperor Maximilian II (1527–1576) between 1573–1576, although no record confirms this hypothesis.[6] Due to his brother's loyal service to the emperor, Jan was appointed in 1576 by Maximilian II as the coadjutor Abbot in the Premonstratensian monastery in Hradisko near Olomouc, on the condition that he undertook a religious profession and adopted the habit.[7] This action was strongly opposed by the canons and the Abbot of the monastery, who claimed that they had the sole right to elect their superior, as had been granted to them by Vladislaus II the Jagiellon (1456–1516). When the Abbot of the monastery, Kašpar from Litovel (Abbot from 1556–1576), died in November 1576, Ponętowski put himself forward as his deputy; the fact that the canons had already elected Pavel Grünwald (*d.* 1593) for this function did not discourage him. Ponętowski was accused by canons of questionable orthodoxy and it was said that he failed to meet the requirements set by the Emperor.[8] However, notwithstanding this, and after the intervention of Rudolf II (1552–1612) and a papal dispensation, Ponętowski adopted a Premonstratensian habit on 14 July 1577. The next day, he was

---

5   Leszek Hajdukiewicz, "Jan Ponętowski—opat hradyski, bibliofil i miłośnik sztuki (materiały do życiorysu)," *Roczniki Biblioteczne* 14 (1970): 494; Danuta Quirini-Popławska claims that Ponętowski also studied in Padua in 1567, "Podróże polskich duchownych do Padwy w XV i XVI wieku; wstępne rozpoznanie," *Itinera clericorum: Kulturotwórcze i religijne aspekty podróży duchownych*, eds. Danuta Quirini-Popławska and Łukasz Burkiewicz (Kraków: 2014), 244. However, there is no known surviving archival evidence for this. Letters from Antonio Maria Graziani to Mikołaj Tomicki, written in 1567, mention several times a Polish nobleman "Ponietowschio" who stayed in Padua but without indicating his first name, see Angelo Mai, *Spicilegium romanum*, vol. 8 (Rome: 1839), 272, 274, 289, 294. Therefore, he could have been Jan's relative, i.e. Wincenty Ponętowski. I would like to thank Danuta Quirini-Popławska for sharing her sources with me.

6   Hajdukiewicz, "Jan Ponętowski—opat hradyski," 504–508. The only reference to Jan Ponętowski from 1573–1576 is his signed poem praising the coat of arms of Henry III of France printed in a Polish Bible translation, the Leopolita Bible in 1575.

7   Prague, Národní archiv (henceforth NA) Morava, inv. no. 2208; the earliest known letters of Maximilian II concerning this matter are dated May 1576. However, quite surprisingly, Serafino Cavalli (*d.* 1578), the master of the Order of Preachers, named Jan Ponętowski an Abbot in February 1576. The latter notice was copied by the monastery's chronicler in the 17th century, and it is possible that the date was mistakenly changed; Brno, Moravský zemský archiv (henceforth MZA), E 55, sig. II 1, inv. no. 199, k. 1, no. 108.

8   NA, Morava, inv. no. 2505; see also letter from Giovanni Delfino to Cardinal Como dated 6 June 1577: Bohumil Navrátil, *Biskupství olomoucké 1576–1579 a volba Stanislava Pavlovského* (Prague: 1909), 260–261.

JAN PONĘTOWSKI'S PRINT ALBUMS

officially appointed Abbot of Hradisko.[9] He received his priestly ordination from the Bishop of Cracow Piotr Myszkowski (*c.*1505–1591) on the 31st of May 1578.[10]

In 1580, Pope Gregory XIII (1502–1585) confirmed that Abbot Jan Ponętowski was entitled to use a miter and a crosier like his predecessors, who had been granted this privilege by Urban VI (1318–1389).[11] In the spring of 1581, Ponętowski was also conferred a title of Protonotary Apostolic and empowered to create notaries (*notaries publicos seu tabelliones*).[12] Henceforth, his armorial blocks (*supralibros*) hold an inscription mentioning both his offices of Abbot and the Protonotary Apostolic along with Ecclesiastical hat, miter, and crosiers. In 1582, a portrait medal of Jan Ponętowski attributed to the Olomouc goldsmith Donát Šolc was created.[13] Before 1587, Ponętowski received another honorary title, Papal Count Palatine.[14] Despite these successive honors, the conflict between the Abbot and his canons did not diminish. It is assumed that the bone of contention was Ponętowski's lavish lifestyle and his squandering of the monastery's demesne.[15] Numerous art and book acquisitions, which formed the

---

9   Cracow, Biblioteka Jagiellońska (henceforth BJ), Cim. 5525, July 1577. Hajdukiewicz, "Jan Ponętowski—opat hradyski," 511–512; probably on behalf of the emperor acted by Vratislav II of Pernštejn (1530–1582) and Hanuš Haugvic of Biskupice (d. 1580). See: MZA, G 12, inv. no. 385, fol. 78.

10 BJ, Cim.8420, fol. Z4; Olomouc, Zemský archiv v Opavě, pobočka Olomouc, fond Arcibiskupství olomoucké (henceforth ZAO-OL, AO), inv. no 2108, sig. Bb126, k. 442, fol. 30r. According to the chronicle of the monastery, Ponętowski took his holy orders three years after his appointment from Bishop Stanisław Pawłowski (*c.*1545–1598), but this source is less reliable, see: MZA, G 12, inv. č. 385, 78; Navrátil, *Biskupství olomoucké 1576–1579*, 260–261.

11 MZA, E 55, inv. no. 262, sig. IV B 4.

12 A letter from Alessandro Farnese (1520–1589), which informs about Ponętowski's new title was dated 19 March 1581, MZA, E 55, sig. II 1, inv. no. 199, k. 1, no. 114.

13 Jan Štěpán, "Olomoucký zlatník Donát Šolc (1575–1588) a olomoucká medailérská škola," *Střední Morava: vlastivědná revue*, 16 (2003): 109. The medals are in the collections of Moravské zemské muzeum in Brno (inv. No. 2968; Antonín Taul, *Olomoucké medaile, plakety, žetony a známky*, Práce odboru společenských věd Vlastivědného ústavu v Olomouci 22 (Olomouc: 1969), cat. 5); Muzeum Sztuki Medalierskiej in Wrocław (inv. No. MSM Mp. 5140; Teresa Bogacz i Jan Sakwerda, *Medale—polonica i silesiaca XVI i XVII wieku w zbiorach Muzeum Sztuki Medalierskiej: katalog zbiorów* (Wrocław: 1999), 17); Zakład Narodowy im. Ossolińskich in Wrocław (inv. no. G 805; Józef Szwagrzyk, *Moneta, medal, order* (Wrocław: 1971), cat. 22); and later copies in Muzeum Emeryka Hutten-Czapskiego in Cracow (inv. MNK VII-MdP-3005; MNK VII-MdP-3007; Emeryk Hutten-Czapski, *Catalogue de la collection des médailles et monnaies polonaises*, vol. 2 (Saint Petersbourg—Paris: 1872), no. 3976).

14 Częstochowa, Biblioteka Jasnogórska (henceforth BJC), Rkps. 1.7. R. 134, fol. 6r.

15 NA, Morava, inv. no. 2685. Information on his debts often recur in other letters from and to the emperor's chancery (fond Morava) and in the correspondence of bishop Stanisław Pawłowski (MZA, G 83, Opisy kopiářů olomouckych biskupů (corespondence from years

216   HERMAN

bulk of his donation to the University of Cracow, probably contributed to his expenditure in Hradisko. In 1587, Ponętowski ostensibly resigned as an Abbot because of bad health, but in fact he was dismissed for getting the monastery into debt.[16] He likely moved back to Cracow in 1588.

We do not have his archival accounts from 1576–1587, but the items preserved from his collection reveal that he was most active as a print collector at that time. The dates 1582 and 1586 are gold-tooled on the bindings of six out of twelve print albums and the majority of the prints housed in Ponętowski's albums are dated between 1570 and 1586, with the earliest engraving dated 1544. However, dates on prints do not always indicate the year that they were issued as publishing houses customarily continued printing from plates in their possession. The examples of worn impressions in Ponetowski's collection indicate that in some cases he acquired prints that were issued years after the dates on them further suggesting that these were all bought between the mid-1570s and late 1580s.[17] Moreover, ten albums have Moravian watermarks dated from the 1570s and 1580s on endpapers, blank folios, pastedowns or margining strips. Only two undated volumes retain end papers bearing Polish 16th-century

---

1579–1588); ZAO-OL, AO, Kopiáře a registra korespondence biskupů, administrátorů, regentů a jiných úředníků—Stanislav Pavlovský). Jan Ponętowski also probably pawned the monastery's assets in Sebetov to his brother. Furthermore, Jakub Ponętowski was accused by the canons of stealing the monastery's valuables; see Hajdukiewicz, "Jan Ponętowski—opat hradyski," 525–526; NA, Morava, inv. no. 2998; see also: Zdeněk Kašpar, "Opat kláštera Hradisko Jan Poniatovský," *Střední Morava: vlastivědná revue* 11 (2000): 128–136.

16   MZA, E 55, sig. II 1, inv. no. 199, k. 1, fol. 241r; G 12, inv. no. 385, fols. 78–79. However, like his appointment, his dismissal could have also been political.

17   Plenty of them were printed from worn plates, and some of them have offsets that indicate late printing. The other case is the impression print from album 211 showing the construction of the vault in the Basilica of Saint Peter in Rome and published by Antonio Lafreri (*c.*1512–1577). Although dated 1561, it is likely to have been printed or have left the printing shop *c.*1574 because on its verso there is a clearly visible offprint of the upper part of the calendar for year 1574 (*Lunario nuovo per anno M D LXXIIII*), Magdalena Herman, "Compiling Standardized *Speculum Romanae Magnificentiae Albums, c. 1575–81*," *Print Quarterly* 41, no. 2 (2024): 147–149. For another example of an offset from album 211, see Hordyński, "Grafika włoskiej proweniencji z kolekcji Jana Ponętowskiego w Bibliotece Jagiellońskiej," in *Amicissima. Studia Magdalenae Piwocka oblata* (Kraków: 2010), 217. Offsets are often used to reveal the sequence of albums. However, great care has to be taken when doing so, as before prints were bound they were stored in a workshop, shipped to or by a buyer, and they could have been stored unbound, so offsets could have been left for a long time before the decision on binding was made. Regarding offsets see Peter Parshall, "Antonio Lafreri's 'Speculum Romanae Magnificentiae'," *Print Quarterly* 23, no. 1 (2006): 20; David Woodward, "The Evidence of Offsets in Renaissance Italian Maps and Prints," *Print Quarterly* 8, no. 3 (1991): 235–51.

watermarks.[18] The prints bound in them are dated between 1564–1589. Ponętowski probably bought most of his prints while still in Moravia, but the presence of the latest prints in the collection, published *c.*1589 that can be found in album 153, indicates that some of them may be later acquisitions that were compiled and bound in Cracow.

Ponętowski's print collection might be described by means of the inventory of his donation to the University of Cracow and the surviving objects themselves. In the inventory, printed images are assigned to three sections. The first section of the inventory, which consists of tapestries and paintings on panel and canvas, also included three monumental prints that still exist in the collection of the Jagiellonian Library.[19] The second section with *Printed Images* ("*Imagines Tipus excussae*") lists eight records. Only one of these entries, the "*Genealogia Austriaca*", can be identified in the Jagiellonian Library's modern collection as a book of portrait engravings of members of the House of Austria by Gaspare Osello (*c.*1536–1590) after Francesco Terzi (*c.*1523–1591) (*Austriace gentis imagines*).[20] Print albums were mostly included among the largest section of the inventory, which was dedicated to books ("*Libri Conscripti*"). Most of them might be identified in the inventory on the basis of their contents and titles (gold-tooled or handwritten on their covers).

The list of surviving albums includes the following (the current albums' numbers are given in parentheses):[21]

---

18   A more detailed description of the bindings, watermarks, and album contents will be given in the Appendix.

19   *The procession of Pope Clement VII and Emperor Charles V after the Coronation at Bologna* (*Divo et invicto Imperatori Carolo V ...*) by Nicolaas Hogenberg, *Magnificent and Sumptuous Funeral of the Very Great Emperor Charles V* (*La magnifique et sumtueuse pompe funèbre faite (...) aux obsèques de l'empereur Charles V*) by the Doetecum brothers, and depiction of the *The funeral procession of emperor Ferdinand I* (*Parentalia divo Ferdinando Caesari Augusto Patri Patriae*) published by Wolfgang II Meyerpeck (1505–1578) and Joachim Sorg. BJ, I.23893, I.23895, I.23894. The types of objects included in this group suggest that they were destined to be hung on walls. The aforementioned printed friezes could have been displayed on the walls of the Collegium Maius in Cracow, as is stated in its inventory compiled in 1801. The frieze of *Parentalia* bears many rust-colored nail holes, indicating that it was fixed to a secondary support for such a display, BJ, Rkps. 918, fol. 14r. See also: Hordyński, "Pochody ceremonialne Habsburgów. Trzy rolki akwafortowe z wieku XVI z kolekcji Jana Ponętowskiego w Bibliotece Jagiellońskiej," in *Tendit in ardua virtus: studia ofiarowane profesorowi Kazimierzowi Kuczmanowi w siedemdziesięciolecie urodzin*, ed. Joanna Ziętkiewicz-Kotz (Kraków: 2017), 107–118.

20   BJ, Album 2 V.

21   Hereafter, the albums will be referred to using their library numbers. Whenever possible, titles are transcribed from the covers of the albums. Albums 154, 1 V, and 2 V do not bear titles on the covers; therefore, their titles from the inventory are listed above.

- *Typus Ecclesiae Catholicae*, 1582 (box 149);
- *Theatrum Legis Divinae*, 1582 (box 150);[22]
- *Theatrum Vitae Humanae*, 1582 (box 152);
- *Speculum Christianae Professionis*, 1582 (box 210);
- *Speculum Romanae Magnificentiae*, 1582 (box 211);
- *Bellum Tuneti, Flandricu*[m], *Gallicu*[m]*que*, 1582 (Album 407–410);
- *Liber Devotus Imaginum*, 1586 (box 151);
- *Acta Apostolorum cum Iconibus*, 1586 (box 154);
- *Liber Divinae Sapientiae*, undated (box 153);
- *Vita Austera Religiosorum*
- *Sanctorum Patrum Heremitarum Monasticae Sacrae Professionis qui Seculores Ignato in Exercitio Spirituale Contemplatine Vixer*[unt], undated (box 209);
- Untitled (Jacques Tortorel, Jean Perrissin, *Der erste tail: Mancher layen gedencwirdiger historien von krierg* [sic]; Album 1 v);[23] and
- *Genealogia Austriaca* (Album 2 v).

We do not know if Ponętowski himself was responsible for naming the albums, but the presence of the titles in the inventory and on the covers acclaims their late 16th-century origin. The prints within print albums reflect to some extent the main topic set by the title. Five album names are derived from the titles of the allegorical engravings or printed sets that they contained (albums 149, 152, 211, 154, 209). The titles of the albums have little descriptive value; instead, they can be described as intellectual, as the album names refer to their content using words popular in book titles (e.g., *speculum, theatrum, liber*).[24] The full scope of the existing print albums from Ponętowski's collection may be summarized in the following categories: ancient and modern history, portraits, moral issues (religious and secular allegories), devotion, the Scripture, divine and earthly law (including political allegories), topographical depictions, and maps. The contents of the thirteenth album, which was lost during World War II, were briefly described in the 19th century by Żegota Pauli as "50 prints, scenes, flowers, colored animals, landscapes" by Philips Galle, Sadelers, Collaerts, Abraham

---

22   Not identified in the inventory.

23   Identified in the inventory by Hordyński as "*Cronica Franciae cum Iconibus sub aureo filo*". However, it is now in a plain cardboard binding with traces of hardly legible 16th-century handwriting which does not seem to include the phrase from the inventory. Only edges of this volume are gilded, Hordyński, "Wstęp do opisu," 79.

24   Herbert Grabes, *The Mutable Glass: Mirror-imagery in Titles and Texts of the Middle Ages and English Renaissance*, transl. Gordon Collier (Cambridge—New York: 1982), 19–65; Markus Friedrich, "Das Buch als Theater: Überlegungen zu Signifikanz und Dimensionen der 'Theatrum'-Metapher als frühneuzeitlichem Buchtitel," in *Wissenssicherung, Wissensordnung und Wissensverarbeitung. Das europäische Modell der Enzyklopädien*, eds. Theo Stammen, Wolfgang E. J. Weber (Berlin: 2004), 207–232.

de Bruyn, after Maarten de Vos, and Hans Bol.[25] The books known only from inventory records and still existing volumes, sometimes lavishly illustrated or even books of prints, also cover a variety of subjects, such as history, topography, cosmography, mathematics, important historical figures, and costumes from around the world, with the strongest emphasis on ecclesiastical and sacred matter. Print albums, books of prints, and books were grouped under one category in the inventory and therefore should be perceived through their relationships to one another. Their grouping shows the twofold character of the printed images as objects of the pictorial arts and a source of knowledge and ideas.[26]

However, in any early modern collection the originality of the albums' structure must be addressed. The prints in all the albums are bound with their own sheets as well as pasted on guards. Only a few were pasted onto extra sheets or onto versos of other prints. Smaller prints have margining strips added to unify the sizes of all the sheets in the album. Prints exceeding the size of the album were folded to fit in or trimmed in some cases. The reparations of the leather and paper as well as uneven gilded edges of sheets reveal past conservation treatments. It cannot be excluded that some unidentified alterations were made to the structure of the volumes during these interventions.[27] Deletions and additions occur very rarely. Narrow, mostly irregular remnants of sheets or empty guards indicate the removal of prints from volumes in a number of places.[28] The exact number of deletions is difficult to establish due to the tight binding of the albums and the lack of a consistent pagination system.[29] Additions tend to have been glued on blank folios, endpapers, versos

---

25   BJ, Rkps. 5446, fol. 11v; not identified in the inventory of 1592. The same information is given by an old inventory card, which also records the old signatures: L 11 6; Artes 496. Before the II World War it was inventoried as box 155 (inv. nos. 9631–9680). The early 20th century library cards list quite precisely its content.

26   Peter Parshall, "Art and the Theater of Knowledge: The origins of Print Collecting in Northern Europe", *Bulletin, Harvard University Art Museums* 2 (1994): 14; Magdalena Herman, "*Cum imaginibus, cum iconibus*: Cataloguing Printed Images in Early Modern Libraries," in *Print Culture at the Crossroads: The Book and Central Europe*, eds. Elizabeth Dillenburg, Howard Louthan, and Drew B. Thomas (Leiden–Boston: 2021), 163–164, 172–174.

27   The salient treatments are those of albums 152 and 407–410 IV. In the latter, the endpapers and blank folios were removed and changed to new ones carrying the same watermark as originally used. The conservation procedure was recorded on the new pastedown in 1936. In the case of the former album new mounting strips and a new guard were used (no watermarks have been identified). Furthermore, in the past, curators of the collection decided to remove two drawings from album 149 (I.R.1961, I.R.1974), and colored woodcuts from the pastedowns of albums 407–410 IV and 149 (I. 14704, I. 9035).

28   However, there is a possibility that some those guards had never been glued to any sheet. On binders' gatherings see: Nicholas Pickwood, "Binders' Gatherings," *The Library: The Transactions of the Bibliographical Society* 15, no. 1 (2014): 63–78.

29   Only in album 154, the deletion of *Vesper* from the *Times of The Day* by Jan Sadeler is revealed by the numbers "8," "9," and "11" written in ink near the bottom right of the platemark of the engravings from this set. These numbers reflect the positions of prints in the

FIGURE 9.1 Numbering on the sheet with Hans Collaert (sculp.), Adriaen Huybrechts (excud.) Corporal and Spiritual Works of Mercy, before 1582, engraving, Jagiellonian Library in Cracow, inv. no 9065, box 149
PHOTOGRAPH: MAGDALENA HERMAN

of impressions already bound in the volume, or on existing guards. All of these extra prints were issued before the collection was donated to the University of Cracow, and it is highly probable that they were introduced by Ponętowski and can thus be seen as reflecting the process of creating and supplementing a print collection. The early stage of assembling and organizing the prints before binding is revealed by the incomplete and dispersed page numbering present in album 149. The numbers written in ink in a 16th-century hand appear only on the very bottom of a few prints bearing sheets.[30] One of numerals was shaved in half during the binding process (Fig. 9.1). Some are covered by the margining strips and visible only in transmitted light. Two others are preserved because the margining strips with a Moravian watermark used after 1581 were added at the bottom of the versos of sheets to adjust them to the size of the album.[31] The strips retain their original gilded edges. All the above

album. The only other sheet number in this album is "68," and this also appears in its actual place.
30 Numerals are present on 8 out of 78 print-bearing sheets. They do not indicate accurately the place of the sheets in the album, but they are relatively close. Furthermore, in three cases, the distance between prints corresponds precisely to the distance set by the numbering.
31 Inv. nos. 9042, 9079; the watermark was used by a papermill in Šumperk. Veronika Stružová, *Filigrány moravských papíren na základě nových zjištění využití papíru v kanceláři olomouckých biskupů* (diploma at University of Pardubice: 2015), 68, fig. 5.

FIGURE 9.2 Dirck Volckertsz. Coornhert (?), *Epitaph of Sigmund Feyerabend's Daughters*, 1576–1582, engraving, Jagiellonian Library in Cracow, inv. no 9058, box 149
PHOTOGRAPH COURTESY OF THE JAGIELLONIAN LIBRARY PHOTOGRAPHIC SERVICES JAGIELLONIAN LIBRARY, CRACOW

implies that those numbers are prior to the binding of album 149, when its organization was being discussed and created.[32] It also reveals that the album composition was carefully considered.

The composition of the albums, which is likely very close to the original dating to pre-1592, indicates that there was an attempt at organizing the prints into groups based mostly on thematic sequences. The subject groups happen to be supplemented with pictorial juxtapositions. For instance, in the group of crucifixions in album 149, narrative and allegorical variants are present; the depiction of the Epitaph of Feyerabend's Daughters attributed to Dirck Volckertsz. Coornhert (1522–1590) is placed in this group because of its main scene, which is the crucifixion (Fig. 9.2). Groups are also formed by print series bound in albums in their original or altered order. Print series are frequently interrupted and enriched with thematic or pictorial allusions to their subjects or compositions. Individual prints from the cycles are sometimes distributed among different thematic groups, as in the case of the four engravings from the series *The Divine Charge to the Three Estates* by Philips Galle after Maarten van Heemskerck (1498–1574), which are dispersed in album 152, and each belongs to a coherent group.[33] Furthermore, this series is an example of duplicates in the collection, as it is also present in album 154.[34] The presence of duplicates in the albums may reveal a mass acquisition of printed images, which finally resulted in the solicitous choice to use an image more than once; alternatively, this could have been the aim of the collector from the very beginning, with duplicates being placed in the albums due to their specific themes. Despite identifiable organization schemes, the sequence in the albums seems haphazard at times, and no common criteria for assembling prints in the specific order can be identified. Similarly, the organizational pattern breaks at the end of some albums (153, 210).

We probably know only part of Ponętowski's collection. He made his generous donation six years before his death on 30 June 1598.[35] It is doubtful that in

---

32 On several pages in albums 149, 150, 152, and 210, other numbers are written in metalpoint or graphite in another hand, but these numbers are repeated multiple times in one album and refer to the predicted number of a sheet in a quire while the album was being organised. Most of them are numbers "2," "4," and "6". The detailed description of this numbering is beyond the scope of this essay.

33 See the Appendix.

34 Duplicates on a larger scale are in albums 153 and 154.

35 The year 1589 was often mistakenly given as his death date, and it probably originates from the transposed digits in the *Liber mortuorum* of Hradiště Monastery. Despite this inaccuracy, the *Liber mortuorum* indicates the date of Ponętowski's death; see: MZA, G 10, kniha 92/1, fol. 361. A slightly different date of Ponętowski's death is given by the

JAN PONĘTOWSKI'S PRINT ALBUMS

1592 he would have divested himself of everything that he had collected over the course of his life. Moreover, contemporary sources suggest that he bought and offered his books as gifts in the late 1590s. Some of his possessions that are now housed in the library are not all listed in the inventory of 1592, and they probably reached the university library much later.[36] For that reason, care needs to be taken in giving an overall assessment of Ponętowski's collection and his patterns of collecting in general. Ponętowski was a generous man, who during his stay in Hradisko made provisions for the Olomouc Jesuit College, young students, travelers, and catholic hierarchs passing through Olomouc.[37] He also donated books to his monastery and commissioned artworks for at least two churches.[38] He also sustained his relationship with academics from the University of Cracow. These contacts may be observed in the journal entries of a rector of the University of Cracow, Marcin Glicius from Pilzno (1528–1591), who wrote about a joint banquet in Cracow in 1577.[39] The Jagiellonian Library and Książnica Cieszyńska still hold individual gifts of books from Ponętowski to professors of the University of Cracow.[40] The donation of his books and art collection in 1592 to the University was the clearest sign of amicable association with his alma mater. The donation consisted of a wide range of objects (including his crosier and liturgical paraments), and it is questionable whether they were amassed solely for the university. Only in two cases is it possible to state that an album and a book were bound for the University of Cracow, as the name of the University was tooled on its upper cover in lettering identical to other inscriptions.[41] However, when the donation was made in 1592, it can be assumed that Ponętowski considered it to be a closed set of art and

---

Cathalogus mortuorum written by the Norbertine nuns in Strzelno: 7 April (without a year). Wrocław, Zakład Narodowy im. Ossolińskich, sig. 5192/I, fol. 115r.

36 See dedication for Adam Bronikowski dated 1596, BJ, Cim.6024. Another gift for Adam Bronikowski has the date 1596 gold-tooled on the binding, Cieszyn, Książnica Cieszyńska, SZ T III 35. Album 150 and the lost 155 album were not listed in the inventory either; therefore, they may not have been part of the donation in 1592.

37 Hajdukiewicz, "Jan Ponętowski—opat hradyski," 517–518; Vatican Library, Chigi.L.III.67, fol. 99 *recto*.

38 Magdalena Herman, "Odrowąż, smok i salamandra. Kreacja wizerunku w herbowych znakach własnościowych ksiąg Jana Ponętowskiego," *Z Badań nad Książką i Księgozbiorami Historycznymi* 13 (2019): 82–83.

39 Hajdukiewicz, "Jan Ponętowski—opat hradyski," 512.

40 These include books for Adam Bronikowski, who was an Augustinian monk and professor of Theology in Cracow (see footnote 36), and the Halle and Wittenberg reliquary book dedicated to the professors of the University of Cracow, which was donated after 1581, BJ, Cim.5746–5747.

41 Album 153 and Cim.5693 (*Cosmographia Apiani*, Antwerp 1540); the latter is not identified in the inventory of 1592.

library items that were given to serve the university. The book-like manner of naming the albums might be familiar to the university audience. The prominence of religious, moral, and historical subjects within the print collection prevails, thereby supplementing the university library with works of an instructive and edifying character. The albums also reveal a strong interest in recent events, especially in religious wars. The presence of prints including definite religious and political matter may be particularly confusing, as the prints in Ponętowski's albums depict standpoints on both sides of the line in the early stage of the Eighty Years War in the Netherlands. The decision to bind prints severely critical of military campaigns and the harsh repression of protestants led by Duke Alva (1507–1582), such as *The Allegorical Comparison between William the Silent and Duke Alva* and Theodor de Bry's *The Evil Rules the World while Truth and Justice Sleep*, is puzzling.[42] However, this might represent an attempt to record all information available. Furthermore, some prints lose their political or religious context in the juxtaposition with other works in an album. Thus, in examples such as *The Watchers on the Walls of Jerusalem* by Hieronymus Wierix, published by Willem van Haecht from album 210 and *The Unhappy Lot of the Rich* by Philips Galle after Maarten van Heemskerck from album 152, they might be devoid of controversial connotations and serve as moral or religious allegories.[43] Placing the depictions of the siege of Haarlem (1573) and the siege of Maastricht (1579) among the battles with the Ottoman Empire (album 150) along with Ponętowski's writings and actions might reveal his anti-protestant attitude.[44] His print albums did not include any works of old masters. Some copies and pastiches are present, but they are allocated to a place in a topical sequence or group. Similarly, mythological scenes are even rarer. It is not clear whether Ponętowski was not interested in acquiring specific types of prints or if he wanted to keep them to himself and therefore excluded some prints from the donation.

The compilation of Ponętowski's albums was a result of the activity and interests of a Polish nobleman who was also entrusted with vital Church functions in post-Tridentine Moravia. This kind of art collecting has not been adequately reflected in the literature, as comparable 16th-century collections of this type are very rare.[45] Furthermore, albums donated to the University of

---

42   Daniel R. Horst, *De Opstand in zwart-wit. Propagandaprenten uit de Nederlandse Opstand (1566–1584)* (Zutphen: 2003), il. 43, 55, 58.

43   See McDonald, "The Print Collection of Philip II," 26.

44   Jan Ponętowski, *Krotki Rzeczy Polskich Seymowych pamięci godnych Commentarz* (Cracow: 1569), quire F1.

45   On the print album that belonged to bishop of Bamberg Johann Georg Zobel (1543–1580) see: Joyce Zelen, "The Venetian Print Album of Johann Georg Zobel von Giebelstadt," *The Rijksmuseum Bulletin* 63, no. 1 (2015): 2–51.

Cracow formed a very early university print collection. Unfortunately, we do not know much about its use and reception by Cracovian academics. Prints collected by Ponętowski stand out for their exquisite artistic quality. On the other hand, the strategies of their organization, placement in the inventory, and the naming of the albums clearly emphasize the library affiliation.[46] The impressions in albums consist of mostly up-to-date and popular productions, but among them there are also rare, precious, and previously unknown impressions.[47] The dates on the bindings and the date of donation provide the *terminus ante quem* for many undated prints and make it possible to place them more precisely within the respective artists' oeuvre—foremost the works by Wierixes, Sadelers, and Collaerts. Ponętowski's albums constitute important, representative material not only for the history of printmaking but also for research on collecting in Europe in the 16th century. The archival sources concerning the early history of the collection are scarce, but close analysis of preserved objects makes it possible to pose and answer many questions. A better understanding of Ponętowski's collection content and its place within the European context will be made possible by means of the forthcoming catalogue.[48] However, the catalogue of Ponętowski's collection requires different strategies from catalogues of modern collections to achieve the aims set above. The approach of ordering records according to the authors will be abandoned in favor of the order and structure of individual albums. The following Appendix to this essay provides only a brief description of individual albums and aims to provide a general view of the collection.

Appendix

Bindings

Ten of Ponętowski's print volumes are in their 16th-century leather bindings (149, 150, 151, 152, 153, 154, 209, 210, 211, Albums 407–410). They can be divided into three groups according to the dates and ornaments on the bindings.

All but one of the albums dated 1582 are gold-stamped with figural blocks (149, 150, 152, 210, 407–410). The exception is album 211, which has ornamental blocks.[49] Figural blocks on the front covers of these albums depict the *Pietas Patris*, which is

---

46 Magdalena Herman, "*Cum imaginibus, cum iconibus*," 172–174.

47 See Appendix regarding i.a. the anonymous *Homini Christiani Ecstasis* printed on silk.

48 Magdalena Herman, *Kolekcja rycin Jana Ponętowskiego w zbiorach Biblioteki Jagiellońskiej w Krakowie*, vols. 1–3 (Warszawa: 2025).

49 Ornamental center tooling consists of four triangular corner-blocks in place of the figural one.

accompanied by the inscription "*ALSO HADT GODT DIE WELDT GELI[e]BT DAS*" ("God so loved the world"). On the back covers, a depiction of King David is accompanied by the inscription "*FAC CUM SERVO TUO SECUNDUM MISERI[cordiam]*" ("Deal with your servant according to [your] mercy"; fig. 9.3).[50] The titles of the albums are gold-tooled on the front covers along with the date followed by the inscription "*ANNO DOMINI*". On the back is the inscription: "*IOHANNES PONETOWSKY / ABBAS GRADICENSIS*" ("Jan Ponętowski, the Abbot of the Hradisko Monastery").

The albums dated 1586 have a more elaborate gilded and tooled ornamental decoration (151, 154). Two of Ponętowski's armorial blocks are stamped on the front and back covers, one with the external ornament of a coat of arms of a protonotary apostolic and the lettering "*I[oannes] P[onetowski] / P[rotonotarius] A[postolicus]*" and the second with ornaments of "*abbas infulatus*" and the inscription "*IOANNES PONETOWSKI D[ei] G[ratia] ABBAS GRADICEN[sis] SEDIS AP[osto]LICAE PROTHONOTARIUS*" ("Jan Ponętowski by the grace of God the Abbot of the Hradisko Monastery [and] Protonotary Apostolic").[51] The album titles are written on the front covers in ink, but they are hardly legible.

Two undated volumes, 153 and 209, form a third group of albums. The similar decoration of these volumes suggests that they were probably produced by the same workshop.[52] The gold-tooled titles of these volumes are accompanied with the same armorial blocks and inscriptions as the albums from 1586 (Fig. 9.4). Album 153 is also tooled with the inscription "*SACRII COLLEGII CRAC[oviensis]*".

Two volumes do not belong to any of the above-described groups. Gaspare Osello's (*c.*1536–1560/1580) engravings from *Austriacae Gentis Imaginum* (Album 2 v) are bound in 16th-century red-stained leather, which has the same figural blocks as Ponetowski's

---

50   The latter is also present on the front covers of books, which belonged to Stanislaw Pawłowski, ZAO-OL, fond Arcibiskupství olomoucké, dodatky, sign. 1451; Knihovna biskupství brněnského, sign. MZK STA3-327. Regarding books that belonged to Stanisław Pawłowski. See: Jan Kašpar, "Exempláře starých tisků s vlastnickými vazbami olomouckého biskupa Stanislava II. Pavlovského dochované na území České republiky," *Sborník Národního muzea v Praze. Řada C—Literární historie* 59 (2014): 13–20.

51   Photographs of the types of signets, and some book bindings, were published in Tadeusz Chrzanowski, "Uwagi o intelektualiście kolekcjonerze w Polsce na przełomie renesansu i baroku," in *Mecenas, kolekcjoner, odbiorca. Materiały Sesji Stowarzyszenia Historyków Sztuki, Katowice, November 1981* (Warsaw: 1984), 134–137. According to the old inventory card, album 155 (untitled), which was lost during World War II, also bore the binding with heraldic supralibros and the date "1586".

52   Anna Lewicka-Kamińska, "Biblioteka Jagiellońska w latach 1492–1655," in *Historia Biblioteki Jagiellońskiej*, vol. 1, ed. Ignacy Zarębski (Kraków: 1996), 163–164.

FIGURE 9.3 Impressions of figural medallions on the front and back covers of the album *Typus Ecclesiae Catholicae*, Jagiellonian Library in Cracow, box 149
PHOTOGRAPH COURTESY OF THE JAGIELLONIAN LIBRARY PHOTOGRAPHIC SERVICES JAGIELLONIAN LIBRARY, CRACOW

FIGURE 9.4 Supralibros on the front and back covers of the album *Vita austera religiosorum sanctorum patrum heremitarum monasticae sacrae professionis...*, Jagiellonian Library in Cracow, box 209
PHOTOGRAPH COURTESY OF THE JAGIELLONIAN LIBRARY PHOTOGRAPHIC SERVICES JAGIELLONIAN LIBRARY, CRACOW.

228   HERMAN

albums dated 1582. It has more intricate ornamental gold-tooling but bears no date nor title. Album 1 v is bound in simple paperboards without any covers.[53]

Moravian watermarks are present on the blank folios, endpapers, pastedowns, and margining strips in the albums from 1582, 1586, and albums 1 v and 2 v. In album 211, two free sheets and the margining strips also carry various Italian watermarks, which suggest it was pre-compiled in Italy. Later it was supplemented with additional sheets with Moravian watermarks and folios bearing Ponętowski's bookplates (*ex libris*) (Fig. 9.5).[54] Volumes 153 and 209 retain their 16th-century end papers bearing Polish watermarks of the Lubicz and Abdank coats of arms, respectively.[55]

Albums
Album 2 v

This album is listed in the inventory as "Genelogia [sic] Austriaca", it includes an incomplete series of portraits of the Habsburg rulers and their relatives after Francesco Terzi engraved by Gaspare Osello. It consists of 55 plates, including a dedication page and title pages of all five parts of the work. The portrait of Archduke Charles II of Austria (1540–1590) is printed on parchment. Some sheets are missing, and this is clearly visible in the case of plate 31, of which only scrap of paper bearing the number is preserved.

---

53 See footnote 23.

54 Watermark from Litovel papermill with two fishes on the crowned shield in 151, 152, 154, and 407–410 (similar to Briquet 2102); Veronika Stružová, *Filigrány moravských papíren*, 61, fig. 3; part of unidentified watermark similar to those of Litovel is in the mounting of a print on silk (inv. no. 12.480) in 210; watermark from Šumperk with half of the eagle and half of the antlers on the crowned shield is on the margining strips of a few prints in 149 (Stružová, *Filigrány moravských*, 68, fig. 5); unidentified watermark with one-headed eagle on a crowned shield that bears a strong resemblance to the watermarks of paper produced in the Olomouc—it has the same shield and lower crown ornaments as the watermarks used in 1568–1572 and a very similar crown to the watermarks used in 1574 . It is present in 211, 1 v, 2 v; see Stružová, *Filigrány moravských*, 48–49, fig. 8, 10; Miroslav Čermák, "Městská papírna v Olomouci (1505–1785)," *Vlastivědný věstník moravský* 30, no. 1 (1978): 36–48 fig. 1.9–1.12; Petr Gajdošík, "Další nově zjištěné filigrány olomoucké papírny," *Olomoucký archivní sborník* 9 (2011): 67–68, fig. 11. Other similar Olomouc watermarks include Briquet nos. 217, 325. A barely visible watermark with a double-headed eagle in a crowned shield on the lower pastedown of 150 and endpapers of 1 v and 2 v also bears a strong resemblance to the Olomouc papers; see Stružová, *Filigrány moravských*, 49, fig. 10. In the margining strips in 211, the most frequently occurring watermarks are of Pilgrim with vertical crook in a shield (in two variants) and Paschal Lamb with bent standard, David Woodward, *Catalogue of Watermarks in Italian Printed Maps. (ca. 1540–1600)* (Florence: 1996), nos. 9 and 46.

55 Karol Badecki, *Znaki wodne w księgach Archiwum miasta Lwowa, 1382–1600* (Lwów: 1928), nos. 74, 88, 116; Jadwiga Siniarska-Czaplicka, *Filigrany papierni położonych na obszarze Rzeczypospolitej Polskiej od początku XVI do połowy XVIII wieku* (Wrocław: 1969), nos. 228, 543.

FIGURE 9.5 Exlibris of Jan Ponętowski, before 1582, woodcut, Jagiellonian Library in Cracow, box 211
PHOTOGRAPH COURTESY OF THE JAGIELLONIAN LIBRARY PHOTOGRAPHIC SERVICES JAGIELLONIAN LIBRARY, CRACOW

Albums 407–410

Listed in the inventory as "Bellum Tuneti cum imaginibus", with BELLUM TUNETI, FLANDRICU[m], GALLICU[m]QUE on the front cover. The album comprises the three groups of broadsheets by Franz Hogenberg (1535–1590) that are bound together in one volume (66 prints). The first group includes eight etchings and the title page from *The Conquest of Tunis by Charles V, 1535* (*Kurtze erzeichnis wie Keyser Carolus der V. in Africa Dem Konig von Thunis...*), the second comprises 25 prints that relate to the religious wars in the Netherlands, and the third includes 33 prints showing the religious wars in

France. The prints generally follow a sequence based on the numbers stamped from the plate. The colored *Turkish galley captured by the Venetians* by Cesare Vecellio was removed from the pastedown and now is stored separately.[56]

Album 1 v

The album consists of 33 woodcuts and etchings with inscriptions in German from a series of 40 depicting the French religious wars by Jacques Tortorel (*act.* 1568–1575) and Jean Perrissin (before 1546–1617).[57] Prints in the volume are preceded and followed by folios with Ponętowski's bookplates. The anonymous *Battle of Moncontour* (*Il ordene del fattodarme fano ira Catolici et Ugonotti ...*), which does not belong to the set, was pasted on the verso of *The Capture of Nîmes* by Jacques Tortorel.[58] Two other additions were pasted on the blank folios at the end, namely, a map by Matthias Zündt (*c.*1498–1572) (*Tabula complectens totam Belgicam ...*, 1568) and the poem *Carmina de humilitate* dedicated to Ponętowski by Michael Prudeker (Mihovil Obratković).

Album 209

This is listed in the inventory as "Vitae Sanctorum Patrum cum imaginibus". Raphael Sadeler (1560–1628) and Johann Sadeler I's (1550–1600) cycle of 30 prints from the *Solitudo sive vitae patrum eremicolarum* is bound as a self-contained suite with its title page. On the cover, it bears another extended title, *Austere lives of the holy monks Hermits of the holy monk vocation who lived their lives in spiritual contemplation after having resigned from their earthly lives.*[59]

Album 149

This is listed in the inventory as "Tipus [sic!] Ecclesiae Catholicae", with TYPVS ECCLESIAE CATHOLICAE on the cover. The earliest dated print is 1566 while the latest is 1581. The colored *Astronomical Clock in the Cathedral in Strasbourg* by Tobias Stimmer (1539–1584) was removed by librarians from the upper pastedown and is now stored separately.[60] The album consists now of 93 prints, mainly Italian large folios, depicting various religious allegories, which are interspersed with the subjects of saints, the Virgin Mary (many in the context of a rosary), Rome, portraits of popes and rulers, a broadsheet with cardinals' coats of arms (published in 1581 by Francesco Zanetti, *fl.* 1563–1591), and numerous representations alluding to the passion of Christ.

---

56   See footnote 27.

57   Rafał Szmytka, "Graficzne przedstawienie przemocy w Quarante tableaux Jeana Perrissina i Jacques'a Tortorela," *Biuletyn Biblioteki Jagiellońskiej* 67 (2017): 129–51.

58   Philip Benedict, *Graphic History: The Wars, Massacres and Troubles of Tortorel and Perrissin* (Travaux D'Humanisme et Renaissance) 431 (Geneva: 2007), 145.

59   VITA AUSTERA RELIGIOSORUM, SANCTORUM PATRUM HEREMITARUM MONASTICAE SACRAE PROFESSIONIS QUI SECULORES IGNATO IN EXERCITIO SPIRITUALI CONTEM-PLATINE VIXER[unt]

60   See footnote 27.

All of them give an elaborate image of the Catholic Church. The most important allegory in this volume is *Typus Ecclesiae Catholicae*, published by Luca Bertelli (*fl.* 1560–1594) in 1574 and accompanied by an extended description published by Bertelli in the following year, because it sets the title for the album.[61] Few groupings can be observed in the album. For instance, the first state of engraving (with no inscriptions), *Six prophets of the Annunciation* (previously attributed to Hendrick Goltzius, 1558–1617), opens the sequence with depictions of the Virgin Mary and Child, among which is a copy of Raphael's (1483–1520) *Madonna of Divine Love* published by Pietro Paolo Palumbo (*fl.* 1562–1586) and *Virgin Mary with Angels*, published by Ferrando Bertelli (*fl.* 1561–1571) after Albrecht Dürer (1471–1528). Engravings after famous authors, such as *The lamentation of the Virgin beneath the cross* by Mario Cartaro (*fl. c.*1560, *d.* 1620) after the design of Sebastiano del Piombo (*c.*1485–1547) (after Michelangelo (1475–1564)), *Resurrection* after Pieter Breughel the Elder (*c.*1525–1569), and the prints copying compositions after Dürer and Raphael mentioned above, are placed in their thematic sequence. The final group in the album consists of portraits of Catholic rulers (mostly the House of Wittelsbach by Peter Weinher, *fl.* 1570–1583) and bishops, with a few insertions of seemingly less relevant subjects, which can be seen in the placement of antique sculptures from the Alessandro Farnese's and Giovan Giorgio Cesarini's collections, and *The Cyclops Forging the Arms of Brescia* by Cornelis Cort (*c.*1533–1578) after Titian (*c.*1490–1576). They may also be viewed as allusions to prominent personages due to their inclusion in the group of portraits. In contrast to portraits of Catholic rulers, there is also the *Sommario et alboro delli principi della casa Othomana* by Niccolo Nelli (*fl.* 1552–1579). On the lower pastedown, there is a woodcut after *Adam with the skull* from Vesalius (1514–1564). This is preceded by an allegory of *Vanitas*, which is the subject of this group.[62] The *vanitas* theme was also represented by two drawings of unrealized projects for Ponętowski's tombstone, which were once at the end of the album; these were removed and are currently stored separately.[63]

---

61   On this composition, Grażyna Jurkowlaniec, "La porpora cardinalizia e l'arte nera dell'incisione: Tomasz Treter tra gerarchie ecclesiastiche e stampatori romani e veneziani," in *Italian music in Central-Eastern Europe. Around Mikołaj Zieleński's 'Offertoria' and 'Communiones'* (*1611*), eds. Tomasz Jeż, Barbara Przybyszewska-Jarmińska, Marina Toffetti (Venezia: 2015), 89–90; Jurkowlaniec, *Sprawczość rycin. Rzymska twórczość graficzna Tomasza Tretera i jej europejskie oddziaływanie* (Kraków: 2017), 93–118; *Eadem*, "Printed Images Crossing Borders: an Allegory of the Catholic Church and Its Dissemination in Late Sixteenth Century Europe," in *Transregional reformations: crossing borders in early modern Europe*, eds. Violet Soen, Wim François, Alexander Soetaert, Johan Verberckmoes (Göttingen: 2019), 205–244.

62   It is probably a 'flap' print with the flap missing. Ponętowski's copy bears a 1578 publisher's signature of Giacomo Franco. The later state was published by Luca Bertelli (Amsterdam, Rijksmuseum, RP-P-2015-14-7).

63   Probably, Ponętowski was not commemorated with any tombstone at all; regarding the designs see: Tadeusz Chrzanowski, "Adoracja czy prezentacja? O dwóch projektach z drugiej połowy XVI wieku nagrobka Jana Ponętowskiego, opata hradyskiego," *Folia Historiae Artium* 2–3 (1997): 83–89.

The publishers represented in album 149 include, among others, Lorenzo Vaccaria (*fl.* 1574–1608), Godevaard (1546–*c.*1599) and Willem (*c.*1527–*c.*1583) van Haecht, Hieronymus Cock (1518–1570), Antonio Caranzano (*fl. c.*1577–*c.*1614), Adriaen Huybrechts (*fl.* 1573, d. *c.*1614), Nicolas Beatrizet (*fl. c.*1540, d. *c.*1566), Benetto Stefani (*fl.* 1570–1580), and Perino de Guarlotti (*fl.* 1567–1574).

Album 150

This album is not in the inventory. Its title, THEATRVM LEGIS DIVINAE, is tooled on the cover. The earliest dated print is 1549 while the latest is 1581. The album has only 53 prints, which broadly refer to the fall and redemption of man, rulers of the Catholic Church, and their enemies according to divine law. Two cycles, *The Four Enemies of Righteousness and the Theological Virtues* by Hieronymus Wierix (1553–1619) after Maerten de Vos (1535–1603) and *The Fall and Redemption of Men* after Ambrosius Francken (*c.*1544–1618), by Willem van Haecht and Hieronymus Wierix, constitute the core of this album and allude to the subject set by its title. Prints from these sets are scattered within the volume among subjects that include depictions of Rome and the papacy published by Bartolomeo Faleti (*fl. c.*1560, d. 1570) and Antonio Lafreri, which were possibly introduced as a sign of the divine law on Earth. An important group in this album comprises maps of Europe and the Holy Land as well as depictions of battles against the Turks and battles of the Eighty Years War in the Netherlands by Mario Cartaro, Balthasar Jenichen (*fl.* 1560, d. 1599), and Matthias Zündt (*c.*1498–1572). There are also three political allegories published by Pieter Baltens (*c.*1526/9–1584), which show Philip II as the author of the long-awaited peace achieved by the Perpetual Edict of 1577. Another political broadsheet published by Adriaen Huybrechts represents metaphorically an appeal for the union of the Netherlands against the Spanish reign, but in Ponętowski's copy the accompanying text is missing.[64] The album also includes a few Italian biblical stories. Gouaches, which depict two common wood pigeons and a great crested grebe, are pasted onto the upper and lower pastedowns, respectively.[65]

Album 151

This is listed in the inventory, and title *Liber Devotus Imagnum* appears also on the cover in handwriting. The earliest dated print is 1582 while the latest is 1585. A few pages are missing from the album. Currently, it consists of 22 prints, which cover biblical and devotional subjects as well as the *Seven Planets and Four Elements*, which follow the *Seven Days of Creation* after Hans Bol (1534–1593). Depictions of Virgin and Passion dominate. Among the devotional subjects are the *Salvator Mundi*, based on the engraving of Lucas van Leyden (1494–1533), and *Nuestra Seniora de l'Antigua*

---

64 Daniel R. Horst, *De Opstand*, il. 66, 68 I, 77 I, 86.

65 The paper of the latter bears an Olomouc watermark with eagle, see footnote 54.

by Hieronymous Wierix. The publishers represented in the album include Eduard Hoeswinckel (*d.* 1583), Philips Galle, and Ferdinand Reael (*fl.* 1560–1600).

Album 152

This is listed in the inventory and its majuscule title *THEATRVM VITAE HVMANAE* is tooled on the front cover. The earliest dated print is 1561 while the latest is 1579. It consists of 216 prints and is mainly organized by published cycles. The first section comprises prints after Virgil Solis (1514–1562), Philips Galle (1537–1612), Johann Bussemacher (*fl.* 1577–*d.* before 1627), Harmen Jansz Muller (*c.*1539–1617), and Hieronymus Wierix, which depict the world and human nature, with subjects ranging from the continents, four elements, four seasons, months, temperaments, and allegories of the *Three Ages of Men* and *Time*.[66] This is followed by moral and religious allegories (such as *Christian Faith, Life and Death* by Hendrick Goltzius after Adriaan de Weerdt (*c.*1510–*c.*1590)), biblical figures, and narratives. The album includes the print cycle *Theatrum Vitae Humanae* by Wierix, published by Pieter Baltens after Hans Vriedeman de Vries (1527–*c.*1607), which sets the title for the whole volume. Interestingly, the four engravings from the series *The Divine Charge to the Three Estates* by Philips Galle after Maarten van Heemskerck (1498–1574) are dispersed in this album and might be ascribed to four groups.[67] *The Lord Assigning Duties to the Three Estates* opens the group, with the cycle *Credo* by Johannes Sadeler after Maarten de Vos and *Ecce Homo* published by Hans van Luyck (*fl.* 1580s) as well as *Imitation of Christ in Bearing the Cross* published by Hieronymus Cock. *The King Administering Justice* opens a group of various suites of virtues and vices including allegories by Willem van Haecht after Ambrosius Francken and ones after Maarten van Heemskerck published by Philips Galle, biblical stories such as *Lucretia* by Hendrick Goltzius and published by Philips Galle, and deadly sins, with thematic conjunctions that encourage the viewer to choose between good and evil, by Johannes Sadeler, Hieronymus Wierix, Hendrick Goltzius, Peter Furnius (*c.*1545–*c.*1610), Lucas van Doetecum (*fl.* 1554–1572), and Hans Collaert (*c.*1525/1530–1580). There are also some series that were later published by Gerard de Jode (1516/1517–1591) in *Thesaurus sacrarum historiarum veteris* [et] *novi testamenti*, such as *The story of Esther* and *The story of Daniel*. The third group begins with *Christ Giving the Symbols of Power to Philip II and Gregory XIII* by Johannes Wierix (1549–*c.*1620), which links this group with the previous one and antecedes *The Pope Performing Religious Duties* from *The Divine Charge to the Three Estates*. This group includes religious prints, a depiction of William the

---

66   *The Thiumphal Processions of the Four Seasons* after Solis are pasted now on front blank folios, previously they were glued on the upper pastedown.

67   Duplicates from this series are also present in album 154.

234 HERMAN

Silent (1533–1584) praying with Charlotte de Bourbon (1546–1582), and the double portrait of Matthias Habsburg (1557–1619) and William the Silent.[68]

The fourth of the above-mentioned groups in this album of the theater of human life consists of depictions of hunting and fishing scenes by both Philips Galle and the monogrammist FML after Jan van der Straet (1523–1605), which come from *Venationes Ferarum, Avium, Piscium*. *The People Labouring in the Fields* from *The Divine Charge...* is also included in this group. Album 152 ends with prints alluding to glorious and condemnable actions, most of which are from the Bible, by Hendrick Goltzius after Jan van der Straet and Philips Galle after Heemskerck, and one anonymous woodcut of the Council of Trent.[69] All have associations with religious or historical subjects and could be interpreted as representations of virtues, warnings, or examples that should be followed.

Album 210

SPECVLVM CHRISTIANAE PROFESSIONIS is tooled on the front cover, and it is listed in the inventory with the annotation "cum imaginibus". The earliest dated print is 1563 while the latest is 1580. The album consists of 182 prints, which can be divided into two main parts that are mixed with diverse religious, moral, and political subjects. According to the title, the first part reflects the teachings of the Catholic Church, as follows: sacraments, acts of mercy, deadly sins, the eight beatitudes, the ten commandments, and prayers by Hans (I) Collaert, Adriaen Huybrechts, Philips Galle, and Hendrick Goltzius. The sequence of the second part is more disturbed, as topical, chronological, and pictorial organizational schemes are mixed and merged together. It is composed of grouped Netherlandish and Italian depictions of the Youth and Passion of Christ, the Pietà, and Virgin Mary, with sub-thematic and pictorial groupings, including annunciations, Virgin and Child, Assumption of Mary, and saints. Various religious allegories, such as the *Allegories of Christian Faith* and the *Allegories on Christ's Life* by Hendrick Goltzius or *Triumphs of Truth* by Dirck Volckertsz. Coornhert after Adriaen de Weerdt, are dispersed throughout the album. Among many anonymous prints, *Homini Christiani Ecstasis*, an engraving on yellow silk, should be mentioned as a rare and luxurious item (Fig. 9.6).[70] The album ends, quite surprisingly, with suites of the

---

68 Horst, *De Opstand*, il. 10, 59, 78. There are also four mythological prints whose compositions are very similar to religious ones, but their presence can hardly be explained.

69 The latter was glued on the lower pastedown. Following conservation treatment, it has been pasted on the free sheet.

70 A reversed version of this engraving published by Adriaen Huybrechts was pasted into a manuscript, Paris, Bibliothèque Sainte-Geneviève, MS. 1413, f. 192. See also: Brussels, La Bibliothèque royale de Belgique, EST 4°—Huberti (A.)—S.I 56210. Another version of this composition was published in 1576 by Giovanni Battista Cavalieri (*c.*1525–1601), see Jesús María González de Zárate, *Real Colección de Estampas*, vol. 2 (Vitoria–Gasteiz: 1992), no. 512 (Esc.28-II-2, fol. 83a). Three other prints on silk from Ponętowski's collection were used as pastedowns for a missals, BJ, Cim.5750, Cim.8426. See also Jurkowlaniec,

FIGURE 9.6 Anonymous, *Homini Christiani Ecstasis*, engraving on silk, before 1582, Jagiellonian Library in Cracow, inv. no 13.476, box 210
PHOTOGRAPH COURTESY OF THE JAGIELLONIAN LIBRARY PHOTOGRAPHIC SERVICES JAGIELLONIAN LIBRARY, CRACOW

Gods of Agriculture by Cornelis Cort, *Persian Kings* with a title page published in 1579 by Gerard de Jode, and *Virtues* by Hans Collaert. The pastedowns are decorated with heraldic prints, the upper of Gregory XIII (1502–1585) and Cardinal Zaccaria Delfino (1527–1583) and the lower with the poem *Cenotaphion of Caspar Cropacius* accompanied by the poet's (1539–1580) coat of arms. At the end of the album, there is a colored and gilded drawing of the Rožmberks' coat of arms.

Album 153

This is listed in the inventory by the title tooled on the cover *LIBER DIVINA*[e] *SAPIENTIAE*. The earliest print dated on the plate is 1564 while the latest 1586. However, the latest datable prints in this album from the series of *Americae retectio* were published *c.*1589.[71] The album consists of 135 prints, 119 of which belong to various series. The prints assembled in this album, in accordance with the title, illustrate aspects of divine wisdom. The first part of the album praises divine creation. It opens with *Adam and Eve in Eden* and impressions from *Credo* by Adriaen Collaert (*c.*1560–1618) after Hans Bol, which are followed by series with personifications of the planets (zodiac), the four elements, times of the day, archangels, temperaments, and the five senses by various Netherlandish artists, including Johann Sadeler, Adriaen Collaert, Philips Galle after Maarten de Vos, Hadrianus Junius, and Theodor Barendszoon (1534–1592). The second part describes the world and humankind in history and contains the *Continents* and the biblical scenes of *Knowledge of Good and Evil* by Johann Sadeler, *The Course of History of all God's Creatures* and *Discovery of America* by Adriaen Collaert, and biblical scenes within landscapes by Lucas and Johannes van Doetecum (*c.*1530–1605). Johannes Wierix's *Hercules at the Crossroads* opens the equivocal series of *Virtues* by Hendrick Goltzius. The *Virtues* series is followed by the biblical scenes in landscapes by Adriaen Collaert and Pieter van der Borcht (*c.*1530–*c.*1611). The next group concerns sin and God's mercy and includes *Examples of Repentant Sinners from the Old and New Testament* after Maarten de Vos by Philips Galle and *The Sorrows of the World*. This group is enriched with *The Divine Charge to the Three Estates* by Adriaen Collaert and depictions of evangelists by Johannes Wierix. *The Repentance of Saint Peter* from *Repentant sinners from the Old and New Testament* initiates the group along with *The Crucifixion and the Martyrdom of the Apostles* by Hendrick Goltzius, which is followed by scenes from the Passion, with a copy of Dürer's *Christ Mocked by a Soldier* from *The Large Passion* by Antoine Wierix. In the album, there are some engravings inserted between the above-mentioned series that could be viewed as occasional thematic or pictorial allusions to the subjects or compositions of prints from cycles. Some

---

Sprawczość rycin, 105–106; *Eadem*, "Geneza i recepcja drzeworytów na kartach tytułowych kazań Lutra o sakramentach z 1519 roku," *Rocznik Historii Sztuki* 42 (2017): 38–39; *Eadem*, "Printed Images Crossing Borders," 213–215.

71   Lia Markey, "Stradano's Allegorical Invention of the Americas in Late Sixteenth-Century Florence," *Renaissance Quarterly* 65, no. 2 (2012): 393.

series, such as the *Repentant Sinners*, are scattered among the others. Nevertheless, the album ends quite surprisingly with three engravings by Philips Galle after Jan van der Straet from the *Mediceae Familiae rerum feliciter gestarum victoriae et triumphi*, two engravings praising William the Silent (one anonymous, one signed by Theodor de Bry, 1528–1598), *The Allegory of Patience in Adversity* by Hans Collaert, which alludes to the Antwerp Spanish Fury of 1576,[72] and *Rhinoceros Abada of Philip II* by Philips Galle. In this album, short notes written by Ponętowski are present beneath a few impressions. These handwritten notes occur very rarely in other albums.

Album 154

This is listed in the inventory as "Acta Apostolorum cum Iconibus". On the cover, there is a barely visible handwritten title, possibly the same as in the inventory. The album takes its title *Acta Apostolorum* from the series of the same name by Heemskerck and Jan van der Straet, published by Philips Galle, which forms a major part of this volume (72 prints).[73] The printed suite (published in 1582) was bound together with duplicates of prints already present in the album *Liber Divinae Sapientiae*. In both of these albums, *Adam and Eve in Eden* after Hans Bol is the first print. Other duplicates include the *Times of the day* by Johann Sadeler, a beautifully hand-colored impression of the *Four elements* by Adriaen Collaert (Fig. 9.7), and *The Crucifixion and the Martyrdom of the Apostles* by Hendrick Goltzius after Maarten de Vos. The set of *Acta Apostolorum* is also enriched at the end with five biblical scenes from the *Flight into Egypt* and the *Story of Jonas* published by Gerard de Jode.

Album 211

This is listed in the inventory, with "Speculum Romanae Magnificentiae" on the cover. Ponętowski's *Speculum* comprises 120 prints that mostly follow the order of the *Indice* published by Antonio Lafreri between 1575 and 1577.[74] There are also impressions published after Lafreri's catalogue was issued and one that was not recorded by Christian Hülsen.[75] The earliest datable print is from 1544 while the latest is from 1575. There are no later etched copies issued by Claudio Duchetti (*fl.* 1565–1585). Most importantly, Ponętowski's volume, dated on the cover as 1582, is an early example of the *Speculum* after the incorporation of the title page.[76] It was most probably compiled by Lafreri

---

72   Horst, *De Opstand in zwart-wit*, figs. 43, 55, 58.

73   Out of 72, 35 prints in the album are from this series.

74   The depictions of the Mausoleum of Augustus and the Port of Ostia (both by Etienne Dupérac, published by Lafreri in 1575, inv. no. 13.531, 13.628) were added after the initial compilation but by Ponętowski as dates indicate.

75   Christian Hülsen, "Das Speculum Romanae Magnificentiae des Antonio Lafreri," in *Collectanea variae doctrinae Leoni S. Olschki sexagenario* (Munich: 1921), 121–170.

76   Parshall, "Antonio Lafreri's 'Speculum Romanae Magnificentiae'," 22–23, 26–28; Birte Rubach, *Ant. Lafreri Formis Romae. Der Verleger Antonio Lafreri und seine Druckgraphikproduktion* (Berlin: 2016), 83–85, 100–104.

FIGURE 9.7 Maarten de Vos (inv.), Adriaen Collaert (sculps.), Gerard de Jode (excud.), *The Allegory of Fire*, hand-coloured engraving, c. 1582, Jagiellonian Library in Cracow, inv. no 9564, box 154
PHOTOGRAPH COURTESY OF THE JAGIELLONIAN LIBRARY PHOTOGRAPHIC SERVICES JAGIELLONIAN LIBRARY, CRACOW

workshop; or, less likely, soon after his death before the division of the plates between his heirs, or soon after the division when Claudio still had in his stock prints issued by Lafreri.[77]

Selected Bibliography

Manuscript Sources

Brno, Moravský zemský archiv, E 55 Premonstráti Klášterní Hradisko, sig. II 1, inv. no. 199, k. 1.

Brno, Moravský zemský archiv, G 12 Cerroniho sbírka, inv. no. 385.

Cracow, Archiwum Uniwersytetu Jagiellońskiego, Akta pap. 16330.

Cracow, Biblioteka Jagiellońska, Rkps. 918.

---

77 Recently: Magdalena Herman, "Compiling Standardized *Speculum Romanae Magnificentiae* Albums, c. 1575–81," 141–156.

Cracow, Biblioteka Jagiellońska, Rkps. 5446.
Prague, Národní archive, Morava, inv. no. 2205.
Prague, Národní archive, Morava, inv. no. 2208.
Prague, Národní archive, Morava, inv. no. 2685.
Prague, Národní archive, Morava, inv. no. 2998.

Printed Sources

Kuntze, Edward, and Nanke Czesław (ed.), *Alberti Bolognetti nuntii apostololici in Polonia, epistolae et acta 1581–1585*, vol. 1 (Monumenta Poloniae vaticana. Series Nuntiaturae Polonae) 5 (Cracow: 1923–1933).

Navrátil, Bohumil, *Biskupství olomoucké 1576–1579 a volba Stanislava Pavlovského* (Prague: 1909).

Ponętowski, Jan, *Krotki Rzeczy Polskich Seymowych pamięci godnych Commentarz* (Cracow: 1569).

Secondary Sources

Benedict, Philip, *Graphic History: The Wars, Massacres and Troubles of Tortorel and Perrissin* (Geneva: 2007).

Chrzanowski, Tadeusz, "Uwagi o intelektualiście kolekcjonerze w Polsce na przełomie renesansu i baroku," in *Mecenas, kolekcjoner, odbiorca. Materiały Sesji Stowarzyszenia Historyków Sztuki, Katowice, November 1981* (Warsaw: 1984), 121–145.

Hajdukiewicz, Leszek, "Jan Ponętowski—opat hradyski, bibliofil i miłośnik sztuki (materiały do życiorysu)," *Roczniki Biblioteczne* 14 (1970): 485–529.

Herman, Magdalena, "Odrowąż, smok i salamandra. Kreacja wizerunku w herbowych znakach własnościowych ksiąg Jana Ponętowskiego," *Z Badań nad Książką i Księgozbiorami Historycznymi* 13 (2019): 67–94.

Eadem, "*Cum imaginibus, cum iconibus*: Cataloguing Printed Images in Early Modern Libraries," in *Print Culture at the Crossroads: The Book and Central Europe*, eds. Elizabeth Dillenburg, Howard Louthan, and Drew B. Thomas (Leiden–Boston: 2021), 158–176.

Herman, Magdalena, "Compiling Standardized *Speculum Romanae Magnificentiae* Albums, c. 1575–81," *Print Quarterly* 41, no. 2 (2024): 141–156.

Eadem, *Kolekcja rycin Jana Ponętowskiego w zbiorach Biblioteki Jagiellońskiej w Krakowie*, vols. 1–3 (Warszawa: 2025); forthcoming.

Hordyński, Piotr, "Grafika włoskiej proweniencji z kolekcji Jana Ponętowskiego w Bibliotece Jagiellońskiej," in *Amicissima. Studia Magdalenae Piwocka oblata*, ed. Grażyna Korpal (Kraków: 2010), 217–221.

Hordyński, Piotr, "Kolekcja Jana Ponętowskiego. Wstęp do opisu zawartości," *Biuletyn Biblioteki Jagiellońskiej* 66 (2016): 69–84.

Horst, Daniel R., *De Opstand in zwart-wit. Propagandaprenten uit de Nederlandse Opstand (1566–1584)* (Zutphen: 2003).

Jurkowlaniec, Grażyna, "L'immagine della Chiesa nelle stampe di Tomasz Treter dedicate a Stanisław, Hozjusz. Contributo polacco alla cultura artistica europea ai tempi della controriforma," in *Atti dell'Accademia Polacca*, ed Leszek Kuk, vol. II, 2011 (Rome: 2012), 130–150.

Eadem, "Printed Images Crossing Borders: an Allegory of the Catholic Church and Its Dissemination in Late Sixteenth Century Europe," in *Transregional reformations: crossing borders in early modern Europe*, eds. Violet Soen, Wim François, Alexander Soetaert, Johan Verberckmoes (Göttingen: 2019), 205–244.

McDonald, Mark P., "The Print Collection of Philip II at the Escorial," *Print Quarterly* 15, no. 1 (1998): 15–35.

Parshall, Peter, "Art and the Theatre of Knowledge: The Origins of Print Collecting in Northern Europe," *Harvard University Art Museums Bulletin* 2, no. 3 (1994): 7–36.

Pickwoad, Nicholas, "Binders' Gatherings," *The Library: The Transactions of the Bibliographical Society* 15, no. 1 (2014), 63–78.

Štěpán, Jan, "Olomoucký zlatník Donát Šolc (1575–1588) a olomoucká medailérská škola," *Střední Morava: vlastivědná revue* 16 (2003): 108–111.

Stružová, Veronika, *Filigrány moravských papíren na základě nových zjištění využití papíru v kanceláři olomouckých biskupů* (diploma at University of Pardubice, 2015).

CHAPTER 10

A "Great and Valuable Collection": Sir Joshua Reynolds (1723–1792) and His Prints

Donato Esposito

1 Introduction[1]

Sir Joshua Reynolds' print collection, formed in company with a gathering of paintings, sculpture, drawings and books, was immense in both size and scope. The pupil of Thomas Hudson (1701–1779), himself a voracious art (and print) collector, Reynolds returned from a sojourn in Italy in 1752 to launch his successful artistic practice, which would see his meteoric rise as the founding President of the Royal Academy of Arts in 1768, and a knighthood. His large print collection was broad in variety and range; it varied in date, subject and quality. The scope of this collection has yet to be fully documented, and his position as a major print collector of the 18th century remains to be properly established. Despite extensive scholarship on Reynolds, little attention has been given to his art collection, especially his prints. For example, Mark Hallett's thorough monograph on Reynolds, published in 2014, fails to mention this aspect at all.[2]

Today, Reynolds' print collection is widely scattered across the globe, as far apart as Edinburgh, Ottawa, San Francisco and Melbourne. Prints from the collection quickly began to enter public collections less than a decade after his death. The bequest to the British Museum in 1799 by the Rev. Clayton Mordaunt Cracherode (1730–1799), who had acquired a number of prints from the collection in the years immediately after the artist's death, began the gradual drift of Reynolds' print collection from private to public ownership. In the following century his prints were routinely found in auctions in London and Paris

---

1 I would like to extend my deepest gratitude to the Metropolitan Museum of Art, New York for supporting my research as an Andrew W. Mellon Fellow in 2012–13, and at the Department of Drawings and Prints warm thanks are due in particular to Stijn Alsteens, Carmen Bambach, George Goldner, Constance McPhee, Furio Rinaldi, and Freyda Spira. I would also like to thank Maggie Allen, Stephanie Dickey, Jim Ganz, Paul Jeromack, MacKenzie Mallon, Caroline Palmer, Anna Schultz, Anita Viola Sganzerla, Ann Shafer, and Kerrianne Stone for invaluable assistance and information.

2 Mark Hallett, *Reynolds: Portraiture in Action* (New Haven; London: 2014).

© KONINKLIJKE BRILL BV, LEIDEN, 2024 | DOI:10.1163/9789004703834_012

and they appeared, for example, in the stock of New York-based art dealers. By 1900, examples had been acquired by other prestigious public collections as far apart as Boston in the United States of America and Adelaide in Australia. The form of Reynolds' original collection is largely unknown, beyond the surviving examples themselves and the three auction sale catalogues from 1792, 1798 and 1821, and the process of reconstruction has been undertaken by the present author from 2009 onwards.[3] The work here aims to extend these modest overviews and incorporates new research undertaken in the United States of America in 2012–13.

2   Content and Dispersal

Reynolds' collection remained intact until his death on 23 February 1792. Shortly afterwards, a small sale took place of "duplicate prints" on 16–18 April 1792, close to Reynolds' former home in Leicester Fields (now Leicester Square).[4] Further sales were held after the death of his main beneficiary Mary Palmer in 1821.[5] But the primary dispersal of the print collection took place over 18 days from 5 March 1798 onward, by the newly established auctioneer Harry Phillips, with premises on 67 New Bond Street in the center of the commercial art world. His two surviving executors, Edmond Malone and Philip Metcalfe (the third, Edmund Burke, had died in 1797) confirmed that his collector's mark was "imprinted on each of the drawings and prints" he had owned and it is this mark that remains the key identifier of the items in his former collection. The placement of the mark on whichever side provides an indication of the relative value of individual sheets, since 'superior' items were stamped on the recto, and 'inferior' ones on the verso.[6] Irrelevant to which side it was stamped, the exact location of Reynolds' collector's mark was itself unimportant.

---

3   Donato Esposito, "'Care, Taste and Judgement': Reynolds' Collection of Works on Paper," in Sam Smiles (ed.), *Sir Joshua Reynolds: The Acquisition of Genius* (Bristol: 2009), 102–58; Donato Esposito, "The Print Collection of Sir Joshua Reynolds", *Print Quarterly* 28 (2011): 376–81. The sales were John Greenwood, London, 16–18 April 1792, followed by Harry Phillips, London, 5–26 March 1798, and Christie's, London, 16–17 May 1821.

4   John Greenwood, London, 16–18 April 1792.

5   Christie's, London, 16–17 May 1821.

6   Donato Esposito, "What's in a Mark, or What Marks Can Tell Us: The Use and Abuse of the Collector's Mark of Sir Joshua Reynolds (1723–1792)", in Peter Fuhring (ed.), *Les marques de collections: II* (Dijon: 2011), 58.

In his 1912 survey of important prints sales over the past two centuries, Howard C. Levis considered the 1798 auction catalogue as "not interesting, as it contains no [detailed] descriptions" but nonetheless demonstrated what a "large collection" had been formed.[7] The sale consisted of 2001 lots and the prints, drawings, and books were grouped in mixed blocks, with prints beginning each day's sale. Most items are found in large groups (sometimes consisting of over 50 items) with very minor descriptions, as Levis had noted, except books of prints, which were lotted separately. For example, one typical mixed lot of prints from the third day's sale was frustratingly elusive, described as "57 ditto [prints], by various masters."[8] Few prints were lotted separately and most of these were by Marcantonio Raimondi, often known simply as Marcantonio (of whom, more later). Until recently, only a single example was known of a print bearing Reynolds' mark on the recto: Rembrandt's etching of *Jan Lutma* printed on Japan paper, now in the British Museum.[9] More have now come to light, including the first monotype to be identified from his collection, a superb example by the originator of the technique, Giovanni Benedetto Castiglione (1609–1664) (Fig. 10.1).[10] The collection also included a related drawing by the same artist, which is now at the Morgan Library and Museum, New York.[11] Reynolds stored his vast print collection at the rear of his property at 47 Leicester Fields, in more than 100 portfolios.[12] From the 1798 sale, which also disposed the portfolios and cabinets that stored the collection, we learn something of its physical housing, including a "mahogany cabinet on a frame, with folding doors enclosing 9 long and 6 short drawers for drawings, &c." and a "dwarf ditto [mahogany cabinet] enclosing 12 drawers."[13] Reynolds avidly pored over his print collection. His pupil James Northcote (1746–1831), who for several years lived with his master from 1771–76, provided an invaluable and fascinating insight into his working habits. He was keen to stress Reynolds' busy and productive attitude to his painterly practice, and evenings after a

---

7   Howard C. Levis, *A Descriptive Bibliography of the Most Important Books in the English Language relating to the Art and History of Engraving and the Collecting of Prints* (London: 1912), 230.

8   Phillips, London, 8 March 1798, lot 297.

9   British Museum, London (inv. PD 1868,0822.696); Esposito, "'Care, Taste and Judgement,'" 147, no. 73.

10 Carmen Bambach and Nadine M. Orenstein, *Genoa: Drawings and Prints, 1530–1800* (New York: 1996), 53, no. 57.

11 Morgan Library and Museum, New York (inv. 1956.6).

12 Donato Esposito, "Artist in Residence: Joshua Reynolds at No 47, Leicester Fields," in *The Georgian London Town House: Building, Collecting and Display*, ed. Susanna Avery-Quash and Kate Retford (New York and London: 2019), 191–210.

13 Phillips, London, 24 March 1798, lots 1844 and 1845 respectively.

FIGURE 10.1 Giovanni Benedetto Castiglione, *Noah and the Animals entering the Ark*, c.1650–55, monotype

day spent in the studio were never "spent in idleness, or lost in dissipation" as by 1762, when Reynolds was living in his large home at 47 Leicester Fields, Northcote recounts:

> after his daily occupation was past, he employed himself in looking over, and studying from, the prints of the Old Masters, of which he had procured a fine collection.[14]

3 Portrait Prints

Unsurprisingly, portrait prints comprised great swathes of Reynolds' print collection, with both historic and contemporary examples. These provide an obvious point of interest for us, in relation to the great artist's own successful portrait practice. Moreover, they were a key source of interest for Reynolds himself in adapting—as was well known in his lifetime—their pose and

---

14 James Northcote, *The Life of Sir Joshua Reynolds*, vol. 1 (London: 1818), 119.

compositions. Most of these were summarily allotted in the posthumous sales in unidentifiable job lots. Typically, one lot of mixed prints in the 1798 sale is described as "5 portraits from C. Marratti."[15] In another example, we find "3 portraits, Titiano" after the Venetian Renaissance painter Titian (1488/90–1576), one of which, a portrait of Charles V, Holy Roman Emperor (1500–1558) by Theodorus van Kessel (1620–1660), is now in the British Museum (Fig. 10.2).[16] This engraved likeness captured with a dazzling technique the array of textures and materials in Titian's painted portrait, from feathers and polished metal to trimmed beard. This print broadened examples of Titian's painted portraits in Reynolds' collection.

Reynolds had a variety of portrait prints, from the *arriviste* evident in the flashy self-portrait of Baccio Bandinelli (1493–1560) engraved by Niccolò della Casa (*fl.* 1543–48) (*c.*1544; National Gallery of Canada, Ottawa), to the reserved *Jan Lutma* etched by Rembrandt (1656; British Museum, London).[17] Bandinelli's confident self-portrait, widely disseminated through della Casa's engraving, displays his unabashed self-awareness and refined cultivation.[18] Reynolds also owned the accomplished portrait engraving of *Louis Dauphin de Bourgogne* (1682–1712), grandson of the French king Louis XIV (1638–1715), by Pierre Drevet (1663–1738) after Hyacinthe Rigaud (1659–1743), in which the Dauphin's cloak is emphatically set against polished armor and cascades over a *trompe-l'oeil* frame (Fig 10.3). The voluminous drapery is a dazzling counterfoil to the rigid pose of the young male in ceremonial armor, whose supercilious gaze confronts the spectator. These portrait prints were designed to impress their respective audiences. Reynolds' possession of them signaled his pedagogic documentation of art history, his appreciation of the many techniques of printmaking, and at the same time aligned the parallel awareness and position of his own very public portrait practice, which could equally dazzle and impress. Reynolds was obviously impressed by the technical accomplishments and variety of compositions in reproductive portrait prints by Drevet, as he owned over 50 examples by the printmaker.[19]

---

15   Phillips, London, 5 March 1798, lot 19.

16   Phillips, London, 5 March 1798, lot 23; British Museum, London (inv. PD 1868,0808.2269).

17   National Gallery of Canada, Ottawa (inv. 41343); British Museum, London (inv. PD 1868,0822.696).

18   David Franklin in David Franklin (ed.), *Leonardo da Vinci, Michelangelo, and the Renaissance in Florence* (Ottawa; New Haven; London: 2005), 274–75, no. 98.

19   For example, Phillips, London, 6 March 1798, lots 242 as "10 foreign portraits, by Drevat [*sic*], &c.," 243 as "8 ditto by ditto," 244 as "20 ditto," and 248 as "13 portraits of artists, by Drevat, &c."

FIGURE 10.2 Theodorus van Kessel after Titian, *Charles V*, engraving

A "GREAT AND VALUABLE COLLECTION" 247

FIGURE 10.3   Pierre Drevet after Hyacinthe Rigaud, *Louis Dauphin de Bourgogne*, 1707, engraving

Reynolds supplemented his Northern Renaissance paintings by Dürer and Gossaert with contemporary Northern prints. The tightly cropped portrait engraving of *Albert van der Helle*, from 1538, by the German Heinrich Aldegrever (1501/02–1555/61), pays excessive attention to the sitter's costume, which parallels Reynolds' own focus on detail in matters of dress.[20] The print was recorded in the collection of the Rev. H. Last of Stony Stratford, Buckinghamshire and, having last been on the London art market in 1921, remains untraced.[21] Sitting alongside these impressive portrait prints were other more intimate and informal examples revealing Reynolds' private, more sensitive taste. Reynolds was deeply interested in the history of British portraiture, and the prints he amassed positioned this area within the broader European context of his wide collection to encompass past British painting and drawing, alongside these portrait prints. Notable clusters of works by (and after) Sir Peter Lely and Sir Anthony van Dyck, illustrious collectors as well as painters, formed the foundation of this aspect of his collection. His etching by Josias English (*fl.* 1649–1705) after the self-portrait by William Dobson (1611–1646) clearly signaled this interest, and formed a natural complement to examples of work by Van Dyck (Fig. 10.4). The figure of Dobson was taken from a large triple portrait, now at Alnwick Castle, showing the artist with Sir Charles Cotterell (1615–1701) and Nicholas Lanier (1588–1666), painted shortly before Dobson's premature death in 1646, and bearing a strong imprint of the portraiture of Van Dyck. In a mezzotint portrait of the political theorist James Harrington (1611–1677) by Giuseppe Marchi (*c.*1721–1808), the 17th and 18th centuries are brought together (Fig. 10.5). Marchi was Reynolds' chief studio assistant, from the time of their meeting in Rome in 1752. As the print's lettering indicates, Marchi's portrait of Harrington is after a painting, then in the collection of John Hudson of Bessingby, Yorkshire. Marchi made many mezzotints after Reynolds' portraits (and other work). Considering the close relationship between Reynolds and his assistant it is likely that he owned many, if not all, of Marchi's prints, although only a few have come to light. The simple, introspective quality of the mezzotint of Harrington contrasts with the more flamboyant examples in Reynolds' collection, such as those by Van Kessel and Drevet outlined above.

---

20   B.8.418.186; NH. 186.

21   Sotheby's, London, 21–22 March 1921, lot 90 as "H. Aldegrever. Albrecht Vander Helle (B. 186); *from the Sir J. Reynolds collection*"; B.8.418.186.

FIGURE 10.4   Josias English after William Dobson, *William Dobson*, c.1649, etching

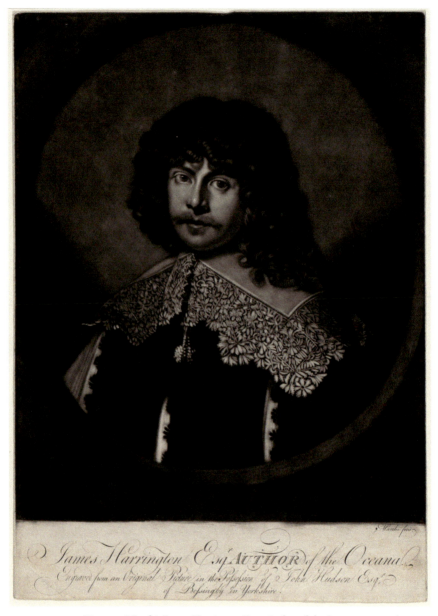

FIGURE 10.5   Giuseppe Marchi, *James Harrington Esqr. Author of the Oceana*, mezzotint

A "GREAT AND VALUABLE COLLECTION" 251

4   Formation

Reynolds must have bought many of his prints, perhaps the majority, in job lots comprising multiple items rather than selecting them one by one. Inevitably this led to duplicate impressions in his collection, and may also account for the wide variety in quality, with sparkling impressions placed together with badly rubbed and creased ones. For example, he owned two impressions of the chiaroscuro woodcut *The Presentation in the Temple* by Niccolò Vicentino (*fl.* 1510–50) after Parmigianino (1503–1540), which are coincidentally both now in the Metropolitan Museum of Art, New York. However, the two impressions are not exact duplicates. One is printed in brown-green ink, acquired by the institution in 1922, and had been owned by the sculptor John Michael Rysbrack (1694–1770) before Reynolds.[22] The other example of Reynolds' Vicentino print, printed in grey-green ink, was acquired in 1962 and had also been previously owned by Rysbrack.[23] Reynolds likely acquired them together at the same time, perhaps at Rysbrack's main sale in February 1764 at Langford's, London. Though modest in size, the subtle variant coloring of Vicentino's woodcuts gave Reynolds an opportunity for direct comparison of their variation, something that he practiced himself as a successful colorist.

Reynolds also procured contemporary prints and volumes at the time of their publication. He owned volumes on art history and theory, including *Principles of Beauty, Relative to the Human Head* (1778) by Alexander Cozens (1717–1786), for which Reynolds was a subscriber.[24] The volume contains prints by Francesco Bartolozzi RA (1727–1815) after Cozens. Reynolds' interest in Old Master drawings extended to collecting noteworthy contemporary sets of prints after them, especially Parmigianino, who was one of his favorite artists. These included, for example, the volume by Conrad Martin Metz (1749–1827) of his *Imitations of Drawings by Parmegiano, in the Collection of His Majesty* from 1790.[25] He also owned a copy of *Imitations of Parmegiano* by John Skippe (1741–1812).[26] Reynolds also owned a copy of the seminal *Anatomy of the Horse* by George Stubbs (1724–1806), an artist Reynolds encouraged by buying one of his paintings from him, and whose volume was a landmark in print production.[27]

---

22   Metropolitan Museum of Art, New York (inv. 22.73.3-39).

23   Metropolitan Museum of Art, New York (inv. 62.635.797).

24   Phillips, London, 13 March 1798, lot 752: "1 [book of prints], the principles of beauty, by Alex. Cozens."

25   Phillips, London, 13 March 1798, lot 754: "1 [book of prints], Imitations of drawings, by Parmegiano, in the collection of His Majesty."

26   Phillips, London, 23 March 1798, lot 1655.

27   Phillips, London, 21 March 1798, lot 1449.

5 Star Prints 1: Marcantonio

The 1798 dispersal was dominated by mixed lots of prints (and drawings), but a few stellar impressions were sold by themselves. These were mostly prints by Marcantonio Raimondi (*c.*1480–1534) made in collaboration with Raphael (1483–1520), who was greatly valued at the time. The printmaker's close association with Raphael's late Roman career was particularly creative in the history of Italian printmaking. For example, two impressions of *The Judgment of Paris* sold separately were described as "1 [print], the Judgment of Paris, from Raphael, by M. Antonio."[28] Marcantonio's magisterial large engraving *Saint Cecilia* was also offered singly in a solitary lot.[29] None of these Marcantonio subjects can be traced today but a few others have come to light. These include a superb impression of *Mars, Venus, and Cupid*, made in Bologna in 1508 prior to the printmaker's relocation to Rome, and now in Boston (Fig. 10.6).[30] The balanced poses of both the leading protagonists in this large print appealed to Reynolds' refined sense of composition. In turn, the manner of work could point to his varied picture-making. He had obtained his example from Rysbrack, whose collection was dispersed in 1764 and 1765.[31] Reynolds had many other prints from this source, including the two chiaroscuro woodcuts by Vicentino after Parmigianino of *The Presentation in the Temple* discussed above.[32] As Vasari famously described in *The Lives of the Artists*, Marcantonio made engraved copies after Dürer's woodcut series from the Passion of Christ (known as the *Little Passion*), and one of these, *The Arrest of Christ* (or *The Betrayal*), owned by Reynolds, is in the Courtauld Gallery, London.[33] Reynolds' own copy of Vasari's expanded second edition from 1568, which includes Marcantonio's biography, is now in the library of the Royal Academy of Arts, London.[34] This signals both an appreciation of the work of Marcantonio and Dürer, and an interest in copies (and copying) that adumbrates an aspect of art education on which Reynolds had ambivalent views. One other 'Marcantonio' print (by a member of his circle, after a woodcut after Parmigianino) from Reynolds' collection is

---

28 Phillips, London, 19 March 1798, lot 1220 and 20 March 1798, lot 1312.
29 Phillips, London, 19 March 1798, lot 1213 as "1 [print], St. Cecilia, from Raphael, by M. Antonio"; B.14.101.116.
30 B.14.257.345.
31 Langford, London, 15 February 1764ff.
32 Metropolitan Museum of Art, New York (inv. 22.73.3-39; 62.635.797).
33 Courtauld Gallery, London (inv. G.1990.WL.3007); B.14.403.595.
34 Royal Academy of Arts, London (inv. 06/3766).

A "GREAT AND VALUABLE COLLECTION" 253

FIGURE 10.6   Marcantonio Raimondi, *Mars, Venus, and Cupid*, 1508, engraving

now in the Ashmolean Museum, Oxford.[35] This indicates his wider interest in Parmigianino, which encompassed many aspects of his collection to include not only prints, but books, drawings and paintings. Copies after Marcantonio in the artist's collection can also be traced, such as the *Bacchanale* by Enea Vico (1523–1567) in San Francisco.[36] Reynolds greatly admired the *Stanze* by Raphael in Rome and he owned a partial engraved copy, now in Melbourne, of the *Battle of the Milvian Bridge* after the fresco in the Sala di Costantino.[37] He also had an 18th-century engraving, by Gaetano Bianchi, after a section of *The School of Athens* now in the Ashmolean Museum, Oxford.[38] Reynolds had a great collection of material related to Rome, where he spent a transformative period in his youth studying the artworks by his favorite artists, Raphael (1483–1520) and Michelangelo (1475–1564). Prints after the Vatican frescoes joined drawn and painted examples by the young student in his research. The print in Melbourne is a rare survival that documents this important early time in his life. For Reynolds, Raphael and Michelangelo constituted the pinnacle of the High Renaissance. Writing in a letter in 1769 to James Barry (1741–1806), then studying in Rome, he iterated his great passion for them and their decorative schemes in the Vatican and elsewhere:

> In other places you will find casts from the antique, and capital pictures of the great painters, but it is *there* only that you can form an idea of the dignity of the art, as it is there only that you can see the works of Michael Angelo and Raffael.[39]

Prints formed for Reynolds, along with other areas of his collection, distinct clusters of material centered on points of his long career. His time spent in Italy as a youth in 1750–52, is expressed in a wealth of printed material on Rome, its ancient history, numerous landmarks and decorative schemes—particularly from the Renaissance—allowing him to construct 'virtual' surrogates of the city after his return to London.[40] Reynolds could also construct 'virtual'

---

35   Ashmolean Museum, Oxford (inv. WA1863.5449); B.12.90.8 [after Antonio da Trento after Parmigianino]. Recently, one of Reynolds' paintings by Parmigianino *Saturn and Philyra* was on the London art market in 2021 (Christie's, London, 8 July 2021, lot 40).

36   Fine Arts Museums of San Francisco (Achenbach Foundation for Graphic Arts), San Francisco (inv. 1963.30.3249); B.15.298.33.

37   University of Melbourne, Baillieu Library (inv. 1959.4489).

38   Ashmolean Museum, Oxford (inv. WA1863.6034).

39   John Ingamells and John Edgcumbe (ed.), *The Letters of Sir Joshua Reynolds* (New Haven; London: 2000), 30, no. 22.

40   Donato Esposito, "The Virtual Rome of Sir Joshua Reynolds," in *The Site of Rome: Studies in the Art and Topography of Rome 1400–1750*, ed. David R. Marshall (Rome: 2014), 76–107.

A "GREAT AND VALUABLE COLLECTION"

surrogates for other important cultural centers such as Venice and Florence, places that had a lasting impact on his artistic experience and outlook and informed his developing art theories and teaching at the Royal Academy. The relationship between the prints and drawings owned by Reynolds remains to be fully explored, but it must have been gratifying to be able to match items in different media and to have, in such examples, the models for prints themselves. From the 1798 sale we learn that Reynolds owned Marcantonio's engraving *Alexander committing to Safety the Writings of Homer* that was listed as "1 [print], Alexander discovering the MSS. of Homer, from Raphael, by M. Antonio."[41] Unfortunately, the impression is untraced. But he also owned Raphael's red chalk drawing, squared for transfer, that served as the model for Marcantonio's print; this drawing is now in the Ashmolean Museum.[42] Both sheets match each other in size and are in the same direction. The composition was first conceived as part of the grisaille fresco below *The Parnassus*, painted in 1509–11, in the Stanza della Segnatura, which Reynolds knew well from many visits to the site during his time in Rome. He also owned an example of Marcantonio's engraving of one of the main compositions in this room, that depicting the mythical Mount Parnassus and Apollo, described in the 1798 auction as "1 [print], Mount Parnassus, from Raphael, by M. Antonio."[43] Sadly this print, like so many others by Marcantonio he once owned, is now untraced. Reynolds also owned other studies for prints, including a sheet by Federico Barocci (1535–1612) which was a study for the kneeling St. Francis, in black chalk on blue paper, for his etching *St. Francis Receiving the Stigmata*, now in a private collection in Canada.[44] The tantalizing interconnections between his prints and drawings remain to be uncovered but show the comprehensiveness of the collection, one of its defining characteristics. This aspect allowed many relationships between artists, artworks, projects, and locations to be made at first hand, and one that placed prints at its center. In addition to drawings made for prints, Reynolds also owned drawn copies from prints, such as a pen-and-ink copy (now in the British Museum) by Parmigianino after the *Massacre of the Innocents*, another of Reynolds' stellar prints by Marcantonio produced after Raphael.[45] The print is now untraced. This drawn copy by

---

41   Phillips, London, 26 March 1798, lot 1878.

42   Ashmolean Museum, Oxford (inv. WA1935.152).

43   Phillips, London, 20 March 1798, lot 1311 and 21 March 1798, lot 1416.

44   Hilliard T. Goldfarb, *From the Hands of the Masters: A Private Collection* (Montreal: 2013), 23.

45   British Museum, London (inv. PD 1905,1110.21); Achim Gnann, *Parmigianino: Die Zeichnungen*, vol. 1 (Petersberg: 2007), 405, no. 350; Phillips, London, 20 March 1798,

Parmigianino was, in turn, itself the model for an etching.[46] However, it is not known if Reynolds owned an example of it.

6 Ornament Prints

The sales catalogues of Reynolds' collection indicate that it included a large number of ornament prints, many of which are today scattered and poorly known. The examples that are documented include the celebrated ten-plate series of engravings, *Antique Vases* (published in 1582) by Cherubino Alberti (1553–1615) after Polidoro da Caravaggio (1499–1543). Polidoro was a pupil of Raphael, and assisted the painting of the Loggia of Pope Leo x. He specialized in *sgraffito*, or monochrome frescoed decorations, on the façades of Roman buildings in imitation of ancient Roman bas-reliefs. Vasari mentioned that he knew virtually every Roman statue, vase, and bas-relief, and Reynolds' own expanded second edition of *The Lives* (which includes the biography of Polidoro) is now, as mentioned earlier, in the Royal Academy.[47] Reynolds often incorporated these vases into his portrait practice, imbuing his varied likenesses with the aura of the Renaissance and, by extension, antiquity. These 'insertions' also served to enliven somewhat monotonous and repetitive compositions. Timothy Clifford has identified a number of portraits into which he introduced these Polidoro vases.[48] Reynolds' sets of *Antique Vases* are no longer complete, and examples are dispersed between several collections, including Plates One and Eight (by Alberti) in the Hunterian Museum and Art Gallery, Glasgow and Plates Four and Six (by Aegidius Sadeler after Alberti) in the Victoria and Albert Museum, London.[49] Reynolds also owned examples of ornament prints by Enea Vico (1523–1567) from the series *Antique Vases* from 1543 as well as ornamental prints by Jacques Stella (1596–1657), judging from

---

lot 1314 as "2 [prints], Mount Parnassus, and the Slaughter of the Innocent, from Raphael, by M. Antonio."

46   B.16.13.11.

47   Royal Academy of Arts, London (inv. 06/3766), 198.

48   Timothy Clifford, "Polidoro and English Design," *Connoisseur* 192, no. 774 (1976), 282–91.

49   Hunterian Museum and Art Gallery, Glasgow (inv. GLAHA 6140 and 6141 respectively); Victoria and Albert Museum, London (inv. E.833D-1888 and E.833F-1888; Elizabeth Miller, *16th-Century Italian Ornament Prints in the Victoria and Albert Museum* (London: 1999), 252, no. 69E and 253, no. 69E respectively). I am grateful to Bryony Bartlett-Rawlings for bringing the examples in London to my attention.

A "GREAT AND VALUABLE COLLECTION" 257

his 'insertions' of their work in his portraits.[50] These ornament prints were supplemented by further German and French examples.[51]

7   Reynolds and Contemporary Printmaking

Reynolds famously knew the power of prints and their role in helping preserve against any subsequent loss or damage to artworks, due to their being produced in multiple impressions. The Irish mezzotinter James McArdell (1729–1765) worked extensively after Reynolds from 1754 onwards, leading him to famously exclaim to Northcote, "by this man I shall be immortalized."[52] Indeed in one obituary, published by the *Morning Chronicle*, which made explicit reference to the common fading of many of Reynolds' paintings (from the use of fugitive carmine pigment, which turned from pink to grey) so "that the mezzotints, so frequently engraved from them, shew us in shadow, that such things were."[53] Reynolds embraced contemporary printmaking wholeheartedly and generously. He allowed many artworks from his collection, including his Old Master drawings and paintings, to be disseminated as prints by a group of mostly young printmakers at the beginning of their careers, thus providing them with many self-publishing opportunities. Reynolds greatly championed their work by allowing his name to be publicly associated with them. The grand move to his permanent home at 47 Leicester Fields encouraged this motive and he regularly opened up his home to art students. In 1765, for example, William Humphrey (1745–1810) published his mezzotint after a painting in Reynolds' collection *A Scholar at his Desk* by Rembrandt, now in Rotterdam.[54] The print, as the lettering declares, had won for Humphrey the first premium awarded by the Society for the Encouragement of Arts, Manufactures and Commerce. In 1769 another example from his collection of paintings by Rembrandt, the large biblical work *Susannah and the Elders*, now in the Gemäldegalerie in Berlin, was made into a mezzotint by Richard Earlom (1743–1822).[55] Reynolds' example of this mezzotint, perhaps one of many reproductive prints after works in

---

50   The seven prints by Vico were on the art market in 1995: Christie's, London, 29 June 1995, part of lot 387 [28 in lot]; B.15.350–52.420, 422, 424, 426, 429–30, 432.

51   For a German example by Hieronymus Hopfer (after Albrecht Altdorfer) see Esposito, "'Care, Taste and Judgement," 122, no. 48.

52   Gordon Goodwin, *British Mezzotinters: James McArdell* (London: 1903), 7.

53   'Sir Joshua Reynolds', *Morning Chronicle*, 29 February 1792, 3.

54   Donato Esposito, "Regarding Rembrandt: Reynolds and Rembrandt," in Tico Seifert (ed.), *Rembrandt: Britain's Discovery of the Master* (Edinburgh: 2018), 96.

55   ibid., 96.

his collection that he owned, survives and is now in the Kupferstichkabinett, Berlin.[56] Later still, in 1788 Caroline Watson (1760–1814) published her stipple engraving after the painting of *St. Matthew* by Rubens (1577–1640) in his collection. The lettering on the print declares: "Engraved from the original Picture in the Collection of Sir Joshua Reynolds." Watson was one of the President's last protégées from the 1780s until shortly before his death in 1792.[57] More extensive publications took place in between. Many of Reynolds' Old Master drawings were borrowed by his friend Charles Rogers (1711–1784), author and publisher of the seminal two-volume *A Collection of Prints in Imitation of Drawings*, for this vast project that began in the 1760s but was not published until 1778. These prints sought to reproduce closely the color and technique of a wide variety of drawings.

Reynolds never mentioned a single episode of his activities as a collector in any of his surviving correspondence. But elsewhere in his published writings we learn of his attitude to prints and printmaking and their relationship to other artworks. During his extended trip to Germany and the Low Countries in 1781 with his friend (and future executor) Metcalfe, we are presented with a great many references to prints after artworks he encountered and sought out, particularly paintings and altarpieces in the many ecclesiastical collections he saw in Holland and Belgium. In St-Antoniuskerk in Antwerp, Reynolds saw the altarpiece *The Apparition of the Virgin to St Francis* by Rubens, which remains *in situ*. He remarked in his notes published to accompany the trip that: "The entire picture is engraved by Zoutman. There is a print of the head of St. Francis alone by Cor. Vischer."[58] Reynolds had confused the publisher with the printmaker, and was referring to the engraving by Cornelis Visscher (1629–1658) and published by Pieter Soutman (1580–1657). Reynolds also misread the reference to the engraved artwork in Jean François Marie Michel's *Histoire de la vie de P. P. Rubens* from 1771, in thinking there were two prints, when in fact there is just one.[59] Reynolds found a great many other artworks by Rubens in Antwerp, where, for example, he went into raptures over the celebrated *The Crucifixion* ('*Le Coup de Lance*') (1619–20; Koninklijk Museum voor Schone Kunsten, Antwerp) then installed in the Recollects Convent. He gushed over "the excellence of its colouring [that] is beyond expression" and

---

56   Kupferstichkabinett, Berlin (inv. 739-32).

57   David Alexander, *Caroline Watson and Female Printmaking in Late Georgian England* (Cambridge: 2014), 49, no. 19.

58   Harry Mount (ed.), *Sir Joshua Reynolds, A Journey to Flanders and Holland* (Cambridge: 1996), 72.

59   ibid., 162, footnote 282.

A "GREAT AND VALUABLE COLLECTION" 259

which rightly deserves "extraordinary attention."[60] In reference to the work, he catalogues the many compositional changes between the painting and the print made after it in 1631 by Boëtius Adams Bolswert (1580–1633):

> This print was undoubtedly done under the inspection of Rubens himself. It may be worth observing, that the keeping of the masses of light in the print differs much from the picture: this change is not from inattention, but design: a different conduct is required in a composition with colours, from what ought to be followed when it is in black and white only. We have here the authority of this great master of light and shadow, that a print requires more and larger masses of light, than a picture.[61]

Reynolds admired the printmaker's "fine effect" observing "I suspect it is as certain, that if this change had not been made, it would have appeared a black and heavy print."[62] In deflecting the illumination away from Christ's body and the grieving Virgin's head and hands, the print reduced the contrast and distributed more evenly the mass of light throughout the monochrome translation.

Reynolds must have owned the print to have studied and known it so well. Indeed, we know from an etching by Rombout Eynhoudts (1613–1680) after Rubens' *Sacra Conversazione with St Bonaventure and St George* that was inscribed and colored *in situ* by Reynolds—this etching is now in the British Museum—that he may well have brought (or obtained) an impression of the print on his trip in order to directly examine the artworks he saw, alongside the prints after them.[63] The impression is heavily annotated by Reynolds with color notes, thus adding what the monochome print left out: "Virgin dark blue/arbour green/sky grey ... The dragon yellow." We know from a lot description in the 1798 sale that Reynolds owned three other such annotated prints after Rubens; the others are as yet unlocated.[64] Feeling the need to apologize or account for his frequent mention of prints during his travels in 1781, Reynolds urged that students of art should "have the print before them" when studying Rubens as a colorist and "for this reason I have mentioned all those prints which have come to my knowledge."[65] As to Rubens, "his works look very well

---

60 ibid., 64, 67.
61 ibid., 66.
62 ibid., 66.
63 British Museum, London (inv. PD 1885,0509.1578); Esposito, "'Care, Taste and Judgement,'" 157, no. 83.
64 Phillips, London, 12 March 1798, lot 640 as "4 [prints] from Rubens, retouched by Sir Joshua Reynolds, with remarks on the margin."
65 Mount, *Journey to Flanders and Holland*, 151.

when engraved from the skill of his engravers" who preserved the black and white so that "nothing is really lost but color."[66]

8   Star Prints 2: Rembrandt and Botticelli

The fate of some of Reynolds' stellar prints punctuates many prominent sales in the century following his death in 1792. Throughout the 19th century, as museum graphic collections were both newly founded and grew, competition among a greater number of collectors drove up prices for particular kinds of prints among a shrinking pool. The prints of Rembrandt (1606–1669), for example, had always been widely collected in Great Britain from the late 17th century onwards.[67] But in the early and mid-19th century, competition in London among collectors for early states on special papers was intense. Distinguished provenance also played a part in the fate of some Rembrandt prints auctioned throughout the 19th century. The five-day sale of the print historian and collector Joseph Maberly (1783–1860) took place at Sotheby's on the 26–30th of May 1851. One of the star lots was the first state of the drypoint *Christ Presented to the People* ('*Ecce Homo*'), from 1655, printed on Japan paper (Fig. 10.7). The print was lauded in the auction catalogue: "MAGNIFICENT IMPRESSION ON INDIA PAPER, IN THE FIRST STATE ... EXCESSIVELY RARE."[68] It sold for £44 10s to the London dealer A. E. Evans & Sons. Maberly had cited the impression in his influential handbook and guide to collecting Old Master prints published in 1844, *The Print Collector*, where it was described as a "fine impression ... perhaps the finest in existence."[69] Moreover, he used it to demonstrate how the print's long provenance over more than a century could be deduced from the mere examination of its collectors' marks. The interest in and knowledge of these collectors' marks was beginning to grow from the late-18th century onwards and Maberly includes a rudimentary list, with reproductions, of some of those more commonly encountered. He included Reynolds in this listing and reproduced his mark more successfully and accurately than his executors had done in 1798, though the initials 'J R' were still clumsily delineated and misaligned. The impression might be one of two such examples of different

---

66   ibid., 150.

67   Tico Seifert (ed.), *Rembrandt: Britain's Discovery of the Master* (Edinburgh: 2018).

68   Sotheby's, London, 26–30 May 1851, lot 500. The provenance outlined for this print here differs somewhat, and is an expansion, from that recently published in 2019. See Stephanie Buck, Jürgen Müller and Mailena Mallach, *Rembrandt's Mark* (Dresden: 2019), 214, no. 51.3.

69   Joseph Maberly, *The Print Collector* (London: 1844), 85.

FIGURE 10.7   Rembrandt, *Christ Presented to the People ('Ecce Homo')*, 1655, drypoint on Japan paper

states of the print lotted together in the Reynolds 1798 sale as "2 [prints], Christ before Pilate, with variations."[70] Maberly had obtained the print in 1841 from Joseph Harding, who had in turn purchased it at the dispersal of the print collection formed by Richard Grenville, Duke of Buckingham (1776–1839) in 1834 for 48 guineas. The print was first securely documented as having been owned by Pierre Rémy (1715–1797) in Paris in 1749. It then passed to Edward Astley (1729–1802) and from him to Reynolds, probably at the dispersal of his prints in 1760. Reynolds had obtained from Astley another superb Rembrandt print, the portrait of *Jan Lutma*, from 1656, also printed on Japan paper, and now—as mentioned earlier—in the British Museum.[71] From Maberly, *Christ Presented to the People* later passed to Samuel von Festetits (1806–1862) in Vienna; Émile Galichon (1829–1875) in Paris; and finally the printmaker and etching apologist

---

70   Phillips, London, 8 March 1798, lot 312.
71   British Museum, London (inv. PD 1868,0822.696).

Francis Seymour Haden (1818–1910), from whom it was acquired by Berlin, via auction in London, in 1892.[72]

Early Italian prints from the 15th century also enjoyed a revival of interest as the 19th century progressed. Reynolds had a number of prized examples by Andrea Mantegna (*c*.1431–1506), Giulio Campagnola (*c*.1482–1516) and the Master of the Rat Trap (or Master NA. DAT). Prints by Mantegna, one of the first *peintre-graveurs* in European art, were found in some numbers in Reynolds' collection, lumped together in large undifferentiated lots such as "16 [prints] by A. Montagna [*sic*]."[73] Among them were rarities such as examples printed in blue ink, and others related to his large painted cycle *The Triumphs of Caesar*, in the Royal Collection, London.[74] In the latter group is an early engraving made before 1500 by a member of Mantegna's circle, *The Elephants*, and now in Kansas City (Fig. 10.8). Campagnola's austere depiction of the solitary St. John the Baptist, standing in a hilly landscape, is another of his superb early Italian prints (Fig. 10.9). The figure's clinging drapery and stately pose would have strongly appealed to Reynolds. But undoubtedly the finest (and largest) print from this area of his collection were the two impressions he owned by Francesco Rosselli (1448–*c*.1513) after Sandro Botticelli (1445–1510), *The Assumption of the Virgin*, one of which is now in the British Museum and the other in the Museum of Fine Arts, Boston. It is remarkable that he should have owned two impressions of such a large, impressive and rare print. The latter was purchased by Boston in 1916 and published by the present author in connection with Reynolds in 2011.[75] The other in London is identified here for the first time as in the collection of Reynolds (Fig 10.10).[76] The print was first documented in the collection of Gilbert Paignon-Dijonval (1708–1792), and at some point passed to Reynolds. How he obtained either of his London or Boston impressions is not known. It was not itemized in the 1798 sale and was stamped by the executors, indicating an 'inferior' value, on the verso. It was subsequently owned by Thomas Lloyd and sold at his sale in 1817 for £33 12s to collector, author and future British Museum curator William Young

---

72 Kupferstichkabinett, Berlin (inv. 93-1892).

73 Phillips, London, 6 March 1798, lot 188. The complier(s) of the 1798 auction catalogue frequently misspell or misidentify artists and here "A. Montagna" is Andrea Mantegna, despite the possibility of them confusing his name with the contemporary printmaker Benedetto Montagna.

74 Esposito, "'Care, Taste and Judgement,'" 109, no. 35.

75 Museum of Fine Arts, Boston (inv. M26109); Esposito, "Print Collection," 380–81.

76 British Museum, London (inv. PD 1895,0915.66); Stephen Coppel, "William Mitchell (1820–1908) and John Malcolm of Poltalloch (1805–93)," in Antony Griffiths (ed.), *Landmarks in Print Collecting: Connoisseurs and Donors at the British Museum since 1753* (London: 1996), 166 cites the 1884 sale but not any (of the long) provenance.

FIGURE 10.8   School of Mantegna, *The Elephants, from 'The Triumph of Caesar'*, c.1484–92, engraving

Ottley (1771–1836).[77] It then found its way into the remarkable collection formed by Sir Mark Masterman Sykes (1771–1823), whose early Italian prints

---

77 Sotheby's, London, 10–12, 14–17 April 1817, lot 781 as Botticelli: "The Assumption of the Madona [sic], on 2 sheets, O[ttley] p. 430" (£33 12s to Ottley).

FIGURE 10.9   Giulio Campagnola, *Saint John the Baptist*, c.1505, engraving

A "GREAT AND VALUABLE COLLECTION" 265

FIGURE 10.10   Francesco Rosselli after Sandro Botticelli, *The Assumption of the Virgin*,
c.1494–95, engraving

were its chief glories. In 1824 at his sale in London the print fetched £42.[78] The print then appeared at further auctions in 1837 and possibly 1857.[79]

The impression of *The Assumption of the Virgin*, now in London, was the subject of much critical attention when it was sold from the collection of the late former army officer St John Dent in 1884. Dent had lived in Bryanston Square, London, but is otherwise poorly known. His print collection, dispersed over seven days and comprising over 1,000 lots, was one of the most spectacular to come to auction in the latter part of the 19th century and the contemporary press of the time eagerly followed its course. Shortly before the auction in March–April 1884, a short piece in the *Pall Mall Gazette* highlighted the 'Botticelli' that had once belonged to Reynolds, indicating that "the gem of the sale is supposed to be the *Assumption of the Virgin*, by Botticelli, a large print on two sheets, of which there is, we believe, only one other example known."[80] Historically, the engraving of the design was attributed to Botticelli himself. The *Athenaeum* also informed its readers ahead of the sale that it was "very nearly the last of its kind likely to be brought before the public."[81] The 19th century had witnessed a revival of interest in the early art of Italy, and Botticelli in particular became something of a cult figure.[82] The emergence of Aestheticism in the 1860s gave this renewed interest an added dynamism and made Botticelli immensely fashionable; consequently, prices for work believed to be by the artist in any medium rose dramatically during this period. The sale catalogue proclaimed the lengthy provenance of the large engraving: "*Collections—Dijonval, Reynolds, Lloyd, Sykes, Ottley, Buckingham and Muns*."[83] The print was bought for £860 by the collector John Malcolm (1805–1893) through his agent Alphonse Wyatt Thibaudeau, but not without fierce competition. The rival underbidder was the Frenchman Eugène Dutuit (1807–1886). It had in the mid-19th century been in the collection of the Duke of Buckingham, where it was briefly united with its star Reynolds 'mate' *Christ Presented to the People* in Berlin. The high price attained by the print tinged with nationalistic tones defined the general coverage of the spectacular sale. Immediately following the sale in the lengthy write-up in *The Times* the battle between the two rival bidders, one from London and the other Paris, was described:

---

78 Sotheby's, London, 24 May–5 June 1824 [Part III], lot 854 as "The Assumption of the Virgin, on two sheets, page 86, No. 4, probably by or after *Sandro Botticelli*" (£42 to Ottley).

79 William Young Ottley, his sale, Sotheby's, London, 1 June 1837, lot 1835 (£22 to White [for McIntosh]); David McIntosh, his sale, Christie's, London, 18–20 May 1857.

80 'Occasional Notes', *Pall Mall Gazette*, 5 January 1884, 4.

81 'Fine Art Gossip', *Athenaeum*, 16 February 1884, 224.

82 Mark Evans and Stefan Weppelmann (ed.), *Botticelli Reimagined* (London: 2016).

83 Sotheby's, London, 28–29, 31 March, 1–4 April 1884, lot 241.

A "GREAT AND VALUABLE COLLECTION"

The first bidding was £250 from M. Thibaudeau, who was at once opposed by M. Clément, and these two, who were the only bidders, kept advancing one against the other, M. Thibaudeau continuing to lead his Paris antagonist up to £800, at which there was a pause, after which M. Clément again advanced to his last bid of £850, but upon this M. Thibaudeau bid £860, and the hammer fell.[84]

The extraordinary high price was immediately seized upon and reported in the contemporary press, with lengthy column inches devoted to the 'Botticelli' that had formerly belonged to Reynolds. The report in *The Standard* is typical of the coverage:

It had already passed through seven famous collections ... It had lain only in the best portfolios. But the first collector whose name is known as its possessor gave only a few pounds for it, and could have little dreamt what a love of rarity, and a probably temporary passion for one of the loveliest of the 'aesthetic' masters, would combine to oblige a really eminent collector to give for the print in the Spring of 1884.[85]

The critic Philip Gilbert Hamerton (1834–1894), writing in the specialist print journal *The Portfolio*, also cited the high prize attained by the print and gave the last occasion that another impression was sold:

The prize of the lot was carried off by Mr. Thibeaudeau [sic], for Mr. Malcolm, of Poltalloch, namely, the rare Botticelli *Assumption of the Virgin*; £860 was the exceptional figure given, the highest price hitherto obtained being £420 for the print once in the Durazzo Collection at Stuttgart [in 1872 or 1873].[86]

The fine condition of the impression and the scarcity of the print must have helped drive up the eventual record price. It was, continued the press coverage in *The Times*, much "universally admired for the great beauty of the design" and the recent rise in the interest attached to anything by Botticelli was also enumerated:

---

84   'Sale of the Dent Collection', *The Times*, 31 March 1884, 8.
85   '[Miscellaneous]', *The Standard*, 3 April 1884, 5.
86   Philip Gilbert Hamerton, 'Art Chronicle', *The Portfolio*, May 1884, 101–04 (103).

The print is regarded as one of the most important of the early examples of engraving in Italy, and must always hold a fascinating spell over those who are interested in the works of Botticelli as a *peintre-graveur*.[87]

The Dent sale also attracted critical notice from the regional press. The *Liverpool Mercury* ruminated on the sale of artworks and their fate in the modern world:

> As for rare and unique prints of the caliber of *The Assumption*, by Botticelli, at the Dent sale, they pass often at distant intervals from one portfolio to another ... But when, owing to death or other causes, they come to be disposed of in this country, it is as natural for them to gravitate back to London, either for private sale or to be disposed of under the hammer, as it is for sparks to fly upward.[88]

The print was bought by the British Museum from Malcolm's son in 1895 and the extensive provenance and the circumstances of the remarkable sale in 1884 overlooked. It remains a highlight of the collection of the British Museum.

Further afield, in 19th-century New York, two prominent print collections were formed that have received little attention. The first was that of the painter Juan Jorge Peoli (1825–1893), and the second that of the shipping magnate Henry Foster Sewall (1816–1896). These two different collections taken together possess characteristic traits and many shared aspects with Reynolds. Indeed, Sewall bought heavily from Peoli's sale in 1894, including prints by Rembrandt, Mantegna and Ribera. Peoli's collection must have been even larger than the 1,000 lots auctioned after his death. In March 1875 the *Brooklyn Daily Eagle* announced:

> John J. Peoli, the artist, leaves for Europe in a short time. His studio is now open to the public for a few days [...] He offers for sale his entire collection of engravings, etchings and watercolors, considered to be one of the best in this country.[89]

Peoli's sale revealed, for example, the dominance of Italian, Dutch and Flemish prints from the 16th and 17th centuries. Peoli owned one drawing and four

---

87   'Sale of the Dent Collection', *The Times*, 31 March 1884, 8.
88   'Engravings, and What Becomes of Them', *Liverpool Mercury*, 11 April 1884, 5.
89   *Brooklyn Daily Eagle*, 29 March 1875, 2.

prints from Reynolds' collection, none of which can now be traced today.[90] Nonetheless the prints reveal the British painter's love for tender figural groupings, which he could absorb into his own art practice, such as the *Holy Family* etched by Sébastien Bourdon (1616–1671).[91] Sewall's larger collection comprised 3,000 prints and, unlike that of Peoli's, has survived intact because it was bought *en bloc* in 1897 from his son Charles Sewall (1848–1898) by the Museum of Fine Arts, Boston. Prints from Reynolds' collection that came to Boston from Sewall include prints by Giorgio Ghisi (1520–1582), Agostino Veneziano (1490–*c*.1540) and Cornelis Cort (1533–1578). Sewall's prints also included Reynolds' example of Rubens' only etching, *Saint Catherine*, which joined dozens of drawings and paintings by the Flemish artist in his collection. Cort's print after Titian's *Diana discovering Callisto's Pregnancy* from 1566, was authorized by the painter himself and in this way exemplifies the thorough coverage of the history of art that Reynolds sought, both with celebrated prints and examples after noteworthy paintings.[92] The ex-Reynolds prints from Sewall were not the first (or last) to arrive at Boston and joined a woodcut that had been acquired in 1889 by Cesare Vecellio (1521–1601), which the museum had bought from the dealer Frederick Keppel & Co., New York.[93] More recently, the same institution acquired in 2012 *The Fall of Man* by Hans Baldung (*c*.1484–1545) from Reynolds' collection, a rare example of a print from the German Renaissance bearing tracing marks.[94]

9 Conclusion

Reynolds' rich print collection offers much material for future study. This survey of its origin and form has discovered aspects that resonate in other areas, and reflect upon his personality and influential art practice. The centrality of Italian art, the deep interest in British portraiture, and figural relationship within compositions, are all demonstrated by the prints he owned. Extensive holdings

---

90 American Art Galleries, New York, 8–12 May 1894, lots 99 (drawing by Luca Cambiaso), 750b (by Sébastien Bourdon), 919 (2 by Agostino Carracci), and 1488b (by Parmigianino).

91 American Art Galleries, New York, 8–12 May 1894, lot 750b. This print might be one of those listed in Reynolds' 1798 sale: Phillips, London, 5 March 1798, lot 60 as "17 historical etchings, by S. Bourdon, &c."

92 Museum of Fine Arts, Boston (inv. P1554).

93 Museum of Fine Arts, Boston (inv. M6219).

94 Museum of Fine Arts, Boston (inv. 2012.467). The print was formerly in the British Museum (inv. PD 1853,0709.19) but de-accessioned as a duplicate in 1910 by Sidney Colvin (1845–1927); B.7.305.1.

of portrait prints revealed vivid likenesses, both celebrated and otherwise, from the past. Prints were important to the artist, as revealed in his comprehensive discussions of them. He used them extensively to plan and research elements of his paintings, but he also enjoyed forming the collection for its own sake. Recent work has also revealed the huge debt to Reynolds from one of his successors as President of the Royal Academy of Arts, Frederic Leighton and his collection.[95] Leighton eagerly sought out paintings by Reynolds himself for display in his home, and complemented these with many prints, drawings, and books that had once belonged to him. Thus Reynolds points forwards as well as back, in his accumulation of historic prints dating from several centuries. Surveys of prints held in public collections across the world, such as that published in 2010 by the Art Gallery of South Australia in Adelaide, will in time reveal other parts of Reynolds' important and extensive collection.[96] And undoubtedly, further scholarly attention will uncover more nuanced aspects of this fascinating print collection, so closely tied to the development of British art, taste and pedagogy.

Select Bibliography

Primary Sources
Maberly, Joseph, *The Print Collector* (London: 1844).
Northcote, James, *The Life of Sir Joshua Reynolds*, 2 vols (London: 1818).

Secondary Sources
Alexander, David, *Caroline Watson and Female Printmaking in Late Georgian England* (Cambridge: 2014).
Avery-Quash, Susanna and Kate Retford, (ed.), *The Georgian London Town House: Building, Collecting and Display* (New York and London: 2019).
Bambach, Carmen and Nadine M. Orenstein, *Genoa: Drawings and Prints, 1530–1800* (New York: 1996).
Bartsch, Adam, *Le Peintre Graveur*, 21 vols (Vienna: 1803–1821).

---

95   Donato Esposito, "The Academy at Home: Art Collecting, Formation and Display by Reynolds and Leighton," in Andrea M. Gáldy and Florian Dobmeier (ed.), *Collecting and Museology* (Newcastle: 2020), 47–71.

96   Maria Zagala, *A Beautiful Line: Italian Prints from Mantegna to Piranesi* (Adelaide: 2010), 135 [Pietro Testa; inv. 095G1570].

Clifford, Timothy, "Polidoro and English Design," *Connoisseur*, 192, no. 774 (1976), 282–91.

Coppel, Stephen, "William Mitchell (1820–1908) and John Malcolm of Poltalloch (1805–93)," in *Landmarks in Print Collecting: Connoisseurs and Donors at the British Museum since 1753*, ed. Antony Griffiths (London: 1996), 159–88.

Esposito, Donato, "The Academy at Home: Art Collecting, Formation and Display by Reynolds and Leighton," in *Collecting and Museology*, ed. Andrea M. Gáldy and Florian Dobmeier (Newcastle: 2020), 47–71.

Esposito, Donato, "Artist in Residence: Joshua Reynolds at No 47, Leicester Fields," in *The Georgian London Town House: Building, Collecting and Display*, ed. Susanna Avery-Quash and Kate Retford (New York and London: 2019), 191–210.

Esposito, Donato, "Regarding Rembrandt: Reynolds and Rembrandt," in *Rembrandt: Britain's Discovery of the Master*, ed. Tico Seifert (Edinburgh: 2018), 93–105.

Esposito, Donato, "The Virtual Rome of Sir Joshua Reynolds," in *The Site of Rome: Studies in the Art and Topography of Rome 1400–1750*, ed. David R. Marshall (Rome: 2014), 76–107.

Esposito, Donato, "What's in a Mark, or What Marks Can Tell Us: The Use and Abuse of the Collector's Mark of Sir Joshua Reynolds (1723–1792)," in *Les marques de collections: II*, ed. Peter Fuhring (Dijon: 2011), 57–63.

Esposito, Donato, "The Print Collection of Sir Joshua Reynolds," *Print Quarterly*, 28, no. 4 (2011), 376–81.

Esposito, Donato, "'Care, Taste and Judgement': Reynolds' Collection of Works on Paper," in *Sir Joshua Reynolds: The Acquisition of Genius*, ed. Sam Smiles (Bristol: 2009), 102–58.

Evans, Mark and Stefan Weppelmann, (ed.), *Botticelli Reimagined* (London: 2016).

Franklin, David (ed.), *Leonardo da Vinci, Michelangelo, and the Renaissance in Florence* (Ottawa; New Haven; London: 2005).

Fuhring, Peter (ed.), *Les marques de collections: II* (Dijon: 2011).

Gáldy, Andrea M., and Florian Dobmeier (ed.), *Collecting and Museology* (Newcastle: 2020).

Gnann, Achim, *Parmigianino: Die Zeichnungen*, 2 vols (Petersberg: 2007).

Goldfarb, Hilliard T., *From the Hands of the Masters: A Private Collection* (Montreal: 2013).

Goodwin, Gordon, *British Mezzotinters: James McArdell* (London: 1903).

Griffiths, Antony (ed.), *Landmarks in Print Collecting: Connoisseurs and Donors at the British Museum since 1753* (London: 1996).

Hallett, Mark, *Reynolds: Portraiture in Action* (New Haven; London: 2014).

Ingamells, John and John Edgcumbe (ed.), *The Letters of Sir Joshua Reynolds* (New Haven; London: 2000).

Marshall, David R. (ed.), *The Site of Rome: Studies in the Art and Topography of Rome 1400–1750* (Rome: 2014).

Miller, Elizabeth, *16th-Century Italian Ornament Prints in the Victoria and Albert Museum* (London: 1999).

Mount, Harry (ed.), *Sir Joshua Reynolds, A Journey to Flanders and Holland* (Cambridge: 1996).

Seifert, Tico (ed.), *Rembrandt: Britain's Discovery of the Master* (Edinburgh: 2018).

Smiles, Sam (ed.), *Sir Joshua Reynolds: The Acquisition of Genius* (Bristol: 2009).

Zagala, Maria, *A Beautiful Line: Italian Prints from Mantegna to Piranesi* (Adelaide: 2010).

Bibliography

Manuscript Sources

Bedford and Luton Archives and Record Service. L30/14/333/345 16 February 1779: Frederick Robinson to his brother Thomas Robinson, 2nd Baron Grantham, Ambassador at Madrid.

British Library, London, Add. Mss 36994 ff. 117–119: 'A Mode of Imitating Drawings on Copper Plates discovered by P. Sandby R. A., in the year 1775, to which he gave the Name of Aquatinta'.

Brno, Moravský zemský archiv, E 55 Premonstráti Klášterní Hradisko, sig. II 1, no. 108.

Brno, Moravský zemský archiv, E 55 Premonstráti Klášterní Hradisko, inv. no. 262, sig. IV B 4.

Brno, Moravský zemský archiv, G 12 Cerroniho sbírka, inv. no. 385.

Cracow, Archiwum Uniwersytetu Jagiellońskiego, Akta pap. 16330.

Cracow, Biblioteka Jagiellońska, Rkps. 918.

Cracow, Biblioteka Jagiellońska, Rkps. 5358.

Cracow, Biblioteka Jagiellońska, Rkps. 5446.

Częstochowa, Biblioteka Jasnogórska, Rkps. 1.7. R. 134.

London, Library of the Society of Antiquaries, Society of Dilettanti archives, Letter Book, p. 221, May 1776.

National Art Library, MSL/1932/1563: Letter from Sandby to Clerk of Eldin, London, 8 September 1775. London, Victoria and Albert Museum.

Prague, Národní archive, Morava, inv. no. 2205.

Prague, Národní archive, Morava, inv. no. 2208.

Prague, Národní archive, Morava, inv. no. 2685.

Prague, Národní archive, Morava, inv. no. 2998.

Primary Sources

Ainsworth, Ralph Fawsett, *De corneis humani corporis excrescentiis adiecta cornu praeputialis observatione* [*etc.*] (Berlin: 1836).

Albinus, Bernard Siegfried, *Dissertatio de arteriis et venis intestinorum hominis* (Leiden, Amsterdam: 1736).

Aselli, Gaspare, *De lactibus, sive lacteis venis, quarto vasorum mesaraicorum genere* (Milan: 1627).

Baglione, Giovanni, *Vite de' Pittori, Scultori et Architetti dal pontefìcato di Gregorio XIII del 1572 in fìno a'tempi di Papa Urbano Ottavo nel 1642* (Rome: 1642).

274   BIBLIOGRAPHY

Baldinucci, Filippo, *Lettera di Filippo Baldinucci Fiorentino nella quale risponde ad alcuni quesiti in materie di pittura* (Rome: 1687).

Baldinucci, Filippo, *Cominciamento e progresso dell'arte dell'intagliare in Rame* (Florence: 1686).

Barocchi, Paola and Rosanna Bettarini (ed.), *Giorgio Vasari. Le vite de' più eccellenti pittori, scultori e architettori nelle redazioni del 1550 e 1568* 6 vols (Florence: 1966–1969).

Bell, C. F. (ed.), *Evelyn's Sculptura. With the Unpublished Second Part* (Oxford: 1906).

Bellori, Giovanni Pietro, *Vite de' pittori, scultori e architteti moderni* (Rome: 1672).

Bellori, Giovanni Pietro, *Descrizzione delle imagini dipinte da Raffaele d'Urbino* (Rome: 1695).

Bellori, Giovanni Pietro, *The Lives of the Modern Painters, Sculptors, and Architects: A New Translation and Critical Edition*, translated by Alice Sedgwick Wohl, notes by Helmut Wohl (Cambridge: 2005).

Billard, Charles, *Traité des maladies des enfans nouveaux-nés et a la mamelle* (Paris, London and Brussels: 1828).

Billard, Charles, *Atlas d'anatomie pathologique, pour servir à l'histoire des maladies des enfans*, 1 vol. in 2 parts (Paris, London and Brussels: 1828).

Billard, Charles, *Krankheiten der Neugebornen und Säuglinge, nach den neuesten klinischen und pathologisch-anatomischen im Hospital der Findelkinder zu Paris gemachten Beobachtungen*, ed. Friedrich Ludwig Meißner (Leipzig: 1829).

Bosse, Abraham, *Traicté des manières de graver en taille douce sur l'airan* (Paris: 1645).

Abraham Bosse, *Sentimens sur la distinction des diverses manières de peinture, dessein & gravure* (Paris: 1649).

Abraham Bosse, Moyen Universel de pratiquer la perspective sur les tableaux ou surfaces irrégulières (Paris: 1653).

Caledonian Mercury, 25 February 1752.

Cellini, Benvenuto, *Due trattati, uno intorno alle otto principali arti dell'oreficeria, l'altro in materia dell'arte della scultura* (Florence: 1568).

de Chambray, Roland Fréart, *Traité de la Peinture de Leonard de Vinci donné au public et traduit d'Italiens en François par R. F. S. D. C.* (Paris: 1651).

de Chambray, Roland Fréart, *L'Idée de la Perfection de la Peinture* (Paris, 1662).

Choulant, Ludwig, *Geschichte und Bibliographie der anatomischen Abbildung nach ihrer Beziehung auf anatomische Wissenschaft und bildende Kunst* (1852; repr. Niederwalluf bei Wiesbaden: 1971).

Cramer, Thomas and Christian Klemm (ed.), *Renaissance und Barock*, in *Bibliothek der Kunstliteratur in vier Bänden*, 1, ed. Gottfried Boehm and Norbert Miller (Frankfurt: 1995).

Cutolo, Paolo (ed.), *Pomponio Gaurico. De Sculptura*, trans. Paolo Cutolo (Naples: 1999).

BIBLIOGRAPHY

Edwards, Edward, *Anecdotes of Painters who have resided in or been born in England with critical remarks on their production* (London: 1808).

Erasmus van Roterdam, *De recta Latini Graecique sermonis pronuntiatione Des. Erasmi dialogus* (Paris: 1528).

John Evelyn, *Sculptura: or the History and art of Chalcography and Engraving in Copper* (London: 1662).

Félibien, André, *Entretiens sur les vies et sur les ouvrages des plus excellens peintres anciens et modernes* 5 vols (Paris: 1666–1688).

Félibien, André, *Entretiens sur le vies et sur les ouvrage de plus excellens peintres ancient et modernes* 5 vols (Paris: 1672–1705).

Félibien, André, *Des principes de l'architecture, de la sculpture, de la peinture, et des autres arts qui en dependent* (Paris: 1676).

Froriep, Robert, *Dissertatio medica de corneitide scrofulosa (etc.)* (Jena: 1830).

Gautier-Dagoty, Jacques-Fabien, 'Lettre à M. de Boze, de l'Académie Françoise, & Honoraire de l'Académie de peinture & sculpture, Garde des médailles & pierreries du Cabinet du Roi, &c', in *Mercure de France* (1749, July), 158–72.

Gautier-Dagoty, Jacques-Fabien (ed.), *Observations sur l'histoire naturelle, sur la physique et sur la peinture* (Paris: 1752–55).

Gautier-Dagoty, Jacques-Fabien (ed.), *Observations périodiques sur la physique, l'histoire naturelle et les arts* (Paris: 1756).

General Advertiser, Friday 6 March 1752.

General Evening Post, 27–29 April 1758.

Gilpin, William, *An Essay on Prints, containing Remarks upon the Principles of picturesque Beauty, the different kinds of prints, and the characters of the most noted Masters* (London: 1768).

Jones, Thomas, "The Memoirs of Thomas Jones" ed. Adolph Paul Oppé, *Walpole Society*, vol. 32 (1946).

Kuntze, Edward, and Nanke Czesław (ed.), *Alberti Bolognetti nuntii apostololici in Polonia, epistolae et acta 1581–1585*, vol. 1 (Monumenta Poloniae vaticana. Series Nuntiaturae Polonae) 5 (Cracow: 1923–1933).

Lampsonius, Dominicus, *Pictorum Aliquot Celebrium Germaniae inferioris effigies* (Antwerp: 1572).

Lomazzo, Giovanni Paolo, *Trattato dell'arte de la pittura, scoltura et architettura* (Milan: 1584).

Lomazzo, Giovanni Paolo, *Idea del tempio della pittura* (Milan: 1590).

London Evening Post, 10–12 May 1757.

London Chronicle or Universal Evening Post, 4–6 October 1774.

Luz, Emanuel, *Dissertatio inauguralis medica exhibens momenta quaedam circa herniotomian praecipue circa evitandam arteriae epigastricae laesionem* [*etc.*] (Tübingen: 1799).

Maberly, Joseph, *The Print Collector* (London: 1844).

Malvasia, Carlo Cesare, *Felsina pittrice: vite de pittori bolognesi* 2 vols (Bologna: 1678).

Mander, Karel van, *Het Schilder-Boeck waer in Voor eerst de leerlustighe Iueght den grondt der Edel Vry Schilderconst in Verscheyden deelen Wort Voorghedraghen* (Haarlem: 1604).

Mariette, Pierre-Jean, *Abecedario de P. J. Mariette*, edited by Charles-Philippe de Chennevières-Pointel and Anatole de Montaiglon 6 vols (Paris: 1851–1860).

Marolles, Michel de, *Catalogue de livres d'estampes et de figures en taille douce* (Paris: 1666).

Martens, Franz Heinrich, *Ueber eine sehr complicirte Hasenscharte oder einen sogenannten Wolfsrachen: mit einer an demselben Subjekte befindlichen merkwürdigen Misstaltung der Hände und Füsse, operirt von Johann Gottlob Eckoldt* (Leipzig: 1804).

Mercure de France (July–December 1741).

Miedema, Hessel (ed.), *Karel van Mander. The Lives of the Illustrious Netherlandish and German Painters*, translated and edited by Hessel Miedema 6 vols (Dornspijk: 1994–1999).

Morning Chronicle and London Advertiser, Wednesday 27 July 1774.

Navrátil, Bohumil, *Biskupství olomoucké 1576–1579 a volba Stanislava Pavlovského* (Prague: 1909).

Northcote, James, *The Life of Sir Joshua Reynolds*, 2 vols (London: 1818).

Observations périodiques, sur la physique, l'histoire naturelle, et les Arts, ou Journal de sciences et arts (Paris: 1757).

Ponętowski, Jan, *Krotki Rzeczy Polskich Seymowych pamięci godnych Commentarz* (Cracow: 1569).

Presbyter, Teophilus, *De diversis artibus*, 3, c.XI.

Public Advertiser, London, Saturday 15 January 1757.

von Kinckelbach, Quad, Matthias, *Teutscher Nation Herligkeitt: Ein außfuhrliche beschreibung des gegenwertigen, alten, vnd vhralten Standts Germaniae (...)* (Cologne: 1609).

"Réponse de M. [Antoine Gauthier] de Montdorge, aux informations de M. Rémond de Sainte Albine, au sujet de la contestation entre deux élèves de feu M. le Blond, sur l'art d'imprimer les tableaux," *Mercure de France* (1749, July), 173–79.

Sandby, Thomas Paul, 'Memoirs of the Late Paul Sandby Esq. R. A.', *Monthly Magazine, or, British Register*, vol. 31 (June 1811), 437–41.

Sander, Georg Karl Heinrich, *Praelectionum et chirurgicarum et physicarum selectus quas in Societate Physico-Medica Brunsvicensi Habuit [etc.]* (Brunswick: 1827).

Sandrart, Joachim von, *Teusche Akademie der Edlen Bau-, Bild, und Mahlerey-Künste* 3 vols (Nuremberg: 1675–1680).

Senff, Karl Friedrich, *Nonnulla de incremento ossium embryonum in primis graviditatis temporibus* (Halle: 1802).

BIBLIOGRAPHY

Stukeley, William, *Of the Spleen, its description and history, uses and diseases, particularly the vapors, with their remedy: Being a lecture read at the Royal College of Physicians* (London: 1723), *To which is added some anatomical observations in the dissection of an elephant* (London: 1723).

"Tableaux imprimés", in *Mercure de France* (1742, August), 1838–43.

The Case of Designers, Engravers, Etchers, &c, Stated in a Letter to a Member of Parliament, cited in David Hunter, 'Copyright Protection for Engravings and Maps in Eighteenth-Century Britain', *The Transactions of the Bibliographical Society Library*, vol. s6-IX, no. 2 (1987), 130.

Vasari, Giorgio, *Le vite de' più eccellenti architetti, pittori, et scultori italiani, da Cimabue insino a' tempi nostri* (Florence: 1550).

Vasari, Giorgio, *Le vite de' più eccellenti pittori, scultori, e architettori* 3 vols (Florence: 1568).

Vesalius, Andreas, *De humani corporis fabrica libri septem* (Basel: 1543).

Vicq-d'Azyr, Félix, *Traité d'anatomie et de physiologie: avec des planches coloriées représentant au naturel les divers organes de l'Homme et des Animaux*, 2 vols (Paris: 1786).

Secondary Sources

Adamczak, Audrey, *Robert Nanteuil, ca. 1623–1678* (Paris: 2011).

Alexander, David, *Caroline Watson and Female Printmaking in Late Georgian England* (Cambridge: 2014).

Alexander, David, and Richard T. Godfrey (ed.), *Painters and Engraving: the Reproductive Print from Hogarth to Wilkie*, exhibition catalogue (New Haven: 1980).

Allgemeines Künstler Lexikon, 115 vols (Berlin, Munich: 1991–2021).

Allgemeines Lexikon der bildenden Künstler von der Antike bis zur Gegenwart, ed. Ulrich Thieme and Felix Becker, 37 vols (1907–50, repr. Leipzig: 1999).

Ames-Lewis, Francis, *The Intellectual Life of the Early Renaissance Artist* (New Haven and London: 2000).

Anselmi, Gian Mario, Angela De Benedictis and Nicholas Terpstra (ed.), *Bologna. Cultural Crossroads from the Medieval to the Baroque: Recent Anglo-American Scholarship* (*Atti del Convegno Internazionale, Bologna 2011*) (Bologna: 2013).

Appuhn-Radtke, Sibylle, *Das Thesenblatt im Hochbarock* (Weissenhorn: 1988).

Ashcroft, Jeffrey, *Albrecht Dürer. Documentary Biography* (New Haven and London: 2017).

Avery-Quash, Susanna and Kate Retford (ed.), *The Georgian London Town House: Building, Collecting and Display* (New York and London: 2019).

BIBLIOGRAPHY

Aymonino, Adriano, "The Musaeum of the First Duchess of Northumberland (1716–1776) at Northumberland House in London", in Susan Bracken, Andrea M. Gáldy and Adriana Turpin (ed.), *Women Patrons and Collectors* (Newcastle: 2012), 101–120.

Baader, Hannah, et al. (ed.), *Ars et Scriptura* (Berlin: 2001).

Bambach, Carmen C. and Nadine M. Orenstein, *Genoa: Drawings and Prints, 1530–1800* (New York: 1996).

Barnes, Carl F. Jr., *The Portfolio of Villard de Honnecourt (Paris, Bibliothèque nationale de France, MS Fr 19093): a new critical edition and color facsimile* (Farnham: 2009).

Barocchi, Paola, "Der Wettstreit zwischen Malerei und Skulptur" in *Ars et Scriptura*, ed. Hannah Baader et al. (Berlin: 2001), 93–106.

Baron, Sabrina, Eric N. Lindquist and Shelvin, Eleanor F. (ed.), *Agent of Change: Print Culture Studies after Elizabeth L. Eisenstein* (Amherst and Boston: 2007).

Bartsch, Adam von, *Le Peintre Graveur*, 21 vols (Vienna: 1802–1821).

Bass, Marisa, "Hieronymus Bosch and his Legacy as 'Inventor'", in *Beyond Bosch. The Afterlife of a Renaissance Master in Print*, exhibition catalogue, edited by Marisa Bass and Elizabeth Wyckoff, Saint Louis Art Museum (Saint Louis: 2015), 11–32.

Baverel, Jean-Pierre, and François Malpé, *Notices sur les graveurs qui nous ont laissé des estampes marquées de monogrammes, chiffres, rébus, lettres initiales, etc.* 2 vols (Besançon: 1807).

Baxandall, Michael, *The Limewood Sculptors of Renaissance Germany* (New Haven and London: 1980).

Belozerskaya, Marina, *Rethinking the Renaissance. Burgundian Arts Across Europe* (New York: 2002).

Belozerskaya, Marina, *Luxury Arts of the Renaissance* (Los Angeles: 2005).

Beltrami, Constanza, "A Print source for a painting by Gerard David", *The Burlington Magazine*, 162, no. 1410 (2020), 748–755.

Benedict, Philip, *Graphic History: The Wars, Massacres and Troubles of Tortorel and Perrissin* (Geneva: 2007).

Benoist, Pierre, "Le père Joseph, l'empire Ottoman et la Méditerranée au début du XVIIe siècle," *Cahiers de la Méditerranée*, 71 (2005), 185–202.

Bertoloni Meli, Domencio, *Visualizing Disease: The Art and History of Pathological Illustrations* (Chicago, London: 2017).

Bianchi, Lidia, "La Fortuna di Raffaello nell'Incisione", in *Raffaello: L'opera, le fonte, la fortuna*, ed. Mario Salmi, 2 vols (Novara: 1969).

Biłozór-Salwa, Małgorzata, "Teoria tworzenia anamorfoz", *Rocznik Historii Sztuki*, 39 (2013): 43–53.

Biłozór-Salwa, Małgorzata, "Paryski Karuzel 1612 roku, czyli skały tryskające winem, grające góry i tańczące konie na usługach propagandy władzy", *Rocznik Biblioteki Narodowej*, 44 (2014), 113–358.

Biłozór-Salwa, Małgorzata, "Anamorphosis as a Tool for Presenting Erotic Subjects: Some Remarks on Jan Ziarnko's Lovers", *"The most Noble of the Senses". Anamorphosis,*

BIBLIOGRAPHY

Trompe-L'Oeil, and Other Optical Illusions in Early Modern Art, ed. Lilian H. Zirpolo (Ramsey: 2016), 29–48.

Biłozór-Salwa, Małgorzata, "The Monogram of the Virgin Mary (1605) by Jan Ziarnko as Maria de Medici's Watchword", in *Polish Emblems*, 1 (2016), http://polishemblems.uw.edu.pl/index.php/en/news-uk/43-news-text-2, accessed June 2017.

Biłozór-Salwa, Małgorzata, *The printed map as a tool of political struggle: Paris is well worth a ... map.* https://www.bl.uk/picturing-places/articles/the-printed-map-as-a-tool-of-political-struggle-paris-is-well-worth-a-map, accessed June 2017.

Biłozór-Salwa, Małgorzata, *Jan Ziarnko czy Jean le Grain? Twórczość lwoskiego artysty w XII-wiecznym Paryżu* (Warszawa: 2021).

Le Blanc, Charles, *Manuel de l'amateur d'estampes contenant le dictionnaire des graveurs de toutes les nations* (Paris: 1854–1890).

De Blauw, Sibel, "Das Hochaltarretabel in Rom bis zum frühen 16. Jahrhundert. Das Altarbild als Kategorie der liturgischen Anlage", *Mededelingen van het Nederlands Instituut te Rome*, 55 (1996), 83–110.

Blockmans, Wim, and Walter Prevenier, *The Promised Lands: The Low Countries under Burgundian Rule 1369–1530* (Pennsylvania: 1999).

Bloemacher, Anne, Mandy Richter and Marzia Faietti ed., *Sculpture in Print 1480–1600*, series editor, Walter Mellion (Leiden and Boston: 2021).

Bloemacher, Anne, "Die Idee als Ware. Marcantonio Raimondis Kupferstiche nach Raffael", *Luxusgegenstände und Kunstwerke vom Mittelalter bis zur Gegenwart. Produktion—Handel—Formen der Aneignung* (Irseer Schriften. Studien zur Wirtschafts-, Kultur- und Mentalitätsgeschichte, Bd. 8), ed. Christoph Jeggle, Andreas Tacke and Markwart Herzog (Konstanz and Munich: 2015), 155–184.

Bloemacher, Anne "Von der Virtuosität bis zum System. Marcantonio Raimondi und das Scheitern des malerischen Kupfstiches", in *Technische Innovationen und künstlerisches Wissen in der Frühen Neuzeit*, ed. Magdalena Bushart and Henrike Haug (Cologne: 2015), 189–204.

Bloemacher, Anne, *Raffael und Raimondi. Produktion und Intention der frühen Druckgraphik nach Raphael* (Berlin and Munich: 2016).

Bloemacher, Anne, "Raphael and Marcantonio Raimondi—the empty tablet as a plurivalent sign", *Chicago Art Journal*, 18, 2008, 20–41.

Blunt, Anthony, *Nicolas Poussin* (London: 1995).

Blum, André, *L'Oeuvre Gravé d'Abraham Bosse* (Paris: 1924).

Bohunovsky-Bärnthaler, Irmgard (ed.), *Streit. Domäne der Kultur* (Klagenfurt: 2006).

Bokody, Peter, *Images-within-Images in Italian Painting (1250–1350)* (Farnham: 2015).

Böker, Johann Josef, *Architektur der Gotik/Gothic Architecture: Bestandskatalog der weltgrößten Sammlung an gotsichen Baurissen im Kupferstichkabinett der Akademie der bildenden Künste Wien* (Munich: 2005).

Boorsch, Suzanne, "Mantegna and His Printmakers", in *Andrea Mantegna*, ed. Jane Martineau (London: 1992), 56–66.

280 BIBLIOGRAPHY

Boorsch, Suzanne, "Mantegna and Engraving: What We Know, What We Don't Know, and a Few Hypothesis", in *Andrea Mantegna: Impronta del Genio (Atti del Convegno Internazional ed Studi: Padova, Verona, Mantova, 8, 9, 10 Novembre 2006)*, i, ed. Rodolfo Signorini, Viviana Rebonato, and Sara Tammaccaro (Florence: 2010), 415–437.

Borea, Evelina, *Lo Specchio dell'Arte Italiana: Stampe in Cinque Secoli*, 4 vols (Pisa: 2009).

Bork, Robert, *Geometry of Creation* (Farnham: 2011).

Bosque, Andrée De, *Quinten Metsys* (Brussels: 1975).

Boutièr, Jean, *Les Plans de Paris des origines (1493) à la fin du XVIIIe siècle: étude, cartobibliographie et catalogue colectif* (Paris: 2007).

Boyer, Jean-Claude, "Les Goûts de Mignard: le 'musée imaginaire' d'un Premier peintre." *Pierre Mignard "le Romain,"* Actes du colloque organisé au musée du Louvre par le Service culturel le 29 septembre 1995, ed. Jean-Claude Boyer (Paris: 1997), 265–302.

Brückner, Wolfgang, *Populäre Druckgraphik Europas. Deutchland von 15. biz zum 20 Jahrhundert* (Munich: 1969).

Burg, Tobias, *Die Signatur. Formen und Funktionen vom Mittelalter bis zum 17. Jahrhundert* (Münster: 2007).

Burg, Tobias, "Signaturen in der frühen Drückgraphik" in *Künstlersignaturen von der Antike bis zur Gegenwart*, ed. by Nicole Hegener (Petersberg: 2013), 284–85.

Burgundian Rule 1369–1530 (Pennsyvania: 1999).

Burke, Peter, *Fabrication of Louis XIV* (London: 1992).

Burns, Howard, "The Painter-Architect in Italy during the Quattrocento and Cinquecento", in: *The Notion of Painter-Architect in Italy and the Southern Low Countries* (Architectura Moderna) 11 (Turnhout: 2014), 1–8.

Bury, Michael, "The Taste for Prints in Italy to c.1600", *Print Quarterly*, 2, no. 1 (1985): 12–26.

Bury, Michael, *The Print in Italy, 1550–1620*, exhibition catalogue (London: 2001).

Bussey, Georges Moir and Thomas Gaspey, *The pictorial history of France and the French people*, 2 vols (London: 1843).

Byrne, Janet S., *Renaissance Ornament Prints and Drawings. The Metropolitan Museum of Art* (New York: 1981).

Canova-Green, Marie-Claude, "Warrior King or King of War? Louis XIII's Entries into his Bonnes Villes (1620–1629)", in *Ceremonial Entries in Early Modern Europe. The Iconography of Power*, ed. J. R. Mulryne, Maria Ines Aliverti and Anna Maria Testaverde (Routledge: 2016), 77–98.

Castor, Markus A., editor, *Druckgraphik zwischen Reproduktion und Invention* (Berlin and Munich: 2010).

Cerboni Baiardi, Anna, and Marzia Faietti, *Marcantonio Raimondi: Il Primo Incisore di Raffaello* (Urbino: 2022).

BIBLIOGRAPHY

de Chantelou, Paul Fréart, *Diary of the Cavaliere Bernini's Visit to France*, edited by Anthony Blunt, translated by Margery Corbett (Princeton: 1985).

Chartier, Roger, "Pamphlets et gazettes", *Histoire de l'édition française. Le livre conquérant du Moyen-Âge au milieu du XVII*^{eme} *siècle*, ed. Roger Chartier, Henri-Jean Martin, vol. 1 (Paris: 1982), 405–425.

Chartier, Roger, "Stratégies éditoriales et lectures populaires, 1530–1660", in *Histoire de l'édition française. Le livre conquérant du Moyen-Âge au milieu du XVII*^{eme} *siècle*, ed. Roger Chartier, Henri-Jean Martin, vol. 1 (Paris: 1982), 585–60.

Chartier, Roger (ed.), *Les Usages de L'imprimé (XV*^{e}*–XIX*^{e} *siècle)* (Paris: 1987).

Chartier, Roger (ed.), *The Culture of Print: Power and the Uses of Print in Early Modern Europe*, trans. Lydia G. Cochrane (Cambridge: 1989).

Chartier, Roger, *Culture écrite et société: L'ordre des livres* (Paris: 1996).

Chartier, Roger, and Henri-Jean Martin (ed.), *Histoire de l'édition française. Le livre conquérant du Moyen-Âge au milieu du XVII*^{eme} *siècle*, vol. 1 (Paris: 1982).

Chastel, André, *Le tableau dans le tableau, suivi de La figure dans l'encadrement de la porte chez Velasquez*, vol. 651 Champs arts (Paris: 2012).

Christiansen, Keith, "The Case for Mantegna as Printmaker", *The Burlington Magazine*, 135, no. 1086 (1993): 604–612.

Chrzanowski, Tadeusz, "Uwagi o intelektualiście kolekcjonerze w Polsce na przełomie renesansu i baroku" in *Mecenas, kolekcjoner, odbiorca. Materiały Sesji Stowarzyszenia Historyków Sztuki, Katowice, November 1981* (Warsaw: 1984), 121–145.

Clayton, Timothy, *The English Print 1688–1802* (New Haven and London: 1997).

Colin, Noémi, *Le pouvoir en images: l'acte de dédicace dans l'iconographie occidentale du VI*^{e} *au début du XIII*^{e} *siècle*, doctoral dissertation (Université de Paris X-Nanterre: 2007).

Dällenbach, Lucien, *Le récit spéculaire. Essai sur la mise en abyme* (Paris: 1977).

Collareta, Marco, "Benvenuto Cellini ed il destino dell' oreficeria", in *Benvenuto Cellini. Kunst und Kunsttheorie im 16. Jahrhundert*, ed. Alessandro Nova and Anna Schreurs (Cologne: 2003), 161–169.

du Colombier, Pierre (ed.), *Lettres de Poussin* (Paris: 1929).

Consagra, Francesca, "The De' Rossi Family Print Publishing Shop: A Study in the History of the Print Industry in Seventeenth-Century Rome" (PhD Thesis, The Johns Hopkins University, Baltimore: 1993).

Coppel, Stephen, "William Mitchell (1820–1908) and John Malcolm of Poltalloch (1805–93)," in *Landmarks in Print Collecting: Connoisseurs and Donors at the British Museum*, ed. Antony Griffiths (London: 1996), 159–88.

Coppens, Joseph (ed.), *Scrinium Erasmianum*, 2 vols (Brussels: 1969).

Clayton, Timothy, *The English Print 1688–1802* (London and New Haven: 1997).

Clifford, Timothy, "Polidoro and English Design", *Connoisseur*, 192 (1976), 282–91.

Dackerman, Susan, *Painted Prints: The Revelation of Color in Northern Renaissance & Baroque Engravings, Etchings & Woodcuts* (Baltimore: 2002).

Dackerman, Susan & Daston, Lorraine (ed.), *Prints and the Pursuit of Knowledge in Early Modern Europe*, exhibition catalogue (Cambridge MA: 2011).

Davidson, Bernice, *Marcantonio Raimondi, The engravings of his Roman Period*. Ph.D. thesis Harvard University, Cambridge, MA, 1954 (unpublished).

Davies, Norman, *God's Playground: A History of Poland*, vol. 1, *The Origins to 1795* (Oxford: 1985).

De Beyer, Marc, Ramade, Patrick and Vlieghe, Hans, *Dans la lumière de Rubens: Peintres baroques des Pays-Bas du Sud*, trans. Joke Muller and Milou Boon, exhibition catalogue (Paris: 2000).

Denaro de, Furio, editor, *Domenico Tempesti: I discorsi sopra l'intaglio* (Florence: 1994).

Denhaene, Godelieve, *Lambert Lombard. De Renaissance en humanisme te Luik* (Antwerp: 1990).

Diu, Isabelle, "Enjeux de pouvoir dans la République des Lettres. Préfaces et dédicaces d'Erasme pour ses éditions et traductions d'œuvres classiques et patristiques", in *Le pouvoir des livres à la Renaissance*, ed. Dominique de Courcelles (Paris: 1998), 65–76.

Donnet, Fernand, *Notice historique sur la chapelle du T. S. Sacrement en l'église cathédrale d'Anvers* (Antwerp: 1924).

Drévillon, Hervé, *Lire et écrir l'avenir. L'astrologie dans la France du Grand Siècle (1610–1715)* (Seyssel: 1996).

Dubois, Christine, "L'image 'abymée'", *Images Re-vues*, 2, no. 8 (2006), accessed December 21, 2014 [http://imagesrevues.revues.org/304].

Dubost, Jean-François, *Marie de Médicis, la rein dévoilée* (Paris: 2009).

Duccini, Hélène, *Faire voir, faire croire. L'opinion publique sous Louis XIII* (Seyssel: 2003).

Edwards, Mark U. Jr., *Printing, Propaganda, and Martin Luther* (Minneapolis: 2005).

Ehrle, Francesco, *Roma Prima di Sisto V: Lapianta di Roma du Perac-Lqfrery del 1577, Contributo alia Storia del Commercio delle Stampe a Roma nel Secolo Sedicesimo et Diciasettesimo* (Rome: 1908).

Eisenstein, Elisabeth, *The Printing Press as an Agent of Change: Communications and Cultural Transformations in Early-Modern Europe* (New York: 1980).

Eisenstein, Elizabeth, "An Unacknowledged Revolution Revisited", *The American Historical Review*, 107, No. 1 (1999): 87–105.

Emison, Patricia, "Marcantonio's Massacre of the Innocents", *Print Quarterly*, 1, no. 4 (1984), 257–267.

Emison, Patricia, *Invention and the Italian Renaissance Print, Mantegna to Parmigianino*. Ph.D. Dissertation, Columbia University (New York, NY: 1985).

Emison, Patricia A., "The Raucousness of Mantegna's Mythological Engravings", *Gazette des Beaux-Arts*, 6, no. 124 (1994): 159–176.

BIBLIOGRAPHY

Emison, Patricia, "Raphael's Multiples", *The Cambridge Companion to Raphael*, ed. Marcia B. Hall (Cambridge: 2005), 186–206.

Eser, Thomas, "Der Gold- und Silberschmied. Edelmetall- und edelsteinverarbeitende Gewerbe", *Handwerk im Mittelalter*, ed. Christine Sauer (Darmstadt: 2012), 43–55.

Eser, Thomas, "A Different Early Dürer. Three Proposals", in: *The Early Dürer*, exhibition catalogue, ed. Daniel Hess and Thomas Eser (New Haven and London: 2012), 18–29.

Esposito, Donato, "'Care, Taste and Judgement': Reynolds' Collection of Works on Paper", in *Sir Joshua Reynolds: The acquisition of genius*, ed. Sam Smiles (Bristol: 2009), 102–58.

Esposito, Donato, "What's in a Mark, or What Marks Can Tell Us: The Use and Abuse of the Collector's Mark of Sir Joshua Reynolds (1723–1792)," in *Les marques de collections: II*, ed. Peter Fuhring (Dijon: 2011), 57–63.

Esposito, Donato, "The Print Collection of Sir Joshua Reynolds," *Print Quarterly*, 28, no. 4 (2011), 376–81.

Esposito, Donato, "The Virtual Rome of Sir Joshua Reynolds," in *The Site of Rome: Studies in the Art and Topography of Rome 1400–1750*, ed. David R. Marshall (Rome: 2014), 76–106.

Esposito, Donato, "Regarding Rembrandt: Reynolds and Rembrandt," in *Rembrandt: Britain's Discovery of the Master*, ed. Tico Seifert (Edinburgh: 2018), 93–105.

Esposito, Donato, "Artist in Residence: Joshua Reynolds at No 47, Leicester Fields," in *The Georgian London Town House: Building, Collecting and Display*, ed. Susanna Avery-Quash and Kate Retford (New York and London: 2019), 191–210.

Esposito, Donato, "The Academy at Home: Art Collecting, Formation and Display by Leighton and Reynolds," in *Collecting and Museology*, ed. Andrea M. Gáldy and Florian Dobmeier (Newcastle: 2020), 47–71.

Evans, Mark and Stefan Weppelmann (ed.), *Botticelli Reimagined* (London: 2016).

Faietti, Marzia, "Intorno a Marcantonio", in *Bologna e l'umanesimo 1490–1510*, exhibition catalogue, ed. Marzia Faietti and Konrad Oberhuber (Bologna: 1988), 213–236.

Faietti, Marzia, "Il segno di Andrea Mantegna", *Andrea Mantegna impronta del genio. Convegno internazionale di studi 2006*, ed. Roberto Signorini, Viviana Rebonato and Sara Tammacaro, 2 volumes (Florence: 2010).

Faietti, Marzia and Konrad Oberhuber, ed., *Bologna e l'umanesimo 1490–1510*, exhibition catalogue (Bologna: 1988).

Falk, Tilmann, "Formschneider—Formschnitt", *Reallexikon zur deutschen Kunstgeschichte*, 110 (2004): 190–224.

Feulner, Karoline, "The *Life of the Virgin*: Marketed, Plagiarized, and Copyrighted", in *Albrecht Dürer: His Art in Context*, exhibition catalogue, ed. Jochen Sander (Munich, London and New York: 2013), 234–259.

Filipczak, Zirka Zaremba, *Picturing Art in Antwerp 1550–1700* (Princeton: 1987).

Fiorenza, Giancarlo, "Marcantonio Raimondi's Early Engravings: Myth and Imitation in Renaissance Bologna", in *Bologna. Cultural Crossroads from the Medieval to the Baroque: Recent Anglo-American Scholarship (Atti del Convegno Internazionale, Bologna 2011)*, ed. Gian Mario Anselmi, Angela De Benedictis and Nicholas Terpstra (Bologna: 2013), 13–25.

Franklin, David (ed.), *Leonardo da Vinci, Michelangelo and the Renaissance in Florence* (Ottawa, New Haven and London, 2005).

Fucci, Robert, *Rembrandt's Changing Impressions*, exhibition catalogue (New York: 2015).

Fuhring, Peter, "'Colligete fragmenta, ne pereant': The Ornament Prints in the Columbus Collection" in: *The Print Collection of Ferdinand Colmumbus 1488–1539: A Renaissance Collector in Seville*, ed. Mark P. McDonald (London: 2004), 206–220.

Fuhring, Peter (ed.), *Les marques de collections: II* (Dijon: 2011).

Fuhring, Peter, et al., editors, *A Kingdom of Images: French Prints in the Age of Louis XIV, 1660–1715*, exhibition catalogue (Los Angeles: 2015).

Gady, Bénédicte, "La gravure dans la gravure: Exercices visuels et sémantiques", in *L'estampe au Grand siècle: Études offertes à Maxime Préaud*, ed. Peter Fuhring, Barbara Brejo de Lavergnée and Marianne Grivel, Matériaux pour l'histoire vol. 9 (Paris: 2010), 449–462.

Gady, Bénédicte, *L'ascension de Charles Le Brun: Liens sociaux et production artistique* (Paris: 2010).

Galavics, Géza, "Thesenblätter ungarischer Studenten in Wien im 17. Jahrhundert: Künstlerische und pädagogische Stragegien," in *Die Jesuiten in Wien. Zur Kunst- und Kulturgeschichte der österreichischen Ordensprovinz der "Gesellschaft Jesu" im 17. Und 18. Jahrhundert*, ed. Herbert Karner and Werner Telesko, Veröffentlichungen der Kommission für Kunstgeschichte, vol. 5 (Vienna: 2003), 113–130.

Gáldy, Andrea M. and Heudecker, Sylvia (ed.), *Collecting Prints and Drawings* (Newcastle: 2018).

Gáldy, Andrea M., and Florian Dobmeier (ed.), *Collecting and Museology* (Newcastle: 2020).

Gardner von Teuffel, Christa, "Raffaels römische Altarbilder: Aufstellung und Bestimmung", *Zeitschrift für Kunstgeschichte*, 50 (1987), 1–45.

Getscher, Robert H., *An Annotated and Illustrated Version of Giorgio Vasari's History of Italian and Northern Prints from his Lives of the Artist (1550 & 1568)* 2 vols (Lewiston: 2003).

Gide, André, *Journal 1889–1939*, Bilbiothèque de la Pléiade, vol. 54 (Paris: 1948).

Giesey, Ralph E., *The Royal Funeral in Renaissance France* (Genava: 1960).

Globe, Alexander, *Peter Stent, London Printseller, a Catalogue Raisonné of his Engraved Plates and Books* (Vancouver: 1985).

Gnann, Achim, *Parmigianino: Die Zeichnungen*, 2 vols (Petersberg: 2007).

Gnann, Achim, David Ekserdjian and Foster, Michael, *Chiaroscuro: Renaissance Woodcuts from the Collections of Georg Baselitz and The Albertina, Vienna*, exhibition catalogue (London: 2014).

Godfrey, Richard, *Printmaking in Britain* (Oxford: 1978).

Goldfarb, Hilliard T., *From the Hands of the Master: A Private Collection* (Montreal: 2013).

Goldstein, Carl, *Print Culture in Early Modern France: Abraham Bosse and the Purposes of Print* (Cambridge: 2012).

González de Zárate, Jesus Maria, *Real Colecciòn de Estampas de San Lorenzo de El Escorial*, 10 vols (Madrid: 1992[–1]996).

Goodwin, Gordon, *British Mezzotinters: James McArdell* (London: 1903).

Gordon, Thomas Crouther, *David Allan, the Scottish Hogarth* (Alva: 1951).

Gramaccini, Norberto and Hans Jakob Meier, *Die Kunst der Interpretation. Italienische Reproduktionsgraphik 1485–1600* (Berlin and Munich: 2009).

Gregory, Sharon, *Vasari and the Renaissance Print* (Farnham: 2012).

Griffiths, Antony, "White Ink", *Print Quarterly*, 8, no. 3 (1991), 286–90.

Griffiths, Anthony, "Print Collecting in Rome, Paris, and London in the Early Eighteenth Century", *Harvard University Art Museums Bulletin*, 2, no. 3 (1994), 37–58.

Griffiths, Antony (ed.), *Landmarks in Print Collecting: Connoisseurs and Donors at the British Museum* (London: 1996).

Griffiths, Antony, *The Print in Stuart Britain 1603–1689* (London: 1998).

Griffiths, Antony, "The Prints of John V of Portugal", *Print Quarterly*, 22, no. 3 (2005), 334–338.

Griffiths, Anthony, *The Print before Photography: An Introduction to European Printmaking, 1550–1820* (London: 2016).

Grivel, Marianne, *Le Commerce de l'estampe à Paris au XVIIᵉ siècle* (Geneva: 1986).

Guichard, Charlotte, *Les amateurs d'art à Paris au XVIIIᵉ siècle* (Seyssel: 2008).

Gunn, Ann V., 'Paul Sandby, William Pars and the Society of Dilettanti', *Burlington Magazine*, 152, no. 1285 (2010), 219–227.

Gunn, Ann V., 'Sandby, Greville and Burdett, and the "Secret" of Aquatint', *Print Quarterly*, 29, no. 2 (2012), 178–80.

Gunn, Ann V., 'Views in and Near Naples: Aquatints by Paul Sandby and Archibald Robertson', *The British Art Journal*, 14, no. 1 (2013), 33–43.

Gunn, Ann V., *The Prints of Paul Sandby, (1731–1809), a Catalogue Raisonné* (Turnhout: 2015).

Hajdukiewicz, Leszek, "Jan Ponętowski—opat hradyski, bibliofil i miłośnik sztuki (materiały do życiorysu)," *Roczniki Biblioteczne*, 14 (1970): 485–529.

Hallett, Mark, *Reynolds: Portraiture in Action* (New Haven and London: 2014).

Harley, John Brian, and Laxton, Paul, *The New Nature of Maps: Essays in the History of Cartography* (London: 2001).

Hartley, Craig, "An Unfinished Fan by Abraham Bosse", *Print Quarterly*, 10, no. 4 (1993), 402.

Helmus, Liesbeth, "Drie contracten met Zilversmeden", in: *In Buscoducis. Kunst uit de Bourgondische tijd te 's-Hertogenbosch*, ed. A. M. Koldeweij (Maarssen: 1990), 473–81.

Hemeldonck, Godelieve Van ed., *Zilver uit de Gouden Eeuw van Antwerpen* (Antwerp: 1988).

Henning, Andreas, and Arnold Nesselrath (ed.), Exh. Cat. *Raffael, Dürer und Grünewald malen die Madonna*, ed. Andreas Henning and Arnold Nesselrath (Munich: 2011).

Herrkinger, Robert, and Marielene Putscher, *Geschichte der medizinischen Abbildung*, 2 vols (Munich: 1967–72).

Hernad, Béatrice, editors, *Die Graphiksammlung des Humanisten Hartmann Schedel* (Munich: 1990).

Higman, Francis, "Le livre et les propagandes religieuses Le levain de l'Évangile," in *Histoire de l'édition française. Le livre conquérant du Moyen-Âge au milieu du XVIIeme siècle*, ed. Roger Chartier, Henri-Jean Martin, vol. 1 (Paris: 1982), 305–321.

Hind, Arthur Mayger, *Marcantonio and Italian engravers and etchers of the Sixteenth Century* (London: 1912).

Hind, Arthur Mayger, *Early Italian Engraving*, 7 vols (London: 1938–1948).

Hind, Arthur Mayger, *A History of Engraving and Etching from the 15th Century to the Year 1914* (London: 1923).

Hinterding, Erik, Ger Luijten, and Royalton-Kisch, Martin (eds.), *Rembrandt the Printmaker*, exhibition catalogue (Chicago: 2000).

Hinterding, Erik, *Rembrandt as an Etcher, Studies in Prints and Printmaking*, vi, trans. Michael Hoyle, 3 vols (Ouderkerk aan den Ijssel: 2006).

Hollstein, Friedrich Wilhelm, *Dutch and Flemish Etchings, Engravings and Woodcutrs, ca. 1450–1700* (Amsterdam: 1949–).

Hollstein, Friedrich W., *German Engravings, Etchings and Woodcuts, ca. 1400–1700* (Amsterdam: 1954–).

Hopkinson, Martin, 'The Burdett–Banks Correspondence', *Print Quarterly*, 24, no. 3 (2007), 269–270.

Hordyński, Piotr, "Grafika włoskiej proweniencji z kolekcji Jana Ponętowskiego w Bibliotece Jagiellońskiej" in *Amicissima. Studia Magdalenae Piwocka oblata* (Kraków: 2010), 217–221.

Horst, Daniel R., *De Opstand in zwart-wit. Propagandaprenten uit de Nederlandse Opstand (1566–1584)* (Zutphen: 2003).

Huffel, Nicolaas Gerhardus van, *Coloritto: bijdrage tot de geschiedenis van de kunst om in drie kleuren te drukken, met een herdruk van het boekje van J. C. Le Blon [Paris 1756]* (Amsterdam: 1916).

Hunter, David, 'Copyright Protection for Engravings and Maps in Eighteenth-Century Britain', *The Transactions of the Bibliographical Society Library*, s6-IX, no. 2 (1987), 128–47.

BIBLIOGRAPHY

Hurx, Merlijn, *Architect en aannemer. De opkomst van de bouwmarkt in de Nederlanden 1350–1530* (Nijmegen: 2012).

Hyde, Sarah and Katie Scott (ed.), *Prints (Re)presenting Poussin* (London and Manchester: 1994).

Hyman, Aaron M., *Rubens in Repeat: The Logic of the Copy in Colonial Latin America* (Los Angeles: 2021).

Ikeda, Mayumi, "The Fust and Schöffer Office and the Printing of the Two-Colour Initials in the 1457 mainz Psalter", in *Printing Colour 1400–1700: History, Techniques, Functions and Receptions* ed. Ad Stijnman and Elizabeth Savage (Leyden, Boston: 2015), 65–75.

Ingamells, John and John Edgcumbe (ed.), *The Letters of Sir Joshua Reynolds* (New Haven and London: 2000).

Ivins, William M., Jr, *Prints and Visual Communication* (Cambridge MA and London: 1969).

Johns, Adrian, *The Nature of the Book: Print and Knowledge in the Making* (Chicago and London: 1998).

Johns, Adrian, "How to Acknowledge a Revolution", *The American Historical Review*, Vol. 107, No. 1 (1999): 106–126.

Jones, Michael, *The Print in Early Modern England: An Historical Oversight* (New Haven and London: 2010).

De Jonge, Krista, "'Scientie' and 'experientie' dans le gothique moderne des Anciens Pays-Bas", in *Le Gotique de la Renaissance*, edited by Monique Chatenet (Paris: 2010), 199–216.

De Jonge, Krista, "The Court Architect as Artist in the Southern Low Countries", *Nederlands Kunsthistorisch Jaarboek*, 59 (Zwolle: 2010): 111–135.

Judson, J. Richard and Carl Van de Velde, *Book Illustrations and Title-Pages, Corpus Rubenianum Ludwig Burchard*, vol. 21 (London: 1978).

Julia, Dominique and Jacques Revel, *Les universités européennes du XVIᵉ au XVIIIᵉ siècle. Histoire sociale des populations étudiantes*, vol. 2, *France* (Paris: 1986–1998).

Jurkowlaniec, Grażyna, "L'immagine della Chiesa nelle stampe di Tomasz Treter dedicate a Stanisław, Hozjusz. Contributo polacco alla cultura artistica europea ai tempi della controriforma," in *Atti dell'Accademia Polacca*, ed Leszek Kuk, vol. II, 2011 (Rome: 2012), 130–150.

Kairis, Pierre-Yves, *Bertholet Flémal (1614–1675): Le "Raphaël des Pays-Bas" au Carrefour de Liège et de Paris* (Paris: 2015).

Karr Schmidt, Suzanne and Nichols, Kimberly (ed.), *Altered and Adorned: Using Renaissance Prints in Daily Life*, exhibition catalogue (Chicago: 2011).

Kavaler, Ethan Matt, *Renaissance Gothic* (New Haven and London: 2012).

Kenz, David El, "La propagande et le problème de sa réception, d'après les mémoires-journaux de Pierre de L'Estoile", *Cahiers d'histoire. Revue d'histoire critique*, 90–91 (2003), 19–32.

Kettering, Sharon, "Gift-Giving and Patronage in Early Modern France", *French History* 2, 2 (1988): 131–151.

Kettner, Jasper, "Die Aufwertung der Kunstschneider. Druckgraphik als Skulptur bei Matthias Quad von Kinckelbach und Paul Behaim", in *Druckgraphik zwischen Reproduktion und Invention*, ed. Markus A. Castor (et al.) (Berlin and Munich: 2010), 241–248.

Kik, Oliver, "From Lodge to Studio: Transmissions of Architectural knowledge in the Low Countries 1480–1530", in *The Notion of Painter-Architect in Italy and the Southern Low Countries* (Architectura Moderna) 11 (Turnhout: 2014), 73–88.

Klinkenberg, Jean-Marie, *Précis de sémiotique Générale* (Brussels: 1996).

Koerner, Joseph Leo, *The Moment of Self-Portraiture in German Renaissance Art* (Chicago: 1993).

Koerner, Joseph Leo, 'Albrecht Dürer: a Sixteenth-Century *Influenza*', in *Albrecht Dürer and His Legacy: The Graphic Works of a Renaissance Artist*, ed. Giulia Bartrum, London: 2002, 18–38.

Kornell, Monique, *Flesh and Bones: The Art of Anatomy*, with contributions by Thisbe Gensler, Naoko Takahatake and Erin Travers, exhibition catalogue (Los Angeles: 2022).

Körner, Hans, *Der Früheste Deutsche Einblattholzschnitt* (Mittenwald: 1979).

Koldeweij, A. M., editor, *In Buscoducis. Kunst uit de Bourgondische tijd te 's-Hertogenbosch* (Maarssen: 1990).

Koldeweij, A. M., "Goud- en zilversmeden te 's-Hertogenbosch" in: *In Buscoducis. Kunst uit de Bourgondische tijd te 's-Hertogenbosch* ed. A. M. Koldeweij (Maarssen: 1990), 464–481.

Kristeller, Paul, *Andrea Mantegna* (London, New York and Bombay: 1901).

Kristeller, Paul, "Marcantons Beziehung zu Raffael", *Jahrbuch der Königlich-Preussischen Kunstsammlungen*, 4 (1907), 199–229.

de Lairesse, Gérard, *A Treatise on the Art of Painting in all its branches*, edited by W. M. Craig (London: 1817).

Landau, David, "Andrea Mantegna as Printmaker", in *Andrea Mantegna*, ed. Jane Martineau (London: 1992), 44–55.

Landau, David, "Revisiting Mantegna", *Print Quarterly*, 38, no. 3 (2021): 251–288.

Landau, David and Parshall, Peter, *The Renaissance Print 1470–1550* (New Haven and London: 1994).

Le Blanc, Marianne, *D'Acide et d'Encre: Abraham Bosse (1604?–1676) et son siècle en perspectives* (Paris: 2004).

Lehrs, Max, *Der Meister W A: ein Kupferstecher der Zeit Carls des Kühnen* (Dresden: 1895).

Lehrs, Max, *Geschichte und kritscher Katalog des deutchen, niederlandischen un franzözischen Kupferstichs in XV. Jahrhundert* 9 vols (Vienna: 1908–34).

BIBLIOGRAPHY

Levenson, Jay A., Konrad Oberhuber and Jacquelyn Sheehan, *Early Italian Engravings from the National Gallery of Art* (Washington DC: 1973).

Lightbown, Ronald W., *Mantegna: With a Complete Catalogue of Paintings, Drawings and Prints* (Oxford: 1986).

Lincoln, Evelyn, *The Invention of the Italian Renaissance Printmaker* (New Haven and London: 2000).

Lomartire, Saverio, *Andrea Mantegna e L'Incisione Italiana del Rinascimento nelle Collezioni dei Musei Civici di Pavia* (Milan: 2003).

Long, Pamela O., *Openness, Secrecy, Authorship. Technical Arts and the Culture of Knowledge from Antiquity to the Renaissance* (Baltimore and London: 2001).

Lothe, José, "Images d'actualité éditées à Paris sous le règne d'Henri IV," in *L'estampe au Grand Siècle. Études offertes à Maxime Préaud*, ed. Peter Fuhring, Barbara Brejon de Lavergnée et al. (Paris: 2010), 55–65.

Louvet, Jehan, "Journal ou Récit véritable de tout ce qui est advenu digne de mémoire tant en la ville d'Angers, pays d'Anjou et autres lieux (depuis l'an 1560–jusqu'à l'an 1634)," *Revue de l'Anjou et de Maine et Loire*, 1, no. 4 (1855).

Love, Harold, *Scribal Publication in Seventeenth-Century England* (Oxford: 1993).

Malni Pascoletti, Maddalena, *Ex universa philosophia: Stampe barocche con le tesi dei Gesuiti di Gorizia*, exhibition catalogue (Monfalcone: 1992).

Mancinelli, Fabrizion, ed., *Raffaello in Vaticano*, exhibition catalogue (Milan: 1984).

Mandroux-França, Marie-Thérèse and Maxime Préaud (ed.), *Catalogues de la Collection d'Estampes de Jean V, Roi du Portugal*, 3 vols (Lisbon and Paris: 1996–2003).

Marin, Louis, "Le cadre de la représentation et quelques-unes de ses figures", *Les cahiers du Musée national d'art moderne*, 24 (1988): 62–81.

Marshall, David R. (ed.), *The Site of Rome: Studies in the Art and Topography of Rome 1400–1750* (Rome: 2014).

Mauss, Marcel, *The Gift. Forms and Functions of Exchange in Archaic Societies*, trans. Ian Cunnison, London, 1966.

McDonald, Mark, P., "The Print Collection of Philip II at the Escorial", *Print Quarterly*, 15, No. 1 (1998): 15–35.

McDonald, Mark, P. (ed.), *The Print Collection of Ferdinand Colmumbus 1488–1539: A Renaissance Collector in Seville* 2 vols (London: 2004), 206–220.

McDonald, Mark P., *The Print Collection of Cassiano dal Pozzo. Part I: Ceremonies, Costumes, Portraits and Genre*, 3 vols (London: 2016).

McDonald, Mark P., *The Print Collection of Cassiano dal Pozzo. Part II: Architecture, Topography and Military Maps*, 3 vols (London: 2019).

McGowan, Margaret M., "The French Royal Entry in the Renaissance: The Status of Printed Text", *French Ceremonial Entries in the Sixteenth Century: Event, Image, Text*, ed. Nicolas Russell, Hélène Visentin (Toronto: 2007), 33–50.

Melion, Walter S., *Shaping the Netherlandish Canon. Karel Van Mander's Schilder-Boeck* (Chicago: 1991).

Melion, Walter S., "Introduction: The Jesuit Engagement with the Status and Functions of the Visual Image", in *Jesuit Image Theory*, ed. Karl Wietse de Boer, A. E. Enenkel, and Walter S. Melion, Intersections 45 (Leiden: 2016), 1–49.

Merlini, Valeria, and Daniele Storti, ed., *Raffaello a Milano. La Madonna di Foligno*, exhibition catalogue (Milan: 2013).

Metze, Gudula, ed., *Ars Nova. Frühe Kupferstiche aus Italien. Katalog der italienischen Kupferstiche von den Anfängen bis um 1530 in der Sammlung des Dresdener Kupferstich-Kabinetts*, exhibition catalogue (Petersberg: 2013).

Meyer, Véronique. "Les Copies de Nicolas Cochin." *Nouvelles de l'estampe*, no. 179–80 (December 2001–February 2002), 33–52.

Meyer, Véronique, *L'illustration des thèses à Paris dans la seconde moitié du XVIIe siècle: Peintres, graveurs, éditeurs* (Paris: 2002).

Meyer zur Capellen, Jürg, *Raphael. A critical catalogue of his paintings. T. II. The Roman religious Paintings ca. 1508–1520* (Landshut: 2005).

Miedema, Hessel, "De ontwikkeling van de kunsttheorie in de Hollandse Gouden Eeuw I: Het Begin; de Zuidelijke Nederlanden", *Oud Holland*, 126, no. 1 (2012): 102–115.

Miller, Elizabeth, *16th-Century Italian Ornament Prints in the Victoria and Albert Museum* (London: 1999).

Monteyne, Joseph, *The Printed Image in Early Modern London: Urban Space, Visual Representation, and Social Exchange* (Aldershot: 2007).

Morét, Stefan, "Der Paragone im Spiegel der Plastik", in *Benvenuto Cellini. Kunst und Kunsttheorie im 16. Jahrhundert*, ed. Alessandro Nova and Anna Schreurs (Cologne: 2003), 203–215.

Morrissette, Bruce, "Un héritage d'André Gide: La duplication intérieure", *Comparative Literature Studies*, 8, no. 2 (1971), 125–142.

Mount, Harry (ed.), *Sir Joshua Reynolds, A Journey to Flanders and Holland* (Cambridge: 1987).

de Mûelenaere, Gwendoline, *Early Modern Thesis Prints in the Southern Netherlands: An Iconological Analysis of the Relationships between Art, Science and Power*, Brill's Studies on Art, Art History, and Intellectual History 60 (Leiden/Boston: 2022).

Nakamura, Jun, "On Hercules Segers's 'Printed Paintings'", in *Printing Colour 1400–1700: History, Techniques, Functions and Receptions* ed. Ad Stijnman and Elizabeth Savage (Leyden, Boston: 2015), 189–195.

Nash, Susie, *Northern Renaissance Art* (Oxford: 2008).

Nesselrath, Arnold, "La Madonna di Foligno.", *Raffaello a Milano. La Madonna di Foligno*, exhibition catalogue, ed. Valeria Merlini and Daniele Storti (Milan: 2013), 63–73.

BIBLIOGRAPHY

Nova, Alessandro and Anna Schreurs (ed.), *Benvenuto Cellini. Kunst und Kunsttheorie im 16. Jahrhundert* (Cologne: 2003).

Oberhuber, Konrad, "Raffaello e l'incisione", in *Raffaello in Vaticano*, exhibition catalogue, ed. Fabrizio Mancinelli (Milan: 1984), 332–342.

Oberhuber, Konrad, "Marcantonio Raimondi", in *Bologna e l'umanesimo 1490–1510*, exhibition catalogue, ed. Marzia Faietti and Konrad Oberhuber (Bologna: 1988), 51–210.

Oberhuber, Konrad, "Mantegna and the Role of Prints: A Prototype for Artistic Innovation in the North and the South", in *Renaissance Venice and the North: Crosscurrents in the Time of Bellini, Dürer, and Titian* ed. Bernard Aikema and Beverly Louise Brown (London: 1999), 145–49.

O'Connell, Sheila, *The Popular Print in England 1550–1850* (London: 1999).

Orenstein, Nadine, Leeflang, Huigen, Ger Luijten and Christiaan Schuckman "Print Publishers in the Netherlands", in *Dawn of the Golden Age: Northern Netherlandish Art 1580–1620*, exhibition catalogue, ed. Ger Luijten, Ariane van Suchtelen, Reinier J. Baarsen, and Walter Kloek (Amsterdam: 1993).

Orenstein, Nadine, *Hendrick Hondius and the Business of Prints in Seventeenth-Century Holland* (Rotterdam: 1996).

Pagani, Valeria, "The Dispersal of Lafreri's Inheritance 1581–89—The De' Nobili-Arbotti-Clodio Partnership", *Print Quarterly*, 28, no. 2 (2011): 119–136.

Pałka, Ada, "Jan Ziarnko's Anamorphic Print A Pair of Lovers Embracing", *Print Quarterly*, 32, no. 1 (2015), 3–13.

Parshall, Peter, "The Print Collection of Ferdinand, Archduke of Tyrol", *Jahrbuch der Kunsthistorischen Sammlungen in Wien*, 78 (1982): 129–190.

Parshall, Peter, "Art and the Theatre of Knowledge: The Origins of Print Collecting in Northern Europe", *Harvard University Art Museums Bulletin*, 2, no. 3 (1994): 7–36.

Parshall, Peter, "Antonio Lafreri's *Speculum Romanae Magnificentiae*", *Print Quarterly*, 23, no. 1 (2006): 3–27.

Parshall, Peter and Rainer Schoch (ed.), *Fifteenth-Century Woodcuts and Their Public*, exhibition catalogue (New Haven and London: 2005).

Partner, Peter, *Renaissance Rome 1500–1559. A Portrait of a Society* (Berkeley: 1976).

Pericolo, Lorenzo, "What is Metapainting? The Self-Aware Image Twenty Years Later," in *The Self-Aware Image: An Insight into Early Modern Metapainting*, ed. Victor Stoichita (London: 2015), 11–31.

Pezzo, Annalisa, *Le tesi a stampa a Siena nei secoli XVI e XVII: Catalogo degli opuscoli della Biblioteca comunale degli Intronati* (Milan: 2011).

Pfisterer, Ulrich, "Dürer in Discourse: Art Theories around 1500 and the Paths they Took North and South of the Alps", in *Albrecht Dürer. His Art in Context*, ed. Jochen Sander (Munich, London and New York: 2013), 376–382.

Pickwoad, Nicholas, "Binders' Gatherings", *The Library: The Transactions of the Bibliographical Society*, 15, no. 1 (2014), 63–78.

Pon, Lisa, *Raphael, Dürer, and Marcantonio Raimondi. Copying and the Italian Renaissance Print* (New Haven and London: 2004).

Popham, Arthur E., and Johannes Wilde, *The Italian drawings of the XV and XVI centuries in the collection of His Majesty the King at Windsor Castle* (London: 1949).

Préaud, Maxime, et al., *Dictionnaire des Éditeurs d'Estampes à Paris sous l'Ancien Régime* (Paris: 1987).

Préaud, Maxime, et al., *L'oeil d'or: Claude Mellan 1598–1688* (Paris: 1988).

Préaud, Maxime, "Intaglio Printmaking in Paris in the Seventeenth Century or, The Fortune of France." In Reed, Sue Welsh (ed.), *French Prints from the Age of the Musketeers*, 6–11 (Boston: 1998).

Préaud, Maxime, "'Nous allons à l'an pire': à propos d'un almanach mural pour 1653 et de sa mise en abyme," *Nouvelles de l'estampe*, 245 (2013), 4–14.

Raabe, Mechtild, *Leser und Lektüre im 17. Jahrhundert: die Ausleihbücher der Herzog August Bibliothek Wolfenbüttel 1664–1713*, 3 vols (Munich: 1998).

Raven, James, *Publishing Business in Eighteenth-Century England* (Woodbridge and Rochester, NY: 2014).

Renouvier, Jules, *Des types et des manières des maîtres graveurs. XVIe et XVIIe siècles*, pt. 2 (Montpellier: 1856).

Reske, Christoph and Wolfgang Schmitz, editors, *Der gegenwärtige Stand der materiellen Aspekte in der Inkunabelforschung* (Wolfenbütteler Schriften zur Geschichte des Buchwesens) (Wiesbaden: 2015).

Rice, Louise, "Jesuit Thesis Prints and the Festive Academic Defence at the Collegio Romano", in *The Jesuits: Cultures, Sciences, and the Arts, 1540–1773*, ed. John W. O'Malley (Toronto: 1999), 148–69.

Riggs, Timothy and Larry Silver (ed.), *Graven Images: The Rise of Professional Printmakers in Antwerp and Haarlem, 1540–1640* (Evaston IL: 1993).

Robert-Dumesnil, Alexandre-Pierre-François, *Le Peintre-graveur français, ou catalogue raisonné des estampes gravées par les peintres et les dessinateurs de l'école française, ouvrage faisant suite au Peintre-graveur de M. Bartsch*, 11 vols in 6. (Paris: 1835–1871). Reprint (Paris: 1967).

Roberts, K. B. and J. D. W. Tomlinson, *The Fabric of the Body: European Traditions of Anatomical Illustration* (Oxford: 1992).

Robertson, Bruce, *Paul Sandby and the Early Development of English Watercolor*, PhD dissertation (Yale: 1987).

Rodari, Florian (ed.) *Anatomie de la couleur: l'invention de l'estampe en couleurs*, exhibition catalogue (Paris and Lausanne: 1996).

Roeck, Bernd, "Venice and Germany: Commercial Contacts and Intellectual Inspirations", in *Renaissance Venice and the North: Crosscurrents in the Time of Bellini, Dürer, and Titian* ed. Bernard Aikema and Beverly Louise Brown (London: 1999), 45–55.

BIBLIOGRAPHY

Rombouts, P., and T. van Lerius, *De Liggeren en andere historische archieven van het Antwerpse Sint-Lukasgilde*, 2 vols (Antwerp: 1864–76).

Rooses, Max, *L'oeuvre de P. P. Rubens. Histoire et description de ses tableaux et dessins* (Antwerp: 1892).

Roover, Raymond de, *Money, Banking and Credit in Medieval Bruges* (Cambridge MA: 1948).

Rosenberg, Pierre and Louis-Antoine Prat, *Nicolas Poussin 1594–1665* (Paris: 1995).

Rouillard, Philippe, "Van Halbeeck et vieilles dentelles," in *L'estampe au Grand Siècle. Études offertes à Maxime Préaud*, ed. Peter Fuhring, Barbara Brejon de Lavergnée et al. (Paris: 2010), 67–78.

Roux, Marcel, *Inventaire du fonds français, graveurs du XVIIIe siècle* 15 vols (Paris: 1931– ongoing).

Rupprich, Hans, *Dürer Schriftlicher Nachlass*, 3 vols (Berlin: 1956–1969).

Russell, Gillian, *The Ephemeral Eighteenth Century, Print, Sociability, and the Cultures of Collecting* (Cambridge: 2020).

Sandby, William A., *Thomas and Paul Sandby, Royal Academicians* (London: 1892).

Salzberg, Rosa, *Ephemeral City: Cheap Print and Urban Culture in Renaissance Venice* (Manchester: 2014).

Sauer, Christine, editor, *Handwerk im Mittelalter* (Darmstadt: 2012), 43–55.

Saunders Magurn, Ruth (ed.), *The Letters of Peter Paul Rubens* (Cambridge MA: 1955).

Savage, Elizabeth, "Jost de Negker's Woodcut Charles V (1519): An Undescribed Example of Gold Printing", *Art in Print*, 5, no. 2 (2015, July/Aug), 9–15.

Savage, Elizabeth, "Colour Printing in Relief before c.1700: A Technical Story", in *Printing Colour 1400–1700: History, Techniques, Functions and Receptions*, ed. Ad Stijnman and Elizabeth Savage (Leyden, Boston: 2015), 23–41.

Savage, Elizabeth, "A Printer's Art: The Development and Influence of Colour Print-making in the German Lands, c.1476–c.1600", in *Printing Colour 1400–1700: History, Techniques, Functions and Receptions*, ed. Ad Stijnman and Elizabeth Savage (Leyden, Boston: 2015), 93–102.

Savage, Elizabeth, "Proto-*à la poupée* Printing in Relief: An Initial 'D' in the Rylands Mainz Psalter, 1457," (unpublished manuscript).

Savage, Elizabeth and Stijnman, Ad, *Printing in Colour 1400–1700* (Leiden: 2015).

Sawicka, Stanisława, "Jan Ziarnko peintre-graveur polonais et son activité a Paris au premier quart du XVIIe siècle", in *La France et la Pologne dans leurs relation artistiques*, 2–3 (1938), 101–257.

Sawyer, Jeffrey K., *Printed Poison. Pamphlet Propaganda, Faction Politics, and the Public Sphere in Early Seventeenth-Century France* (Oxford: 1990).

Schandel, Pascal, "Les images de dédicace à la cour des ducs de Bourgogne. Ressources et enjeux d'un genre," in *Miniatures flamandes, 1404–1482*, ed. Bernard Bousmanne and Thierry Delcourt, exhibition catalogue (Paris: 2011), 66–80.

Signorini, Roberto, Viviana Rebonato and Sara Tammacaro, ed., *Andrea Mantegna impronta del genio. Convegno internazionale di studi 2006*, 2 volumes (Florence: 2010).

Simonsfeld, Henry, *Der Fondaco dei Tedeschi in Venedig und die Deutsch-Venetianischen Handelsbeziehungen* (Stuttgart: 1887).

Scheller, Robert W., *Exemplum. Model-Book Drawings and the Practice of artistic Transmission in the Middle Ages* (Amsterdam: 1995).

Teyssèdre, Bernard, *Roger de Piles et les Débats sur le Coloris au siècle de Louis XIV* (Paris: 1957).

Schemmel, Bernhard and Wolfgang Seitz, *Die graphischen Thesen- und Promotionsblätter In Bamberg* (Wiesbaden: 2001).

Schleif, Corine, "Kneeling on the Threshold: Donors Negotiating Realms Betwixt and Between", in *Thresholds of Medieval Visual Culture: Liminal Spaces*, ed. Elina Gertsman and Jill Stevenson (Woodbridge: 2012), 195–216.

Schoch, Rainer, Matthia Mende and Anna Scherbaum, editors, *Albrecht Durer: das drucksgraphische Werk*, 3 volumes (Munich: 2001).

Scolia, Gianni Carlo & Caterina Volpi, *Da van Eyck a Brueghel. Scritti sulle arti di Domenico Lamsonio* (Turin: 2001).

Seifert, Tico (ed.), *Rembrandt: Britain's Discovery of the Master* (Edinburgh: 2018).

Sheehan, Jacquelyn L., "Andrea Mantegna" in Jay A. Levenson, Konrad Oberhuber and Jacquelyn L. Sheehan, *Early Italian Engravings from the National Gallery of Art* (Washington: 1973).

Shelby, Lon, *Gothic Design Techniques: The Fifteenth-Century Design Booklets of Mathes Roriczer and Hanns Schmuttermayer* (Carbondale: 1977).

Shennan, Joseph H., *The Bourbons: the history of a dynasty* (London: 2009).

Shoemaker, Innis H., "Marcantonio and his Sources. A Survey of His Style and Engraving Techniques", in *The engravings of Marcantonio Raimondi*, exhibition catalogue, ed. Innis H. Shoemaker and Elizabeth Broun (Lawrence: 1981), 3–18.

Shoemaker, Innis H. and Elizabeth Broun (ed.), *The engravings of Marcantonio Raimondi*, exhibition catalogue (Lawrence: 1981).

Silver, Larry, *The Paintings of Quinten Massys with Catalogue Raisonné* (Oxford: 1984).

Silver, "Massys and Money: The Tax Collectors Rediscovered", *Journal of Historians of Netherlandish Art*, vol. 7, no. 2 (2015).

Slachmuylders, Raoul, "De Triptiek van de Maagdschap van de Heilige Anna", *Quinten Metsys en Leuven* (Arca Lovaniesis artes atque historiae restans documenta) vol. 33 (Leuven: 2007), 85–120.

Smentek, Kristel, *Mariette and the Science of the Connoisseur in Eighteenth-Century Europe* (Farnham: 2014).

Smiles, Sam (ed.), *Sir Joshua Reynolds: The acquisition of genius* (Bristol: 2009).

BIBLIOGRAPHY

Smolderen, Luc, "Quintin Metsys Médailleur d'Erasme", *Scrinium Erasmianum*, ed. Joseph Coppens (Brussels: 1969), vol. 1, 513–525.

Sounders, Alison, *The Seventeenth-century French Emblem: A Study in Diversity* (Geneva: 2000).

Steadman, David W., *Abraham van Diepenbeeck: Seventeenth-Century Flemish Painter* (Ann Arbor: 1982).

Štěpán, Jan, "Olomoucký zlatník Donát Šolc (1575–1588) a olomoucká medailérská škola," *Střední Morava: vlastivědná revue*, 16 (2003): 108–111.

Stielau, Allison, "Intent and Independence: Late Fifteenth-Century Object Engravings" in *Visual Acuity and the Arts of Communication in Early Modern Germany*, ed. Jeffrey Chipps Smith (Farnham: 2014), 21–42.

Stijnman, Ad, "White Ink", *Print Quarterly*, 9, no. 2 (1992), 181–83.

Stijnman, Ad, "Another Clair-obscur Etching", *Print Quarterly*, 10, no. 1 (1993), 58–59.

Stijnman, Ad, *Engraving and Etching 1400–2000: A History of the Development of Manual Intaglio Printmaking Processes* (London and Houten: 2012).

Stijnman, Ad, "Thoughts on art history from the perspective of the maker," in *Art in Print*, vol. 6, no. 3 (2016), 16–17.

Stijnman, Ad, "Hercules Segers's Printmaking Techniques", in *Hercules Segers: Painter, Etcher*, exhibition catalogue, ed. Huigen Leeflang and Pieter Roelofs (Amsterdam: 2017), 62–77.

Stijnman, Ad, *Johannes Teyler and Dutch Colour Prints c.1700*, ed. Simon Turner (The new Hollstein Dutch & Flemish etchings, engravings and woodcuts: 1450–1700) (Ouderkerk aan den IJssel: 2017).

Stijnman, Ad and Elizabeth Savage, *Printing Colour 1400–1700: History, Techniques, Functions and Receptions* (Leiden: 2015).

Stijnman, Ad and Elizabeth Savage, "Materials and Techniques for Early Colour Printing", in Ad Stijnman and Elizabeth Savage (ed.), *Printing Colour 1400–1700: History, Techniques, Functions and Receptions* (Leiden: 2015), 11–22.

Stock, Jan Van der, *Cornelis Metsys. Grafisch Werk* (Brussels: 1985).

Stock, Jan van der, *Printing Images in Antwerp. The Introduction of Printmaking in a City: Fifteenth Century to 1585* (Rotterdam: 1998).

Stoichita, Victor, *L'instauration du tableau: Métapeinture à l'aube des temps modernes* (Geneva: 1999).

Stoichita, Victor, "L'effet Don Quichotte. Le problème de la frontière esthétique dans L'œuvre de Murillo", in *Cadre, seuil, limite. La question de la frontière dans la théorie de l'art*, ed. Thierry Lenain and Rudy Steinmetz, Essais (Brussels: 2010), 51–99.

Stoltz, Barbara, "Das Bild-Druckverfahren in der frühen Neuzeit", *Marburger Jahrbuch für Kunstwissenschaft*, 39 (2012), 93–117.

Stoltz, Barbara, "*Disegno* versus *Disegno stampato*: printmaking theory in Vasari's *Vite* (1550–1568)", *Journal of Art Historiography*, 7, December (2012) (e-journal), 1–20.

Stoltz, Barbara, "Ars Nova? Die Neue Kunst? Die Bedeutung der Druckgraphik in der Kunstliteratur des 15. und des frühen 16. Jahrhunderts", *Ars Nova. Frühe Kupferstiche aus Italien*, ed. Gudula Metze (Petersberg: 2013) 19–29.

Strange, Robert , *An inquiry into the rise and establishment of the Royal Academy of Arts. To which is prefixed, A Letter to the Earl of Bute* (London: 1775).

Strutt, Joseph, *A Biographical Dictionary containing an historical account of all the engravers, from the earliest period of the art of engraving to the present time* (London: 1785).

Stružová, Veronika, *Filigrány moravských papíren na základě nových zjištění využití papíru v kanceláři olomouckých biskupů* (diploma at University of Pardubice, 2015).

Suykerbuyck, Ruben, *Sign of Times. A concise history of the signature in Netherlandish painting 1432–1575* (Unpublished MA Thesis; Utrecht: 2013).

Tahon, Eva, *Lanceloot Blondeel* (Bruges: 1988).

Takahatake, Naoko, *The Chiaroscuro Woodcut in Renaissance Italy*, exhibition catalogue (Los Angeles: 2018).

Talbot, Charles, "Dürer and the High Art of Printmaking," in *The Essential Dürer*, ed. Larry Silver and Jeffrey Chipps Smith (Philadelphia: 2010), 35–61.

Tanner, Paul, *Das Amerbach-Kabinett. Die Basler Goldschmiederisse* (Basel: 1991).

Telfer, William, *The treasure of São Roque: A sidelight on the counter-reformation* (London: 1932).

Timmermann, Achim, *Real Presence: Sacrament Houses and the Body of Christ, c.1270–1600* (Architectura Medii Aevi) 4 (Turnhout: 2009).

Tourneur, Victor, "Quintin Metys, Médailleur", *Revue Belge de Numismatique*, 72 (1920), 139–160.

Velden, Hugo Van der, "Defrocking St Eloy: Petrus Christus's Vocational portrait of a goldsmith", *Simiolus*, 26 (1998): 243–269.

Velden, Hugo van der, *The Donor's Image. Gerard Loyet and the Votive Portraits of Charles the Bold* (Turnhout: 2000).

Velden, Hugo van der, "Diptych Altarpiece and the Principle of Dextrality," in *Essays in Context. Unfolding the Netherlandish Diptych*, ed. John Oliver Hand and Ron Spronk (Cambridge: 2006), 124–155.

Véliz Bomford, Zahira, "The Authority of Prints in Early Modern Spain", Hispanic Research Journal, Iberian and Latin American Studies, 9 (2008), 416–436.

Verreyt, Christian, "Allart du Hamel of du Hameel", *Oud Holland*, 12 (1894), 1–8.

Vibanti, Corrado, "Henry IV, the Gallic Hercules", *Journal of the Warburg and Courtauld Institutes*, 30 (1967), 176–197.

Vouilloux, Bernard, *L'œuvre en souffrance: Entre poétique et esthétique*, L'extrême contemporain (Paris: 2004).

BIBLIOGRAPHY

Waal, Jan van der, *Prints in the Golden Age: From Art to Shelf Paper*, exhibition catalogue (Rotterdam: 2006).

Wegener Sleeswyk, André, "De Graveur WA: een speurtocht", *Gens Nostra*, 49 (1994), 1–14.

Weijers, Olga, *In Search of the Truth: A History of Disputation Techniques from Antiquity to Early Modern Times* (Turnhout: 2013).

Weigert, Roger-Armand, and Maxime Préaud, *Inventaire du fonds français, graveurs du XVIIe siècle*, vols. 1–13 and 17 (Paris: 1939–).

Whatling, Stuart, "Putting Mise-En-Abyme in its (Medieval) Place," lecture at the workshop *Medieval Mise-En-Abyme: The Object Depicted within Itself*, online article of the Courtauld Institute, February 2009, accessed March 17, 2014, 1–10 [http://www.courtauld.ac.uk/researchforum/projects/medievalarttheory/documents/Mise-en-abyme.pdf].

White, Christopher, *Rembrandt as an Etcher: A Study of the Artist at Work* (London: 1969).

White, John J., "The Semiotics of the *Mise-en-Abyme*," in *The Motivated Sign*, ed. Olga Fischer and Max Nänny (Amsterdam: 2001), 29–53.

Widauer, Heinz (ed.), *Die französischen Zeichnungen der Albertina: vom Barock bis zum beginnenden Rokoko* 10 vols (Vienna: 2004).

Wildenstein, Georges, 'Les graveurs de Poussin', *Gazette des Beaux-Arts*, XLVI, 1955, pp. 77–371.

Witcombe, Christopher. L., *Print Publishing in Sixteenth-Century Rome: Growth and Expansion, Rivalry and Murder* (Turnhout: 2008).

Wouk, Edward H., "Reclaiming the antiquities of Gaul: Lambert Lombard and the history of northern art", *Simiolus*, 36 (2012): 35–65.

Wouk, Edward H., "Introduction: Marcantonio Raimondi, Raphael and the image multipled", in *Raphael, Raimondi and the image multiplied*, ed. Edward H. Wouk and David Morris, exhibition catalogue (Manchester: 2016), 10–11.

Wouk, Edward H., and David Morris (ed.), *Raphael, Raimondi and the image multiplied*, exhibition catalogue (Manchester: 2016).

Wyss, Beat, "Der Paragone. Spielregeln des Kunstsystems" in *Streit. Domäne der Kultur*, ed. Irmgard Bohunovsky-Bärnthaler (Klagenfurt: 2006), 31–55.

Zagala, Maria, *A Beautiful Line: Italian Prints from Mantegna to Piranesi* (Adelaide: 2010).

Zelen, Joyce G. H., "Zum Verhältnis des frühen Kupferstichs zur Goldschmiedekunst: der Salzburger Hausaltar des Meisters Perchtold", in *Mit den Gezeiten. Frühe Druckgraphik der Niederlande*, ed. Tobias Pfeifer-Helke (Petersberg: 2013), 25–31.

Ziolkowski, Jan, *The Medieval Latin Past of Wonderful Lies* (Michigan 2009).

Zorach, Rebecca and Elisabeth Rodini (ed.), *Paper Museums. The Reproductive Print in Europe, 1500–1800* (Chicago: 2005).

Zorach, Rebecca, *The Virtual Tourist in Renaissance Rome: Printing and Collecting the Speculum Romanae Magnificentiae*, exhibition catalogue (Chicago: 2008).

Zucker, Mark J., *Early Italian Masters*, vol. 25 (Commentary). Formerly Volume 13 (part 2). The Illustrated Bartsch, ed. Walter L. Strauss (New York: 1984).

Online Sources

http://www.nationalarchives.gov.uk/currency/.

Index

L'Admiral, Jan   123–124, 129
Ainsworth, Radulph Fawsett   132
Allan, David   96, 101, 106, 108, 109
Alberti, Cherubino   256
Albinus, Bernard Siegfried   123n25, 129
Aldegrever, Heinrich   248
Allais, Angélique (see: Briceau, Angelique)   131
Apelles   48–49, 56
Anne of Austria   164, 183–184
Aselli, Gaspare   125–126
Astley, Edward   261
Austin, William   103

Baglione, Giovanni   57, 59, 60n16, 69
Baldinucci, Filippo   57, 60n16, 62, 68n52, 71, 79, 80n15
Baldung, Hans   269
Baltens, Pieter   232–233
Bandinelli, Baccio   245
Barbari, Jacopo de'   49
Barberini, Maffeo   81
Barendszoon, Theodor   236
Barocci, Federico   255
Barry, James   254
Bartolozzi, Francesco   94n4, 110, 251
Bartsch, Adam von   5, 69, 70n57, 80n25, 146, 149n12, 153–154, 156n29
Beatrizet, Nicolas   232
Bell, Andrew   96
Bellori, Giovanni Pietro   57, 61n20, 70–71, 84, 90–91
Benazech, Paul   104
Berey, Nicolas   183
Bernini, Gian Lorenzo   81–82
Bertelli, Ferrando   231
Bertelli, Luca   231
Billard, Charles   126–128, 131–132
Blaeu, Willem Janszoon   184
Bloemart, Cornelis   78–80
Blondeel, Lanceloot   48, 49n63
Bobrek Ligeza, Gabriel Kilian de   192, 193
Bol, Hans   219, 232, 236–237
Bolswert, Boetius Adams   259
Bolswert, Schelte Adamsz.   77, 192

Boncompagni, Ugo (Pope Gregory XIII)   215, 233, 236
Borcht, Pieter van der   236
Bosse, Abraham   1–3, 16, 56, 64n37, 83–84, 86–90
Botticelli, Sandro   260, 262, 266–268
Bourdon, Sébastien   269
Brescia, Giovanni Antonio   17, 146, 154, 156nn29–30, 158n33, 159, 231
Breughel, Pieter the Elder   231
Briceau, Alexandre   131–132
Briceau, Angélique   131–132
Bronikowski, Adam   223n36, 223n40
Brunelleschi, Fillipo   51n72
Bry, Theodor de   224, 237
Bruyn, Abraham de   219
Buonarotti, Michelangelo   58n10, 84, 231, 245n18, 254
Buckingham, Richard Grenville, Duke of   261, 266
Burckhardt, Jacob   41
Burdett, Peter Perez   105–106
Burke, Edmund   242
Bussemacher, Johann   233

Callot, Jacques   88
Campagnola, Giulio   262
Canot, Pierre Charles   102, 110
Capieux, Johann Stephan   132
Caranzano, Antonio   232
Carracci, Agostino   70nn58–59, 86, 269n90
Carracci, Annibale   61n20
Cartaro, Mario   231–232
Caravaggio, Polidoro da   256
Casa, Niccolò della   245
Castiglione, Giovanni Benedetto   243
Chambray, Roland Fréart de   79, 83–87, 90
Chantelou, Paul Fréart de   75, 76n4, 80–81, 82n18, 83, 90
Charles the Bold, Duke of Burgundy   32, 37–38
Chasteau, Guillaume   77
Christus, Petrus   39, 44
Cellini, Benvenuto   16, 57, 58n10, 64–66, 72
Clérisseau, Charles Louis   96, 106

300 INDEX

Clerk of Eldin, John   105
Cock, Hieronymus   6, 50, 84*n*25, 232–233
Cockburn, William   123
Collaert, Adriaen   236–237
Collaert, Hans   233–234, 236–237
Collalto, Claudius of   206
Collin, Richard   191
Collins, John   95, 101, 103
Concini, Concino (*alias* Marshal d'Ancre)
      169–170
Cooper, Richard   96
Coornhert, Dirck Volckertsz.   222, 234
Corneille, Pierre   1, 177
Cort, Cornelis   49*n*63, 86, 231, 236, 269
Coter, Coleyn de   45
Cotes, Francis   104
Cozens, Alexander   251
Cracherode, Rev. Clayton Mordaunt   241
Cropacius, Caspar (Kropáč Kaspar)   236

Da Cortona, Pietro   77, 79
Da Vinci, Leonardo   83
Dal Pozzo, Cassiano   12, 75–76, 83
David (bible figure)   177
David, Gerard   34*n*16, 44
Dent, St John   266, 268
Delfino, Zaccaria   268
Del Pò, Pietro   77
Demansan, Monsieur   172
Dene, Eduard   48
Dente, Marco (Marco da Ravenna)   65
Dheulland, Guillaume   180*n*42
Diepenbeeck, Abraham van   190–192, 206
Dobson, William   248
Doetecum, Johannes van   236
Doetecum, Lucas van   233
Drevet, Pierre   245, 248
Du Cerceau, Jacques Androuet   180*n*42
du Perron, Jacques   172
Dürer, Albrecht the Elder   28, 44
Dürer, Albrecht   8, 10–11, 41–42, 44–46,
      48–49, 56, 61, 64*n*35, 65–66, 86, 89,
      156*n*29, 231, 236, 248, 252
Dutuit, Eugène   266
Du Val, Jean-Baptiste   165
Dyck, Sir Anthony van   77, 248

Earlom, Richard   257
Elizabeth of France   164
Elliot, William   104
English, Josias   248
Erasmus, Desiderius   48, 56, 174, 190
Errard, Charles   83, 85
Estienne, Robert II   179
Evelyn, John   16, 56–57, 60–61, 62*n*24, 79, 83,
      89*n*38, 90
Eyck, Jan van   39, 44–45, 195

Fabris, Pietro   96, 101, 106, 108
Faleti, Bartolomeo   232
Félibien, André   68, 70–71, 88
Ferdinand of Austria, Archduke   206
Ferdinand II of Tyrol, Archduke of Austria
      12, 213, 214
Ferdinand III of Habsburg, Emperor   203
Ferrari, Giovan Battista   78
Feyerabend, Sigmund   222
Flémalle, Bertholet   202
Floris, Frans   50
Francken, Ambrosius   232–233
Froriep, Robert   132–133
Furnius, Peter   233
Fust, Johann   122

Galle, Philips   218, 222, 224, 233–234,
      236–237
Gaston de France (*alias* Gaston
      Jean-Baptiste/ duc d'Orléans)   170
Gaurico, Pomponio   56*n*2, 59*n*15
Gautier-Dagoty, Arnaud-Éloi   131
Gautier-Dagoty, Eduard   131
Gautier-Dagoty, Fabien   131
Gautier-Dagoty, Jacques-Fabien   123, 129
Gautier-Dagoty, Jean-Baptiste-André   130
Gautier-Dagoty, Louis-Charles   131
Ghisi, Giorgio   84, 269
Gilpin, William   93, 102
Giotto di Bondone   200
Glicius, Martin (of Pilzno)   223
Goltzius, Hendrick   7, 11, 61, 77, 86, 231,
      233–234, 236–237
Goes, Hugo van der   38
Goliath (bible figure)   177

INDEX

301

Graf, Urs 37
Grünwald, Pavel 214
Greville, Charles 101, 106, 108,110
Guarlotti, Perino de 232
Gutenberg, Johann 121n16

Haden, Francis Seymour 262
Haecht, Godevaard van 232
Haecht, Willem van 224, 232–233
Hameel, Alart Du 15, 30, 32, 34, 36n19,
　45–46, 51
Hamilton, Sir William 101
Hanuš Haugvic of Biskupice 215n9
Harding, Joseph 261
Harrington, James 248
Hatzfeldt, Heinrich von 202
Heemskerck, Maarten van 222, 224,
　233–234, 237
Helle, Albert van der 248
Henri II de Bourbon (*alias* Prince of
　Condé) 164, 169–170, 183
Henry IV [King of France] (*alias*
　Henri IV) 162–163, 165–166, 175, 177–181,
　183, 185
Hoeswinckel, Eduard van 233
Hogarth, William 96, 109
Hogenberg, Nicolaas 217n19
Hogenberg, Franz 229
Honnecourt, Villard de 27
Howell, James 88
Hudson, Thomas 241, 248
Humphrey, William 257
Huybrechts, Adriaen 232, 234
Huygens, Christiaan 190n9

Immerseel, Théodore d' 190n9

Jefferys, Thomas 104
Jenichen, Balthasar 232
Jode, Gerard de 233, 236–237
Jones, Thomas 95
Junius, Hadrianus 236

Kašpar of Litovle 214
Kessel, Theodorus van 245–246
Key, Willem 50

Kirkall, Elisha 131
Kraft, Adam 40–41

Lafreri, Antonio 7, 216n17, 232, 237–238
Lagniet, Jacques 175
Lairesse, Gérard de 85
Lallemand, Jean Baptiste 96, 106
Lampsonius, Domenicus 50–51
Last, Rev. H. 248
Layens, Mathes de 32
Le Blon, Jacob Christoff 14, 122–123, 126,
　129–130
Le Clerc, Jean IV 165, 170, 179
Leopold I, Emperor 200, 202
Leeuw, Jan de 39, 44
Leo X, Pope 150, 156n29, 256
Leyden, Lucas van 11, 29, 61–62, 232
Lloyd, Thomas 262, 266
Lomazzo, Giovanni Paolo 57, 63–64
Lombard, Lambert 50
Loyet, Gerard 37–38
Luyck, Hans van 233
Louis XI [King of France] 174
Louis XIII [King of France] (*alias* Louis
　Bourbon/*Ludovicus Borbonius*) 163–165,
　167, 175, 177, 179, 183–185
Loyens, Henri 202
Luther, Martin 162
Lutma, Jan 243, 245, 261
Luz, Emanuel 129

Maberly, Joseph 260–261
McArdell, James 257
Malcolm, John 262n76, 266–268
Malone, Edmond 242
Mander, Karel van 57, 61–63
Mantegna, Andrea 8–10, 51n72, 69, 156n29,
　262, 268
Marchi, Giuseppe 248
Mariette, Pierre-Jean 8
Martens, Frans Heinrich 133
Mason, James 102
Master IAM of Zwolle 29
Master FVB 29
Master WA 32, 34, 46, 51
Mathonière, Michel de 177

302 INDEX

Maximilian, II Habsburg 214
Mazarin, Jules 183
Meckenem, Israel van 34, 37, 44–45
Medici, Marie de' [Queen of France] (*alias*
  Queen Mother/ Regent) 163–165, 172,
  179–181, 183, 185
Mellan, Claude 16, 80–82, 88, 90
Memling, Hans 195
Merian, Mattheus 183
Metcalfe, Philip 242, 258
Metsys, Cornelis 48n59
Metsys, Cristina 48
Metsys, Quinten 46–48, 49n63, 50–51, 195
Metz, Conrad Martin 251
Meyerpeck, Wolfgang (II) 217n19
Mezoulle, Bonaventure 175
Miron, Robert 167
Monogrammist FML 234
Muller, Harmen Jansz. 233

Nanteuil, Robert 16, 87n34, 89
Natalis, Michel 202–203
Nelli, Niccolo 231
Nockart, Simon 199
Northcote, James 243–244, 257
Nuvolstella, Giorgio 59

Ottley, William Young 263, 266

Pacioli, Luca 49
Pader, Hilaire 75
Paignon-Dijonval, Gilbert 262
Palumbo, Pietro Paolo 231
Parasole, Leonardo 59
Parler, Peter 39, 41
Parmigianino 251–252, 254–256, 269n90
Pars, William 96, 106–108
Pauli, Żegota 218
Peake, James 104
Peoli, Juan Jorge 268–269
Père Joseph (*alias* Leclerc du Tremblay) 175
Perrissin, Jean 218, 230
Perrochel, Charles 172
Pesne, Jean 76–77
Philip II (King of Spain) 12, 213, 232
Philip IV (King of Spain) 164
Philip the Good (Duke of Burgundy) 199
Phillips, Harry 242
Piles, Roger de 82–83

Pilgram, Anton 41
Piombo, Sebastiano del 231
Pirckheimer, Willibald 48
Pliny the Elder 72
Poilly, François de 75–77
Ponętowski, Jakub 214, 216n15
Ponętowski, Jan 17, 213–218, 220, 222–226,
  228, 230–232, 234n70, 237
Pontius, Paulus 77, 206
Poussin, Nicolas 16, 75–83, 85, 87, 90
Prince Rupert of the Rhine 90
Prudeker, Michael 230

Quad von Kinckelbach, Mathias 16, 67, 72
Quellinus, Erasmus 190
Quesnel, François 180

Raimondi, Marcantonio 8, 10, 17, 62n25, 65,
  84, 86, 143, 146, 148–149, 152–154, 156,
  158–159, 243, 252, 254–255
Raphael (Raffaello Sanzio) 10, 17, 84, 86,
  143, 146, 148–150, 152–154, 158–159,
  230–231, 252, 254, 255–256
Ratdoldt, Erhard 119
Rémy, Pierre 261
Reynolds, Sir Joshua 17, 94, 241–245, 248,
  251–252, 254–262, 266–270
Richelieu, Cardinal 175
Rigaud, Hyacinthe 245
Rijn, Rembrandt van 11, 174, 243, 245, 257,
  260–1, 268
Ring, Ludger Thomas the Elder 34
Rogers, Charles 258
Roncherolle, Pierre V de, baron du Pont S.
  Pierre 167
Rooker, Edward 101–103, 111
Rosenberg, George and Wolffgang of 203,
  206
Rosselli, Francesco 262
Rubens, Peter Paul 77, 190, 192, 258–259,
  269
Rysbrack, John Michael 251–252
Royal Academy 9n26, 13, 93–96, 108, 110,
  241, 252, 255–256, 270
Ruysch, Frederick 129

Sacchi, Andrea 78
Sadeler, Johannes (I) 230, 233, 236–237
Sadeler, Raphael 230

INDEX 303

Saint-Bonnet de, Jean Caylar d'Anduze (*alias* Marshal de Toiras) 177
Sallaert, Antoon 190
Sandby, Paul 16, 93, 95–97, 99–106, 108–112, 114
Sandby, Thomas 95, 97
Sander, Georg Karl Heinrich 132
Scheuss, Hermann 78
Schmuttermayer, Hans 27–28, 34
Schöffer, Peter 122
Schongauer, Ludwig 45
Schongauer, Martin 37, 45, 65
Schut, Cornelis 190, 203
Schröter, Johann Friedrich 131
Schweiger, Jörg the Elder 37
Seghers, Daniel 190n9
Senff, Karl Friedrich 132
Sewall, Charles 268–269
Sewall, Henry Foster 269
Sigismund III, King of Poland and Sweden 192, 194
Skippe, John 251
Society of Artists 93–94, 96, 104
Society of Dilettanti 100, 106
Solis, Virgil 11, 233
Sorg, Joachim 217n19
Soutman, Pieter 194n17, 258
Spierre, François 79
Stefani, Benedetto 232
Stefaneschi, Giacomo 200
Stella, Jacques 256
Straet, Jan van der 234, 237
Strange, Robert 94
Strutt, Joseph 93, 108
Stubbs, George 251
Stukeley, William 131–132
Sykes, Mark Masterman 263, 266
Syrlin, Jörg the Younger 37

Tacquet, André 190n9
Tempesti, Domenico 82, 87n34
Teyler, Johannes 121, 126
Titian (Tiziano Vecellio) 231, 245, 269
Tortorel, Jacques 218, 230
Treter, Tomasz 231n61

Van Dyck, Anthony 77, 248
Vaccaria, Lorenzo 232
Vasari, Giorgio 16, 50, 57, 58n9, 60–62, 66–69, 72, 84, 146, 147n5, 148n7, 252, 256
Vassallieu, Benedit dit Nicolay 180
Vecellio, Cesare 230, 269
Velázquez, Diego 195
Veneziano, Agostino 269
Vesalius, Andreas 133, 231
Vicentino, Niccolò 251–252
Vico, Enea 254, 256, 257n50
Vicq-d'Azyr, Félix 132
Villamena, Francesco 69n56, 86
Vivares, Francis 99, 102–104, 110
Visscher, Claes Jansz. 7
Visscher, Cornelis 258
Vladislaus II, the Jagiellonian 214
Vlueten, Willem van 39
Vorsterman, Lucas 77
Vos, Maarten de 219, 232–233, 237
Vouet, Simon 77
Vriedeman de Vries, Hans 233
Vratislav II of Pernštejn 215

Watson, Caroline 258
Weerd, Adriaan de 233–234
Wierix, Antoine 236
Wierix, Hieronymus 224, 232–233
Wierix, Johannes 233, 236
Weyden, Rogier van der 199
Wilson, Richard 95
Woollett, William 95, 110

Zanetti, Francesco 230
Zarlino, Gioseffe 80
Zechariah 177
Ziarnko, Jan (*alias* Jean le Grain) 17, 164–167, 169–172, 174–175, 177, 179–180, 182–183, 185
Zündt, Matthia 230, 232